Business Plans Handbook

Business Plans Handbook

A COMPILATION OF BUSINESS PLANS DEVELOPED BY INDIVIDUALS THROUGHOUT NORTH AMERICA

VOLUME

45

GALE
A Cengage Company

Farmington Hills, Mich • San Francisco • New York • Waterville, Maine
Meriden, Conn • Mason, Ohio • Chicago

Business Plans Handbook, Volume 45

Project Editor: Donna Craft

Manufacturing: Rita Wimberley

©2019 Gale, Cengage Learning

WCN: 01-100-101

For product information and technology assistance, contact us at
Gale Customer Support, 1-800-877-4253.
For permission to use material from this text or product,
submit all requests online at **www.cengage.com/permissions.**
Further permissions questions can be emailed to
permissionrequest@cengage.com

Gale, A Cengage Company
27500 Drake Rd.
Farmington Hills, MI 48331-3535

ISBN-13: 978-1-4103-6339-8
1084-4473

This title is also available as an e-book.
ISBN-13: 978-1-4103-6343-5
Contact your Gale sales representative for ordering information.

Printed in Mexico
1 2 3 4 5 6 7 23 22 21 20 19

Contents

CONTENTS

APPENDIXES

Highlights

Business Plans Handbook, Volume 45 (BPH-45) is a collection of business plans compiled by entrepreneurs seeking funding for small businesses throughout North America. For those looking for examples of how to approach, structure, and compose their own business plans, *BPH-45* presents 20 sample plans, including plans for the following businesses:

- Automobile Detailing Service
- Educational Resources
- Gift Box Subscription Business
- Graphic Designer
- Home Winterizing Services Company
- Nonprofit Family Counseling Service
- Online Nutrition Coach
- Social Media Consultant
- Vacation Planning
- Youth Outreach Center

FEATURES AND BENEFITS

BPH-45 offers many features not provided by other business planning references including:

- Twenty business plans, including coverage of two non-profit companies, each of which represent an attempt at clarifying (for themselves and others) the reasons that the business should exist or expand and why a lender should fund the enterprise.

- Two fictional plans that are used by business counselors at a prominent small business development organization as examples for their clients. (You will find these in the Business Plan Template Appendix.)

- A directory section that includes listings for venture capital and finance companies, which specialize in funding start-up and second-stage small business ventures, and a comprehensive listing of Service Corps of Retired Executives (SCORE) offices. In addition, the Appendix also contains updated listings of all Small Business Development Centers (SBDCs); associations of interest to entrepreneurs; Small Business Administration (SBA) Regional Offices; and consultants specializing in small business planning and advice. It is strongly advised that you consult supporting organizations while planning your business, as they can provide a wealth of useful information.

- A Small Business Term Glossary to help you decipher the sometimes confusing terminology used by lenders and others in the financial and small business communities.

- A cumulative index, outlining each plan profiled in the complete *Business Plans Handbook* series.

- A Business Plan Template which serves as a model to help you construct your own business plan. This generic outline lists all the essential elements of a complete business plan and their components, including the Summary, Business History and Industry Outlook, Market Examination, Competition, Marketing, Administration and Management, Financial Information, and other key sections. Use this guide as a starting point for compiling your plan.

- Extensive financial documentation required to solicit funding from small business lenders. You will find examples of Cash Flows, Balance Sheets, Income Projections, and other financial information included with the textual portions of the plan.

Introduction

Perhaps the most important aspect of business planning is simply doing it. More and more business owners are beginning to compile business plans even if they don't need a bank loan. Others discover the value of planning when they must provide a business plan for the bank. The sheer act of putting thoughts on paper seems to clarify priorities and provide focus. Sometimes business owners completely change strategies when compiling their plan, deciding on a different product mix or advertising scheme after finding that their assumptions were incorrect. This kind of healthy thinking and re-thinking via business planning is becoming the norm. The Editor of *Business Plans Handbook, Volume 45 (BPH-45)* sincerely hopes that this latest addition to the series is a helpful tool in the successful completion of your business plan, no matter what the reason for creating it.

This volume, like each volume in the series, offers business plans created by real people. *BPH-45* provides 20 business plans. The business and personal names and addresses and general locations have been changed to protect the privacy of the plan authors.

NEW BUSINESS OPPORTUNITIES

As in other volumes in the series, *BPH-45* finds entrepreneurs engaged in a wide variety of creative endeavors. Examples include a Bookkeeping Services, Fundraising Program Developer, Handmade Knitted Items, and a Web Site Improvement Business, among others. This edition also includes coverage of non-profit organizations.

Comprehensive financial documentation has become increasingly important as today's entrepreneurs compete for the finite resources of business lenders. Our plans illustrate the financial data generally required of loan applicants, including Income Statements, Financial Projections, Cash Flows, and Balance Sheets.

ENHANCED APPENDIXES

In an effort to provide the most relevant and valuable information for our readers, we have updated the coverage of small business resources. For instance, you will find a directory section, which includes listings of all of the Service Corps of Retired Executives (SCORE) offices; an informative glossary, which includes small business terms; and a cumulative index, outlining each plan profiled in the complete *Business Plans Handbook* series. In addition we have updated the list of Small Business Development Centers (SBDCs); Small Business Administration Regional Offices; venture capital and finance companies, which specialize in funding start-up and second-stage small business enterprises; associations of interest to entrepreneurs; and consultants, specializing in small business advice and planning. For your reference, we have also reprinted the business plan template, which provides a comprehensive overview of the essential components of a business plan and two fictional plans used by small business counselors.

SERIES INFORMATION

If you already have the first forty-four volumes of *BPH*, with this forty-fifth volume, you will now have a collection of over 800 business plans (not including the updated plans); contact information for hundreds of organizations and agencies offering business expertise; a helpful business plan template; more than 1,500 citations to valuable small business development material; and a comprehensive glossary of terms to help the business planner navigate the sometimes confusing language of entrepreneurship.

ACKNOWLEDGEMENTS

The Editor wishes to sincerely thank the contributors to *BPH-45*, including:

- Francis R. Fletcher

- Paul Greenland Communications, Inc.

- Zuzu Enterprises

COMMENTS WELCOME

Your comments on *Business Plans Handbook* are appreciated. Please direct all correspondence, suggestions for future volumes of *BPH*, and other recommendations to the following:

Project Editor
Business Plans Handbook
Gale, A Cengage Company
27500 Drake Rd.
Farmington Hills, MI 48331-3535
Phone: (248)699-4253
Toll-Free: 800-877-GALE
URL: www.gale.com

Automobile Detailing Service

JPs Auto Clean

7776 W Oldham Dr.
Warren, MI 48090

Zuzu Enterprises

JPs Auto Clean will provide automobile detailing services to clients in Warren, Michigan, and the surrounding Detroit Metropolitan Area.

EXECUTIVE SUMMARY

Most people "live" in their cars and, as a result, car interiors are some of the dirtiest places you will ever encounter. Between the hours people spend sitting in their cars to the things they haul, car interiors take a lot of abuse. Hair, dust, food, gum, oils, sweat, dirt, spillage, and pet hair all permeate the interior and detract from the aesthetic and practical value of the car. An auto detailing business provides a thorough cleaning, inside and out, of the vehicle being serviced, including waxing, polishing, vacuuming, odor removal, and any extras the client requests.

JPs Auto Clean will provide these services to clients in Warren, Michigan, and the surrounding Detroit Metropolitan Area. Owner JP Stevenson is an avid car enthusiast and has thirty years' experience working in the auto industry as a design engineer. He recently accepted an early retirement package from Ford, but isn't ready to stop working. He is excited to venture out on his own and loves the satisfaction of seeing a job well done.

INDUSTRY ANALYSIS

Often, people think that Car "Wash" and Car "Detail" are synonyms, when in fact they are very far from it. Auto detailing involves a thorough cleaning and reconditioning of both the interior and exterior of your vehicle. It is a meticulous step-by-step process to restore your vehicle's beauty and protect your investment. Detailing services can extend beyond automobiles, and could include trucks, buses, SUVs, RVs, boats, motorcycles, or even airplanes. Most detailing companies can handle some, or all, of these types of vehicles.

The single and most important aspect of auto detailing is your vehicle's need for protection from the elements. A common misconception is that a vehicle's "clear coat" protects the exterior finish, and thus regular maintenance is not required. In reality, a wax coat should be applied at least twice a year to the painted surfaces to protect the finish from contaminants and oxidation.

Since what is included in a "detailing" service can vary, an important consideration is to determine the specific services that you would like to have performed on your vehicle. There may be multiple levels of detailing packages available that vary in services performed and cost. Unfortunately, as there are no uniform guidelines for the detailing industry, you may encounter wide variations in service packaging and pricing. Contributing factors to these variations can include: different levels of training, quality of service, professionalism, and the products and equipment utilized.

A thorough and high-quality detailing job should take several hours, depending on the prior condition of the vehicle being detailed. The results of a detailing job will also vary based on the level of service provided and the age and condition of the vehicle. Basically, you should expect that every detail of your vehicle will be assessed and cleaned, including all cracks and crevices. Whether you've just purchased a previously owned vehicle, are getting ready to sell your vehicle, or simply want to have your vehicle looking great again by restoring its original beauty, professional auto detailing can take your vehicle from ordinary to extraordinary.

The Car Wash and Auto Detailing Industry in the United States consists of full-service clean (conveyor car washes), exterior only clean (conveyor car washes), in-bay automatic car washes, automobile detailing, hand washing, and self-service bay.

This industry has experienced steady growth over the five years to 2018, as the economy continues to grow, and industry operators reaped the benefits of rising employment and per capita disposable income.

Over the past five years, the Car Wash & Auto Detailing industry has grown by 3.6 percent to reach revenue of $11 billion in 2018. In the same timeframe, the number of businesses has grown by 1.6 percent and the number of employees has grown by 2.8 percent.

There are more than 66,000 businesses in the industry, employing approximately 215,000 people. The median annual wage of those working in the industry is $23,360.

MARKET ANALYSIS

JPs Auto Clean is located in Warren, Michigan. The 2010 census places the city's population at 135,069, making Warren the largest city in Macomb County, the third largest city in Michigan, and Metro Detroit's largest suburb.

The median age of the population of Warren is 39.2 years old. The average cars per household in Warren is 1.73, while only 7.2 percent of households don't have a car.

The city of Warren is home to:

FCA Sherwood National Parts Distribution Center—142 employees

FCA Warren Complex Parts Distribution Center—80 employees

FCA Warren Stamping Plant—1,945 employees

FCA Warren Truck Assembly Plant—6,378 employees

GM Global Technical Center—22,764 employees

GM Van Dyke Office Center—812 employees

GM Warren Company Vehicle Operations—123 employees

GM Warren Transmission/GM Global Propulsion Systems—581 employees

In, 2017, car sales in Michigan totaled $21.48 billion, with more than 635,000 new cars sold in that time. There was a total of 3,687,119 car registrations in the state, with the average age of vehicles 10.7 years, down from the national average of 11.2 years.

New and used cars aren't the only vehicles in the state. The area is well-known for its historical vehicles and the shows and cruises to exhibit them. The Woodward Dream Cruise alone attracts upwards of one million visitors a year from across the globe who pack the sidewalks with rows upon rows of lawn chairs. The hub of the event is at 13 Mile and Woodward in Royal Oak, but the entire loop goes from Ferndale to Pontiac, and includes Berkley, Royal Oak, and Huntington Woods.

Eighty-two percent of the workforce in Michigan drives alone to work, with only nine percent carpooling and one percent using public transportation, meaning most citizens own their own car and use it daily. Michigan consumers spend fourteen percent of their monthly income on auto payments, while the national average is twelve percent.

Michigan automaker facilities total 2,454, employing nearly 395,000 people. Suppliers, dealers, auto supply stores, gas stations, rentals, parking, repair shops, and carwashes and other services round out the total number of people employed in automobile-related positions. There are nearly 1 million auto jobs in the state of Michigan, or about 20 percent of the state's workforce. They are employed at the more than 53,000 auto-related employers in the state.

There is a reason Michigan is known as the nation's and the world's automotive capital.

SERVICES

JPs Auto Clean offers a variety of services to car owners in the area. Depending on the specific service or package clients choose, a full detail can take from two to five hours. Quality is the key, and we don't leave until the vehicle meets our strict quality standards and the client's expectations. After the vehicle looks perfect, JPs can then set clients up on a regular maintenance schedule to keep it that way. The complete line of services includes:

- Apply fabric stain and water repellent
- Apply leather conditioner and protectant
- Clean and shine tires and rims
- Clean door jambs
- Clean headliner
- Clean interior and exterior windows
- Clean wheel wells
- Dust all vinyl and plastic, including dashboard and console
- Hand wash car's exterior
- Machine buff and wax
- Pet hair removal
- Removal of tar or tree sap
- Remove odors
- Restore headlights
- Shampoo and clean engine
- Vacuum, steam clean, and shampoo carpets and seats
- Wax, polish, and seal

Apply Fabric Stain and Water Repellent

A colorless and odorless solvent fabric protection product that works great on natural and synthetic fabrics. Provides a high degree of water repellency and does not hinder the fabrics breathing ability in any way. This is a commercial grade product that provides automotive carpet and fabric upholstered seats the very best protection against stains and spills.

Apply Leather Conditioner and Protectant

Leather surfaces are just like beautiful, delicate skin. They must be carefully cleansed before being properly conditioned. As leather ages, it loses essential protectants that were infused into it during the manufacturing process, leaving it susceptible to dirt, oils, and UV damage. To keep leather looking and feeling its best, you must first clean it and then replace the lost moisture and protection. It's much easier to spend a little time protecting and conditioning your fine leather upholstery than spending the energy and money to salvage it.

Clean and Shine Tires and Rims

Cleaning your wheels and tires regularly is not just an appearance issue—it's preventative maintenance! If you allow brake dust to sit on your wheels for a prolonged period, it can eat into the coating and pit the metal. Brake dust is made of an adhesive and carbon fibers that come off the brake pad and tiny metal shavings from the rotor. The intense heat and friction generated by the wheels makes this mixture highly corrosive. Because clients probably drive every day, more brake dust is constantly being made. Frequent cleaning is the only way to keep the wheels safe.

Clean Door Jambs

While most car owners rarely thinking about door jambs when doing regular car cleaning, they provide housing for parts of a car that are essential for the door to open and close properly. That includes things like the hinges, strikers, and guides. A filthy jamb certainly detracts from a car's overall appearance, especially when the contrast is underscored by the car's sparkling-clean exterior. In addition, it's all too easy for that grit and grime to transfer to clothing, causing permanent stains. The dirt, grease, and moisture found on door jambs create the perfect breeding ground for rust, one of a car's deadliest enemies. Finally, door jambs camouflage areas that have excessive wear and other developing problems, and therefore it's important they get the attention they need.

Clean Headliner

The headliner insulates the car from cold, muffles outside noise and vibrations, and creates a clean, finished look to the car. Despite this, it is one of the vehicle's components that receives little attention. It is often neglected when the car is washed and detailed and it can become dirty and discolored. Its exposed surface is porous and absorbs smells and smoke, retaining the odor for days, weeks, or even permanently.

Clean Interior and Exterior Windows

Dirty, hazy, water-spotted glass can be a safety hazard, but car windows are often neglected when detailing your own car. In addition to being a hazard, the effect of dirty glass will quickly ruin the appearance of a perfectly polished and waxed automobile.

Clean Wheel Wells

Wheel wells that have been neglected may look almost black from the buildup of break dust and grime. Much of the buildup on wheel wells is from brake dust; this is a by-product of the braking process, and if left un-treated over a significant period of time, the corrosive qualities of it can permanently damage the finish of the wells as well as the wheels. Since much of the undercarriage can be seen when simply walking around a car, neglecting this area can negate the visual effects of all other auto detailing.

Dust All Vinyl and Plastic

Dust and dirt on the car's dash and center console stares you in the face every time you get in the vehicle. In addition to being unsightly, it's unhealthy to breathe in day after day. To combat this, it is necessary to wipe down all vinyl and plastic surfaces with a damp microfiber detailing towel leaving a lint-free, dust-free finish. A small hand vac may also be helpful to reach each and every crevice. Interior cleaners may also be used to remove built-up grime in minute cracks as well as shine the surfaces.

Hand Wash Car's Exterior

The single most important thing you can do to keep your car's finish looking great is to wash it regularly because dirt, bird droppings, dead bugs, road gunk, tree sap, and other contaminants can harm the paint if left on for too long. This leads to annoying blemishes in the finish at best, and expensive repairs at worst. Drive-through and automated car washes may introduce fine scratches, called swirl marks, into the car's paint finish, especially if it's an old-fashioned brush-type wash or one that's not well maintained. If you really want to keep that like-new look, it pays to hand wash the car.

Machine Polish, Buff and Wax

Keeping a car's finish looking new is easy with wheeling or polishing the vehicle with a rotating wheel. This process works by temporarily heating the paint's clear coat until it softens into a viscous liquid that fills in and dissipates blemishes. To prevent permanent damage to the paint, this method of polishing should be limited to once a year, while buffing and waxing can be done every couple of months.

Pet Hair Removal

Pets can leave behind unwanted gifts in our cars, such as ground-in dog hair on the upholstery and down between the seats. Pet hair on car upholstery is common among pet owners and it can be difficult to remove. Steps to do this successfully include removing loose pet hair; vacuuming; using special gloves, stones, and brushes; and shampooing.

Removal of Tar and Tree Sap

Tar and tree sap can be very difficult to remove, especially the longer it has been on the car; removing them requires special techniques to protect the exterior's paint and clear-coat.

Remove Odors

Our Ozone Treatment is for strong offensive odors and smell from cigarettes, smoke damage, decaying matter, pets, urine, food, beverages, vomit, mold and mildew. Our Ozone treatment permanently kills the odor. Ozone, a colorless gas made up of three atoms of oxygen, occurs quite readily in nature, at the beach, in the forest, or near waterfalls. Since Ozone is the second most powerful sterilant in existence, it can easily destroy bacteria, viruses, mold, mildew, and odors in one to four hours.

Restore Headlights

Headlight restoration is the process of removing oxidation and re-applying a protective UV coating. Not only do unrestored headlights take away from the look of the vehicle, they also reduce the efficiency of the headlight itself. Headlight lenses are deteriorated over time by the sun's harmful UV rays. This causes headlights to appear cloudy, dull, hazy, yellow, discolored, and foggy. In addition to decreased visual appeal this also diminishes night driving visibility, which is a safety concern not only for you, but the other drivers as well. It has been well documented by safety industries that dim headlights have played a serious role in major car accidents.

Shampoo and Clean Engine

Recommended once a year by auto manufacturers, not only will it make your engine compartment look awesome but keeping your vehicle's engine clean will allow it to run at a cooler temperature, while making it easier to work on and increasing resale value. The engine compartment is first shampooed using special degreasers and cleaners to break down built-up grime and grease build-up on liquid containers, firewalls, and valve covers. We then dress the engine compartment with a low sheen non-silicone dressing.

Vacuum, Steam Clean, and Shampoo Carpets and Seats

Vacuuming and a thorough scrubbing are done on the all carpets, mats, and seats in order to remove any stains and blemishes that may have accumulated over the past years. To be more effective, a steam-cleaner should be used. Carpets, mats, and seats should be left to dry completely to avoid mildew.

Wax, Polish, and Seal

The original polish can fade over time, making the car look dull. Polishing the car's exterior can restore the original polish, and sealing or waxing can give the car a glossy shine.

Pricing

Pricing may be done by the individual service or as a package. Individual prices include:

Apply fabric stain and water repellent, starting at $19.99

Apply leather conditioner and protectant, starting at $19.99

Apply trim protectant, starting at $19.99

Clean and shine tires and rims, starting at $19.99

Clean door jambs, starting at $4.99

Clean headliner, starting at $29.99

Clean interior and exterior windows, starting at $4.99

Clean wheel wells, starting at $9.99

Dust all vinyl and plastic, including dashboard and console, starting at $9.99

Hand wash car's exterior, starting at $19.99

Machine buff and wax, starting at $49.99

Pet hair removal, starting at $39.99

Removal of tar or tree sap, starting at $29.99

Remove odors, starting at $99.99

Restore headlights, starting at $39.99

Shampoo and clean engine, starting at $39.99

Vacuum, steam clean, and shampoo carpets and seats, starting at $39.99

Wax, polish and seal, starting at $59.99

Jobs that require additional labor will be billed at $39.99 per hour.

Packages are available and include interior detail service, exterior detail service, and full service. Packages start at $75 and run to $250 or more. Larger vehicles or those in bad condition may require an additional charge.

OPERATIONS

JPs Auto Clean has been established as a Limited Liability Company (LLC). This type of business has very few downsides and allows for liability protection and flexible tax filing. The business is fully licensed and insured. As an automotive business in the state of Michigan, this means that JPs Auto Clean is licensed by the Bureau of Driver and Vehicle Programs (BDVP) and registered by the Michigan Department of State, as required by Section 6 of the *Motor Vehicle Service and Repair Act* (MCL 257.1306). This act says that all persons who repair motor vehicles for compensation, including the reconditioning, replacement, diagnosis, adjustment, or alteration of the operating condition of the vehicle or any component or sub-assembly, in any category of major repair, must be certified by the State of Michigan.

Start-Up Needs

JPs Auto Clean will require several tools to begin business operations. These tools include:

- Applicators and brushes
- Auto detailing light
- Blower
- Buckets
- Buffer and pads
- Car wash mitts and sponges
- Carpet cleaner
- Detailing aprons and belts
- Dusters
- Gloves
- Hand strap applicator
- Hose slides
- Hot water extractor
- Long-reach scraper
- Microfiber cloths
- Mobile cart
- Pet hair detailer and removal stone
- Plastic razor blades
- Polisher and pads
- Shop-Vac
- Sprays and bottles
- Squeegee
- Steam cleaner
- Storage containers
- Tire brush
- Towels, chamois, and drying tools
- Vacuum
- Wash mop with telescoping handle
- Wheel and body brush
- Window cleaner, polishes, etc.

The tools will be stored in appropriate containers and transported in the company truck when traveling to off-site locations. JP will transfer his personal truck, a Ford F-450, to the business to use for all business travel.

Location

JPs Auto Clean will run from the home of owner JP Stevenson. JP has a large three-car garage that will easily accommodate any size car as well as his tools and adequate space to work. It is equipped with suitable power supply and is heated, making working in the garage possible throughout the winter. JP is also willing to travel to work directly at the client's home or place of business, provided the weather and available amenities are adequate to do the job well. A dedicated home office has also been set up for scheduling, billing, and communicating with clients.

Hours

JPs Auto Clean will operate Monday through Friday, from 9 a.m. to 5 p.m. Requests for weekend or evening hours may be accommodated for an additional charge.

Insurance

JPs Auto Clean has procured a full line of insurance to cover the business in case of loss or injury. Insurance coverage includes:

Business General Liability Insurance

Liability insurance is overall protection policy for the business. It covers if someone is hurt on our property or on a property where we are performing a service. It also provides legal representation in the case of a lawsuit and will pay damages if we are found negligent.

Garage Keeper's Policy

The garage keeper's policy was created to cover businesses like detailing, auto body, and mechanic shops. The policy covers any damage that might occur to a customer's vehicle while in our possession. That could mean while driving it, working on it, or while it sits.

Business Property Insurance

Business property insurance is similar to the insurance you would have on your own house. It covers the property itself and anything that is contained inside or on it. This would include equipment, products, and fixtures. It will cover such things as accidental direct physical damage, fire, and theft.

Commercial Vehicle Policy

Like any normal auto policy, this will cover the vehicle against accidents or vandalism. It will also cover any equipment that is a permanent fixture of the vehicle (i.e. bolted down) against theft or loss.

Worker's Compensation Insurance

Workers' compensation provides medical expenses, lost wages, and rehabilitation costs to employees who are injured or become ill "in the course and scope" of their job. It also pays death benefits to families of employees who are killed on the job.

This might appear to be a lot of coverage, but insurance is not that expensive when broken out over the course of a year. A few hundred dollars a month might seem like a lot to a small business, but if something does happen, and you do not have the proper insurance, you will find out the hard way just how expensive it is NOT to have insurance.

Proof of the insurance coverage will be provided to all clients before we begin work.

Business Bank Account

JPs Auto Clean has established a business bank account with First State Bank. Having a separate business bank account keeps the corporate liability protection intact, protecting owner JP Stevenson from creditors, including the IRS, from pursuing his personal assets. It also makes business accounting much easier by running all purchases and payments through one account, especially in the event of an audit. Establishing a business relationship with the local bank may also be useful in the future if JP decides to expand the business and requires a loan to purchase a business location, vehicle, or additional equipment.

Methods of Payment

JPs Auto Clean accepts cash, check, and all major credit cards. Gift Certificates are available and will be accepted as payment as well.

Service Agreement

With the help of a local lawyer, JPs Auto Clean has established a service agreement that clients will be required to sign before starting each new project. This agreement clarifies client expectations and minimize the risk of legal disputes by setting out payment terms and conditions, service level expectations, and intellectual property ownership.

PERSONNEL

JP Stevenson is owner and operator of JPs Auto Clean. JP is an avid car enthusiast and has thirty years' experience working in the auto industry as a design engineer. He recently accepted an early retirement package from Ford, but he isn't ready to stop working. He is excited to venture out on his own and loves the satisfaction of seeing a job well done. The buyout package will help lessen the financial burden of starting a new business venture.

ASSOCIATIONS

JPs Auto Detailing is a member of the International Detailing Association in Saint Paul, Minnesota. The IDA offers members information regarding how to get started, advice on managing your business, and the latest in industry trends. IDA membership benefits include educational resources, networking opportunities, professional development, local, regional, and national events, online registry, and recognition.

JPs Auto Clean has earned the designation of IDA Certified Detailer by successfully completing the Certified Detailer exam and attending Skills Validated testing. The certification exam consists of ten exams in these subject areas: Equipment, Chemicals, Glass, Interior Detailing, Leather, Paint Correction & Protection, Wheels & Tires, Prep Wash/Wash Bay, Detailing Terminology, Safety & Compliance. The Skills Validated test represents the four primary categories that each candidate must demonstrate their "hands on" ability to perform. The detailer must perform each phase of the testing on their own, and meet the minimum proficiency expected in order to pass. The exam is presented in a scenario-type format to afford the detailer the opportunity to demonstrate the abilities expected of the advanced detailing professional. The categories covered include: Wash Bay/Prep, Interior, Exterior Correction, and Finishing Steps.

The Certified Dealer designation is a great achievement and demonstrates a basic mastery of the knowledge and applied skills needed by the detailing professional. Earning the CD designation places that detailing professional among a group at the top of their profession; CDs have not only demonstrated competency, but they have shown determination and commitment in completing the certification process. CDs are dedicated individuals who believe strongly in improving themselves and their profession.

The cost for certification was $350 and membership in the IDA costs $110 per year.

MARKETING & SALES

JPs Auto Clean will employ several different tactics in marketing the business. This includes:

- **Defining our brand**. The JPs brand is what the company stands for, as well as how the business is perceived by the public. A strong brand will help the business stand out from competitors.

- **Establishing a web presence**. A business website allows customers to learn more about JPs Auto Clean and the services we offer. We can use social media to attract new clients or customers. We can keep our clients apprised of the latest industry news and company specials by regularly posting on our website as well as apps such as Facebook, Instagram, Twitter, and LinkedIn.

- **Performing services free of charge for a select group of family and friends in exchange for referrals and testimonials**. The appointments will be set up during regular business hours, preferably at their workplace, which offers an instant opportunity to showcase our talent and gain their co-workers as new customers.

- **Having a cache of business cards and promotional materials**. Business cards and promotional brochures will always be on-hand because you never know when you might meet your next best customer.

- **Mailing promotional brochures to local businesses and homes in the area, as well as local car enthusiasts**. The professional brochure will highlight the available services and testimonials from satisfied customers; several methods of contacting the company for service will also be prominently displayed.

- **Employing mobile advertising**. A magnetic vehicle sign will be procured and proudly displayed on the company truck, which will be kept in immaculate condition.

- **Doing our best work every time**. In this industry, it is critical to always provide excellent service. When it comes to "luxury" services, one poor job will leave a lasting impression.

FINANCIAL ANALYSIS

Start-Up Costs

The car detailing business requires very little investment capital, requiring money only for training, insurance, promotional materials, and tools. An initial budget of $17,500 has been established, which will cover these items.

License fee—$100

Training and certification—$350

Membership fees—$110

Insurance—$3,440

Business cell phone—$1,000

Computer and office equipment—$1,500

Promotional items (including business cards, brochures, website creation, and mobile advertisement) —$1,000

Tools—$10,000

TOTAL—$17,500

Ongoing Expenses

Ongoing expenses included in the monthly budget are:

Fuel costs—$200

Replenishment of supplies—$100

Routine upkeep on vehicle—$50

Equipment maintenance—$50

Insurance—$300

Marketing—$50

Cell phone—$100

TOTAL—$850

Insurance was paid upfront for the year in order to receive a more favorable rate; it is included in the monthly ongoing expenses to accrue to funds to pay in full at the beginning of Year Two. Payroll and taxes will be determined after all the expenses are paid and may vary from month to month.

SWOT ANALYSIS

Strengths

- Demand for car wash and detailing services depends on the level of per capita disposable income because these services are generally considered discretionary. Growth in disposable income boosts discretionary spending and demand for industry services. Per capita disposable income is expected to increase in 2018, representing a potential opportunity for the industry.

- JPs Auto Clean is investing in high-quality detailing supplies that should last for years to come.

- Services are priced comparably with competitors.

Weaknesses

- There are other auto detailing services in the area that are more established and well-known.

Opportunities

- JPs Auto Clean will consider utilizing waterless car wash products.

- We will ask used car dealerships about detailing for them. While the pay is low, the work is consistent, and it will offer immeasurable experience and a potential customer base for repeat customers.

- We may explore the possibility of partnering with local hotels to offer concierge services.

- We will also explore the possibility of partnering with car shows, auto and RV dealerships, car rental companies, and limousine companies.

- We could expand into RV and boat detailing as an additional line of revenue.

- We could invest in a water reclamation system/strategy, which will significantly boost our profit margins.

Threats

- Rising gas prices typically encourage consumers to carpool or use public transportation, reducing demand for industry services. Furthermore, as gas prices climb, consumers' disposable incomes fall, reducing their ability to spend on discretionary services such as car washes. The world price of crude oil is expected to increase in 2018, posing a potential threat to the industry.

Bookkeeping Services
CR Bookkeeping & Tax Services

9982 Maple Ridge Place
Kettering, OH 45429

Zuzu Enterprises

CR Bookkeeping & Tax Services is a freelance bookkeeping service in the greater Dayton Metropolitan Area. As a bookkeeping and tax service, the company will help small businesses to create balance sheets, provide income statements, and create various monthly, quarterly, and annual financial reports, in addition to other tasks. Hiring an outside professional to perform these tasks will allow small businesses to focus on their core business while having an objective and impartial ally to ensure accuracy and guidance, as well as compliance. CR Bookkeeping & Tax Services is invested in our clients' success. Their success is our success.

EXECUTIVE SUMMARY

CR Bookkeeping & Tax Services is a freelance bookkeeping service in the greater Dayton Metropolitan Area. As a bookkeeping and tax service, the company will help small businesses to create balance sheets, provide income statements, and create various monthly, quarterly, and annual financial reports, in addition to other tasks.

Small businesses are more successful with an accounting professional to help and CR Bookkeeping & Tax Services is invested in our clients' success. Hiring an outside professional to perform bookkeeping tasks will allow small businesses to focus on their core business while having an objective and impartial ally to ensure accuracy and guidance, as well as compliance. Our role is to create clarity to help businesses make better decisions by providing expert advice and direction. Their success is our success.

INDUSTRY ANALYSIS

Workers in the bookkeeping and accounting industry engage in a wide range of tasks from maintaining an entire organization's books to handling more specific, targeted tasks. These tasks include:

- Use bookkeeping software, spreadsheets, and databases
- Enter (post) financial transactions into the appropriate computer software
- Receive and record cash, checks, and vouchers
- Put costs (debits) and income (credits) into the software, assigning each to an appropriate account
- Produce reports, such as balance sheets (costs compared with income), income statements, and totals by account

- Check for accuracy in figures, postings, and reports
- Reconcile or note and report any differences they find in the records

The widespread use of computers also has enabled bookkeeping, accounting, and auditing clerks to take on additional responsibilities, such as payroll, billing, purchasing (buying), and keeping track of overdue bills.

The median income for people working in the industry is $39,240 a year, or roughly $19 per hour. This is higher than the total for all occupations.

Bookkeeping, Accounting, and Auditing Clerks

Median annual wages, May 2017

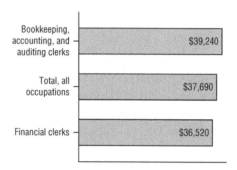

Note: All Occupations includes all occupations in the U.S. Economy.

SOURCE: U.S. Bureau of Labor Statistics, Occupational Employment Statistics

Bookkeeping, accounting, and auditing clerks held about 1.7 million jobs in 2016. This employment level is projected to show little or no change through the year 2026. Technological change and automation are expected to reduce demand for these workers. Software innovations, such as cloud computing, have automated many of the tasks performed by bookkeepers. As a result, the same amount of bookkeeping work can be done with fewer employees, which is expected to lead to job losses for bookkeepers over the next ten years. But, because bookkeeping, accounting, and auditing clerks constitute a large occupation, there will be a large number of job openings from workers leaving the occupation. Thus, opportunities to enter the occupation should be plentiful, despite the slight projected decline in employment.

Quick Facts: Bookkeeping, Accounting, and Auditing Clerks

2017 median pay	$39,240 per year
	$18.87 per hour
Typical entry-level education	Some college, no degree
Work experience in a related occupation	None
On-the-job training	Moderate-term on-the-job training
Number of jobs, 2016	1,730,500
Job outlook, 2016–26	−1% (Little or no change)
Employment change, 2016–26	−25,200

The largest employers of bookkeeping, accounting, and auditing clerks were as follows:

Professional, scientific, and technical services	12%
Retail trade	10
Wholesale trade	7
Healthcare and social assistance	7
Finance and insurance	7

Most bookkeeping, accounting, and auditing clerks work full time, with only about one in four working part time in 2016. They may work additional hours to meet deadlines at the end of the fiscal year, during tax time, or when monthly or yearly accounting audits are done. Independent or freelance bookkeeping companies typically work for multiple firms and may visit their clients' places of business in addition to working remotely.

In May 2017, the median annual wages for bookkeeping, accounting, and auditing clerks in the top industries in which they worked were as follows:

Professional, scientific, and technical services	$41,260
Finance and insurance	40,910
Wholesale trade	39,870
Healthcare and social assistance	38,430
Retail trade	34,580

With more routinized tasks automated, bookkeepers are expected to take on a more analytical and advisory role over the next ten years. For example, rather than performing manual data entry, bookkeepers will focus more on analyzing their clients' books and pointing out potential areas for efficiency gains.

MARKET ANALYSIS

The primary target market for CR Bookkeeping & Tax Services is the city of Dayton, Ohio. Dayton is a located in Montgomery County, Ohio. It borders Drexel, Huber Heights, Kettering, Moraine, Oakwood, Montgomery County, Riverside, Trotwood, and Vandalia.

The population of Dayton was 140,371 in July 2017. Eighty-three percent of the population has a high school diploma, and only 17.7 percent have earned a college degree.

There are more than 10,000 businesses in the city. The largest industries in Dayton are Healthcare and Social Assistance (9,468), Manufacturing (7,091), and Accommodation and Food Service (6,339); and the highest paying industries are Utilities ($48,438), Management of Companies and Enterprises ($44,091), and Finance and Insurance ($32,815).

This market is expanded when one considers the larger Dayton Metropolitan Area; this area is the fourth largest metropolitan area in Ohio with a population of more than 800,000. It includes Montgomery County, Greene County, and Miami County, as well as Dayton, Kettering, and Beavercreek. More than 90 percent of the population has a high school diploma, while nearly 30 percent have earned a college degree.

In 2013-2017, the region saw the best three to four year stretch in employment growth since the late 1990's. Regional successes were notable in both the logistics and financial sectors. The Dayton Area Chamber of Commerce's Research Advisory Council (RAC) notes a sense of optimism for businesses, especially startups and entrepreneurs. The region has the necessary tools like workforce training, easy access to interstates, and a variety of properties ready for redevelopment to attract new businesses and support the growth of established companies.

Forbes rates the Dayton Metro Area as 130th in Best Places for Business and Careers; it jumps to 4th in the state of Ohio. It ranks 112th in Cost of Doing Business (6th in Ohio), and 148th in Job Growth (4th in Ohio).

According to The Entrepreneurs Center, the Dayton entrepreneurial ecosystem mirrored the national trend of increasing start-up activity and, along with it, community support and enthusiasm for entrepreneurs. The year 2016 showed incredible growth and development, and that trend shows no sign of slowing down.

The largest industries in the Dayton Metro Area are Healthcare and Social Assistance (57,090), Manufacturing (56,189), and Retail trade (43,970), and the highest paying industries are Professional, Scientific, Tech Services ($54,565), Utilities ($53,656), and Management of Companies and Enterprises ($47,368).

Employment by Industry in the Dayton Metropolitan Area

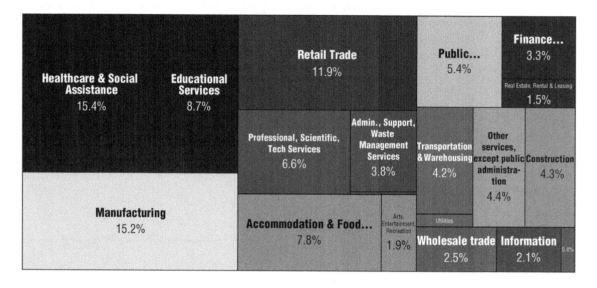

There are even more opportunities if one considers the entire state of Ohio as our potential target market, especially for future growth.

In the third quarter of 2015, Ohio grew at an annual rate of 2.3 percent, which was faster than the overall U.S. growth-rate of 1.9 percent. By comparison, Ohio's 2014 growth of 3.4 percent; was up from the 2013 level of 2.2 percent.

The employment situation in Ohio has also improved. At the close of 2015, unemployment was 4.8 percent, down from 5.1 percent at the close of 2014. This was below the national unemployment rate of 5.0 percent.

Indeed, there are 927,691 small businesses in the state of Ohio. These small businesses employed 2.1 million people, or 46.2 percent of the private workforce, in 2013. Firms with fewer than 100 employees have the largest share of small business employment with 31.8 percent of all firms being in this category.

Ohio Employment by Firm Size, 2000–2013

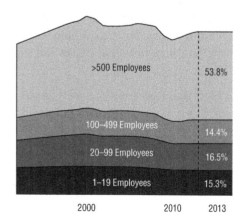

SERVICES

CR Bookkeeping & Tax Services specializes in bookkeeping and tax preparation services for small businesses, particularly those who utilize QuickBooks. QuickBooks is an established and well-known system that provides everything a small business would need to operate successfully. It is relatively inexpensive, starting at only $10 a month for basic service.

QuickBooks can be used to:

- Manage bills
- Track income and expenses
- Track mileage
- Create invoices
- Process payments
- Manage contractors
- Pay workers
- Track time
- Manage inventory
- Create reports
- Process sales and remit sales tax
- Create estimates
- Manage tax deductions
- Track projects

Clients using QuickBooks can invite CR Bookkeeping & Tax Services to access their books for seamless collaboration.

A complete list of services performed by CR Bookkeeping & Tax Services includes:

- Check financial records for accuracy
- Create financial statements
- Create invoices
- Keep track of overdue accounts
- Make purchases
- Prepare bank deposits by compiling data from cashiers, verifying receipts, and sending cash, checks, or other forms of payment to the bank
- Prepare the general ledger—record all transactions and post debits (costs) and credits (income)
- Prepare profit and loss statements to show the organization's financial health
- Prepare various reports, such as balance sheets (costs compared with income), income statements, and totals by account
- Process payroll
- Run accounts payable, or bills that need to be paid
- Track accounts receivable including invoices, or what other people owe the organization
- Track receipts, or money that comes in

In addition to these tasks, CR Bookkeeping & Tax Services will take on a more analytical and advisory role, preparing long-term comparisons, noting trends, and otherwise guiding companies. Hiring an outside professional to perform these tasks will allow our clients to focus on their core business while having an objective and impartial ally to ensure accuracy and guidance, as well as compliance. Our role is to create clarity to help businesses make better decisions by providing expert advice and direction.

Small businesses are more successful with an accounting professional to help. CR Bookkeeping & Tax Services is invested in our clients' success—their success is our success.

OPERATIONS

Location

CR Bookkeeping & Tax Services is operated from the dedicated home office of owner Cynthia Rogers, located at 9982 Maple Ridge Place in Kettering, Ohio. The office is outfitted with a desk, computer, multiuse printer/scanner/copier, and dedicated phone line. Although most work will be done in the office, Cynthia may also meet with clients at their place of business as needed.

Hours

CR Bookkeeping & Tax Services will generally maintain normal business hours of 9 a.m. to 5 p.m., Monday through Friday. Additional hours may be needed at month- and year-ends, as well as tax season.

PERSONNEL

Cynthia Rogers is the owner and sole employee of CR Bookkeeping & Tax Services. She has more than ten years' experience in the industry where she was employed as a bookkeeper for a medium-sized corporation, having been promoted from intern to clerk and finally to head of the department. She has been helping family and friends with their small business needs for the past several years and has decided to venture out on her own to expand these services. Her extensive knowledge, training, and credentials, as well as her contact list and networking skills will help the business to succeed.

In addition to this, Cynthia possesses the following skills:

- **Computer skills**. Cynthia is comfortable using computer spreadsheets and bookkeeping software.

- **Detail oriented**. Cynthia is detail-oriented, which helps her to avoid making errors and recognize errors that others have made.

- **Integrity**. Cynthia is trustworthy. Having control of an organization's financial documentation, it is imperative that she use the information properly and essential that she keep it completely confidential. It is vital that she keep transparent records and guard against anyone misusing an organization's funds.

- **Math skills**. Cynthia is comfortable with basic arithmetic, as well as noticing trends and making predictions.

Certification

Cynthia has three certifications that will help her business succeed, providing both the expertise and knowledge to get the work done, as well as the status and reputation to attract new clients.

To start, Cynthia is a QuickBooks Certified ProAdvisor. A ProAdvisor is a QuickBooks-certified independent accounting professional who can provide strategic insights to drive small business success. This certification boosts customer confidence, demonstrates proficiency, and earns client trust. It sets CR

Bookkeeping & Tax Services apart from other accountants and establishes our expertise to prospective clients. It will also attract new clients by publishing our free profile on "Find-a-ProAdvisor" on the Quick-Books website, which is visited by more than 700,000 small businesses each year. In addition, being a certified ProAdvisor will provide unlimited access to accountancy experts whenever additional expertise is needed.

The QuickBooks Online Advanced Certification includes training to:

- Gain most-used knowledge to serve clients
- Learn setup, navigation, and features
- Manage sales, purchases, payroll, and payments
- Learn about reporting, apps, and troubleshooting
- Gain ultimate knowledge to serve clients
- Manage complex conversions
- Learn special transactions and advanced features
- Learn advanced reporting and problem solving

Cynthia has also earned the Certified Bookkeeper (CB) designation awarded by the American Institute of Professional Bookkeepers. This designation shows that those who have earned it have the skills and knowledge needed to carry out all bookkeeping tasks, including overseeing payroll and balancing accounts, according to accepted accounting procedures. The cost of certification was $479 for members.

Finally, Cynthia has earned the Certified Public Bookkeeper (CPB) certification from the National Association of Certified Public Bookkeepers. To earn this certification, candidates must have at least two years of full-time bookkeeping experience or equivalent part-time work, pass a four-part Uniform Bookkeeper Certification Examination, and adhere to a code of ethics.

ASSOCIATIONS

CR Bookkeeping & Tax Services is a member of the American Institute of Professional Bookkeepers (https://www.aipb.org/).

The American Institute of Professional Bookkeepers was established in 1987 to:

- Recognize bookkeeping as a profession and bookkeepers as professionals.
- Keep employed and freelance bookkeepers current on important revisions to federal and state laws, regulations, and procedures.
- Answer bookkeepers' everyday bookkeeping and accounting questions on a free Members Only telephone AnswerLine.
- Deliver high-quality continuing education for professional bookkeepers.
- Provide job opportunities to professional bookkeepers and help employers find them on a free Jobs Site devoted exclusively to the bookkeeping profession.
- Create a high-level certification of elite professional bookkeepers.
- Provide online forums for professional bookkeepers to exchange information, help and ideas.

CR Bookkeeping & Tax Services is also a member of the National Association of Certified Public Bookkeepers (https://www.certifiedpublicbookkeeper.org/). NACPB serves bookkeepers providing bookkeeping services to the public; it protects the public interest by helping to ensure that only qualified bookkeepers provide public bookkeeping services and assures the public that licensed CPBs are trustworthy and competent. NACPB trains, certifies, and licenses bookkeeping students, employees, and professionals in bookkeeping, accounting, payroll, QuickBooks, tax, and Excel. It provides anytime, anywhere access via an Internet-connected computer or mobile device to:

- Training Videos
- Certified Professional Education (CPE) or Continuing Education (CE)
- Checklists
- Training Courses
- Certifications
- Licensing
- Certification and License Exam Preparation Programs

Annual membership dues are $100.

MARKETING & SALES

CR Bookkeeping & Tax Services will employ several different tactics in marketing the business. This includes:

- **Defining our brand.** The brand is what the company stands for, as well as how the business is perceived by the public. A strong brand will help the business stand out from competitors; it will heavily feature our lengthy experience and many certifications.

- **Establishing a web presence.** A business website allows customers to learn more about CR Bookkeeping & Tax Services and the services we offer. We can use social media to attract new clients or customers. We can keep our clients apprised of the latest industry news and company specials by regularly posting on our website, as well as apps such as Facebook and LinkedIn.

- **Utilizing friends and family for whom pervious work was done for referrals and testimonials.** Cynthia Rogers has been providing bookkeeping services for friends and family who own small businesses for some time. She will ask these contacts for referrals and testimonials to build her reputation and confirm her character.

- **Having a cache of business cards and promotional materials.** Business cards and promotional brochures will always be on-hand because you never know when you might meet your next best customer.

- **Mailing promotional brochures to businesses in the area.** The professional brochure will highlight the available services and testimonials from satisfied customers; several methods of contacting the company for service will also be prominently displayed.

- **Doing our best work every time.** In this industry, it is critical to always provide excellent service. Clients are relying on the services we provide and errors could have lasting cnsequences.

FINANCIAL ANALYSIS

There is little overhead in starting a freelance bookkeeping service. The startup costs are minimal, requiring only the costs to set up the office and obtain certification. The specific breakdown includes:

Start-Up Costs

AIPB Membership, $40

NACPB Membership, $100

QuickBooks Class, $550

QuickBooks Certification, $150

AIPB CB Certification, $480

NACPB CPB Certification, $100

QuickBooks Software, $1,000

Office furniture, $1,020

Office electronics, $3,660

Website, $150

Logo creation, $500

Marketing materials, $250

TOTAL, $8,000

Educational Resources

The Learning Tree

84557 Buccanneer Court
Tampa, Florida 33603

Fran Fletcher

The Learning Tree creates and sells educational resources for use by homeschool families and teachers in Tampa, Florida.

BUSINESS SUMMARY

The Learning Tree is an educational resource business owned and operated by Laurie Jones and Holly Morgan. The Learning Tree will offer lesson kits, activities, games, project ideas, and supplies for every school subject imaginable. Each summer, The Learning Tree will offer camps for elementary and middle school students with age appropriate skills to give them a head start on the upcoming school year.

Ms. Jones, a native of Alachua, Florida, has fifteen years of experience as an elementary school teacher. During her career, she has received recognition for going the extra mile to make learning fun for her students. She was named Teacher of the Year three years in a row. Ms. Morgan is a native of Tampa, Florida. She has nine years of experience as a middle school teacher. Like Ms. Jones, she also has received recognition for the creative ways she engages her students to learn.

The Learning Tree will market its online products to homeschooling families and teachers. The business will also market its products and services locally to Tampa residents by operating a brick and mortar store and by hosting summer camps and teacher workshops.

There are currently over two million homeschool students in the United States that purchase curriculum and related materials each year. Additionally, there are over one million elementary school teachers in the country who often purchase products that complement the national teaching standards. The Learning Tree's products will meet the needs of both groups with its vast selection of supplemental learning supplies.

There are two major competitors in the online teaching products industry:

- Teachers Help Teachers
- Materials For Teachers

What makes The Learning Tree stand out?

- It will use national standards as a guide so that its content is applicable.
- It will offer customized games and activities for a variety of subjects.

- It will offer teacher guides to help explain difficult concepts.

- It will offer summer camps.

- It will offer monthly kits delivered automatically.

The Learning Tree will advertise through:

- Social media

- Homeschool blogs

- Education blogs

- Newspapers

- Fliers

The owners wish to rent a building where they can develop teaching kits and conduct summer camp. The owners are seeking financing in the form of a business line of credit in the amount of $50,500. This amount will cover start–up costs and expenses for the first two months of operation. Financial projections indicate that The Learning Tree will be able to pay back the line of credit in five years.

COMPANY DESCRIPTION

Location

The Learning Tree will rent a building in Tampa, Florida. The owners have found a nice building that will meet their needs. This building is spacious and includes a supply room, work area, conference room, large open area, and eight large office spaces.

Hours of Operations

Monday–Thursday 9 a.m.–4 p.m.

Personnel

Laurie Jones (co–owner)
Ms. Jones has a Master's Degree in Education from Florida State University. She has fifteen years of experience working as an elementary school teacher. She has been recognized for her ability to engage students and teach difficult subjects in a fun way. She was named Teacher of the Year for her school district three years in a row. She will serve as the main creative force behind the business. She will create games, activities, and teaching kits.

Holly Morgan (co–owner)
Ms. Morgan has a Master's Degree in Education from the University of Florida. She has nine years of experience working as a middle School teacher. She has been recognized for her ability to teach difficult subjects using games and activities. She will write teacher help pages that will explain how to teach difficult subject matter in a fun and engaging way. She will also review federal standards to determine what teachers will need to enhance learning.

Products and Services

Products

- Science Kits

- History Kits

- Social Studies Kits

- Math Kits
- Writing Kits
- Reading Kits
- Language Arts Kits
- Foreign Language Kits
- Games
- Activities
- Worksheets

Services

- Teacher workshops
- Homeschool workshops
- Summer camps

MARKET ANALYSIS

Industry Overview

According to the U.S. Department of Education, it is estimated that two million children are homeschooled in the United States each year. Homeschool families often look for extra materials to go with their curriculum, materials that can be used for multiple grade levels, and for materials and activities that can be completed with minimal help.

According to the National Center for Education Statistics, there are over three million public school teachers in the United States. One third of these are elementary school teachers. National and state standards dictate the curriculum. Teachers are left without much time to spend on preparing supplemental learning materials. They depend on outside sources to create and prepare these materials.

The online store will be available around the clock for customers all over the country. The Learning Tree's brick and mortar store will be located in Tampa within five miles of five public elementary schools, one magnet school, one charter school, and one middle school. The Learning Tree will be visible to teachers and students who attend these nearby schools.

Target Market

The Learning Tree will focus on four target markets:

- Homeschool Families in the United States
- Teachers in the United States
- Students in Tampa
- Teachers in Tampa

The primary target market will be online product sales to homeschool families. Local customers will be targeted mainly during the summer months.

Competition

There are currently two major online competitors.

1. Teachers Help Teachers—Online marketplace where teachers can sell materials
2. Materials For Teachers—Online retailer for various teaching supplies

GROWTH STRATEGY

The overall strategy of the company is to produce quality teaching materials at an affordable price. The Learning Tree will work to gain notoriety in the homeschool community for offering affordable teaching materials. The Learning Tree would ultimately like to create its own brand of curriculum. The owners will be working toward this goal along with its regular business operations.

Additionally, the owners would like to obtain a portion of the online market for teacher supplies.

Locally, the owners want to establish a presence in the community by offering workshops and summer camps for local students. They will also sell their products in their brick and mortar store.

The owners expect that income will stem from the following streams:

Income Sources Projection

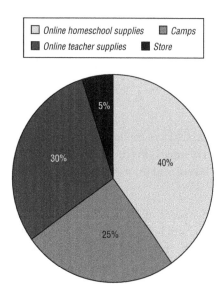

Sales and Marketing

The company will maintain a presence on social media in various homeschool and education groups. Products will be sent to ten notable homeschool and education bloggers in exchange for product review and promotion.

Marketing to gain notoriety in the homeschool community will include product promotion at two homeschool conventions each year. Additionally, the owners will offer monthly workshops for area homeschoolers, summer camps for area students, and summer workshops for area teachers.

Advertising

Advertising products and services to the homeschool community will be very important to the growth of the company, both online and locally. Advertising will include:

- Maintaining a social media presence

- Promotion by homeschool bloggers

- Product promotion at homeschool conventions

Local community support will also be important to the company's success. Advertising products and services to the local community will include:

- Maintaining a social media presence
- Advertising in Tampa newspapers
- Sending fliers and information to area schoolteachers and students

FINANCIAL ANALYSIS

Start–up costs

Estimated Start–up Costs

Building lease advance	$ 2,000
Office furniture	$10,000
Supplies	$10,000
Computers	$ 5,000
Website	$ 2,000
Graphic design software	$ 2,000
Advertising	$ 500
Total	**$31,500**

Estimated Monthly Income

Monthly income will be determined by online sales. The owners conservatively estimate that they will host one homeschool workshop each month. They project that online sales will start slowly, but will ramp up and level out.

Prices for Products

Products	Mailed	Digital Download
Subject kits (10 lessons)	$ 50	$20
Supplemental kits	$ 50	$20
Lesson kits (1 lesson)	$ 25	$ 8
Games	$ 25	$10
Worksheets	$ 2	$ 1
Monthly kits	$480	N/A

Prices for Services

Services	Price
Summer camp	$30 per student
Homeschool workshops	$30 per student
	$50 per family
Teacher workshops	$35 per teacher

Estimated Monthly Expenses

Printer rental	$ 100
Bank loan	$ 800
Electricity	$ 250
Insurance	$ 50
Phone/Internet	$ 100
Advertising	$ 100
Supplies	$ 100
Wages for Ms. Jones (est.)	$4,000
Wages for Ms. Morgan (est.)	$4,000
Total	**$9,500**

Profit/Loss

The owners conservatively estimate modest profits for the first two months while their business is getting publicity from online blogs. They estimate a steady increase in online sales for the third through fifth months. During the summer months, the owners expect the majority of their income to stem from summer camps and teacher workshops. August and September are estimated to be the largest sales months since homeschool families and teachers are getting ready for the new school year. Then, sales are expected to decrease but remain steady during the last three months of the year. The second and third year are expected to see profits similar to the first year minus the losses experienced in the first few months of operation.

Estimated Monthly Profits

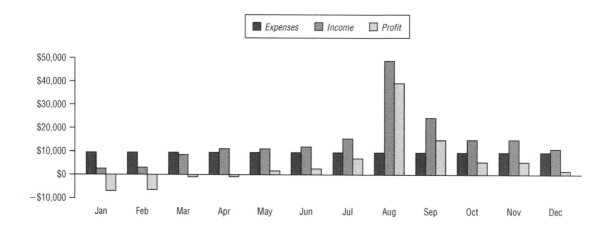

Estimated Profits Years 1–3

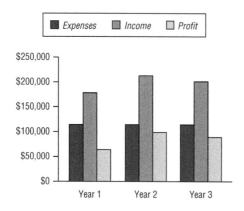

Financing

The owners would like to obtain a business line of credit for $50,500. This will cover the start–up costs and operating expenses for the first two months.

Repayment Plan

The business will make payments of $800 each month. The loan will be repaid in approximately five years.

Loan Repayment Plan

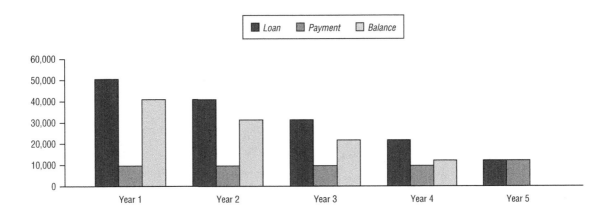

Fundraising Program Developer

Thorpe Consulting Inc.

9554 Charlotte Dr.
Brighton, IL 62558

Paul Greenland

Thorpe Consulting specializes in designing, planning, executing, and managing creative fundraising programs for charities and nonprofit organizations.

EXECUTIVE SUMMARY

Fundraising is the lifeblood of nonprofit organizations. Thorpe Consulting helps nonprofits develop and manage programs, from small events to longer campaigns, that achieve goals creatively and successfully. The business has been established by Amanda Thorpe, an experienced event planner with a passion for the nonprofit sector. Prior to establishing her own consulting business, Thorpe served as director of corporate events and exhibits for a large university. Additionally, she has extensive experience volunteering and serving on the boards of several charities. With more than 1.5 million nonprofit organizations in the United States, significant opportunities exist for growing Thorpe Consulting into a thriving enterprise.

INDUSTRY ANALYSIS

Citing data from the National Center for Charitable Statistics, GrantSpace revealed that the number of nonprofit organizations in the United States exceeded 1.5 million during the late 2010s. Operating at the local, state, regional, national, and international levels, these organizations not only included foundations and charities, but also fraternal organizations, civic leagues, and chambers of commerce.

Thorpe Consulting is part of the broader consulting industry. According to data from the U.S. Bureau of Labor Statistics, approximately 806,400 management consultants were employed in 2016. By 2026, an additional 115,200 positions were expected to develop within the industry, fueled by an above-average growth rate of 14 percent. In 2017, median annual pay for management consultants was $82,450. One of the key factors driving growth was the need for businesses to control costs and improve efficiency. Approximately 17 percent of management consultants are self-employed. A key professional association for consultants is the Institute of Management Consultants (https://www.imcusa.org), which has served more than 10,000 members since its formation in 1968.

With its focus on event planning, Thorpe Consulting was also a part of the event planning industry. In addition to independent consultants, professionals in the field are employed by conference centers, hotels, and organizations. The industry includes several trade and professional organizations. Established in 1972, Meeting Professionals International (MPI) (https://www.mpiweb.org) claims to be the world's largest association in the meeting and event industry. Its 17,000 members belong to approximately 90 clubs and chapters in 19 different countries and benefit from "innovative and relevant education, networking opportunities and business exchanges." Another organization is the Event Planners Association (https://www.eventplannersassociation.com), which offers "legal contracts/templates, business optimization, networking, done for you marketing, software, certification programs, and valuable discounts" to its members.

MARKET ANALYSIS

Thorpe Consulting initially will serve customers in the states of Illinois, Iowa, Wisconsin, and Minnesota. Prospective customers fall into many different categories, including:

- Chambers of Commerce
- Charities
- Civic Leagues
- Colleges & Universities
- Foundations
- Fraternal Organizations
- Healthcare Systems
- Hospitals
- Museums
- Private Schools
- Public School Districts
- Religious Organizations
- Sports Clubs

Because she has extensive experience working at a large university and serving on the boards of charitable organizations focused on illiteracy and homelessness, Amanda Thorpe will concentrate her marketing efforts on these types of organizations, which will be Thorpe Consulting's primary target markets. Key secondary target markets include private schools, public school districts, and sports clubs. Using resources available at her public library, Amanda Thorpe has compiled a detailed list of prospects in each category, which are available upon request.

SERVICES

Thorpe Consulting specializes in designing, planning, executing, and managing creative fundraising programs for charities and nonprofit organizations. Some clients may require assistance in only one of these areas, while others need an outside resource to conceptualize, create, and run turnkey programs. Whether a client only needs a few hours of consulting time to identify creative possibilities for a potential event or campaign, or a trusted partner to plan and handle a major event from soup to nuts, Thorpe Consulting is an ideal solution.

Campaigns & Events
The types of campaigns and events that Thorpe Consulting can assist with are limited only by the imagination. They include, but certainly are not limited to:

- Advocacy Events
- Annual Events

- Bake Sales
- Bowling Tournaments
- Carnivals
- Charity Auctions
- Crowdfunding Campaigns
- Dances
- Date Night Auctions
- Donation Kiosks
- Family Fun Days
- Fashion Shows
- Galas
- Golf Tournaments
- Jail & Bail Events
- Local Athletic Competitions
- Networking Dinners
- Obstacle Courses
- Peer-to-Peer Fundraising (Fun Runs, Walkathons, Bike-a-Thons)
- Pub Crawls
- Raffles
- Recycling Drives
- Scavenger Hunts
- Special Themed Events
- Speed Dating
- Talent Show
- Tree-Planting Parties
- Trivia Tournaments
- Variety Shows
- Videogame Tournaments
- Virtual Bake Sales
- Wacky Sports Contests
- Work-a-Thons
- World Markets
- Yard Sales

Process

After connecting with a potential client, Amanda Thorpe will discuss their specific goals and objectives, and determine how her consulting services fit into the picture. Once this has been determined, Thorpe Consulting will follow a process that may involve a few or all of the following steps:

- Developing, alone or in collaboration with the client, one or more potential event/campaign ideas or themes.

- Developing project timelines and checklists.

- Selecting event venues.

- Identifying required resources and vendors.

- Securing estimates.

- Booking and managing vendors.

- Coordinating and managing available internal resources.

- Producing room/location diagrams and maps.

- Overseeing event planning, coordination, and set-up.

- Providing on-site supervision of events to ensure customer satisfaction.

- Overseeing event breakdown/cleanup.

- Settling vendor accounts.

- Gathering input and feedback.

- Measuring results (attendance, funds raised, etc.).

- Reporting/sharing results.

External Resources

In addition to utilizing a customer's available internal resources, Thorpe Consulting will identify, book, and manage outside vendors on behalf of its clients in a variety of categories, including:

- Audio-visual (lighting, sound, videography, photography)

- Business/Corporate Event Insurance

- Catering

- Decorations (balloons, table decorations, plants)

- Entertainment (musicians and performers, photo booths, comedians, guest speakers)

- Equipment Rental (tents, chairs, podiums, staging)

- Marketing (print advertising, Web promotion, social media)

- Media Relations (news releases, interview coordination)

- Premiums (T-shirts, pens, and other promotional items)

- Registration

- Security (loss prevention, traffic/parking control, guest safety)

Fees & Rates

Thorpe Consulting charges an hourly rate of $125 for all consulting and event management services.

OPERATIONS

Location

To keep overhead low during its initial years of operations, Thorpe Consulting will operate as a home-based business. This type of arrangement is ideal because Amanda Thorpe typically will meet with her clients off-site, at their place of business or event venue, doing away with the need for dedicated office facilities.

Communications

Thorpe Consulting has secured a low-cost toll-free number with auto attendant capabilities and dedicated extensions, allowing clients to speak with Amanda Thorpe directly or reach her virtual assistant, Patricia Ludlow, who can assist with scheduling meetings, fielding calls, coordinating arrangements with vendors, etc.

Business Structure

Thorpe Consulting is structured as an S corporation, which provides its owner with certain tax and liability advantages. Amanda Thorpe established her S corporation as cost-effectively as possible by using a popular online legal document service.

Liability

In conjunction with a reputable insurance agency, Amanda Thorpe has secured an appropriate level of liability coverage for her firm.

PERSONNEL

Amanda Thorpe (President)

Prior to establishing her own consulting business, Amanda Thorpe served as director of corporate events and exhibits for Crandon University. Additionally, she has extensive experience volunteering and serving on the boards of several charities, including Parkwood Rescue Mission and Literacy Champions. After earning an undergraduate degree from the University of Minnesota, Thorpe earned an MBA from Lakewood University. She possesses many of the qualities needed to run her own enterprise successfully. In addition to having excellent time, project, and budget management skills, Thorpe is able to communicate effectively with individuals at all levels, from C-suite executives to operations-level staff, and has a strong reputation for facilitating information exchange between various teams, partners, departments, vendors, and other stakeholders.

Professional & Advisory Support

Thorpe Consulting has established a business banking account with Green Forest Bank. The business has hired virtual assistant Patricia Ludlow to assist with scheduling meetings, fielding calls, coordinating arrangements with vendors, etc. Tax advisory and bookkeeping services are provided by Evans Financial Services LP.

MARKETING & SALES

Thorpe Consulting will use the following primary tactics to market its services:

1. A monthly fundraising program development podcast, featuring guest interviews with nonprofit leaders, vendors, and event planners.

2. A content marketing strategy featuring free checklists, guides, and articles that nonprofit executives and educators can download in exchange for joining the firm's mailing list.

3. A media relations strategy that promotes Amanda Thorpe as a thought leader and expert source to industry publications.

4. A quarterly direct response campaign targeting the primary and secondary target markets identified in the Market Analysis section of this plan.

5. A presence on LinkedIn, including the posting of occasional guest articles.

6. A Web site featuring downloadable content, including articles and podcasts; Amanda Thorpe's bio; testimonials and success stories; an opt-in newsletter; social media links; and complete details about the firm and the services it provides.

7. Networking and presentations at important nonprofit conferences and events.

GROWTH STRATEGY

Amanda Thorpe is fortunate to begin operations with two clients, with whom she has worked as an independent contractor. Understanding that she will need to devote uncompensated time to the business (e.g., for marketing and administrative tasks), Thorpe has identified what she feels are realistic and conservative targets for billable hours during the consultancy's first three years of operations. These projections are based on 50 work weeks annually:

Year One: Begin operations with two initial clients. Launch marketing campaign to primary and secondary target markets. Achieve an average of 20 billable hours per week. Generate gross revenue of $125,000.

Year Two: Expand services to the state of Indiana. Continue sustained marketing efforts to primary and secondary target markets. Achieve an average of 25 billable hours per week. Generate gross revenue of $156,250.

Year Three: Expand services to the state of Ohio. Begin evaluating the possibility of adding a second consultant to the firm. Achieve an average of 30 billable hours per week. Generate gross revenue of $187,500.

FINANCIAL ANALYSIS

Following are the firm's projected revenue and expenses for the first three years of operations:

	2020	2021	2022
Revenue	**$125,000**	**$156,250**	**$187,500**
Expenses			
Salaries	$ 80,000	$ 85,000	$ 90,000
Employment tax	$ 12,000	$ 12,750	$ 13,500
Home office reimbursement	$ 650	$ 650	$ 650
Insurance	$ 750	$ 850	$ 950
Office supplies	$ 450	$ 450	$ 450
Equipment	$ 500	$ 500	$ 500
Marketing & advertising	$ 7,500	$ 10,000	$ 12,500
Telecommunications & Internet	$ 1,800	$ 2,000	$ 2,200
Professional development	$ 1,500	$ 1,500	$ 1,500
Travel & entertainment	$ 3,500	$ 4,000	$ 4,500
Subscriptions & dues	$ 325	$ 400	$ 475
Miscellaneous	$ 500	$ 500	$ 500
Total expenses	**$109,475**	**$118,600**	**$127,725**
Net income	**$ 15,525**	**$ 37,650**	**$ 59,775**

Gift Box Subscription Business

Adventure Box

20056 Oakwood Ave.
Butte, MT 59703

Paul Greenland

Adventure Box sells subscription-based hunting, fishing, and camping-themed gift boxes.

EXECUTIVE SUMMARY

In addition to owning Jake's Outdoor Adventure, an independent hunting, camping, and fishing retailer, Jake Benton publishes the highly successful blog, AdventureLand, where he covers topics regarding outdoor adventures of all kinds. With more than 30,000 followers, the blog has provided him with a strong platform for reaching lots of outdoor enthusiasts. About 70 percent of his subscribers are men. To build on the success of his retail store and blog, Jake has decided to launch Adventure Box, a related gift box business. Tapping into existing connections with suppliers, wholesalers, and craftspeople, Jake will benefit by launching Adventure Box to his existing customers and blog followers. Although Adventure Box will operate as division of Jake's Outdoor Adventure, Inc., it easily could be operated as a standalone enterprise.

INDUSTRY ANALYSIS

Adventure Box is part of the U.S. retail industry, which generated annual revenue of approximately $5.45 billion in 2018, according to IBISWorld. The industry includes 2.71 million businesses that collectively employ 18.67 million people. The researcher anticipated annual growth of 1.2 percent would occur through 2023. During the late 2010s, retailing was in a state of transition. Many traditional brick-and-mortar stores had closed or scaled back locations as a result of e-commerce. In its "2019 Retail Outlook," Deloitte indicated that changes would likely continue to unfold in the coming years. "Consumers realize they can have it all," the firm explained. "Today's digital consumer is increasingly connected, has more access to information, and expects businesses to react to all their needs and wants instantly. Many shoppers have an increased desire for personalized services."

MARKET ANALYSIS

According to the Hitwise report, "Subscription Boxes in 2018," the U.S. market has achieved explosive growth in just a few short years, with online visits to pure-play companies increasing from 4.7 million visits in early 2014 to 41.7 million in early 2018. During the first quarter of 2018 alone, a record

18.5 million people visited at least one subscription site, according to Hitwise, reflecting a 24-percent increase over the previous year. Although the market was maturing, ample opportunity still existed for innovative new businesses.

Hitwise indicated that food, beauty, and kids were the market's top three categories during the late 2010s. The following companies were identified as market leaders:

1. ipsy
2. Blue Apron
3. Hello Fresh
4. Stitch Fix
5. Dollar Shave Club
6. Home Chef
7. FabFitFun
8. Birchbox
9. Loot Crate
10. Groove Collaborative

Mobile strategies are essential for marketing subscription box services. Hitwise revealed that about 65 percent of traffic on subscription box sites originates from tablets or smart phones. This is a much higher percentage compared to the overall retail industry (53%). Additionally, mobile access within the lifestyle category is even higher, at 68 percent.

Although the gift market was once considered to be highly seasonal, it has become more of a year-round opportunity for retailers in recent years. As Pamela N. Danziger explained in the October 29, 2017, issue of *Forbes*: "In retail today the fourth quarter's importance is greatly overrated. Since 1992 the contribution of the fourth quarter to annual sales has been on the decline, shifting from 32.8% of total sales to 28.9% in 2016.... The gift market represents an enormous opportunity for retailers not just at holiday time, but throughout the rest of the year. What makes the gift market so powerful is that it is a unique marketing opportunity to touch two target consumers at once—the gift buyer who makes the purchase and the gift recipient who receives the gift."

Competition

Gift box subscriptions are growing in popularity, and many other sellers offer various types of gift boxes targeted toward outdoor enthusiasts. However, Adventure Box will stand out from the competition by leveraging the trust and loyalty that Jake Benton enjoys with his existing retail customers and blog followers. Rather than throwing together random compilations of items, Jake will use knowledge gained from personal experience and operating his retail store to develop gift boxes that offer extremely popular items that are high in quality and available at the lowest possible price. He will put his personal reputation behind every box. By welcoming feedback from his followers and customers, Jake will continuously improve Adventure Box's offerings and seek out new items to include.

PRODUCTS

Overview

Adventure Box sells gift boxes for hunting, fishing, and camping enthusiasts in several different categories. Customers purchase competitively priced annual subscriptions and receive a different themed gift box every three months (four per year). All products are of the highest quality and are personally selected by Jake Benton. Subscriptions require prepayment and renew automatically unless canceled prior to the renewal date.

Subscriptions

Adventure Box offers three different themes/price points, including:

1. **The Fly Fisher ($60)**—A trout fisher's dream, this package includes 12 trout flies per box, attractively packaged in a reusable metal tin.

2. **The Knife Collector ($100)**—For those with an affinity for sharp things, this package delivers a different type of knife every time, including pocketknives, hunting knives, tactical knives, and more. This option also is delivered in a reusable metal tin.

3. **The Camper ($140)**—Outdoorsy types will eagerly await this selection of 8–10 useful camping items, such as flashlights, journals, thermoses, first aid kits, hand warmers, and water purification tablets.

In the future, gift boxes focused on snacks (nuts, jerky, etc.) and clothing items will be introduced based on customer feedback.

OPERATIONS

Adventure Box will operate as division of Jake's Outdoor Adventure, Inc. Owner Jake Benton will work with existing suppliers and wholesalers to purchase high quality items at the best possible price for his gift box operation. Many of the same items featured in Adventure Box's subscription packages will also be sold individually via Jake's Outdoor Adventure brick-and-mortar store and its corresponding e-commerce site. In addition to working with existing suppliers, Benton also will buy goods through international channels like Alibaba.com, where merchandise and packaging supplies can be purchased in bulk quantities for deep discounts. The existing staff at Jake's Outdoor Adventure will arrange, package, and ship gift boxes directly to customers.

PERSONNEL

Jake Benton (owner)

In addition to owning Jake's Outdoor Adventure, an independent hunting, camping, and fishing retailer, Jake Benton publishes the highly successful blog, AdventureLand, where he covers outdoor adventures of all kinds, along with related topics like outdoor cooking. With more than 30,000 followers, the blog has provided him with a strong platform for reaching lots of outdoor enthusiasts. A modern day Renaissance man, Jake has many interests, ranging from carpentry and woodworking to cross country skiing and model railroading.

After earning undergraduate and graduate business degrees from the University of Colorado, Jake spent fifteen years serving as a management consultant in the retail industry. During that time, he had the privilege of working with big-box retailers, e-commerce pioneers, and many entrepreneurs and independent retailers. His experience provided him with a holistic view of retailing, and a hunger to get involved. An avid outdoorsman, Jake ultimately decided to combine his passion for hunting, camping, fishing, and outdoor sports with his knowledge of retailing to establish Jake's Outdoor Adventure. What began as a humble storefront shop ultimately evolved into a thriving retail destination that attracts thousands of customers per year. Outdoor enthusiasts appreciate Jake's Outdoor Adventure for its competitive pricing, commitment to quality, and knowledgeable staff. By forming Adventure Box, Jake Benton has the opportunity to extend the geographic reach of an already thriving retail enterprise.

GROWTH STRATEGY

The following growth strategy has been developed for Adventure Box's first three years of operations:

Year One: Launch Adventure Box with an initial marketing push to customers of Jake's Outdoor Adventure and subscribers to the Adventureland blog. Initially offer three gift box packages: The Fly Fisher, the Knife Collector, and the Camper. Generate net profit of $25,000 from the sale of 532 annual subscriptions.

Year Two: Based on customer feedback, introduce an outdoor snack-themed (nuts, jerky, etc.) gift box package. Investigate opportunities to expand the business through affiliate marketing relationships. Generate net profit of $50,000 from the sale of 1,064 subscriptions.

Year Three: Consider introducing an outdoor clothing-themed (T-shirts, stocking caps, camo, etc.) gift box package. Generate net profit of $75,000 from the sale of 1,595 subscriptions.

As Adventure Box evolves, numerous opportunities exist for expanding the business' selection of gift boxes to other closely related categories such as mountain climbing, hiking, kayaking, and skiing. Secondary categories that also may be popular with customers include hand tools, grilling (barbecue supplies, wood chips, seasonings, spices, etc.), shaving (razors, beard care, grooming kits, etc.), and exercise/fitness (gym accessories, protein powders, supplements).

MARKETING & SALES

Adventure Box will benefit from dedicated marketing tactics, as well as cross-promotional opportunities it will enjoy as a division of Jake's Outdoor Adventure, including:

1. In-store promotions within Jake's Outdoor Adventure.

2. Special discounts and offers to members of the Jake's Outdoor Adventure loyalty club.

3. Promotion throughout the mobile and regular versions of the Jake's Outdoor Adventure Web site.

4. Exposure on Jake Benton's Adventureland blog.

5. Dedicated social media promotion via Facebook, Instagram, Twitter, Pinterest, and Youtube.

6. Displays at regional outdoor, hunting, camping, and fishing shows.

7. Search engine optimization.

8. Paid search advertising.

9. Word-of-mouth marketing

FINANCIAL ANALYSIS

The following table provides an average estimated per-unit breakdown of gift boxes in each of Adventure Box's three subscription categories, including wholesale price, associated costs (e.g., packaging, shipping, and labor), and net profit:

Item	Description	Wholesale	Retail	Packaging	Shipping	Labor	Total Cost	Net Profit
Fly fisher	12 trout flies	$1.55	$15	$0.05	$2.00	$0.50	$ 4.10	$10.90
Knife collector	1 knife 8–10 camping	$9.50	$25	$0.05	$3.00	$0.50	$13.05	$11.95
Camper	items	$ 15	$35	$0.10	$7.00	$0.50	$22.60	$12.40

Including all categories, the owner has prepared the following five-year sales targets for Adventure Box's gift box subscriptions:

All	2020	2021	2022	2023	2024
Unit volume	532	1,064	1,595	2,128	2,660
Net profit	$25,000	$50,000	$75,000	$100,000	$125,000

Graffiti Removal Business

Graffiti Action Network, Inc.

2147 Cedar St., Ste. 303
Preston, Pennsylvania 15010

Paul Greenland

Graffiti Action Network, Inc. is a nonprofit organization focused on removing graffiti from residential, commercial, and municipal properties.

EXECUTIVE SUMMARY

Graffiti Action Network, Inc. is a nonprofit organization focused on removing graffiti from residential, commercial, and municipal properties. The organization's mission is to preserve the beauty and pride of its community by removing graffiti "tags," which are problematic for towns and cities of all sizes. In some cases, graffiti is the result of street gangs marking their territory. In other instances, it is viewed as an outlet for artists to express social, political, or artistic viewpoints. Most communities view graffiti as a form of vandalism that has real economic and social costs. With a small but dedicated administrative staff, Graffiti Action Network provides graffiti removal using teams of volunteers. The following plan outlines the organization's strategy for its first three years of operations.

MARKET ANALYSIS

Nationwide, between $12 and $20 billion is spent every year on graffiti removal, according to the company, ALPOLIC Materials. Costs are higher in larger cities, with Los Angeles spending approximately $7 million annually to clean up more than 30 million square feet of graffiti. Graffiti Action Network serves the community of Preston, Pennsylvania, which has struggled with rising levels of vandalism for 10 consecutive years. The city had a population of 150,131 people (58,296 households) in 2017. That year, nearly $312,483 was spent on the removal of 4,130 graffiti "tags," compared to $250,505 and 3,126 graffiti tags in 2016, respectively. In the previous 10 years, more than 650 vandals (or "taggers") have been arrested for graffiti-related crimes. Preston also has intensified its prevention efforts by developing an outreach program that targets students at the elementary, junior high, and high school levels. However, the problem not only remains, but continues to grow, requiring additional resources like Graffiti Action Network, which inspires and mobilizes the community to address this problem at a grassroots level.

SERVICES

Project Planning

Graffiti Action Network's administrative staff facilitates communications with city officials, residents, and business owners to discuss graffiti abatement issues. Potential projects typically are referred by the City of Preston, which receives graffiti reports from the community via a 24-hour hotline and Web site. Referrals are evaluated by the organization's executive director, who meets with property owners or managers, determines the scope of required work (e.g., number of volunteers, supplies, equipment, etc.), takes representative photographs, and calculates related costs to formulate a budget. Projects are classified by size (small, medium, large, and very large), entered into a database, and prioritized at the organization's monthly board meeting. The board of directors develops a quarterly project schedule, providing staff with enough time to organize volunteer groups and procure necessary supplies and equipment.

Removal Process

Graffiti Action Network will perform graffiti removal services according to the aforementioned quarterly project schedule approved by its board of directors. The City of Preston will be notified of all projects, and arrangements will be made beforehand with property owners/managers. The methods and equipment needed for graffiti removal will vary from project to project and will be defined by the executive director during her initial assessment. In some cases, the removal process may be completed using a hot water (190 degrees) pressure washer, working from the bottom of the surface to the top. In other cases, solvents or chemicals will be applied to services beforehand and agitated with nylon or bristle brushes. Care will be taken when scrubbing graffiti with brushes so that the surface eventually regains its original color after exposure to the elements. Removing graffiti on porous surfaces (e.g., cinderblock walls) may be impossible, requiring painting instead of removal. In this case, preparation (e.g., sanding, washing, etc.) may be required prior to painting with brushes, rollers, or sprayers (depending on the size and scope of the job). Some projects will be more complicated and time-intensive than others if there is no access to power (requiring a generator) or water (requiring a portable supply), or if the graffiti is difficult to reach.

Abatement Categories

The organization will remove graffiti from a wide variety of surfaces, including but not limited to:

- Telephone Poles
- Street Curbs
- Building Exteriors
- House Exteriors
- Stone Surfaces
- Decorative Rocks
- Wood Fences
- Concrete
- Brick Walls
- Mailboxes
- Utility Boxes
- Garage Doors
- Sheds
- Lampposts

OPERATIONS

Location

Graffiti Action Network's office is in Wellington Place, a former YWCA facility that was converted into a community center in 2005. Dormitory rooms on the building's upper floors have been converted into cost-effective office space, which mainly is occupied by community and nonprofit organizations. Graffiti Action Network occupies two adjoining rooms in the building. While small, the footprint is large enough to accommodate the organization's three staff members. Additionally, there are several meeting rooms in the building, which are available to tenants. Equipment storage space has been provided by the City of Preston, which has given the organization access to a lockable storage cage in its municipal building at no charge, as well as garage space to store its trailers.

Equipment

Graffiti Removal Equipment

Graffiti Action Network will require some or all of the following equipment when working on community projects. The organization will begin operations with four trailers, which have been donated by the City of Preston. Each trailer will be equipped with a pressure washer, generator, and most of the items on the following list. Volunteers (typically team leaders) will use their own vehicles to tow supply trailers to graffiti abatement sites.

- 3000 PSI Pressure Washer (Hot/Cold)
- Trailers
- Spray Bottles
- Safety Glasses
- Paint Brushes
- Paint Rollers
- Respirators
- Wire Brushes
- Hoses
- Nylon Bristle Brushes
- Buckets
- Air Compressors
- Paint Spray Guns
- Extension Cords
- Generators
- Ladders

Graffiti Removal Supplies

- Aerosol Solvents
- Cotton Rags
- Trash Bags
- Paint Containers
- Paints

- Paint Scrapers
- Dust Masks
- Paint Roller Heads
- Kitchen Cleaners
- Biodegradable Emulsifiers
- Water

Office Equipment

- Phone System with Voicemail
- Computer
- Productivity Software (for Word Processing and Database Management)
- Multifunction Device (Print/Fax/Copy)
- Desks
- Filing Cabinets

Office Supplies

- Plain Paper
- Forms
- Stationary
- Pens
- Pencils
- Markers

PERSONNEL

Graffiti Action Network employs a small staff consisting of an executive director, volunteer coordinator, and an administrative assistant:

Executive Director: Held by former 12th Ward Alderman Janet Cabello, the responsibilities of this position include communications with the board of directors, government officials, community leaders, area residents, and local business owners. Additionally, the executive director oversees the organization's budget, fundraising, and promotional activities.

Volunteer Coordinator: This position, held by Gary Green, is responsible for organizing groups of volunteers for graffiti removal projects and providing them with hands-on training. However, the volunteer coordinator also is responsible for purchasing supplies and equipment, facilitating equipment maintenance and repairs, and assisting the executive director with communications tasks.

Administrative Assistant: The administrative assistant position, held by Jennifer Shepard, is responsible for frontline communications (e.g., answering phones, responding to e-mails, managing the organization's social media platforms, ordering office supplies, and providing general administrative support to the executive director and volunteer coordinator).

Volunteers: The organization will rely on community volunteers to complete graffiti removal projects. In general, volunteers will fall into one of two categories (team leaders and general volunteers). All volunteers will complete an orientation that includes extensive safety training. Team leaders will be provided with a more in-depth orientation program that covers basic leadership and communication skills, as well as technical training pertaining to graffiti removal methods, including related supplies and equipment.

Salary Costs

The following salaries have been budgeted for Graffiti Action Network's first year of operations:

Executive Director ($35,000)

Volunteer Coordinator ($24,500)

Administrative Assistant ($18,700)

Total salary costs: ($78,220)

Board of Directors

Graffiti Action Network's board of directors is responsible for establishing policies and making all major decisions for the organization, in conjunction with Executive Director Janet Cabello. The board's members, several of whom were part of a steering committee responsible for its establishment, have been carefully chosen. Each member possesses specific knowledge, skills, and expertise that will be of great benefit to Graffiti Action Network. In 2019, the organization's board members included:

Candace Adams—the City of Preston's Director of Public Works.

Brice Amdur—a certified public accountant and well-known member of the business community.

Jamal Williams—Executive Director of the Preston Chamber of Commerce.

Margaret P. Davis—Worthington County Board Chairwoman.

Larry Holmes—Preston Neighborhood Watch Director.

Peter Graham—Manager of Public Information for Preston Community Health System.

Denver H. McCoy—Executive Director of Keep Eastern Pennsylvania Beautiful.

Douglas Perry—a real estate attorney with the firm of Jensen, Sully & Tate.

Tracey Englewood Price—City of Preston Chief of Police.

MARKETING & SALES

Graffiti Action Network has developed a marketing plan that includes the following tactics:

1. **Public Meetings:** Graffiti Action Network will host a series of public meetings to garner public support, volunteers, and media coverage for its programs.

2. **Media Relations:** The organization will issue press releases on a periodic basis to announce the completion of successful graffiti abatement projects, and will seek to procure television news stories showcasing its volunteers in action, volunteer recruitment drives, etc.

3. **Newsletter:** An e-newsletter (e-mail and mobile-friendly format) will be developed to keep potential supporters, volunteers, partners, and community members informed of programmatic developments, success stories, progress, special events, and fundraising opportunities.

4. **Volunteer Drives:** Graffiti Action Network will host quarterly volunteer drives throughout the City of Preston and the surrounding region.

5. **Public Service Announcements:** The organization will solicit public service announcements from local radio and television outlets to stay visible with community members and potential fundraising sources.

6. **Web Site:** A Web site will be developed for Graffiti Action Network that offers key information regarding the organization, contact information, volunteer opportunities, press releases, social media links, and a link to the city's graffiti reporting page/database.

7. **Social Media:** The organization will maintain a presence on several social media channels, including Twitter, Facebook, Instagram, and LinkedIn.

8. **Direct Mail:** In partnership with a reputable list broker and mail house, Graffiti Action Network will conduct a semiannual direct mailing to prospective individual and corporate donors (seeking monetary donations, as well as supplies and equipment).

GROWTH STRATEGY

Prior to commencing operations, Graffiti Action Network devoted the previous year to planning and preparation. During this time, the organization was incorporated, its bylaws were established, a board of directors was elected, initial grant funding was received, and this business plan was developed. With enough funds to begin operations, Graffiti Action Network has now procured equipment and supplies and established office operations.

During its first year of operations, Graffiti Action Network will complete an estimated 172 projects (approximately 3–4 per week). The organization has established a goal of increasing total project volume by 15 percent annually, as reflected in the following chart:

Project Size	2019	2020	2021
Small	146	168	193
Medium	18	21	24
Large	7	8	9
Very large	1	2	3
	172	**199**	**229**

Following is a summary of Graffiti Action Network's growth targets for its first three years of operations:

Year One: Begin operations with a three-member administrative staff, including the executive director, volunteer coordinator, and administrative assistant. Recruit and train four volunteer team leaders and 20 general volunteers. Complete 172 graffiti removal projects.

Year Two: Procure two additional trailers. Increase total fundraising by 10 percent over the previous year. Recruit and train an additional two volunteer team leaders and 16 general volunteers. Complete 199 graffiti removal projects. Evaluate opportunities to assist the City of Preston with graffiti prevention/youth outreach efforts.

Year Three: Procure two additional trailers. Increase total fundraising by 15 percent over the previous year. Recruit and train two volunteer team leaders and 16 general volunteers. Complete 229 graffiti removal projects. Begin assisting the City of Preston with graffiti prevention/youth outreach efforts. Explore opportunities to assist the city with other beautification projects.

LEGAL

With the assistance of a local business attorney, Graffiti Action Network has been organized as a nonprofit corporation in the state of Pennsylvania and is a tax-exempt 501(C)(3) organization. A Federal Employer Identification Number (FEIN) has been obtained. The corporation's bylaws have been reviewed by its legal counsel to ensure they adhere to state law. An appropriate level of liability insurance coverage has been obtained. Related policies are available for review upon request.

FINANCIAL ANALYSIS

Income & Expenses

The following table provides a summary of Graffiti Action Network's total income and expenses for the first year of operations:

Income

Grant funding	$ 75,000
Individual fundraising	$ 25,000
Corporate fundraising	$ 75,000
Total income	**$175,000**

Expenses

Insurance	$ 3,500
Equipment	$ 8,500
Rent	$ 4,200
Telecommunications	$ 1,150
Utilities	$ 1,000
Equipment maintenance	$ 2,000
Audit/990 fees	$ 2,500
Office supplies	$ 475
Newsletter	$ 750
Advertising and promotion	$ 3,250
Postage	$ 1,600
Fuel	$ 3,250
Events	$ 4,000
Supplies	$ 45,000
Salaries	$ 78,220
Payroll taxes	$ 11,733
Misc.	$ 450
Total expenses	**$171,578**
Operating profit	**$ 3,422**

Funding

Approximately 43 percent of Graffiti Action Network's funding will come from grants, including a substantial matching grant from the City of Preston. A like amount has been raised from local corporations and business owners (a detailed list is available upon request), with the remaining 14 percent coming from individual donors.

Projected Abatement Costs

Graffiti Action Network has determined that, in most cases, it can provide graffiti removal services at an average cost of $1.50 per square foot, most of which is attributable to supplies and equipment. On average, chemicals represent approximately 10 percent of the cost of each project. In most cases, the organization's volunteer coordinator will be on-site for at least a portion of every project, or in regular communication with the volunteer team leader, resulting in some labor-related costs.

The organization estimates that its abatement costs will fall into the following ranges, based on project size:

Small Projects (1–249 SF; $1.50–$374)

Medium Projects (250–499 SF; $375–$749)

Large Projects (500–999 SF; $750–$1,499)

Very Large Projects (1,000 SF+; $1,500–$5,000+)

Based on feedback with local law enforcement and government officials, Graffiti Action Network anticipates that 55 percent of the projects it performs will fall into the small category. Medium projects will account for about 20 percent of the organization's services, followed by large projects (15%), and very large projects (10%).

Graffiti Removal Budget

For its first year of operations, Graffiti Action Network has developed the following budget for graffiti removal projects:

Small Projects: $27,500

Medium Projects: $10,000

Large Projects: $7,500

Very Large Projects: $5,000

Total: $50,000

Graphic Designer

Bergeon Graphic Design Services LLC

PO Box 44901
Kalamazoo, MI 49005

Zuzu Enterprises

Bergeon Graphic Design Services LLC is a freelance graphic design firm specializing in creating digital content for use on social media for advertising and brand promotion. It is owned and operated by Elizabeth Bergeon.

EXECUTIVE SUMMARY

Graphic designers create visual concepts to communicate ideas that inspire, inform, and captivate consumers. They develop the overall layout and production design for various applications such as advertisements, brochures, magazines, and corporate reports. Technology plays a major role in the creation of digital work available in graphic design.

Bergeon Graphic Design Services LLC is a freelance graphic design firm specializing in creating digital content for use on social media for advertising and brand promotion. It is owned and operated by Elizabeth Bergeon.

INDUSTRY ANALYSIS

Graphic designers combine art and technology to communicate ideas through images and the layout of websites and printed pages. They may use a variety of design elements to achieve artistic or decorative effects. Graphic design is important to marketing and selling products and is a critical component of brochures and logos. Graphic designers often work closely with people in advertising and promotions, public relations, and marketing to create a cohesive message and strong brand.

Graphic designers work with both text and images. They often select the type, font, size, color, and line length of headlines, headings, and text. Graphic designers also decide how images and text will go together on a print or webpage, including how much space each will have. Through the use of images, text, and color, graphic designers can transform statistical data into visual graphics and diagrams, which can make complex ideas more accessible.

The scope of the work of a graphic designer includes:

- Meeting with clients to determine the scope of a project

- Using digital illustration, photo editing software, and layout software to create designs

- Creating visual elements such as logos, original images, and illustrations that help deliver a desired message

- Designing layouts and selecting colors, images, and typefaces to use

- Presenting design concepts to clients

- Incorporating changes recommended by clients into final designs

- Reviewing designs for errors before printing or publishing them

Over the past five years, the Graphic Design industry in the United States has grown by 2.4 percent to reach revenue of $15 billion in 2019. In the same timeframe, the number of businesses has grown by 1.5 percent and the number of employees has grown by 1.5 percent. There are more than 136,000 graphic design businesses in the United States, employing nearly 266,000 people.

The median annual wage for graphic designers was $48,700 in May 2017. In 2016, about 1 in 5 graphic designers were self-employed.

Employment of graphic designers is projected to grow four percent from 2016 to 2026, slower than the average for all occupations. Graphic designers are expected to face strong competition for available positions, but the work of graphic designers will continue to be important in the marketing of products throughout the economy as high-quality graphic design services will become increasingly integral for companies seeking to develop brand awareness.

Employment Projections Data for Graphic Designers, 2016–26

Occupational Title	SOC Code	Employment, 2016	Projected Employment, 2026	Change, 2016–26	
				Percent	Numeric
Graphic designers	27-1024	266,300	277,400	4	11,100

SOURCE: U.S. Bureau of Labor Statistics, Employment Projections program

By digging deeper into the numbers, we find that the projected change in employment of graphic designers from 2016 to 2026 varies greatly by industry. For example, employment of graphic designers in newspaper, periodical, book, and directory publishers is projected to decline 22 percent from 2016 to 2026. However, employment of graphic designers in computer systems design and related services is projected to grow 20 percent over the same period. Companies are continuing to increase their digital presence, requiring graphic designers to help create visually appealing and effective layouts of websites and social media accounts. Growth in advertising expenditures and an explosion in mobile media has helped sustain demand for skilled designers. As expenditures on advertising increase, so does demand for graphic design services; total advertising expenditure is expected to increase in 2018, representing a potential opportunity for the industry.

MARKET ANALYSIS

The market for freelance graphic designers is limitless, especially in the creation of online digital content for websites and social media platforms. Freelance graphic designers can be helpful to companies of all sizes and in all industries and, because they are not dependent on physical space, they can be located anywhere in the world to help companies across the globe. The can be contracted to create specific, individual projects or hired on an ongoing basis to create various content over a longer period of time. Freelance graphic designers are valuable employees that can be utilized to save time and money to companies of all sizes and budgets.

SERVICES

Companies depend on successful marketing efforts to tap into their target audience's decision-making process. Great marketing engages people based on the wants, needs, awareness, and satisfaction they have about a product, service, or brand. Since people will always find visual content more engaging, graphic design helps organizations promote and communicate more effectively.

Technology has enabled brands to have more exposure online, allowing businesses to interact with their clients and consumers in new ways. Technology has also created the ability to review and analyze real-time data to measure and see what sources are driving more traffic. We can digitally analyze the type of content and graphics that are getting more media impressions, more likes, more saves and, ultimately, are more appealing and converting to an audience. Content marketing and the evolution of graphic design for digital marketing is continuing to rise with the internet as the major source of marketing and exposure and increased company investment.

The rise of content marketing and good design is going to continue to make an impact on businesses' bottom-line revenue. Graphic design will always be a necessary tool for artistic, economic, marketing, and architectural expression and will continue to evolve as a result of advances in technology and online mediums.

Bergeon Graphic Design Services LLC will focus on online marketing and advertising, including such things as:

- Digital brochures
- Email marketing templates
- Images for websites and blogs
- Infographics
- Social media ads, banners, and graphics
- Website design

Pricing

Individual projects are priced based on the average of $40 per hour, including consultation, design, review, and correction/adjustment. Ongoing projects are quoted based on the anticipated number of hours to complete, using the same base price of $40 per hour.

OPERATIONS

Location

Graphic designers are no longer glued to their workstations. With graphic design software now readily available on laptops and mobile phones through apps, it is much easier for designers to work anywhere in the world, and easier for companies to outsource talent without having to hire in-house.

As such, Bergeon Graphic Design Services LLC will be operated from the home office of owner Elizabeth Bergeon. A dedicated home office has been set up with all the equipment she will need to create digital content as well as operate the business, from billing and taxes to customer communications.

The office is equipped with a desk and ergonomic chair, design table, adequate lighting, Apple iMac Pro with 5K retina display, MacBookPro, HP PageWide Pro Color Multifunction Business Printer, as well as a dedicated phone line and answering system.

Hours

As with most independent freelance businesses, there is no such things as regular or set hours. Generally, email and phones are regularly checked from 8 a.m. to 6 p.m., but work is being done throughout all hours of the day as necessary to meet project deadlines.

PERSONNEL

Owner Elizabeth Bergeon earned a bachelor's degree in graphic design from the Frostic School of Art at Western Michigan University. She has five years' experience working for an in-house graphic design department of a local corporation as well as doing side jobs on her own for the past twelve months. This side business steadily took off as her work became more well-known; her winning design for a local community campaign added to her recognition and prompted her to strike out on her own.

Ms. Bergeon is a lifelong learner who is adaptable to the ever-changing demands of her career and the industries she serves. She has a professional portfolio (online and print) to demonstrate to potential clients her creativity, originality, and appeal to a wide range of customers.

Ms. Bergeon is also certified in Adobe Creative Cloud and Creative Suite. She is proficient in SEO and earned a certification in Google AdWords. She also has a working knowledge of Java and is certified in JavaScript. Coupled with her strong written and verbal communication skills, Ms. Bergeon is well equipped to succeed as a freelance graphic designer.

ASSOCIATIONS

Bergeon Graphic Design Services LLC is a member of AIGA (https://www.aiga.org/). As the profession's oldest and largest professional membership organization for design—with more than 70 chapters and more than 25,000 members—AIGA advances design as a professional craft, strategic advantage, and vital cultural force.

Specifically, AGIA:

- Advocates for a greater understanding of the value of design and designers in government, business, and media.

- Enhances professional development through enriching learning opportunities at all levels.

- Inspires designers and the public by sharing the most exciting design work and engaging in thoughtful, provocative discussion on pressing issues.

- Hosts a robust calendar of events as well as programming and initiatives to serve a wide range of special interest groups.

- Defines global standards and ethical practices.

- Makes powerful tools and resources accessible to all.

Membership benefits include a job board, access to a standard form of agreement, member portfolios, a designer directory, product discounts, and opportunities for professional development. Cost of a sustaining membership is $250 a year.

MARKETING

As a graphic design firm that specializes in creating digital content for website and social media platforms, these same avenues will be used to market the business. It has the added benefit of being free and easily and regularly updated. A website has been created for the business as well as a blog, LinkedIn profile, Facebook page, and accounts on Twitter, Instagram, Snapchat, and Pinterest. All profiles and accounts are linked back to the website, which contains a list of services, testimonials, and a digital portfolio in addition to contact information.

Of these, particular attention will be paid to Pinterest as a primary mode of exposure and exhibition. Because of the visual nature of the site as well as being the third largest online media platform, Pinterest is even more important than Twitter and Facebook. Marketing success on Pinterest includes the following tasks:

Utilize Search Engine Optimization

We will optimize our Pinterest account so that our pins will pop up when users are searching for our specific type of pins. In our "About" section, we will include an informative description of the business and include relevant keywords, our website URL, and a main hashtag or two.

Include Web Address with Pins

Our work will first be placed on our website and then pinned to Pinterest. This ensures that our URL is permanently attached to that pin, no matter how many times it is repinned. Pinned images will also include our website URL in the caption.

Add "Pin It" Button to All Images

The "Pin It" button will be added to every image on our website so that viewers can easily share it on their Pinterest accounts. This ensures that our image still has our website URL attached, meaning that our site gains backlinks with each pin.

Protect Images with Watermark

We will create a watermark that will be added to every image we put online. This helps protect our intellectual property whether it's on Pinterest, Twitter, Facebook, or if someone simply shares it via email with a friend. The watermark will include the copyright symbol, our URL, and the year. To avoid annoying Pinterest users, the watermark will be placed along the top or bottom of the image.

Use Humor and Inspiration to Draw Attention

We will design several humorous and inspirational designs specifically for Pinterest; these are more readily shared with users and are an easy way to gain interest and brand awareness.

Create Content for Target Audience

We will create content and market our pins to our target audience. Since our ideal customers are businesses needing digital marketing content, we will make sure that a majority of our pins are something they could use in this capacity.

Pin Blogs Posts

Our blog posts will be pinned to our Pinterest account. Each will include a graphic image to draw users in and prompt them to click through to the blog.

Repin Other's Pins

Repinning other's related pins will help us build a community and create relationships within Pinterest, similar to reposting on Facebook or retweeting on Twitter.

FINANCIAL ANALYSIS

The cost to start a freelance graphic design company are relatively low. A breakdown is included below:

Start–Up Costs

Office furniture, $1,500

Apple iMac, $5,000

MacBook Pro, $2,400

HP PageWide Pro Color Multifunction Business Printer, $500

Membership fees, $250

Software, $1,000

Phone and data plan, $1,500

Internet service, $800

Wifi hotspot, $600

Antivirus software, $150

Promotional materials, $500

Website and social media creation with branding, $800

Total, $15,000

SWOT ANALYSIS

Strengths

- The owner is self–motivated.
- The work can be done from anywhere in the world.
- Experience and exposure from winning community contest has increased awareness and interest in the company.
- More and more companies are realizing the outsourcing graphic design is much more cost–efficient than hiring someone in-house.

Weaknesses

- Building the business will take time.
- Unpredictable and changing pay may make budgeting difficult.
- To remain competitive, we will need to keep up–to–date with the latest software and computer technologies.

Opportunities

- Total advertising expenditures are increasing, so demand for graphic design services will increase, as well.
- The increase in online and social media marketing efforts will increase the market for our services.

- We can expand our services to include user interface graphic design to make them easy to use and provide a user–friendly experience. This includes game interfaces and apps.

Threats

- Freelance graphic designers must compete with in–house designers working within the markets they serve.

Handmade Knitted Items

Mama Knit Shop

2486 Milner St.
St. Clair Shores, MI 48081

Zuzu Enterprises

Mama Knit Shop makes unique, handmade knitted hats, scarves, and related items. Each item is lovingly made in a smoke-free home in a variety of colors and styles to fit each and every customer's desire.

EXECUTIVE SUMMARY

Mama Knit Shop makes unique, handmade knitted hats, scarves, and related items. Each item is lovingly made in a smoke-free home in a variety of colors and styles to fit each and every customer's desire. Some of our signature items support our local sports teams and universities from the state of Michigan, including Lake Shore High School, Lakeview High School, South Lake High School, the Detroit Tigers, Detroit Lions, Detroit Pistons, Detroit Red Wings, Michigan State University, Wayne State University, and the University of Michigan. Custom orders are also welcomed.

Handmade shopping has grown in popularity in recent years thanks to the introduction of online marketplaces like Etsy, along with some consumers' increasing desire to support independent businesses and entrepreneurs. In fact, as reported by Handshake, there's a rising demand for handmade items in the gift industry as a whole. Handmade products and the artisans who craft them have a unique skill that others admire and go out of their way to support.

INDUSTRY ANALYSIS

The nature of commerce is continuing to evolve: more people are choosing to purchase goods online and many consumers are looking for unique items as an alternative to mass produced goods. Indeed, market demand in the gift industry for handmade goods has risen exponentially in the last few years. With the rise of online e-commerce sites, consumers have become very aware of the value of owning things that are not mass produced and can now purchase handmade goods directly from the people who make them. According to eMarketer, a market research company, worldwide retail e-commerce sales are expected to be $2.3 trillion in 2017, up from $1.9 trillion in 2016. Further, eMarketer estimates that worldwide retail e-commerce will generate double-digit growth each year through 2021, and that worldwide retail ecommerce sales will reach $4.5 trillion by the end of 2021.

The most important reason behind the rise in popularity in handmade goods is simply access. Not so long ago, consumers were basically forced to buy what was available at stores in their area. Most people did not have access to unique handmade gift items unless they lived in or traveled to the areas where the goods were made and bought them directly from the makers. Now, with e-commerce sites available on the web or via mobile app that connect consumers directly to the artisans and craftspeople that make handmade items, coupled with the ability to ship nearly anywhere by air, ground, or sea transportation relatively quickly and cheaply, consumers can learn about and access fine, handmade gifts much more easily than ever before.

Social media including Pinterest, Instagram, Facebook, blogs, and the Internet also make it easier for makers themselves to directly access their target markets.

People like to know that the products they bought were made by a real person—that the products they're spending money on have a sense of authenticity attached to them.

The ability to purchase custom-made items particularly appeals to Millennials. They decry mass-produced, impersonal products whether they be intended for themselves or as gifts to others. They would rather purchase one-of-a-kind, special items that cost a little more than off-the-shelf or uninspiring items.

Handmade items are often perceived to be higher quality than mass-produced items, further adding to their appeal. In addition, when it comes to gift giving, consumers enjoy being able to give items that are unique, special, and memorable. Handmade gift items are believed to be special, something that only a fortunate few people will ever own.

Consumers will be increasingly mindful of their purchases. More and more shoppers are choosing products that are sourced responsibly and are good for their bodies and the environment. When they are able purchase beautiful, unique items while also addressing environmental concerns such as the desire to reduce the consumer's overall carbon footprint, then purchasing handmade goods is a very attractive option. Handmade goods created by human beings outside of a factory environment seem more environmentally conscious to many consumers, and in many cases may be.

The ability to make a difference in the lives of makers by providing them opportunities to be paid for meaningful work is very attractive to consumers as well. They enjoy the idea of being able to make a difference in other people's lives simply by purchasing items they likely would have bought anyway.

Personalization that enables shoppers to build products and customize them to the very last detail will be a key retail trend in 2019 and beyond, so retailers that enable shoppers to build and customize products will prosper.

In a 2016 study by Ask Your Target Market (aytm.com) which asked consumers about their spending habits for handmade items, they found:

- 30% of respondents said that they've purchased handmade items many times, and 40% have done so at least once or twice.

- Of those who have purchased handmade items, 53% have done so at craft fairs.

- 51% of handmade shoppers said that they have purchased handmade fashion accessories.

- 46% have purchased home items.

- 42% have bought holiday items or decorations.

- 81% said that they chose to buy handmade because they could get items that were truly unique.

- 51% said they like that buying handmade items allows them to support small businesses.

- 38% have chosen to buy handmade because of the quality behind the products.

- 72% of all respondents think that handmade items are generally more special than mass produced items.

- 58% think that handmade items are higher quality than mass produced items.
- 55% think that handmade items are more stylish than mass produced items.

MARKET ANALYSIS

One of the main markets for Mama Knit is the city of St. Clair Shores, Michigan, as some of our signature items include those in colors and designs supporting our three local, rival high schools.

St. Clair Shores includes 59,798 people, 26,977 households, and 15,932 families as of the most recent census (2010). The population density was 5,139.4 per square mile and there were 28,467 housing units. Of the 26,977 households, 22.6 percent had children under the age of 18 living with them. The population spread includes:

21.1% under the age of 20

4.9% from 20 to 24

24.9% from 25 to 44

29.7% from 45 to 64

19.2% who were 65 years of age or older

The median income for a household in St. Clair Shores was $52,775, and the median income for a family was $67,311.

Our second main market is the Detroit metropolitan area, as another signature line of Mama Knit is local sports teams and universities. Detroit is home to four professional U.S. sports teams, one of only twelve cities in the United States to have representation in all four major North American sports, all of which play within the downtown district area.

The Detroit metropolitan area is home to just over 4.3 million people. The median age is 40, with 62 percent of the population aged 18-64. The median household income for the entire metro area was $58,411, which was slightly higher than the state. There were 1.7 million households in the area, and the median homeowner-occupied home value was $171,600. Sixty-three percent of the population has at least some college, if not a bachelor's degree or post-graduate degree.

The third market for Mama Knit is harder to quantify, as customers may come from across the United States and even the world as a result of our online presence and world-wide shipping.

Competition

The competition for Mama Knit is substantial due to the online nature of sales in the global marketplace. Therefore, Mama Knit will have to differentiate itself with unique designs, quality workmanship, attractive and appealing marketing, and excellent communication and customer support.

PRODUCTS

Mama Knit prides itself on providing high quality items for our customers. If it isn't something owner Justine Lashbrook would want for her child or for herself, she won't sell it.

Yarns

Mama Knit uses both natural fibers and acrylic yarns in the creation of its products. Natural fibers are preferred, but acrylics are employed to appeal to those with allergies or those who are looking for easier washing and drying for products that may require it often, especially those made for children.

Natural fibers are locally-sourced and include wool and alpaca yarn. Alpaca yarn is known as the affordable luxury yarn because it is softer than cashmere without the high price. Natural fibers offer these benefits:

- It is a great insulator
- It is breathable
- It is naturally fire-resistant
- It uses natural dyes
- It is resilient
- It is a renewable resource
- It is biodegradable; scraps can be composted
- Natural fibers have a distinct beauty and feel
- It is purchased from local sources, so we know the source and how it is produced
- We love to support fellow craftspeople
- Supporting a local yarn shop is one of the best ways you can contribute to keeping handcraft traditions alive and well
- Locally sourced yarns keep money closer to the community
- Using natural fibers provides a sense of connection to human history, as it links us with generations before us who depended on natural fibers to stay warm

On the other hand, items made with natural fibers require hand washing and air drying and they cost marginally more to make.

Acrylic yarn is also purchased from a local store and it has its own benefits, including:

- It is machine washable and dryable
- It is widely available
- It is durable
- It is affordable
- It is nonallergenic

On the other hand, acrylic fibers tend to be rougher than natural fibers.

Knitted items

Our current list of available items includes:

- Baby blankets
- Beanie hats
- Bonnets
- Boot toppers/cuffs
- Bows
- Coffee sleeves
- Cowl
- Crowns
- Ear warmer/scarf sets

- Ear warmers
- Fingerless gloves
- Flapper hats
- Gloves
- Hat/scarf sets
- Hats
- Hats with ear flaps
- Headbands
- Infinity scarves
- Lap/throw blankets
- Mermaid tails
- Mittens
- Newborn hat/diaper cover sets
- Newsboy hats
- Patterns
- Pompom hats
- Pony tail/bun hats
- Scarves
- Shawls
- Slouchy hats
- Socks
- Stocking caps

Personalization

Each item may be personalized with a wide variety of colors and adornments. Possible adornments include:

- Flowers
- Bows
- Patches
- Buttons
- Pompoms
- Ruffles
- Jewels

Themes

In addition to colors and adornments, Mama Knit offers signature items in a variety of themes. These include:

- Animals—bears, unicorns, pandas, cats, dogs, dinosaurs, bunnies, turkeys
- Characters—Frozen, Tangled, Very Hungry Caterpillar

- Colleges—Michigan State Spartans (green and white), University of Michigan Wolverines (maize and blue), Wayne State University Warriors (green and gold)

- High schools—Lake Shore Shorians (red, white, and black), Lakeview Huskies (blue, grey, and white), South Lake Cavaliers (blue, yellow, and grey)

- Professional sports teams—Detroit Tigers (orange and blue), Detroit Lions (Honolulu blue, silver, and white), Detroit Red Wings (red and white), Detroit Pistons (royal blue and red)

- Superheroes—Superman, Batman, Wonder Woman

- Other—Footballs, baseballs, crowns, mermaids

Sizes

Wearable items are available in several sizes as well. These sizes include:

- Newborn

- Baby

- Toddler

- Child

- Adult

Special orders are always available. Customers are free to design their own item, from styles, colors, and sizes to adornments. Mama Knit will work with custom order customers to make sure they get exactly what they are expecting, from yarn color to button selection.

SALES VENUES

Sales will be made through a variety of different venues including Etsy, Amazon Handmade, retail consignment in local brick and mortar stores, and crafts and holiday fairs. Each is described in more detail.

Etsy

Etsy is probably the most well-known craft selling website, and for good reason. The website makes it easy to set up your own shop for free, and crafters are making excellent money selling their one-of-a-kind items. You can get paid in several ways, including Google Pay and PayPal.

An Etsy store called Mama Knit has been established. Etsy is the most well-known and popular avenue for sales of handmade items and is a natural fit for our products. Etsy boasts:

- 54 million members

- 33.4 million active buyers

- 1.9 million sellers

- Over 50 million items for sale

- 2016 gross merchandise sales of $2.84 billion

- 2017 gross merchandise sales of $3.25 billion

Etsy statistics on sellers include:

- 87% of sellers are women

- Median age of Etsy sellers is 37

- 73% consider their Etsy shop to be a business

- 97% run their shops from their homes

- 81% aspire to grow their sales in the future

- 62% started their Etsy shop to supplement income

- Sellers come from 83 countries

Sales statistics from Etsy include:

- 81% of sales come from repeat purchasers

- 67% of visits come from mobile devices

- 60% of Etsy sellers sell in other venues, but Etsy remains their largest source of sales

- Of 50 retail categories on Etsy, Clothing and accessories is the top retail category, followed by home and living

Etsy has a very reasonable fee structure, charging only a 3.5 percent commission and a flat $0.20 listing fee, allowing sellers to maximize profits. Etsy also offers many free tools and support guides to make sales go as smoothly as possible.

Amazon Handmade

A second online retail presence is also being explored at Amazon. Amazon is the largest online retailer in the world generating $177.9 billion in revenue in 2017 and a net income growth of 27.8 percent. In 2016, the ecommerce company's net revenue was $135.99 billion, up from $107.01 billion in 2015. Around 50 percent of all sales on Amazon marketplaces come from third-party sellers.

Handmade is a store on Amazon for Artisans to sell their unique, handcrafted goods reaching hundreds of millions of customers worldwide. An Amazon Handmade store provides access to over 95 million Amazon Customers in the United States alone and over 250 million worldwide. Amazon Handmade premiered in fall 2015 as an alternative to Etsy and is growing fast and making an impact; the available categories of items for sale were expanded in 2017 to include clothing and accessories. Many handmade business owners are welcoming the opportunity to sell their wares on Amazon in addition to Etsy. Amazon is certainly much, much bigger and the additional exposure for artisan items is good.

Amazon Handmade offers:

- More than one million handcrafted items across all 50 U.S. states and more than 60 countries.

- 15% of the top sellers are Clothing, Shoes, & Jewelry

- 13% of the top sellers are Home & Kitchen

- Since the beginning of 2018, there has been a 100-percent increase in handmade artisans taking advantage of its service to deliver items quickly to customers

- It provides artisans a richer storefront for handcrafted items where they can showcase their work and make more sales

- Amazon can fulfill your orders for you, so you can focus on creating products; you can get a Prime badge on your listings

- Customizations that you define for each item are available right on the product page

- Zero upfront costs; you pay only when you make a sale

Compared to Etsy, Amazon charges about a fifteen-percent commission on most products in its marketplace, although it brings this percentage slightly lower for its Handmade service in order to appeal to small businesses in the artisan space. This is significantly higher than Etsy, which is a tradeoff for the added exposure and Prime shipping.

Retail consignment

A third retail outlet is retail consignment in local stores and boutiques, including places like the Post Detroit, Rust Belt Market in Ferndale, Nora Detroit, and the Rail and Anchor in Royal Oak. These retailers select a diverse array of unique specialty items that appeal to the same customer as Mama Knit. While big box department stores are on the way out, this type of specialty store is poised to succeed. These retailers thoughtfully curated products that are sourced from small business makers that offer organic, fair trade, and handmade items. The company also collaborates with artists to offer exclusive products. Because of this, the stores' items are unique, high quality, and oozing with personality.

Craft shows

Mama Knit will also participate in a small number of different craft fairs, but we will be very selective when doing so. Each potential craft fair will be evaluated on attendance, quality of offerings, and time of year. The craft fairs identified in which we will participate include:

Detroit Urban Craft Fair

Ann Arbor Art Fair

Lac Ste. Claire Fine Art Fair

Holiday Markets

Holiday markets like the Lakeview Marching Band Christmas Craft Show will also be attended. Home-made items with a high local interest such as our local sports teams will do well in holiday markets as people want cute, unique winter accessories for themselves and their loved ones.

Pricing

While consumers may be willing to pay a little more for unique, handmade items, pricing is still an important factor. In general, items will be priced based on type of yarn used and time needed to create them. Most items run between $20 and $35, with something like a coffee sleeve running as low as $10 and a scarf/mitten set may be upwards of $65.

OPERATIONS

Location

All items are constructed with love in my smoke-free home. The portability of yarn and knitting needles mean the actual product creation can be done anywhere and at any time, while watching a movie or waiting in the car to pick up the kids from practice.

A dedicated home office with a desktop computer and multi-function printer as well as storage has been established to process orders, prepare shipments, communicate with clients, photograph items for sale, and all other administrative activities in addition to storing raw materials, mailing materials, and completed items.

Hours

Manufacture of items will be done at all times throughout the day. Listings will be posted on a weekly basis, and communication with clients will be done within 5-8 hours, if not sooner. The flexibility of an at-home, creative business requires that it be checked and updated frequently, so there are no "off" hours.

PERSONNEL

All items are made by owner Justine Lashbrook. Justine has three school-age children and needs the flexibility of a job that can accommodate raising children and keeping a home. She has always loved knitting and took great enjoyment making various items for her own brood over the years, as well as luxury items for herself, her family, and her friends. She always received compliments for her work as well as requests to make items, so she decided to turn this into a business. This way, she can earn extra income for her family while still being available for sick/snow days, homework help, or anything else that may come up with having kids. It is the best of all possible worlds.

BUSINESS/GROWTH STRATEGY

Social media is the key to future growth, whether sales are in brick-and-mortar stores or e-commerce. Mobile commerce is on the rise and social media is likely to be a bigger part of that in the future; brand awareness is essential and there is no easier or better way to establish and reinforce that as through social media. The rise of Instagram Stories, Facebook Live, and messenger apps will fundamentally change how retailers interact with consumers online. Simply posting photos or updates to a branded social profile won't cut it anymore. Mama Knit will need to up our social media game and use social networks and apps to tell stories and engage with fans in real time. We will need to make sure customers find all important releases, restock, and sale info there first. We need to include links to make it easy for people to shop directly, and location filters to raise brand awareness in key cities.

Listing a lot of items on both Etsy and Amazon Handmade and renewing them often is very important to drive interest and attention.

Great photography is also key. If you don't have good photographs of your items, you are going to be passed over for those that do. A neutral and simple background with necessary props will be utilized as well as a light box for higher-quality photos. Flickr will be used to store and edit shop photos because it has an included editing software that works very well; because you can list your shop URL with the photos, it is also a great marketing tool. Photos will also include:

- Vibrant colors
- Contextual background
- Red tones
- Lightness

Google analytics will be utilized to track shop views and sales. It helps to see what items are getting the most views, where your traffic is coming from, and the key times customers are visiting your shop.

Facebook and Instagram will also be used as well as contacts/word of mouth to generate sales.

A blog about crafting will also be established. Craft blogging is huge right now, since blogs are the perfect place to post crafting tutorials. A blog can help potential customers "know" you and feel good about their purchase. It can establish the owner as an "expert" and point followers to new items and sales. It is also possible to earn money through advertisements or affiliate links to crafting products that we recommend, or even to posts that may be sponsored by different brands who seek out crafters who can do creative things with their products to make them even more appealing to potential customers.

Finally, our products will be promoted using Pinterest. Pinterest was the fastest growing social network in 2014 and growth is still going strong. It's safe to say it isn't going anywhere anytime soon. Pinterest is huge for crafts, and crafters can make a lot of money by driving traffic to their blog or shop through the app. There's significant power behind using Pinterest to drive traffic to your blog, because:

- A pin is 100 times more spreadable than your average tweet

- Each pin can drive up to 2 page visits and 6 pageviews

- E-commerce sites benefit from pinning as each pin can generate 78 cents

- The life of a pin is one week! Compare that to 24 minutes for Twitter and 90 minutes for Facebook

Mama Knit will sign up for a Pinterest business account, which will give us access to Pinterest analytics. We will explore the possibility of applying for Rich Pins, that have real-time pricing and direct links to our sales venue for our products, and article pins for our blog posts. We will pay attention to our concise description copy and create striking pin images utilizing great photography and text.

For high engagement our pins need to be:

- Helpful—make it easy for pinners to find our pins with a spot-on description. According to Pinterest, helpful pins receive 30% more engagement.

- Detailed—in a sentence or two explain what our pin is about. Give enough information to entice a pinner to click through to our blog.

- Interesting—draw on the emotions of the pinner by using sensory-related words and positive sentiments.

- Actionable—include a call-to-action in your description. Using phrases like, "check out" or "click to find out more" can generate an 80% increase in engagement.

Most pins will be added on the weekends, any time after 3 p.m. on Fridays, but preferably Saturday mornings.

MARKETING & SALES

Advertising costs have never been lower, because of the power of social media. Mama Knit can develop a following at a relatively low cost if we have a great product that we are passionate about and we utilize all the tools available to us. The cost to use them is low, but the time needed to maximize their effectiveness is where the investment comes in. Each of the various social media components described above will be evaluated periodically to ensure the results they enact are worth the effort.

SWOT ANALYSIS

Strengths

- Unique, customizable products

- Variety of retail channels

- Handmade items

- Quality items

- Social media knowledge and expertise will increase exposure and sales

- Environmentally-friendly products

Weaknesses

- Many other players in the market

Opportunities

- Classes, whether in person or online may be a way to expand services in the future
- Meet and greets and process demonstrations at local stores that carry our wares is a way to garner exposure and increase sales. It appeals to the experiential side of retail where customers can get experiences that they won't find anywhere else
- An expanded offering list may include stuffed animals, dolls, puppets, popular characters, hot water bottle/heating pad covers, and holiday ornaments

Threats

- Times of economic uncertainty may make items luxuries rather than necessities

Home Winterizing Services Company

Pierce Home Winterizing Services

PO Box 77661
Sterling Heights, MI 48313

Zuzu Enterprises

Pierce Home Winterizing Services specializes in helping homeowners prepare their homes for the harsh winter months in the Midwest. Services range from blowing out sprinklers and cleaning gutters to cleaning and storing outdoor furniture, window screens, and screen doors.

EXECUTIVE SUMMARY

Pierce Home Winterizing Services specializes in helping homeowners prepare their homes for the harsh winter months in the Midwest. Services range from blowing out sprinklers and cleaning gutters to cleaning and storing outdoor furniture, window screens, and screen doors. Mike Pierce owns a lawn service company, Pierce Lawn Care, that operates in the spring and summer months and is starting this business so that he can expand his services into the fall and early winter. He will begin marketing his new venture to his current lawn care customers, offering them a ten-percent discount as a reward.

INDUSTRY ANALYSIS

Your home is the most expensive asset you have; it is important to protect your most valuable investment by maintaining it and keep it looking good and running well. Doing so will make sure your home is safe and your investment is protected, but it requires constant upkeep.

Maintenance takes some money, dedication, and hard work, but in the long run you save much more money than if you didn't do maintenance. Keeping up a regular maintenance schedule can:

- Lower utility bills.
- Reduce the number of repairs needed. If you keep an eye on your home at regular intervals, things are less likely to go wrong. Staying on top of things with minor fixes will help you to avoid big problems later down the line.
- Lessen costs of repairs that are needed. Repairs that are needed are less costly; it can be more expensive to fix something that goes wrong rather than prevent it from failing.
- Increase the value of your home. The more maintenance and home improvement projects you do, the more equity you have in your home; maintenance adds value to your home.

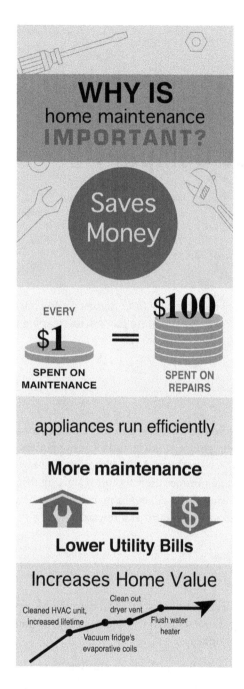

The easiest way to keep up regular maintenance is to conduct seasonal maintenance checks. By establishing a set routine, the work will be completed more quickly and timely. Hiring an outside service to help with the tasks is also beneficial, as they can ensure that all necessary checks and repairs are done right and in a timely manner.

The home services industry constitutes businesses whose main purpose is working on residential homes, and includes such work as plumbing, HVAC, flooring, landscaping, concrete, moving and storage services, and more—including the tasks related to home maintenance and repair. The industry is growing and with the explosion of online and mobile booking services, major companies such as Google and Amazon are diving into the estimated $400-billion market.

It makes sense. Our economy is growing. Our society is becoming less and less handy. Houses are getting more complex. And people are outsourcing more of their lives every day in an attempt to get everything done and finally have some time left over for family, friends, relaxing, and hobbies. Indeed, it used to be uncommon to hire a housecleaner; it was something only wealthy families did. Now it's normal for a middle-class family to hire not only a housecleaner, but to hire mobile dog groomers, carpet cleaners, painters, lawn care services, dog walkers, nannies, and just about anything else they can easily outsource.

Handyman services are another component in the home services industry. Home ownership comes with an endless list of things to fix, improve, and put together, and finding the time to get it all done is a common challenge for homeowners. Plus, some of the items on the typical homeowner to-do list may require more than your average do-it-yourself knowledge. How better to deal with these issues than to hire a handyman?

The handyman service industry is part of the overall home services industry. It has sales of $5 billion a year in the United States and has grown 8.1 percent over the past five years. There are more than 1,400 businesses in the handyman industry, employing more than 20,000 people.

MARKET ANALYSIS

Our target market is the city of Sterling Heights, which is located in Macomb County, Michigan. The population of Sterling Heights is 131,674 spread between 49,754 households.

The median property value is $154,000, with 4.27 percent average growth. The Zillow home value index is $202,400, which is below the national average of $220,100 but above the Michigan average of $146,600. The 10-year appreciation rate is 2.68 percent, which is higher than both Michigan and the national averages. The homeownership rate of Sterling Heights, Michigan, is 71.5 percent, which is higher than the national average of 63.6 percent.

The following chart displays the property values in Sterling Heights, Michigan, in 2016 compared to other geographies.

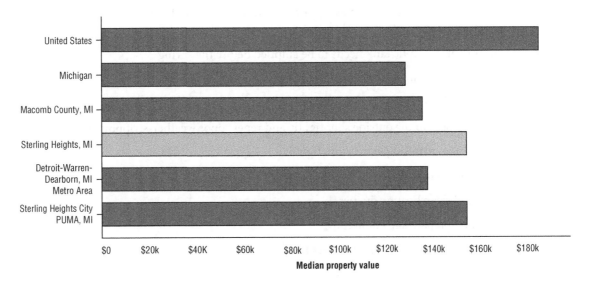

Sterling Heights borders Clinton Township, Fraser, Madison Heights, Rochester Hills, Troy, Utica, and Warren. These cities, along with adjacent cities of Royal Oak, Ferndale, Birmingham, Bloomfield Hills, and Beverly Hills will serve as our secondary markets. The populations, home values, and income levels vary greatly in these cities, but each offers a significant potential market.

SERVICES

Pierce Home Winterizing Services offers a wide variety of services to help homeowners prepare for the harsh winter months. A complete list of services includes:

- Bleed air from hot water radiators
- Caulk or apply weather-stripping in drafty areas such as doors and windows
- Change batteries in smoke and carbon monoxide detectors
- Check flashing around chimneys and other roof projections and make necessary repairs
- Check flue damper operation
- Check for carbon monoxide leaks
- Check the roof for missing or damaged shingles
- Check water pressure and pressure-reducing valves
- Clean and cover air conditioning unit and turn off power at the breaker
- Clean and maintain grills
- Clean and maintain lawnmowers and trimmers, including draining gas
- Clean furnace and change filter
- Clean gutters and downspouts
- Clean heating vents and make sure they are not covered or obstructed
- Clean refrigerator coils
- Clean window weep holes
- Cover plants and trees as needed; bring others indoors
- Cut/stack wood for fireplace, making sure it is separated from the house by at least 20-30 feet and covered with a plastic tarp or other moisture barrier
- Determine if the septic tank needs to be emptied before the spring
- Drain sediment from water heater
- Drain water fountains and unplug pumps
- Ensure all doors to the outside shut tightly and renew door weather-stripping if required
- Ensure windows and skylights close tightly
- Inspect and clean dryer vents
- Inspect and clean heating ductwork
- Inspect and prepare snowblowers
- Install insulated blankets on hot water tanks
- Install insulated cover for hose bib
- Install leaf guards on gutters
- Install outdoor lights and flood lights
- Install programmable thermostat
- Insulate exposed pipes

- Lube garage door springs
- Open furnace humidifier damper and clean humidifier
- Prepare ice melt and salt buckets
- Put up holiday decorations and lights
- Remove and store hoses
- Remove and store window air conditioning units
- Remove, wash, and store window screens and screen doors
- Replace window screens and screen doors with storm windows and storm doors
- Reverse ceiling fans
- Seal deck to protect it from winter elements
- Store or cover outdoor furniture, grills, portable firepits, cushions, and umbrellas
- Test sump pump
- Trim tree branches hanging over the house, electrical wires or outbuildings; remove dead and damaged trees and branches
- Turn off water supply to exterior faucets and drain any remaining water
- Turn off water supply to sprinklers and blow compressed air through the lines to purge them of water

Pricing

Pricing is generally done on an hourly basis at the rate of $75 an hour, with actual cost of all materials being paid for by the homeowner. Clients may choose precisely which services they want, and time and cost estimates will be prepared taking into account the size and condition of the home as well as any other pertinent factors. The homeowner must sign off on the quote before any work may commence; any deviations or additional charges will be communicated and approved before they are enacted.

OPERATIONS

Location

Pierce Home Winterizing Services is operated from a private office in the home of owner Mike Pierce. Mike currently owns and operates Pierce Lawn Care, which is active in the spring and summer months, but winds down in the fall as winter approaches. The office is also used for this business and is set up and ready to go.

Hours

Pierce Home Winterizing Services generally operates from 8 a.m. to 5 p.m., Monday through Friday. Clients that absolutely require nighttime or weekend appointments may be accommodated for an additional fee.

Equipment

Mike Pierce already owns a company vehicle for Pierce Lawn Care; this truck will be modified to include the Pierce Home Winterizing Services company name and contact information. Other than transportation, the business will require the following tools:

- Air compressor
- Brooms
- Buckets

- Carbon monoxide detector
- Caulking gun
- Clamps
- Drill bits
- Electric voltage tester
- Extension ladder
- Hammer
- Hand truck
- Hoses
- Level
- Pliers
- Power drill
- Ratchet set
- Screwdrivers of various sizes and heads
- Shop Vac
- Shovels
- Staple gun
- Step ladder
- Tape measure
- Tree trimmers
- Wrench set

PERSONNEL

Mike Pierce has owned and operated Pierce Lawn Care for the past six years. He received numerous inquiries from clients over the years to help with winterizing their homes and decided this was a logical next step in the expansion of his business. He already has a dedicated client base to market his new services, and the lawn care business naturally slows at exactly the same time winterizing services are needed.

In anticipation of the opening of Pierce Home Winterizing Services, Mike has completed sixty hours of training and obtained his Maintenance & Alteration Contractor License from the State of Michigan.

INSURANCE

A full line of liability insurance has been procured from Simmons Insurance Agency. The policy covers things like property damage, settlements, legal fees, judgments, damage to property, and medical expenses. It includes the following coverage:

- $1,000,000 liability coverage per claim
- $2,000,000 per year aggregate coverage limit
- $1,000 deductible

MARKETING & ADVERTISING

Word-of-mouth advertising from satisfied customers is one of the best and most effective forms of advertising. Pierce Home Winterizing Services is well poised to begin operations by marketing its services to satisfied customers of Pierce Lawn Care.

In addition to this, Pierce Home Winterizing Services will also heavily utilize the internet and social media to market its services. It's no secret that the internet is the best way to reach potential customers and, since the home service industry as a whole is relatively unsophisticated when it comes to marketing, it's surprisingly easy to stand out online if you're willing to learn how to leverage the tools available to you.

Building a strong online presence is an investment in the business that will pay huge dividends. As compared to more traditional marketing strategies of procuring mailing lists or sending blanket advertisements to all homeowners in a given area, online marketing has the following benefits:

- Lower cost to acquire a customer
- Higher profits (you don't have to buy leads)
- Higher quality customers (customers who are more aligned with your business)
- More security with market shifts
- More control over your business and customer experience

GROWTH STRATEGY

In this day and age, customers want to move fast, and successful businesses need to keep up. People are busier than ever and have more demands on their time and attention. Businesses that find ways to make better use of their client's time will be remembered for it—this is the key to the growth strategy for Pierce Home Winterizing Services. Specifically, we will employ a number of different strategies to prove invaluable to clients, including:

- Clients inquiries will be responded to within 8 hours.
- An online appointment booking system will be utilized so potential clients can easily see open time availabilities for consultations and work appointments.
- Work estimates will be provided within 48 hours. Using tablet computers and portable printers, Pierce Home Winterizing Services will have the ability to create estimates on the fly directly after the consultation process that determines what work is to be done and when. They can then be emailed directly to the clients for electronic signature, or printed in hard copy for a physical signature, depending on client preference.
- As next day service is the new norm, clients will expect service to be performed relatively quickly. If Amazon can deliver a package within 24 hrs or the same day, why can't home service businesses deliver on the same time frame? This is the mindset that Pierce Home Winterizing Services will embrace.
- Technology is key to beat out competition. Pierce Home Winterizing Services will utilize technology on the business-side of their company to save time, freeing it up to be able to offer faster client service.
- Pierce Home Winterizing Services will implement Jobber's service scheduling software; it is the touted as a very efficient way to organize visit scheduling, quotes, invoicing, and billing.

- Mobile apps are essential to the future success of the business. They allow Pierce Home Winterizing Services to provide quick communication with clients while on the road and will be essential in the future as more business is done with Millennials who have grown up with the technology and expect it to be utilized in every aspect of the business transaction.

- Pierce Home Winterizing Services will make it a priority to stay in touch with clients on a regular basis, via phone, emails, and text messages.

- We will explore the possibility of maximizing exposure by working with services like Amazon and Google, making it easy for potential customers to purchase or order our services through these venues as they do other items and services.

- Pierce Home Winterizing Services will be available to clients via numerous communication channels such as text, phone, email, Facebook messages, website inquiries—any way that is convenient and easy for them. All channels will be regularly monitored and responded to in a timely manner.

- Pierce Home Winterizing Services will find a way to earn a customer's loyalty, from repeat customer and referral discounts to personalized service that makes them feel special and appreciated.

- Pierce Home Winterizing Services will focus on building our online reputation, online reviews, and connect with younger customers on social media.

- Social media channels such as Instagram will be heavily employed to market the business. We will edit and create professional photos while also using hashtags, stories, and location tags to appeal to younger homeowners.

- Video will be an important media both on Facebook and Instagram posts for Pierce Home Winterizing Services. We will post authentic content that explains the business and how we can help homeowners.

- Pierce Home Winterizing Services will employ AdWords for many key category Google searches, thus boosting our exposure to potential clients.

SWOT ANALYSIS

Strengths

- Startup costs are relatively low
- The business is easily scalable
- Overhead expenses are generally low
- Word-of-mouth and referrals are great marketing tools
- Seasonal work fits into the schedule of Pierce Lawn Care
- There is potential for high profit margins

Weaknesses

- The work requires good physical condition, so injuries or illness would cripple the business
- State licensing is intensive

Opportunities

- The client base for Pierce Lawn Care is an excellent place to begin marketing for Pierce Home Winterizing Services

- Creating an online presence and utilizing social media will be very effective in marketing our services and garnering attention
- Many of the winterizing services will need to be reversed in the Spring (putting screens in, getting outdoor furniture out of storage, etc.), thus creating an opportunity for future business

Threats

- In tough economic times, handyman services may be seen as a luxury rather than a necessity

Mosquito Abatement Business

Morton's Mosquito Shield LLC

77889 Vine Terrace NE, Ste. 8
Wrightville, IN 48060

Paul Greenland

Morton's Mosquito Shield LLC is a mosquito abatement business established by Jack Morton, the owner of a thriving lawn care business in Wrightville, Indiana.

EXECUTIVE SUMMARY

Consumers are increasingly concerned about mosquitoes and mosquito bites because of the diseases they carry, including the Zika and West Nile viruses. Mosquito abatement services can be provided as part of a standalone business, or as an addition to an existing pest control or lawn care company. Morton's Mosquito Shield LLC is a mosquito abatement business established by Jack Morton, the owner of Morton's Landscaping Inc., a thriving lawn care business in Wrightville, Indiana. Morton's Landscaping already provides some lawn treatments to control insects such as grub worms, Japanese beetles, fleas, and ticks. However, until now Jack Morton has referred customers to dedicated pest control businesses for mosquito control. Realizing that significant demand exists for these services, and that cross-selling them to existing lawncare customers would be quite easy, Jack Morton has decided to establish a dedicated sister business. This business plan outlines his strategy for growing the new business during its initial three years of operations.

INDUSTRY ANALYSIS

Mosquito abatement services typically are provided by pest control or landscaping businesses, although some are stand-alone enterprises. Pest control is big business. According to *Market Share Reporter*, the pest control industry generated revenues of approximately $12 billion during the mid-2010s. Residential homes accounted for 65.6 percent of the market, while commercial establishments accounted for 31.8 percent and government institutions for 2.6 percent. Some pest control businesses focus on either residential or commercial markets, while others serve both. Seasonal fluctuations can affect sales depending on the region of the United States in which a business operates, and its corresponding climate.

Generally speaking, consumers and businesses spend a significant amount of money to repel and control mosquitoes. While mosquito bites are an annoyance, efforts to prevent them are based largely on public health concerns, because mosquitoes contribute to the spread of the Zika and West Nile viruses. According to a 2018 Grand View Research report, in North America the market for mosquito repellents (sprays, mats, coils, vaporizers, candles, and bands) was expected to reach $1.9 billion by 2025, following compound annual growth of 7.5 percent.

Although specific figures for abatement services are difficult to find, many pest control companies anticipated that their mosquito control revenues would increase from 2016 to 2017. The "2017 State of the Mosquito Market Report," compiled by Readex Research and sponsored by MGK, surveyed 2,321 pest control businesses regarding mosquito control services. Based on a 10-percent response rate (224 respondents), the report indicated that 28 percent of respondents expected revenues to increase 15 percent or more. Another 26 percent foresaw revenues increasing 10 percent–14 percent, and 29 percent expected revenues to increase 5 percent–9 percent. About 15 percent of respondents expected revenues to increase between 1 percent and 4 percent, and 3 percent of respondents did not provide an answer.

MARKET ANALYSIS

National Market Overview

The "2017 State of the Mosquito Market Report," also indicated that, compared to 38 percent in 2014, 55 percent of businesses offered mosquito control in 2016. The largest percentage of respondents (55%) were in the South, followed by the Midwest (19%), Northeast (17%), and the West (10%). Of those companies offering mosquito control services, 65 percent saw their revenues increase in 2016, while revenues were flat for 28 percent of respondents. Only 7 percent of respondents saw mosquito control revenues decrease.

Local Market Overview

Morton's Mosquito Shield is located in Wrightville, Indiana, near the Ohio River. Mosquito treatments are seasonal in the business' market, typically lasting from April through October. In warmer climates, services may be provided year-round or during additional months.

In 2018 Wrightville was home to a population of 127,387 people (61,146 households). The total employed civilian population was 76,908. Approximately 79 percent of the community's 72,016 housing units were owner-occupied and 21 percent were renter-occupied. Wrightville's average household income was $79,142.

The business will target the following three market segments:

Residential

- Weddings
- Picnics
- Birthday Parties
- Block Parties

Commercial

- Business Complexes
- Churches
- Restaurants
- Tent Rental Companies
- Special Events
- Sports Venues

Government

Many local, state, and federal agencies need assistance providing adequate service coverage within their respective mosquito control districts (in residential zones and public recreation areas), providing lucrative opportunities for companies such as Morton's Mosquito Shield.

Competition

Established national brands offering mosquito abatement services include:

- Mosquito Authority

- Mosquito Barrier

- Mosquito Joe

- Mosquito Squad

- Orkin

- Terminix

- TruGreen

In addition, several local pest control companies in the Wrightville market already provide mosquito abatement services. Morton's Mosquito Shield has been a regular referral partner to the most reputable of these providers for the past eight years, including:

- Winters Pest & Termite Control

- Johnston Pest Services LLC

- Parkway Landscaping Co.

- Thornton Services Inc.

By offering mosquito abatement services directly, Morton's Mosquito Shield not only will have an opportunity to increase its revenue through cross-selling, it also will be able to provide a more comprehensive array of services to its customers and better control their overall experience (e.g., instead of relying upon subcontractors).

SERVICES

Completely eliminating mosquitoes from any environment is impossible. However, Morton's Mosquito Shield provide services that minimize the annoyance and protect customers from the health risks associated with these pests. The business' services, which also target fleas and ticks, include:

Abatement

Residual Barrier Sprays: This involves the application of different treatments in a residential or commercial area, including on shrubbery, trees, landscaping, bushes, etc. Applications, which generally are effective for up to 21 days, include a combination of adulticide (immediately kills adult mosquitoes), insect growth regulators (sterilizes adult mosquitoes/reduces number of eggs), and synergists (improves effectiveness by preventing insecticide breakdown/population resistance).

Mosquito Trapping Products: These feature insect growth regulators and are an alternative to chemicals/pesticides.

Natural/Organic Mosquito/Tick Sprays: These are a more expensive, but environmentally friendly alternative to synthetic applications.

Prevention & Education

Spraying for mosquitoes is only one part of the solution. Morton's Mosquito Shield will educate its customers on steps they can take to minimize mosquito populations on their property. This typically involves eliminating sources of standing water where mosquitoes breed. Sources of standing water may be found in a variety of places, including:

- Birdbaths
- Buckets
- Children's Pools
- Clogged Rain Gutters
- Downspout/Sump Discharge Areas
- Flowerpots
- Leaf Piles
- Patio Furniture
- Pet Water Bowls
- Pool Covers
- Rain Barrels
- Tires
- Toys
- Water Bottles
- Watering Cans
- Wheelbarrows
- Wood Piles

Some potential problem areas for standing water are more specific to commercial locations, including:

- Construction Material
- Dumpsters
- Flat Roofs
- Gravel Parking Lots/Tire Ruts
- Outdoor Drains
- Sewers/Drainage Ditches
- Truck/Vehicle Beds

Safety

Morton's Mosquito Shield will take great care when spraying customers' property. The company will avoid areas such as:

- Decorative Ponds
- Fruit and Nut Trees
- Vegetable Gardens
- Wetlands

Generally speaking, a 20-foot range will be maintained around sensitive areas. Morton's Mosquito Shield also will take steps to prevent applications from contaminating these types of areas on adjoining properties (e.g., neighbors' yards). When necessary, tarps will be used to cover areas such as small ponds and swimming pools. Environmental factors, such as the direction and strength of the wind, will be considered prior to all applications.

Pricing

Morton's Mosquito Shield will provide customers with a time and cost estimate prior to service. Typically, a popular online real estate Web site will be used to remotely evaluate a prospective property, along with details provided by the customer. Morton's Mosquito Shield considers more than square footage when estimating a job. This is because applications typically are made to trees, shrubbery, landscaping, and other areas where mosquitoes breed. Additionally, while a customer may have a very large property, the desired treatment footprint may be limited to a smaller area where they spend most of their time outdoors (e.g., a patio area, deck, etc.). For this reason, an on-site pre-inspection will be performed for all customers who schedule service.

For residential applications, Morton's Mosquito Shield has a minimum $50 charge. Large properties with more extensive landscaping may cost as much as $150 per application. However, on average, Morton's Mosquito Shield will charge $85 per half-acre. As an incentive, the business will provide new customers with their initial application for only $45. Although it will provide one-time applications, Morton's Mosquito Shield will attempt to secure contracts from customers for monthly or bimonthly applications. Considering the local climate, Morton's Mosquito Shield will provide mosquito control services from April to October. Although recurring customers may want anywhere between 6 and 12 treatments per season, on average Morton's Mosquito Shield estimates that it will provide 9 treatments for most recurring customers.

Callbacks

Morton's Mosquito Shield will re-treat an area for customers who are unsatisfied. To avoid callbacks, mosquito applications will be rescheduled if rain is in the forecast.

MARKETING & SALES

When marketing it services, Morton's Mosquito Shield will attempt to position itself as the trusted local expert for mosquito prevention and abatement. The following key tactics have been identified to promote the business:

1. Web Site

2. Consumer Surveys

3. Mobile Advertising (mainly on the music streaming site, Pandora)

4. Cross-Selling Strategies to Existing Lawncare Customers

5. Referral Bonuses

6. Pay-Per-Click Advertising

7. Brochures

8. Public Relations (to capitalize on opportunities regarding mosquito borne illnesses and diseases)

9. Facebook Page

10. Discounted Initial Application

11. Community Presentations

12. Mosquito Prevention Blog

OPERATIONS

The following items will need to be purchased for the business at startup (total cost of $3,305):

Equipment

- Heavy-Duty Tarp (40'x60') (2): $300/each
- Heavy-Duty Tarp (50'x50') (2): $500/each
- Tank Sprayers (3): $50/each
- Backpack Sprayers (2): ($650/unit)
- Safety Equipment: $125
- Work Gloves (2): $20
- Spill Kit: $110

Supplies

Morton's Mosquito Shield will need supplies on an ongoing basis, the majority of which will be pesticides and other chemicals needed for treatment applications. The owners have determined that they will need the following startup supply inventory ($525):

- Sprayer Cleaner: $25
- Pesticides: $150
- Fumigants: $350

Morton's Mosquito Shield has identified a number of potential suppliers for chemicals and other products, including:

- AllPro Vector
- Babolna-Bio
- BASF
- Bayer Environmental Science
- Central Life Sciences
- Clarke
- Kadant GranTek
- MGK
- Summit Chemical (AMVAC)
- Univar
- UPL
- Valent BioSciences
- Westham

Location

Morton's Mosquito Shield will share facilities with its sister company, Morton's Landscaping Inc., which is located in an industrial area of Wrightville. The facility includes a small office area, a kitchenette, bathroom facilities, a storage area for chemicals and equipment, and garage space for up to eight commercial vehicles.

Vehicles

A late-model used pickup truck has been purchased for the exclusive use of Morton's Mosquito Shield. The owner feels that this will be sufficient for initial operations, since the majority of applications will be made using backpack sprayers. In the future, the business will purchase additional trucks, as well as trailers to accommodate mounted tank sprayers needed for large commercial/government contracts.

Hours of Operations

The nature of the landscaping and pest management business requires service providers to work evenings and weekends, based on weather patterns and the needs of their customers. Morton's Mosquito Shield will maintain a flexible service call schedule based on customer demand. Generally, the owner will be available to answer calls from, and establish appointments with, new customers during regular business hours.

PERSONNEL

Morton's Mosquito Shield will be led by Jack Morton, who has established the operation as a sister company to his existing landscaping business, Morton's Landscaping Inc. The business will begin operations by hiring Myles Adams, an experienced technician, who formerly worked for a national mosquito abatement competitor. This individual will then train Morton's Mosquito Shield's other field technicians.

Although employment is seasonal, Morton's Mosquito Shield will make every effort to provide most of its employees with year-round work. During the late winter months, as spring approaches, existing customers who have not responded to direct mailings requesting service renewal will need to be contacted for follow-up by phone. Additionally, Morton's Mosquito Shield's sister landscaping company, Morton's Landscaping Inc., often needs additional staff members to provide snow removal and salting (during icy conditions) during the winter season.

Professional & Advisory Support

Morton's Mosquito Shield has established a business banking account with Wrightville Community Bank, including a merchant account for accepting credit card payments. Tax advisement is provided by Horace Freeman Tax Service.

GROWTH STRATEGY

Based on his knowledge of the local market, the regional climate, feedback from his existing landscaping customers, and other factors, Jack Morton has developed the following growth targets for Morton's Mosquito Shield's initial three years of operations:

Year One: Begin operations with an experienced full-time lead technician and two seasonal field technicians. Introduce Morton's Mosquito Shield to the local market. Cross-sell services to existing customers of sister business, Morton's Landscaping Inc. via a preseason direct mail/online campaign. Secure an initial 75 residential contracts and five commercial contracts.

Year Two: Hire an additional two seasonal field technicians (total of four). Secure five additional commercial contracts (total of 10). Increase residential contracts to 150.

Year Three: Hire an additional two seasonal field technicians (total of six). Secure an additional five commercial clients (total of 15). Begin exploring opportunities to win municipal/government mosquito abatement contracts. Evaluate the cost of purchasing a truck-mounted spraying system for larger government/commercial jobs.

LEGAL

Morton's Mosquito Shield has obtained all necessary licenses, certifications, and registrations. The business has obtained a five-year license from the Indiana Department of Agriculture. In addition, an adequate level of liability insurance ($100,000/property damage, $300,000/bodily injury), has been secured.

FINANCIAL ANALYSIS

Morton's Mosquito Shield has prepared a complete set of pro forma financial statements, which are available upon request. Following is a breakdown of projected revenue and expenses for the first three years of operations:

	2019	2020	2021
Income			
Residential contracts	$ 57,375	$ 95,625	$133,875
One-time residential applications	$ 12,750	$ 17,000	$ 21,250
Commercial contracts	$ 15,300	$ 30,600	$ 45,900
One-time commercial applications	$ 17,000	$ 34,000	$ 51,000
Gross revenue	**$102,425**	**$177,225**	**$252,025**
Cost of goods sold	$ 20,485	$ 35,445	$ 50,405
Labor cost	$ 46,091	$ 79,751	$113,411
Total cost of goods sold	**$ 66,576**	**$115,196**	**$163,816**
Gross profit	**$ 35,849**	**$ 62,029**	**$ 88,209**
Expenses			
Advertising & marketing	$ 15,000	$ 20,000	$ 25,000
Accounting & legal	$ 700	$ 800	$ 900
Insurance	$ 626	$ 743	$ 874
Vehicle financing	$ 2,600	$ 7,200	$ 7,200
Fuel	$ 2,800	$ 5,600	$ 9,500
Mobile telecommunications	$ 900	$ 1,800	$ 2,700
Office supplies	$ 325	$ 350	$ 375
Equipment	$ 2,500	$ 2,500	$ 2,500
Postage	$ 1,500	$ 2,000	$ 2,500
Fees & regulatory	$ 500	$ 500	$ 500
Total expenses	**$ 27,451**	**$ 41,493**	**$ 52,049**
Net income before taxes	**$ 8,398**	**$ 20,536**	**$ 36,160**

Nonprofit Family Counseling Service

Ledgewood Family Counseling, Inc.

89 Smith Ave.
Ledgewood Springs, OH 43466

Paul Greenland

Ledgewood Family Counseling, Inc. is a nonprofit family counseling service devoted to providing affordable and accessible counseling services to those in need.

EXECUTIVE SUMMARY

Nationwide, significant demand exists for mental health services provided by licensed counselors. Unfortunately, several roadblocks make accessing these services difficult or impossible for some. Financial barriers represent a major obstacle for low- and middle-income individuals—especially those with no or inadequate insurance coverage. Ledgewood Family Counseling, Inc. is a nonprofit family counseling service devoted to providing affordable and accessible counseling services to those in need. The organization is being established by four recently retired licensed professional counselors, who initially will operate Ledgewood Family Counseling as a local clinic in a physical location, but plan to expand the service into a statewide virtual network of professionals who will provide counseling hours in their local market at a significantly reduced rate. In addition to benefiting underserved individuals in their communities, members of this counseling network will receive several perks in exchange for participating. This plan outlines the founders' strategy for establishing Ledgewood Family Counseling and growing the organization during its formative years.

INDUSTRY ANALYSIS

Counseling is big business in the United States. According to a 2018 IBISWorld report, in 2018 revenues generated by providers of family counseling and crisis intervention services totaled $34.7 billion, following five years of nearly 1.8 percent annual growth. "Despite overall economic growth over the five years to 2018, the industry has expanded mainly due to budget increases at the state and local level, as well as an expanding budget for social services at the federal level," the researcher explained. During the late 2010s, approximately 87,087 organizations comprised the U.S. counseling industry, employing 484,456 people.

MARKET ANALYSIS

Community Profile

The organization operates in the city of Ledgewood Springs, Ohio. Located in the southwestern region of the state, the Ledgewood Springs population included 284,848 people (117,020 households) in mid-2018.

At that time the total employed civilian population was 123,840. Approximately 85 percent of the community's 137,795 housing units were occupied, with a vacancy of about 15 percent. Approximately 53 percent of housing units were owner occupied and 47 percent were renter occupied.

In 2018 Ledgewood Springs' median household income was $36,716 and specific income brackets broke down as follows:

- $0–$9,999 (13.3%)
- $10,000–$14,999 (8.4%)
- $15,000–$24,999 (14.0%)
- $25,000–$34,999 (12.5%)
- $35,000–$49,999 (14.4%)
- $50,000–$74,999 (18.0%)
- $75,000–$99,999 (9.2%)
- $100,000–$124,999 (5.4%)
- $125,000–$149,999 (2.3%)
- $150,000+ (2.7%)

The population's ratio of income to poverty level broke down as follows:

- Less than .50 (36,894)
- .50–.99 (39,331)
- 1.00–1.24 (17,922)
- 1.25 –1.49 (16,870)
- 1.50 –1.84 (22,603)
- 1.85–1.99 (8,933)
- 2.00+ (142,295)

SERVICES

Overview

Ledgewood Family Counseling's primary objective is to provide affordable and accessible counseling services to those in need. The organization works with individuals who either do not have health insurance, or whose policy does not provide affordable mental health coverage. Ledgewood Family Counseling directly provides counseling services to individuals and families in Ledgewood Springs. In time, the organization will expand its business model to include mental health professionals in other areas of the state, who will agree to provide a dedicated block of counseling hours (within their existing practices) at a reduced rate.

Fees & Rates

Ledgewood Family Counseling's counselors will provide services at a rate of $25–$45 per session ($25–$75 for families/couples). Within these ranges, individual providers will determine an affordable rate in conjunction with clients, based on their unique needs and circumstances. Clients are asked to pay a one-time $30 registration fee, which will help to support the organization's operations.

No insurance payments are submitted or accepted as part of the Ledgewood Family Counseling program. Additionally, no financial background checks are performed on clients, who are expected to be truthful about their financial circumstances on an ongoing basis, notifying their provider if their financial position worsens or improves. Providers have the right to increase or decrease rates within the aforementioned ranges, and may transition the client to a full-fee situation should their income improve substantially or their insurance coverage changes.

Conditions Treated

The services provided by Ledgewood Family Counseling's counselors, and eventually the counselors in its broader network, will address a variety of mental health conditions, including:

- ADHD
- Anxiety Disorders
- Bipolar Disorder
- Borderline Personality Disorder
- Depression
- Dissociative Disorders
- Panic Disorder
- Psychosis
- Eating Disorders
- Obsessive-Compulsive Disorder
- Posttraumatic Stress Disorder
- Schizoaffective Disorder
- Schizophrenia
- Social Phobias

Services typically will be provided in the form of one-on-one mental health or substance abuse counseling. Additionally, providers also will offer marriage and family counseling services.

Education & Training

In addition to providing counseling services, another aspect of Ledgewood Family Counseling's mission is to provide educational opportunities to interns in the field of mental health. Whether they provide services at the organization's physical clinic in Ledgewood Springs, or in conjunction with a participating provider in the Ledgewood Family Counseling network, qualified interns will have completed their postgraduate educational requirements and have the appropriate internship-related state licensure.

OPERATIONS

Location

Ledgewood Family Counseling is located in Ledgewood Springs, Ohio, where it operates from donated space in the Ledgewood Community Center. In addition to a dedicated office for its operations, the center has provided the organization with several private rooms that can be used for counseling sessions, as well as shared conference room space, bathroom facilities, and ample parking. The community center is used by a number of area nonprofit organizations and programs, which is ideal for networking and referral purposes.

Intake & Scheduling Process

Potential patients can register on Ledgewood Family Counseling's Web site by completing a secure intake form. Patients will be considered on a first-come, first-served basis, with consideration given to their circumstances and financial need. Ledgewood Family Counseling's staff will respond to all registration requests. Patients accepted into the program will agree upon an affordable fee within a preestablished range. After payment of a one-time registration fee is received, appointments will be scheduled according to the availability of Ledgewood Family Counseling's providers. Space for counseling sessions is available at the Ledgewood Community Center during the day on Monday, Wednesday, and Friday, with evening availability on Tuesday and Thursday. An arrangement has been made with an answering service, which will handle all front-line telephone communications. Special software will be used to manage scheduling and records for patients seen directly at the Ledgewood Community Center.

Licensure

All of Ledgewood Family Counseling's founding members exceed the minimum requirements established by the state of Ohio's Counselor, Social Worker & Marriage and Family Therapist Board, and maintain an adequate level of liability insurance coverage. As the organization grows, professional members who wish to become part of its network will be required to meet or exceed these same standards.

PERSONNEL

Ledgewood Family Counseling has been founded by four recently retired licensed professional counselors. Although the founding members will each commit to providing a limited number of counseling hours to the service, they will devote significant time and attention to the establishment of Ledgewood Family Counseling as a virtual network, using their extensive contacts in the mental health profession. Following are brief descriptions of Ledgewood Family Counseling's four founders and their respective positions within the organization:

Marion Ceterra, MA, LMFT-t, Executive Director: With 37 years of experience, Marion's career began in an inpatient setting, where she worked with adolescents and young adults at a psychiatric facility in Michigan. However, the majority of her career was spent as a marriage and family counselor in private practice. Marion has extensive experience in the area of couples and relationships, as well as children and adolescents. After earning an undergraduate psychology degree from Ohio State University, Marion received a graduate marriage and family therapy degree from Central State University. She will take a lead role as the executive director of Ledgewood Family Counseling, with primary responsibility for the organization's administrative and financial activities.

Lawrence Rice, MA, LMHC, Grant Administrator: Following a long career in community mental health, Lawrence eventually went into private practice, where he specialized in providing counseling for veterans, adolescents, and children. He has specialized expertise in posttraumatic stress disorder, loss/grief, and the use of Trauma Focused Cognitive Behavioral Therapy. Lawrence graduated from Upper Ridge University, where he earned a Master's degree in mental health counseling. As grant administrator, he will play a key role in pursuing funding for Ledgewood Family Counseling.

Dr. Betsy Parker, PhD, Network Development Officer: With more than three decades of experience, Betsy Parker specializes in sexual abuse, eating disorders, and depression and anxiety. In addition to many years working for the Trenton Residential Treatment Center, Parker's career includes nearly a decade with River Valley College's counseling center in Trenton, New Jersey. After earning an undergraduate degree from Eastern New York College, Betsy earned a PhD in clinical psychology from Northeastern University. As the organization pursues its growth strategy, Betsy will lead its efforts to build a virtual network of providers throughout Ohio.

Jonathan Stehman, MA, LMHC, Outreach Officer: Specializing in cognitive behavioral therapy and adaptive behavior functioning, Jonathan has been a professional counselor for more than 25 years.

Most of his career has been spent in private practice, where his focus has been on patients with depression and anxiety. Jonathan graduated from Upper State University in Idaho, where he earned a Master's degree in mental health counseling. In conjunction with Executive Director Marion Ceterra, Jonathan will play a key role in promoting Ledgewood Family Counseling and engaging with various constituencies.

Board of Directors

Ledgewood Family Counseling's board of directors is responsible for establishing policies and making all major decisions for the organization, in conjunction with Executive Director Marion Ceterra and the organization's founders. The board's members, several of whom were part of a steering committee responsible for its establishment, have been carefully chosen. Each member possesses specific knowledge, skills, and expertise that will be of great benefit to Ledgewood Family Counseling. In 2019, the organization's board members included:

Janice Lipke—Executive Director of the mental health advocacy group, Ohio Action Network.

Donna Brighton—a certified public accountant and well-known member of the Ledgewood Springs business community.

Lisa Seaton—Executive Director of the Ledgewood Springs Chamber of Commerce.

Jeremy Deville—CEO of the Southwestern Ohio Health Coalition.

Bill Gorton—President and CEO of Ledgewood Springs Community Health System.

Heather Marcellas—General Manager of WTYU TV.

Percy Traub—a real estate attorney with the firm Swift, Traub & Jenkins.

Network Providers

After establishing itself locally, Ledgewood Family Counseling will focus on expanding throughout Southwestern Ohio, and eventually the entire state, via the formation of a virtual network of qualified mental health professionals. These individuals will not be employees of Ledgewood Family Counseling, but members of a referral network who agree to provide counseling services within established fee ranges to individuals of limited means. In exchange for their participation, network members will receive several benefits, including:

1. A profile page on the Ledgewood Family Counseling Web site, linking back to the professional's own practice site.

2. Inclusion in Ledgewood Family Counseling's public relations initiatives, which will promote the involvement of professionals in the network.

3. Access to a private Facebook community reserved exclusively for Ledgewood Family Counseling providers.

4. Discounted practice management software from a leading provider.

5. Deeply discounted continuing education unit (CEU) opportunities.

6. A subscription to *The Ledgewood Provider*, a quarterly e-newsletter exclusively for participating providers, with contributions from network members, Ledgewood Family Counseling's founders, and outside sources.

7. Three hours of complimentary consulting hours with one of Ledgewood Family Counseling's founding partners, who have agreed to assist network members when needed by sharing insight from their many years of practice.

GROWTH STRATEGY

Ledgewood Family Counseling's founders have established the following growth strategy for the organization's initial three years of operations:

Year One: Establish Ledgewood Family Counseling as a nonprofit counseling service in the local (Ledgewood Springs) market, with services provided by the founders at the Ledgewood Community Center. Concentrate on establishing efficient operations (e.g., appointment scheduling, marketing, payment, etc.). Directly provide weekly counseling sessions to 20 patients.

Year Two: Directly provide weekly counseling sessions to 30 patients. Establish a virtual model that will enable Ledgewood Family Counseling to expand both locally and regionally, with mental health professionals other than the founders becoming part of a service network that provides a dedicated block of counseling services for a reduced fee. The founders will use their extensive contacts in the mental health field to build the network, with an initial goal of 10 network partners each agreeing to provide at least 12 hours of discounted counseling per month.

Year Three: Directly provide weekly counseling sessions to 40 patients per month. Develop a branding strategy that will allow the founders to expand the Ledgewood Family Counseling concept statewide. Continue building the service's virtual network of mental health professionals, with a goal of adding 15 additional network partners (total of 25).

MARKETING & SALES

Ledgewood Family Counseling has developed a marketing plan that includes the following tactics:

1. **Public Meetings:** Ledgewood Family Counseling will host a series of public meetings to garner public support and media coverage for its programs.

2. **Media Relations:** The organization will issue press releases on a periodic basis to announce the addition of new providers to its network (providing them with valuable exposure in exchange for their participation), and will seek to procure television news stories showcasing the critical services it provides to residents of Ledgewood Springs, Ohio, and the surrounding region.

3. **Provider Newsletter:** An e-newsletter (e-mail and mobile-friendly format) will be developed and distributed to participating providers, with contributions from network members, Ledgewood Family Counseling's founders, and outside sources.

4. **Public Service Announcements:** The organization will solicit public service announcements from local radio and television outlets to stay visible with prospective patients, mental health professionals, fundraising sources, and the community at large.

5. **Web Site:** A Web site will be developed for Ledgewood Family Counseling that offers key information regarding the organization, its founders, how its services work (for both patients and providers), contact information, educational opportunities, press releases, and social media links.

6. **Social Media:** The organization will maintain a presence on social media for members of its provider network, including pages on both Facebook and LinkedIn.

7. **Word-of-Mouth:** Ledgewood Family Counseling will rely heavily upon word-of-mouth referrals and promotion to build its provider network and patient base.

8. **Professional Presentations:** Ledgewood Family Counseling's founders will give presentations regarding nonprofit counseling at regional, state, and national conferences, positioning themselves as experts in the field.

LEGAL

With the assistance of a local business attorney, Ledgewood Family Counseling has been organized as a nonprofit corporation in the state of Ohio and is a tax-exempt 501(C)(3) organization. A Federal Employer Identification Number (FEIN) has been obtained. The corporation's bylaws have been reviewed by its legal counsel to ensure they adhere to state law. An appropriate level of liability insurance coverage has been obtained. Related policies are available for review upon request.

FINANCIAL ANALYSIS

Ledgewood Family Counseling's founders have each committed to directly provide 10 hours of counseling service per week (total capacity of 40 hours per month). Using $35 per session as an average figure for calculation purposes, annual revenue of $35,000 is projected for the first year of operations, according to the targets outlined in the Growth Strategy section of this plan, and $70,000 if full capacity is reached in year three.

The founders have agreed to forgo any compensation during Ledgewood Family Counseling's first three years of operations, providing maximum funding to cover operational expenses such as scheduling/practice management software, marketing, the answering service, Web site development, administrative fees, etc. The owners may opt to receive modest compensation when funding allows, but will prioritize the statewide growth and development of the Ledgewood Family Counseling provider network during the organization's formative years.

In addition to revenue from counseling sessions, Ledgewood Family Counseling will generate income from one-time patient registration fees, grant funding, and individual and corporate donations. Ledgewood Family Counseling will begin operations with $10,000 in startup funding, collectively provided by its founders, as well as a $10,000 matching grant from the Ohio Community Health Foundation. A detailed breakdown of projected first-year expenses is available upon request.

Online Grocery Delivery Assistance Service

PantryPower LLC

2786 Adams Street
Appleton, WI 54911

Paul Greenland

PantryPower LLC provides kitchen and grocery-related assistive services to senior citizens, disabled individuals, and those with other types of special needs.

EXECUTIVE SUMMARY

Based in Appleton, Wisconsin, PantryPower LLC provides kitchen and grocery-related assistive services to senior citizens, disabled individuals, and those with special needs. The business functions as a trusted third-party, helping its clients to place and receive orders for groceries and basic household goods. Although many leading retailers and services offer grocery delivery, PantryPower adds value to the process by providing a range of assistive services, including meal planning, pantry management, coupon research, online grocery order placement and fulfillment help, and household grocery restocking. PantryPower emphasizes assistance with online shopping from existing retailers, but also will conduct personal shopping on behalf of customers who wish to purchase goods from retailers that do not offer online ordering/delivery. Trust is a key element of PantryPower's business model. For this reason, customers will enjoy access to a dedicated associate with whom they feel comfortable and can establish trust with. PantryPower's goal will be to provide total satisfaction to its customers. Success will be determined by a customer's willingness to refer PantryPower to a friend or family member. PantryPower is the brainchild of Patricia Smith, who was inspired to establish the business after taking the hassle out of grocery shopping for her older parents and enabling them to take advantage of online ordering.

INDUSTRY ANALYSIS

Although the scope of its services go beyond grocery shopping, PantryPower's primary focus will be assisting customers with, or enhancing, online grocery delivery services. According to a November 2018 report from Hexa Research, the amount of groceries being sold through online channels was on the rise during the late 2010s thanks to the convenience afforded by related services, which were becoming available in a rising number of markets nationwide. In 2018 Hexa Research indicated that in the United States alone, the number of consumers purchasing grocery products online had increased fourteen percent since 2014. By 2025, U.S. online grocery sales were projected to reach $26.87 billion.

The majority of PantryPower's customers will be senior citizens. Toward the end of the decade, services that helped seniors live independently were growing. According to a 2018 analysis from

MarketLine, significant opportunity existed for businesses aimed at the senior market. The firm explained: "Seniors in society have long been known to possess extensive spending power—more per capita than younger generations have on tap—yet much of the consumer society focuses upon the desires of millennials and the emerging 'generation z'. Many businesses have so far proven themselves to be largely insouciant towards the commercial opportunities available through appealing to the over-65-year-old age group."

MARKET ANALYSIS

Overview

PantryPower is located in Appleton, Wisconsin. According to an April 26, 2018, article in *USA Today*, about 13 percent of Appleton's residents are over the age of 65, and the city is on the list of the top U.S. 30 cities in which to retire, ranking seventh overall behind Casper, Wyoming. The newspaper's analysis indicated that Appleton's average retirement income is $20,693, placing it in the bottom 25 percent nationwide. At the same time, the city ranks in the top 25 percent for fitness centers per 100,000 people over age 65 (95.6) and physicians per 100,000 people over age 65 (69.6).

PantryPower will concentrate on providing services to:

- Senior Citizens (age 65-plus).
- Disabled Individuals.
- Individuals with Special Needs.

PantryPower will rely heavily on word-of-mouth referrals to reach customers in each category.

In addition to marketing directly to its target market, the company also will promote its services to:

- Adult Children of Senior Citizens
- Social Service Agencies
- Churches
- Community Organizations

The owner has conducted online and library research to compile lists of organizations in the aforementioned categories, which are available upon request.

Online Grocery Providers

By 2019, many leading companies offered online grocery delivery options. Some of these were pure-play grocery delivery companies, others were traditional grocery stores, and some were leading retail enterprises that sold much more than just groceries. Examples include:

- Amazon.Com, Inc.
- Meijer, Inc.
- Target Corp.
- Peapod, LLC
- Walmart
- The Kroger Co.
- Fresh Direct, LLC

Businesses like these are an important aspect of PantryPower's business model, which focuses on enhancing existing offerings through value-added services.

Competition

Currently, several "senior helper" companies operate in the local market. While these businesses sometimes aid with grocery shopping and light meal preparation, their business models are broader in focus and include other services such as housekeeping and companionship. PantryPower will differentiate itself by specializing in the grocery services category and leveraging its collective experience and expertise for the benefit of all customers (e.g., staying abreast of special promotions, sales, coupons, etc.).

SERVICES

Overview

PantryPower is a trusted third-party service provider specializing in kitchen and grocery-related assistive services for senior citizens, disabled individuals, and those with other special needs. Although many leading retailers and third parties offer grocery delivery services, PantryPower adds value to the process by providing:

- Meal Planning

- Light Recipe/Meal Preparation

- Pantry Organization & Management

- Coupon Research

- Online Grocery Order Placement/Fulfillment

- Household Grocery Restocking

- Personal Shopping

Trust is a key element of PantryPower's business model. For this reason, customers will enjoy access to a dedicated associate with whom they feel comfortable and can establish trust with. PantryPower's goal will be to provide total satisfaction to its customers. Success will be determined by a customer's willingness to refer PantryPower to a friend or family member.

Process

Owner Patricia Smith will personally meet with all new potential clients during PantryPower's formative years, with a focus on establishing a lasting relationship with them. She will provide prospective customers with a free 45-minute meeting, during which she will describe the services provided by the business and answer any questions. If a prospect is interested in moving forward, Smith will work with the client to determine exactly what services they require. Some clients may only want assistance in establishing an online account, building a grocery list, and scheduling orders. Others may need help receiving deliveries and putting away items. For customers who shop at stores that offer online ordering, but not delivery, PantryPower can arrange for convenient pickup and delivery.

Once Smith understands the client's needs, he or she will be provided with an estimate outlining the hours required. Options for paying hourly or subscribing to a discounted service package (see below) will be presented. During PantryPower's first several years of operations, Smith likely will be the one providing services to the client. Some customers will work with one of her two children, who will join the business on a part-time basis. In either case, the client will know exactly who they will be working with from day one. Smith's ultimate goal will be to help her customers make planning, ordering, and organizing groceries as easy as possible. Eventually, Smith will provide services such as meal planning and light meal/recipe preparation for customers who need an extra hand with these activities.

Fees & Rates

PantryPower charges a flat fee of $30 per hour for all services. Once established, some customers may only need a few hours of assistance per month, while others will have more extensive needs. On average, Smith estimates that most customers will require eight hours of assistance per month ($240). PantryPower has established three service packages that provide customers with maximum value:

Deluxe Package ($315/month)

The Deluxe Package provides 13 hours of service at a savings of $75 and includes:

- Meal Planning

- Light Recipe/Meal Preparation

- Pantry Management

- Coupon Research

- Online Grocery Order Placement/Fulfillment

- Household Grocery Restocking

- Personal Shopping

Standard Package ($250/month)

The Standard Package provides 10 hours of service at a savings of $50 and includes:

- Pantry Management

- Coupon Research

- Online Grocery Order Placement/Fulfillment

- Household Grocery Restocking

- Personal Shopping

Economy Package ($155/month)

The Economy Package provides 6 hours of service at a savings of $25 and includes:

- Online Grocery Order Placement/Fulfillment

- Household Grocery Restocking

- Personal Shopping

*All service packages require a three-month minimum and must be paid for in advance.

OPERATIONS

Location

Smith will operate PantryPower as a home-based business. During its formative years, she will personally meet with all potential and existing clients in their homes.

Hours

PantryPower typically will provide services between the hours of 8 a.m. and 6 p.m., Monday through Friday, and 8 a.m. and 2 p.m. on Saturday. The business will make every effort to accommodate special requests for early morning and evening services if needed.

Communications

Smith will serve as the key point of contact for all prospective and existing customers. She will obtain a dedicated phone number for the business from her Internet service provider that is accessible via voice or text from her home office and mobile device. If she is unable to answer a phone call or text message immediately, Smith will attempt to respond within two hours between 8 a.m. and 6 p.m. All messages received outside of normal business hours will be returned promptly the morning of the next business day. A dedicated e-mail address also will be established for PantryPower.

PERSONNEL

Patricia Smith, Owner

PantryPower is the brainchild of Patricia Smith. Several years ago, Smith began providing extra support to her elderly parents. Though living independently, they needed help with everyday tasks, including getting groceries. Not tech savvy, they desired to take advantage of the convenience afforded by online grocery services, but were unable to do so on their own without Internet access. They turned to Patricia, who helped them establish an account and place online orders with a local grocery store. There were other challenges, though. The grocery service's policy prevented its delivery person from coming into their home, and did not include assistance putting items away. With each order, a different independent delivery person brought their groceries. When items on their list were unavailable and required substitution, communication with independent contractors who were unfamiliar with their preferences was sometimes frustrating. Smith began managing the ordering process on her parents' behalf, picking up items from other stores that did not offer online delivery, organizing their pantry and cupboards so that frequently used items were more easily accessible, searching for coupons and online-only deals to save them money, and more. Ultimately, Smith helped her parents take the hassle out of grocery shopping, while enabling them to take advantage of the savings and convenience available through online ordering. Recognizing that other people in her community would benefit from the same type of assistance, she was inspired to establish PantryPower.

Employees

Smith's daughter, Stacy, and son, Blake, both students at the nearby University of Wisconsin Oshkosh, will provide a limited number of hours to the business during its first year. As PantryPower grows, they hope to each provide fifteen hours of weekly service by the third year of operations.

Professional & Advisory Support

PantryPower has established a business banking account with Appleton Community Bank, including a merchant account for accepting credit card payments. The owner will initially use a popular accounting software application for bookkeeping purposes.

MARKETING & SALES

PantryPower will rely heavily on word-of-mouth marketing to generate customer referrals. Additionally, owner Patricia Smith will promote the business personally by giving presentations to community groups and local agencies that serve senior citizens and disabled individuals. The business will employ other low-cost, high-impact marketing tactics, including:

1. A color flier describing the business and the services it provides, emphasizing local ownership and Chamber of Commerce membership.

2. Membership in the Appleton Chamber of Commerce.

3. A Web site with complete details about PantryPower and the services it provides.

4. Participation in events targeted toward older citizens (e.g., health fairs, senior expos, etc.).

5. Placemat advertising at a local family restaurant.

6. A small advertisement in the *Appleton Senior Times* newspaper, which is distributed freely throughout the community.

7. Magnetic signage for employees' vehicles.

8. A Facebook page to connect with prospective customers and, in some cases, their adult children.

GROWTH STRATEGY

Patricia Smith has established the following growth strategy for PantryPower's first three years of operations:

Year One: Establish PantryPower as a part-time operation in the Appleton market. Develop a simple Web site and brand identity with assistance from a local graphic design student. Focus on establishing an initial customer base through word-of-mouth referrals and advertising in the *Appleton Senior Times*. Emphasize trust building and customer loyalty to produce positive buzz throughout the community. Become a member of the Appleton Chamber of Commerce and the Better Business Bureau. Generate gross revenue of $43,440.

Year Two: Continue to focus on building trust and loyalty among PantryPower's customers. Expand the business' target market to include disabled individuals and begin promoting the service to local organizations that serve this community segment. Sell the very first Deluxe Service Package by introducing premium services such as meal planning and light meals/recipe preparation. Generate gross revenue of $71,370.

Year Three: Achieve service volume capable of providing the owner with full-time employment (40 hours per week) and two part-time employees with 15 hours per week. Based on customer demand, evaluate plans for adding 1–2 additional part-time employees. Generate gross revenue of $94,440.

The following table provides a snapshot of the company's volume targets (service hours and package sales) for the first three years of operations:

Service Hours & Package Sales (Years 1–3)

	2019	2020	2021
Hourly service	714	1,071	1,428
Economy packages	84	132	168
Standard packages	36	60	72
Deluxe packages	0	12	24

LEGAL

PantryPower has been established as a limited liability company (LLC) in the state of Wisconsin. This type of business provides certain liability protections without the complexities of forming a corporation. The owner established her LLC cost effectively using a popular online legal document service. PantryPower will maintain appropriate liability and automotive insurance coverage (policies available upon request).

FINANCIAL ANALYSIS

PantryPower estimates that about 60 percent of its customers will purchase one of its service packages, as opposed to paying for services on an hourly basis. Of those customers that opt for a service package, PantryPower anticipates that 50 percent will opt for the Economy Package, 35 percent for the Standard Package, and 15 percent for the Deluxe Package. The following table provides a snapshot of the business' projected revenue during its first three years of operations:

Projected Revenue Years 1–3

	2019	2020	2021
Hourly service	$21,420	$32,130	$42,840
Economy packages	$13,020	$20,460	$26,040
Standard packages	$ 9,000	$15,000	$18,000
Deluxe packages	$ 0	$ 3,780	$ 7,560
Total	**$43,440**	**$71,370**	**$94,440**

PantryPower requires virtually no overhead and only minimum startup capital. The business will begin operations with $3,500 in startup funding from the owner. Smith will focus on keeping expenses to a minimum for her business. Approximately 15 percent of sales will be devoted to marketing purposes. With the exception of expenses for her business telephone line, insurance, mileage reimbursement, and Web site hosting, the owner anticipates that salaries will account for the majority of PantryPower's expenses.

Online Nutrition Coach

NutritionOnline LLC

51 Parker Ave.
Iowa City, IA 55240

Paul Greenland

NutritionOnline LLC provides online nutrition consulting packages and related subscription-based services.

EXECUTIVE SUMMARY

NutritionOnline LLC provides online nutrition consulting packages and related subscription-based services. The business has been established by Nancy Louden, a registered dietitian with an entrepreneurial spirit who plans to eventually give up her day job at a local hospital to run her own virtual practice, capitalizing on the burgeoning popularity of telemedicine. Louden has devised a strategy for establishing the practice as a part-time enterprise, allowing her to provide general, subscription-based nutrition consultations while growing the business. Long-term, NutritionOnline will offer services beyond its home state of Iowa and provide specialty consultations in categories such as sports nutrition and obesity and weight management.

INDUSTRY ANALYSIS

According to the U.S. Bureau of Labor Statistics, in 2016 the nation employed approximately 68,000 dietitians and nutritionists. By 2026 this figure is expected to reach 77,900, a 15 percent increase (much greater than the average for all occupations). Health and wellness promotion, along with the provision of nutrition services for individuals with illnesses such as heart disease and diabetes, are among the key factors contributing to the profession's growth. Only six percent of dietitians are self-employed, providing significant opportunity for entrepreneurs like Nancy Louden. Most states require dietitians to be licensed, and many dietitians hold the Registered Dietitian Nutritionist (RDN) credential, which is administered by the Academy of Nutrition and Dietetics' credentialing agency, the Commission on Dietetic Registration (CDR).

Based in Chicago, the CDR's mission is to administer "rigorous valid and reliable credentialing processes to protect the public and meet the needs of CDR credentialed practitioners, employers and consumers." In addition to Registered Dietitian (RD) or Registered Dietitian Nutritionist (RDN), the organization awards other credentials, including those for Dietetics Technician, Registered (DTR) or Nutrition and Dietetic Technician, Registered (NDTR), along with specialized board certifications in Renal Nutrition (CSR), Pediatric Nutrition (CSP), Sports Dietetics (CSSD), Gerontological Nutrition (CSG), Oncology Nutrition (CSO), Obesity and Weight Management (CSOWM), and Advanced Practice Certification in Clinical Nutrition (RDN-AP or RD-AP).

NutritionOnline provide services remotely via "telemedicine," offering consultations that otherwise would require an office visit to customers at flexible times and in remote locations. According to a 2018 P&S

Market Research report cited in *Becker's Hospital Review*, by 2023 the global market for telemedicine is projected to reach $48.8 billion, following compound annual growth of 14.8 percent. The increasing prevalence of lifestyle-associated and chronic diseases, along with the need for remote services and an aging population, were among key factors named in the report's growth projections.

MARKET ANALYSIS

Toward the end of the decade, the United States was in urgent need of healthier lifestyles and better nutrition. Obesity, in particular, was a pressing problem nationwide. According to The State of Obesity (https://www.stateofobesity.org/adult-obesity), by late 2018 obesity rates exceeded 25 percent in 48 states and 30 percent in 29 states. Seven states had obesity rates of more than 35 percent. Rates were highest in the states of West Virginia (38.1%), Mississippi (37.3%) Oklahoma (36.5%), Iowa (36.4%), and Alabama (36.3%). NutritionOnline's services are sorely needed in its home state of Iowa—especially in rural communities where access to nutrition professionals is either limited or nonexistent.

SERVICES

Overview

NutritionOnline provides online nutrition consulting to customers in three distinct packages, including:

Bronze (four-week program, $189)—Includes a three-day dietary analysis, 45-minute consultation, meal plans, grocery list, and two 20-minute follow-up consultations.

Silver (eight-week program, $289)—Includes a three-day dietary analysis, 45-minute consultation, meal plans, grocery list, and four 20-minute follow-up consultations.

Gold (12-week program, $389)—Includes a three-day dietary analysis, 45-minute consultation, meal plans, grocery list, and six 20-minute follow-up consultations.

After completing a given program, customers are able to become a monthly NutritionOnline subscriber ($45/month, minimum three-month commitment required) to help maintain their healthy diet. The owner estimates that 50 percent of nutrition package customers will become subscribers, and that the retention rate for subscribers will be approximately 70 percent. Subscribers receive the following benefits:

- One 20-minute follow-up consultation (per month)

- One three-day dietary analysis (every three months)

- Access to a growing selection of exclusive articles, videos, and e-books written by Nancy Louden and other authors

- Access to a private members-only Facebook community

Process

Customers will complete a secure online questionnaire and a three-day dietary intake form. This information will be used to generate reports by the software application that NutritionOnline is using under license. Nancy Louden will discuss the results via an online (audio or video) consultation with her clients. During the consultation, Louden will discuss the client's health and nutritional needs, their budgetary situation, and goals.

NutritionOnline will help customers identify the right dietary approach based on their specific situation and goals, including:

- General Weight Loss

- Healthy Cholesterol

- Low-Carbohydrate Diet
- Increasing Muscle Mass
- Vegetarian Diet
- Vegan Diet
- Healthy Aging
- Gluten-Free Diet
- Sports Nutrition
- Cardiac Health

In addition to providing general information about healthy eating and exercise habits, Louden will develop a nutritional plan tailored specifically for the customer, including suggested meals and convenient grocery lists based on templates included in the software. Through follow-up visits every two weeks, Louden will monitor her customers' progress and make changes or adjustments as needed.

MARKETING & SALES

NutritionOnline has developed a marketing plan that includes a number of key tactics:

1. A Health Insurance Portability & Accountability Act (HIPAA)-compliant, e-commerce-enabled Web site, integrated with licensed software for performing nutritional analysis, that provides a secure channel for sharing information with clients. Customers will be able to learn about the benefits that NutritionOnline provides and subscribe to a package that meets their needs and budget. Additionally, the site will provide access to proprietary content for subscribers, including articles, videos, and e-books produced by owner Nancy Louden.

2. Online advertising and search engine optimization (SEO).

3. The use of Facebook for promoting the business and hosting private members-only groups.

4. A quarterly e-mail newsletter, for both customers and noncustomers, which includes free nutrition tips, articles, and special customer offers.

5. A public relations campaign that involves the submission of customer success stories to nutrition blogs, publications, and other media outlets.

PERSONNEL

Nancy Louden, RDN

Nancy Louden, RDN is a registered dietitian with seventeen years of professional experience. She holds a bachelor's degree in clinical nutrition from Central State University and is licensed to practice in the states of Iowa and Illinois. During the course of her career, the owner has worked for several leading hospitals, including Lancaster General Health System, Providian, and Midwestern Memorial Health. In her role as a hospital dietitian, Louden works extensively with older adults. While she enjoys working in a hospital setting, Louden has long desired to establish her own practice. In addition to academic credentials in her chosen field, Louden has pursued additional education in business administration to prepare her for establishing and growing her own business.

As a dietitian, entrepreneur, and business owner, Louden possesses many of the qualities necessary for success. She is very warm and personable, which goes a long way in helping her to connect with patients, many of whom are apprehensive about changing their dietary habits or self-conscious about their weight.

She is a good listener, communicator, and problem solver. At the same time, Louden possesses exceptional organizational skills, which will help her to manage a growing customer base and meet their needs successfully while also building NutritionOnline into a successful enterprise.

In addition to providing consultations, Louden will be responsible for handling all administrative aspects of NutritionOnline, including:

- Appointment Scheduling
- Record-Keeping
- Content Development
- Marketing
- Professional Networking
- Information Technology

In some cases, she will rely upon outside resources to handle certain tasks (namely information technology). She has identified a Web site developer for assistance in this area.

Independent Contractors

Louden eventually will utilize a network of registered dietitians throughout Iowa to expand her practice's capacity. Contractors will be paid for providing consultations and will share a portion of their revenue with the business in exchange for being part of its network. Contractors will be responsible for providing documentation regarding their education and training, along with references, and must maintain current state certification to work with NutritionOnline.

Professional & Advisory Support

NutritionOnline has established a commercial checking account with Iowa City Credit Union, along with a merchant account for accepting credit card payments. Tax advisory services are provided by Crestview Accounting Services. Finally, NutritionOnline works with Firebrand Technologies for ongoing Web site development and hosting, as well as assistance with online advertising and search engine optimization.

GROWTH STRATEGY

The following growth strategy has been developed for NutritionOnline's first three years of operations:

Year One: Establish NutritionOnline as a part-time, subscription-based virtual enterprise, allowing the owner to earn additional income while establishing the framework for a full-time enterprise. Sell a total of 60 nutrition packages and 30 new monthly subscriptions. Generate gross revenue of $29,290.

Year Two: Continue to operate NutritionOnline as a part-time operation. Sell a total of 120 nutrition packages and 60 new monthly subscriptions. Generate gross revenue of $68,345.

Year Three: Transition to full-time operations. Toward the end of the year, establish relationships with 3–5 Registered Dietitians in Iowa who can serve as independent contractors in year four. Begin investigating opportunities to offer specialized obesity and weight management and sports nutrition consulting packages. Sell a total of 240 nutrition packages and 120 new monthly subscriptions. Generate gross revenue of $136,690.

In addition to continued organic growth, NutritionOnline has excellent opportunities for long-term expansion. Geographically, the practice can expand by forming relationships with independent contractor dietitians who are licensed in neighboring states. Additionally, the practice likely will contract with registered dietitians who also are board-certified in Sports Dietetics (CSSD) and Obesity and Weight Management (CSOWM), enabling it to provide highly specialized expertise to individuals with unique needs.

The following graph provides a projected percentage breakdown of NutritionOnline's nutrition package sales during its initial years of operations:

**Annual Nutrition Package Sales
(Percentage Breakdown by Category)**

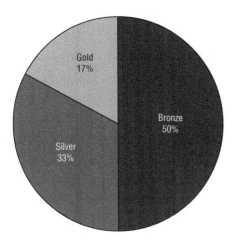

OPERATIONS

Location

NutritionOnline will begin as a home-based business to minimize expenses. Nancy Louden will utilize a spare bedroom in her home for operations. The business will maintain it servers in an off-site data center with HIPAA-compliant security.

Hours of Operation

As an online business focused on providing customers with maximum convenience, NutritionOnline will offer consultations seven days per week, at variable times.

Communications

Nancy Louden will communicate with customers through a secure area of the NutritionOnline Web site. She will attempt to answer all questions promptly (within 24 hours). All communications and consultations will be provided through the Web site, via secure audio or video chat, based on customer preference.

Billing & Payment

NutritionOnline will require all customers to pay in advance for services by credit card or PayPal; insurance coverage will not be accepted. Customers may submit NutritionOnline's charges to their insurance plan for potential reimbursement.

LEGAL

NutritionOnline has been established as a limited liability company (LLC) in the state of Iowa. This type of business structure provides certain liability protections without the complexity of incorporating. The owner used a popular online legal document service to establish her LLC as cost-effectively as possible. NutritionOnline complies with the Health Insurance Portability & Accountability Act of 1996 (HIPAA), a public law passed by Congress that protects the privacy of health information. Nancy Louden meets all certification and licensure requirements in the states of Iowa and Illinois. She has secured an appropriate level of business and malpractice coverage, based upon the recommendations of a business attorney.

FINANCIAL ANALYSIS

Start-up Costs

Nancy Louden will incur the following startup costs ($14,330) to establish NutritionOnline:

1. **Software License ($1,250/year):** The business will use hosted dietary analysis software, which can be customized to reflect the NutritionOnline brand. The application includes access to meal plans and thousands of recipes.

2. **Web Development ($7,000):** Nancy Louden has identified a local Web development firm that can create a secure, HIPAA-compliant online platform for her business.

3. **Launch Campaign ($4,500):** A launch campaign, focused heavily on online advertising and social media promotion, will be developed for NutritionOnline in conjunction with a paid intern ($1,000) at a local university.

4. **LLC Formation & Fees ($1,200)**

5. **Printer ($380)**

Projected Annual Income & Expenses

Projected Annual Income & Expenses, 2020–2022

	2020	2021	2022
Revenue			
Bronze packages	$ 5,670	$11,340	$ 22,680
Silver packages	$ 5,780	$11,560	$ 23,120
Gold packages	$ 3,890	$ 7,780	$ 15,560
Monthly subscriptions	$13,950	$37,665	$ 75,330
Total	**$29,290**	**$68,345**	**$136,690**
Expenses			
Salaries	$ 7,500	$35,000	$ 70,000
Payroll taxes	$ 1,125	$ 5,250	$ 10,500
Insurance	$ 1,100	$ 1,200	$ 1,300
Office supplies	$ 400	$ 450	$ 500
Web hosting & development	$ 1,000	$ 1,250	$ 1,500
Equipment	$ 700	$ 700	$ 700
Marketing & advertising	$ 8,500	$ 9,500	$ 10,500
Telecommunications & Internet	$ 1,500	$ 1,700	$ 1,900
Professional development	$ 750	$ 750	$ 750
Subscriptions & dues	$ 300	$ 300	$ 300
Licensure & fees	$ 175	$ 175	$ 175
Total	**$23,050**	**$56,275**	**$ 98,125**
Net profit	**$ 6,240**	**$12,070**	**$ 38,565**

Startup Funding

Nancy Louden will fund all startup costs from her own personal savings. She will draw a nominal salary during the first year of operations and expects to recoup her investment during year two.

Packing Business
Affordable Packing Services, LLC

2132 Andrews Parkway
Santa Fe, New Mexico 87500

Paul Greenland

Affordable Packing Services LLC provides cost-effective packing and unpacking services to residential and commercial customers.

EXECUTIVE SUMMARY

Affordable Packing Services LLC provides cost-effective packing and unpacking services to residential and commercial customers. In addition to individuals and families who are moving into a new apartment or house, or who need assistance packaging items for storage, the business also assists organizations and corporate customers with relocations and department/staff moves. Affordable Packing Services' competitive differentials will include highly personalized service and prices that are lower than those of larger competitors (without compromising quality). The business is being established by Roger Lane, a former professional mover, and his daughter, Lynette Cox. The following business plan outlines the owners' plan for establishing and growing the business during its first three years of operations.

INDUSTRY ANALYSIS

According to a June 2017 Technavio report, the U.S. market for moving services was projected to reach $16.11 billion by 2021, following compound annual growth of nearly four percent over the previous five years. In 2016 the corporate sector accounted for 45 percent of the market, followed by residential (30%), military and government (15%), and other (10%). Technavio indicated that growth in the rental market was resulting in more residential relocations, supporting projected growth in this category of 3.13 percent. Compared to 32.13 percent in 2006, the percentage of renters in the United States had increased to 41.23 percent by 2016. At the same time, corporate relocations also were on the rise. The sector was expected to achieve the strongest growth (4.18%) between 2017 and 2021, thanks in part to an uptick in both domestic and international short-term assignments.

MARKET ANALYSIS

Overview

Affordable Packing Services is located in Santa Fe, New Mexico. According to the Santa Fe Chamber of Commerce (http://www.santafechamber.com), the community "has a long-standing reputation as a great place to visit, to live and to retire. A diverse economy, moderate climate and great quality of life make Santa Fe an ideal place to do business, raise children or enjoy the retirement years in a stimulating cultural environment."

Residential Market

In 2018 Santa Fe was home to a population of 149,457 people (64,563 households). The total employed civilian population was 76,908. Approximately 72 percent of the community's 72,016 housing units were owner-occupied and 28 percent were renter-occupied. Santa Fe's average household income was $84,122.

The owners estimate that most of their customers will be at least 35 years in age. Senior citizens, specifically, will represent a key market segment for Affordable Packing Services. In 2018, nearly 41 percent of the local population was over the age of 55. That year, specific age brackets broke down as follows:

- 35–44 (11.4%)
- 45–54 (11.7%)
- 55–64 (14.7%)
- 65–74 (16.2%)
- 75–84 (7.5%)
- 85+ (2.2%)

In addition to older individuals, Affordable Packing Services also will be an invaluable resource to busy households (especially two-income families) that, due to work or other obligations, are either too busy to pack their belongings, or overwhelmed by the prospect of doing so.

Commercial/Organizational Market

Santa Fe has a thriving business community. Formed in 1882 as the Santa Fe Board of Trade, the Santa Fe Chamber of Commerce included approximately 1,000 businesses among its members toward the end of the decade. According to research conducted by the owners at their local public library, in 2018 Santa Fe was home to 7,905 business establishments that collectively employed 82,357 people.

Several key corporate/organizational prospects have been identified for Affordable Packing Services, including:

- Century Bank
- CHRISTUS St. Vincent Regional Medical Center
- City of Santa Fe
- El Castillo LifeCare/LifePlan Community
- New Mexico Department of Cultural Affairs
- New Mexico Department of Health
- Pacifica Senior Living
- Santa Fe Community College
- Santa Fe County
- Santa Fe Imaging
- Santa Fe Indian School
- Santa Fe Public Schools
- Santa Fe University of Art and Design
- State of New Mexico
- Thornburg Investment Management

SERVICES

Affordable Packing Services provides cost-effective packing and unpacking services to residential and commercial/organizational customers. In addition to individuals and families who are moving into a new apartment or house, or who need assistance packaging items for storage, the business also assists organizations and corporate customers with relocations and department/staff moves. Affordable Packing Services provides services in a 60-mile radius surrounding the city of Santa Fe, New Mexico.

Affordable Packing Services charges both residential and corporate customers on an hourly basis. Customers are provided with a free time and cost estimate prior. Estimates may involve an on-site visit (for the greatest accuracy). Alternatively, customers can provide a general description of the project by phone. In either case, Affordable Packing Services will do its best to estimate the amount of time required. If additional hours are required, clients can decide whether to pay for additional time. If Affordable Packing Services completes a job sooner than estimated, the customer will only be billed for the number of service hours actually provided. According to some estimates, national averages for packing/unpacking services are approximately $60 per hour (per packer). Affordable Packing Services will charge $50 per hour.

Typically, 3–4 hours will be required to pack a one-bedroom apartment. A two-bedroom home will take 3–5 hours, a three-bedroom home will require 3–6 hours, and a four-bedroom home will take 5–6 hours. Two professional packers can often handle a one-bedroom apartment or two-bedroom home, while three or four professional packers will be needed for larger homes (e.g., requiring independent contractor labor). The cost of packing materials for a one-bedroom apartment averages $125–$175, while costs for homes are slightly higher: two-bedroom homes cost $175–$275, three bedroom homes $275–$375, and four-bedroom homes $325–$475.

Typically, the services provided by Affordable Packing Services will include the following physical tasks:

- Folding
- Organizing/Sorting
- Packing/Unpacking
- Labeling/Marking

Affordable Packing Services' owners will lend their specialized expertise when providing packing services. For example, when wrapping fine china, newspaper (the ink from which can stain dishes) will be avoided. Boxes made especially for dishes will be used whenever possible, and the owners will stack dishes in an upward direction to minimize potential damage.

In addition to packing and unpacking services, the business also will provide customers with an option to purchase packaging materials (e.g., bubblewrap, tape, cardboard boxes, etc.), for a flat fee, based on the size and scope of the project. When possible, Affordable Packing Services will purchase these items online (in bulk) to procure them cost-effectively. In the case of extremely valuable items, such as chandeliers, antiques, and artwork, the business will contract with a carpenter to build custom wooden crates on a case-by-case basis.

OPERATIONS

Location

To keep overhead low, Affordable Packing Services will operate as a home-based business. Roger Lane and Lynette Cox will meet prospective customers on-site or discuss projects via phone or e-mail. Dedicated office space will be maintained within Roger Lane's residence at 2132 Andrews Parkway in Santa Fe.

A dedicated business phone number has been obtained from the owners' Internet services provider, which is accessible via a traditional landline phone or via the owners' mobile devices (making communications easy when they are out in the field).

Equipment

Other than a tablet computer, desk, and filing cabinet, which Roger Lane already had on-hand, no additional equipment is needed for this low overhead business other than a portable dolly to move heavier items within a customer's home.

Supplies

Whenever possible, the owners will attempt to purchase packing materials for specific projects on an as-needed basis, several days beforehand (a nonrefundable prepayment from customers will be required). Examples of packaging materials include:

- Cardboard Boxes
- Packing Paper
- Wardrobe Boxes
- Packing Peanuts
- Bubblewrap
- Packing Tape
- Marking Pens

PERSONNEL

Roger Lane knows a thing or two about moving, packing, and unpacking. For seventeen years, he worked for a leading moving company, which typically required him to be on the road and away from home for lengthy periods of time. Now in his late fifties, Lane wants to remain in the moving industry, but take advantage of an opportunity that is less physically demanding, and which will allow him to stay closer to home. His daughter, Lynette Cox, also is interested in establishing a family-owned business that will provide her with a flexible schedule. A natural organizer, Cox has learned a great deal about packing and unpacking from her father. While both owners will be hands-on, in terms of providing services to customers, Roger Lane will take the lead with new business development, while Lynette Cox will focus on customer relations. Lane and Cox both have attributes necessary for success in running a packing services business. In addition to excellent organization skills, both are detail-oriented and efficient workers.

The owners of Affordable Packing Services have taken several steps to ensure their success as new small business owners. In addition to completing courses at Santa Fe Community College, they took advantage of free small business counseling from the Santa Fe Small Business Development Center, whose mission is "to strengthen the economy of New Mexico by providing direct assistance, entrepreneurial education and resource linkages to promote the retention and expansion of existing small businesses and the creation of new businesses." Lane and Cox also attended several business skills workshops offered by the Northern New Mexico Service Corps of Retired Executives (SCORE).

Independent Contractors

Roger Lane and Lynette Cox will provide most packing/unpacking services for their customers directly. However, for larger jobs, the owners will retain the services of independent contractors, allowing them to affordably scale up their workforce when needed without maintaining a large payroll.

Professional & Advisory Support

Affordable Packing Services has established a business checking account with Santa Fe Community Bank, along with a merchant account for accepting credit card payments. Tax advisory services are provided by Tennyson Accounting & Tax Inc.

MARKETING & SALES

Affordable Packing Services has developed a marketing plan that includes the following tactics:

1. **Networking:** The business will become a member of the Santa Fe Chamber of Commerce and obtain a listing in its online Santa Fe Business Directory.

2. **Flyers:** The owners will post four-color flyers in locations such as laundromats, apartment complexes, condominiums, office buildings, supermarkets, and coffee shops.

3. **Event Marketing:** Affordable Packing Services will participate in the Santa Fe Chamber of Commerce's annual Santa Fe Business Expo in April, which features hundreds of local businesses.

4. **Online Advertising:** The business will use paid search advertising to connect with prospective customers.

5. **Direct Mail:** Targeted direct mailings (letter/promotional flyer) will be sent to leasing offices, insurance agents, moving companies, and real estate agents in the Santa Fe area to generate referrals.

6. **Sales Calls:** To maintain visibility with Santa Fe area real estate offices, insurance agents, leasing offices, and moving companies, Roger Lane will visit these locations regularly.

7. **Content Marketing:** The owners will develop several moving and packing/unpacking-related tip sheets and guides, which they will provide to prospective customers free of charge in exchange for their contact information, which will be entered into the business' marketing database.

8. **Web Site:** A Web site will be developed for Affordable Packing Services that offers key information regarding the business, its services, contact information, testimonials from satisfied customers, and a link to its social media accounts.

9. **Social Media:** The organization will maintain a presence on several social media channels, including Facebook and LinkedIn.

GROWTH STRATEGY

Following is a summary of Affordable Packing Services' conservative growth targets for its first three years of operations:

Year One: Establish the business in the Santa Fe market. Obtain membership in the Santa Fe Chamber of Commerce. Launch targeted direct mail campaign. Market heavily to key referral sources (real estate offices, insurance agents, leasing offices, and moving companies). Bill 2,500 hours of work (approximately 50 hours per week). Generate gross packing/unpacking revenues of $125,000.

Year Two: Secure one exclusive business relationship with a local moving services provider. Bill 3,000 hours of work (approximately 60 hours per week). Generate gross packing/unpacking revenues of $150,000.

Year Three: Evaluate the possibility of hiring one additional full-time staff member. Bill 3,500 hours of work (approximately 70 hours per week). Generate gross packing/unpacking revenues of $175,000.

LEGAL

Affordable Packing Services has been established as a limited liability company in the state of New Mexico. This type of business structure provides certain liability protections without the complexity of incorporating. The owners used a popular online legal document service to establish their LLC as cost-effectively as possible. Additionally, customer agreements have been obtained from the same service, which have been customized to meet the business' needs. Professional liability insurance has been obtained from a reputable agent in the Santa Fe area.

FINANCIAL ANALYSIS

Affordable Packing Services has prepared a complete set of pro forma financial statements, which are available upon request. Following is a breakdown of projected revenue and expenses for the first three years of operations:

	2019	2020	2021
Revenue			
Packing services	$125,000	$150,000	$175,000
Packing supplies (markup)	$ 6,250	$ 6,875	$ 7,500
Total	**$131,250**	**$156,875**	**$182,500**
Expenses			
Salaries	$ 80,000	$ 90,000	$100,000
Payroll taxes	$ 12,000	$ 13,500	$ 15,000
Independent contractors	$ 13,125	$ 15,688	$ 18,250
Mileage	$ 2,000	$ 2,250	$ 2,500
Office supplies	$ 350	$ 400	$ 450
Telecommunications	$ 1,100	$ 1,100	$ 1,100
Legal & regulatory	$ 750	$ 250	$ 250
Accounting	$ 1,050	$ 1,150	$ 1,250
Postage	$ 650	$ 750	$ 850
Internet	$ 1,100	$ 1,100	$ 1,100
Marketing	$ 10,500	$ 11,500	$ 12,500
Total expenses	**$122,625**	**$137,688**	**$153,250**
Net profit	**$ 8,625**	**$ 19,187**	**$ 29,250**

Social Media Consultant

Social Media Masters

PO Box 3312
Austin, TX 78704

Zuzu Enterprises

Social Media Masters specializes in helping companies navigate the ever–changing world of social media and use platforms to increase brand awareness and drive their business. The company is owned and operated by Tessa Crowner.

EXECUTIVE SUMMARY

Social media consultants help guide businesses in managing their social media strategy and achieve success. By hiring a social media specialist, companies will be able to manipulate social media tools that are available to help a business grow. Social media consultants understand how to drive traffic to social media networks and, ultimately, to a business' website. Being a specialist in social media marketing is more than posting text, pictures, and videos to social media sites; it's providing a special service that increases a business' online presence, which in turn brings more potential clients to a business.

Social Media Masters specializes in helping companies navigate the ever–changing world of social media and use platforms to increase brand awareness and drive their business. The company is owned and operated by Tessa Crowner.

INDUSTRY ANALYSIS

Social media consulting is the process of reaching out to and engaging with customers using social networking channels on behalf of a brand. As such, a social media consultant is essentially the eyes, ears, and voice of a company online. They can and should raise brand awareness, deliver traffic to a company's website, and boost their bottom line, all while keeping the company's reputation top–of–mind. With the growth and boom in social media users and increase in online shopping, social media consultants are always in demand. As a newly emerging field, however, social media consultants are not covered by the U.S. Bureau of Labor Statistics (BLS). Instead, statistics about the industry must be gleaned from other measurements.

Both for businesses and consumers, social media is absolutely essential and it's not going away anytime soon. At the same time, many businesses and brands don't understand social media so there is—and will continue to be—an increase in the need for social media consultants.

In fact, the push toward social media advertising is no longer an option for most businesses. It is essential for success. Consider this:

- The number of social media users worldwide in 2018 was 3.196 billion, up 13 percent year–on–year

- The number of mobile phone users in 2018 was 5.135 billion, up 4 percent year–on–year

- Social media is now the number one source of traffic to websites, accounting for more than search engines

- 83.0% of Americans use some form of social media

- 50.0% of millennials use the internet to research products before purchasing

- 73.4% of users follow a brand because they're interested in the product or service

- 46.0% will unfollow a brand on social media for posting too many promotional messages

- 70.0% of Gen Xers are more likely to make purchases from brands they follow on social media

- 59.0% of Americans agree that customer service via social media is essential

Because of this, social media marketing is on the rise. Investments in social advertising worldwide are forecast to grow from around $32 billion in 2017 to approximately $48 billion in 2021.

The United States is, by far, the largest social media advertising market in the world, as more than $14.80 billion was spent on social media ads in the country in 2016 alone, up from a mere $7.52 billion in 2014. By 2019, this figure is expected to rise by almost 10 billion to $17.34 billion.

Despite the overall marketing budget devoted to social media, more than doubling from 2015 to 2020 (from 11 percent to 24 percent), 53 percent of businesses do not know whether social media is working for them. In many cases, it's not. Consider customer care; the top choice for a customer care channel is social media. Despite this, 89 percent of social media messages to brands go ignored and the average response time for a brand to reply on social media to a user is 10 hours, while the average user will only wait 4 hours. This is only one area where social media consultants could drastically impact a business' social media acumen.

People's Top Choice for Customer Care
Q1 2016

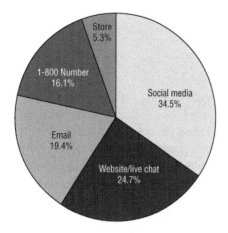

In addition to improved customer care, there are many other benefits for businesses using social media, ranging from increased exposure and website traffic to developing a loyal fan base and generating leads.

Benefits of Social Media Marketing

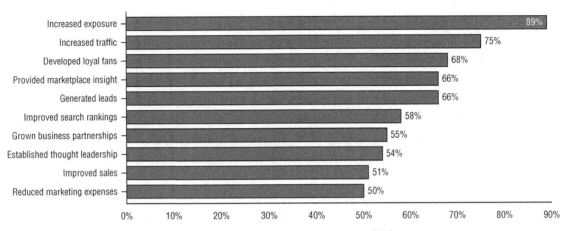

SOURCE: http://www.socialmediaexaminer.com/social-media-marketing-industry-report-2016

MARKET ANALYSIS

Social media is ubiquitous. There are no borders; apps are used by people the world over. As such, the market for a successful social media consultant is unlimited. They can be helpful to companies of all sizes and in all industries. Because they are not dependent on physical space, they can be located anywhere in the world to help companies across the globe. Social media consultants are valuable partners that can be utilized to increase traffic and sales to companies of all sizes and budgets.

SERVICES

Social Media Masters offers a wide variety of services to companies who want to establish or increase their social media presence to benefit their bottom line. Such services include:

- Analyzing the competition's social media presence

- Collaborating with marketing and sales staff to create consistent message delivery across platforms

- Connecting to industry influencers who can help build awareness of a company's products and services

- Creating, curating, and managing all published content (images, video, and written)

- Determining what customers like about an organization and identify areas for improvement

- Developing and overseeing social media communities dedicated to an organization's brand

- Developing methods to analyze the performance of social media campaigns

- Developing relevant content topics to reach the company's target customers

- Evaluating industry best practices and implementing them for the benefit of the clients

- Experimenting with different tactics that can leverage social media activities

- Listening to the client's requirements and delivering the product as per the specifications

- Monitoring, listening, and responding to users in a social way while cultivating leads and sales

- Noting and making companies aware of developments in the industry, including social media trends and trend changes

- Recommending improvements to organizational management

- Reviewing the monthly performance of social media activity in accordance with best practices and trends, analyzing any shortfall, providing suggestions for improvement, and choosing the best possible alternative

- Utilizing social media tools and social media marketing knowledge appropriately to form effective online marketing strategies

- Working with the social media management team to incorporate various social media tactics into the marketing strategy, which can also be reflected in the company's products and services

In this position, we will focus on areas like customer engagement, brand management, and organizational communications. To do this successfully, we must thoroughly understand each client's specific industry and their specific target market.

One of the most important things we need to do is back up our accomplishments with metrics and analytics that quantify return on investment. In addition to simple tallies of likes, followers, and fans, we need to analyze and provide lead conversion rates. To do this, we may use our own custom tracking methods, or we may utilize popular tools like Google Analytics, Facebook Insights, and Klout. This is imperative to prove our worth and encourage companies to continue to use our services.

Our process for accomplishing our tasks and services includes an audit of the current social media policy and presence, creating and setting up social media accounts, writing a social media policy, mapping the social media strategy, analyzing data, and ultimately integrating the content.

Social Media Audit

Social Media Masters will undertake an audit to understand the business and its target audience, the present social media strategy and presence, and other relevant information. We will create an unbiased opinion of the social media strategy, analyzing what works, what doesn't, potential weaknesses, and any other issues that need to be fixed.

Account Creation and Setup

Based on the audit, Social Media Masters may recommend creating various social media accounts. These accounts can be created and set up to be ready for content.

Social Media Policy

Social Media Masters will then prepare a tailored social media policy, which is specifically designed to help managers and employees of the business to understand the expectation of the company while using social media to grow its business.

Create or Update Social Media Strategy

Social Media Masters will prepare a comprehensive social media strategy that includes programs that define the best possible use of social media marketing techniques that help in increasing visibility, followers, and traffic. The strategy is prepared in accordance with the impact of social media on the overall marketing efforts of the company. Being strategic in utilizing social media includes noting the best times to post, balancing marketing campaigns, and keeping an eye on what everyone else is talking about. If a company already has a social media strategy, then Social Media Masters may re-draft a social media strategy report according to the objectives of the businesses.

Analyze Data

Social Media Masters will examine monthly analytics reports to make sure the company's social media strategy is on the right track. We will determine what type of posts have been performing well, and what type have not.

Integrate Content

Social Media Masters will synergize social marketing efforts across all social media platforms seamlessly. It is imperative to ensure that every page on each of the social sites includes a link back to the main company website.

SOCIAL MEDIA PLATFORMS

Social Media Masters covers all social media platforms from Facebook to LinkedIn. It is important to know where each stands in terms of audience, purpose, and potential for businesses to reach customers and increase sales leads. The most common platforms are described below.

Leading Social Media Platforms Used by Marketers Worldwide as of January 2018

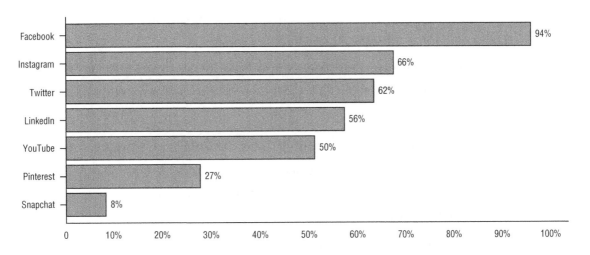

Facebook

- Facebook isn't going anywhere; Facebook still sees the most interactions and is the preferred network among millennials, Gen Xers, and baby boomers
- Facebook still reigns as the most popular social media network with 79% of internet users in the United States logging on to the site
- Facebook was estimated to generate $21.57 billion in U.S. ad revenues in 2018, which would account for 83% of the total social media ad spend throughout the nation
- Facebook ad revenue in the United States was expected to outpace total print ad spending by 2019
- 100 million hours of video is viewed daily on Facebook

Instagram

- New Instagram users increased by 150 million year over year in 2014 and has since successfully grown by 100 million new users each year
- Instagram added 100 million users in roughly six months during 2016, which coincided with the launch of Instagram Stories
- 35% of Instagram users check Instagram multiple times a day and 51% open the app daily
- Nearly a fourth of social media influencers believe Instagram is the top avenue for influencer marketing strategies

- Instagram drives the most engagement per post compared to any social network—84 times more than Twitter, 54 times more than Pinterest, and 10 times more than Facebook

Twitter

- New Twitter users grew by 43 million year over year in 2014, but only by 9 million in 2016
- More businesses are turning to Twitter for faster customer service actions
- Twitter is accessed through a mobile device by 82% of its monthly active users
- 47% of marketers agreed Twitter was the best social media channel for customer engagement
- 81% of millennials view their Twitter account on a daily basis
- Tweets with images are 150% more likely to get retweets than text–only tweets

LinkedIn

- More businesses are starting to use LinkedIn as a marketing channel
- There are more than 450 million LinkedIn user accounts
- The typical LinkedIn user only uses the network for an average of 17 minutes per month
- 94% of B2B organizations rely on LinkedIn for content marketing and distribution

YouTube

- There are 1.9 billion monthly active YouTube users and 30 million daily active users
- More than five billion videos have been shared as of June 2018
- The average viewing session is 40 minutes, up 50% year–over–year
- 62% of YouTube users are male
- Only 9% of small businesses are on YouTube
- 35+ and 55+ age groups are the fastest growing demographic groups using YouTube
- Millennials prefer YouTube over traditional television 2 to 1

Pinterest

- 29% of adults in the United States use Pinterest
- 50% of millennials use Pinterest every month
- 93% of active pinners use Pinterest to plan for purchases
- 50% of users have made a purchase after seeing a promoted pin
- Most people (85%) access Pinterest via their mobile device
- 78% of Pinterest users say it's useful to see content from brands
- Pinterest delivers $2 in profit for every $1 spent on advertising
- Pinterest had a 27.49% increase in social referral traffic from 2016 to 2017

Snapchat

- There are more than 300 million active monthly users on Snapchat
- 45% of Snapchat users are aged between 18–24
- 71% of Snapchat users are under age 34

- People under the age of 25 use Snapchat for 40 minutes on average every day, more than Instagram's latest stat for the same demographic

Knowing who uses what social media platform, how they use it, and for how long they use it is essential to creating a social media marketing strategy that is unique to the needs of each individual client.

OPERATIONS

Hours

Social media is a 24/7/365 job; there is no 9–5 in this industry. Content building, audience building, interaction, and communication, can happen at any moment, so there is no set schedule of hours for the business. We are working all the time, no matter where we are in the world.

Location

Social Media Masters is operated from the home office of owner Tessa Crowner in Austin, Texas. It is set up with all the needed office furniture and equipment including laptop computer, internet access, wifi hotspot backup, and mobile device.

Pricing

Social Media Masters will price according to the general premise of earning $50 per hour. We can charge by the hour, by the project, or offer a monthly block of hours on retainer. In this way, we can adjust to the unique needs, wants, and budget of each specific client.

All time spent on various tasks will be tracked to make sure companies are charged correctly and projects are costed appropriately. Invoices will be submitted with relevant analytics to provide context and prove value.

Invoice payments are due within sixty days, and there is a three percent late charge on all overdue invoices.

Referrals for new clients will be rewarded with a credit of five free hours.

BUSINESS APPLICATIONS

Several business applications are essential to the success of Social Media Masters. These applications include GroupHigh, Mention, and Cyfe. Each is described in detail below, as noted in an article in *Adweek* (https://www.adweek.com/digital/harald-merckel-guest-post-7-apps-you-need-as-a-social-media-consultant/).

GroupHigh (www.grouphigh.com)

The difference between a successful social media strategy and an unsuccessful one often lies in the involvement of influencers. Have the support of the right influencers, and your reach suddenly expands—you can make your message heard at any time.

With GroupHigh, you can find bloggers and social media influencers at any time; you can also sort these influencers by their influence, segment influencers with filters, and have regularly up-to-date information on the influencers you research. This makes it easy for you to be more efficient about who you connect with.

Mention (https://mention.com/en/)

It's a well-established fact that customers overwhelmingly expect a response on social media when they complain about a brand. Part of our work as a social media consultant is to help brands track complaints and facilitate a response as soon as possible, and nothing can damage a brand more than a complaint—in which you're not tagged—that goes viral.

Mention does just one thing—it helps you track mentions of your brand everywhere online, especially on social media. It also helps you find influencers in your clients' niches that they can connect with. With their dashboard, you can monitor what people are saying about the brand in real–time, and you can respond accordingly. More important, you can create reports to share with your clients so that they see that you're actually working and getting them results.

Cyfe (https://www.cyfe.com/)

One of the very first things real business leaders worry about is how their social media activities integrate with their overall business and marketing strategies. How can you know if social media is working? How do your clients know how much sales and traffic your activities as a consultant are generating?

With Cyfe, letting your clients see the results of what you're doing is extraordinarily easy. Cyfe is a dashboard builder that allows you to monitor all your business data in one visualization; this can include social media activity, website traffic analytics and other essential data. Reports are also updated in real–time, and you can share them privately with anybody you want, including your clients.

Some key features include the ability to see historical data, schedule email reports of your data and export your data in a variety of formats.

PERSONNEL

Owner Tessa Crowner has a bachelor's degree in communications and marketing from the University of Texas at Austin. She minored in business management. Tessa has excellent digital acumen, including an understanding of various social media platforms and their benefits as well as how to utilize social media reporting tools and analyze the results. She has excellent communication skills and strong project management abilities, which will help when overseeing multiple social media campaigns. Tessa is empathetic, articulate, and easily adaptable to changing trends. Her creative flair and sense of humor will only add to her success.

Translation Services

CB Lane Translation Services

1612 Cherry Blossom Lane
Winston-Salem, NC 27127

Zuzu Enterprises

To reach a global cultural market as well as communicate with a changing workforce, businesses of all types may need translation and localization services for their websites, software, and documents, including in-house documents such as employee materials. CB Lane Translation Services will address these needs by offering Spanish translation services, primarily to the manufacturing and related industries.

EXECUTIVE SUMMARY

To reach a global cultural market as well as communicate with a changing workforce, businesses of all types may need translation and localization services for their websites, software, and documents, including in-house documents such as employee materials.

CB Lane Translation Services will address these needs by offering Spanish translation services, primarily to the manufacturing and related industries. We work with clients to ensure that the content is accurately translated, published in the right format, on-time, and within budget.

Owner Lucia Reyes is proficient is Spanish, having grown up in a household where it was the only language spoken, and has more than ten years' experience in the manufacturing industry where she was employed as a project manager. Interpretation services will also be available on a limited basis.

CB Lane Translation Services will help customers break the language barrier, get their message across, and make communication easier. We are a one-stop solution for manufacturing translations.

INDUSTRY ANALYSIS

Interpreters and translators convert concepts in the source language to equivalent concepts in the target language and compile information and technical terms into glossaries and terminology databases to be used in their oral renditions and translations. Successful translators and interpreters must be able to speak, read, and write fluently in at least two languages, accurately, quickly, and clearly. In addition, they must be able to relay the style and tone of the original language and apply their cultural knowledge to render an accurate and meaningful interpretation or translation of the original message. To do that, the translator must be able to write in a way that maintains or duplicates the structure and style of the original text while keeping the ideas and facts of the original material accurate. Translators must properly transmit any cultural references, including slang, and other expressions that do not translate literally. The goal of a translator is to have people read the translation as if it were the original written material.

Nearly all translation work is done on a computer, and translators receive and submit most assignments electronically. Translations often go through several revisions before becoming final. Translation may be done with the help of computer-assisted translation (CAT) tools, in which a computer database of previously translated sentences or segments (called a "translation memory") may be used to translate new text. CAT tools allow translators to work more efficiently and consistently. Translators also edit materials translated by computers, or machine translation. This process is called post-editing.

Interpretation and translation services are needed in virtually all subject areas. Although most interpreters and translators specialize in a particular field or industry, many have more than one area of specialization.

Employment of interpreters and translators is projected to grow 18 percent from 2016 to 2026, much faster than the average for all occupations. Currently, there are more than 68,000 people employed in the industry, and this growth rate will increase that number to more than 80,000 by 2026. Globalization and large increases in the number of non-English-speaking people in the United States will drive employment growth. Job prospects should be best for those who have professional certification.

Interpreters and Translators

Percent change in employment, projected 2016–26

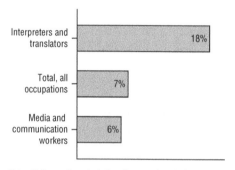

Note: All Occupations includes all occupations in the U.S. Economy.

SOURCE: U.S. Bureau of Labor Statistics, Employment Projections program

Employment projections data for interpreters and translators, 2016–26

Occupational Title	SOC Code	Employment, 2016	Projected Employment, 2026	Change, 2016–26	
				Percent	Numeric
Interpreters and translators	27–3091	68,200	80,300	18	12,100

SOURCE: U.S. Bureau of Labor Statistics, Employment Projections program

The largest employers of interpreters and translators were as follows:

Professional, scientific, and technical services	30%
Educational services; state, local, and private	23
Self-employed workers	22
Hospitals; state, local, and private	8
Government	6

The median annual wage for interpreters and translators is more than $47,000, which is significantly higher than the average for all occupations at $37,690.

Interpreters and Translators

Median annual wages, May 2017

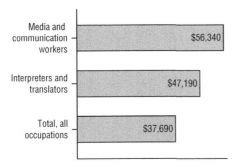

Note: All Occupations includes all occupations in the U.S. Economy.

SOURCE: U.S. Bureau of Labor Statistics, Occupational Employment Statistics

Demand will likely remain strong for translators of frequently translated languages, such as French, German, Portuguese, Russian, and Spanish. Interpreters and translators of Spanish in particular should have good job prospects because of expected increases in the population of Spanish speakers in the United States. Similarly, job opportunities should be plentiful for interpreters and translators specializing in healthcare and law, because of the critical need for all parties to understand the information communicated in those fields.

MARKET ANALYSIS

In the 1990s, North Carolina led in Latino population growth as new immigrant arrivals and their families moved there to pursue job opportunities in agriculture and manufacturing. As of July 2017, the population of Winston Salem was 244,605, with nearly 15 percent being Hispanic or Latino. The median household income was $42,219. The median value of homes in the area was $142,200. There are more than 94,000 households in the city, and 10-20 percent of them speak a language other than English at home; the primary language other than English that is spoken at home is Spanish.

Language at home, children 5–17

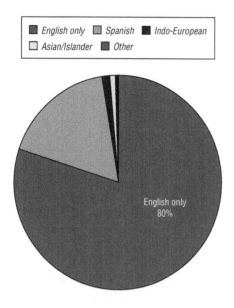

Language at home, adults 18+

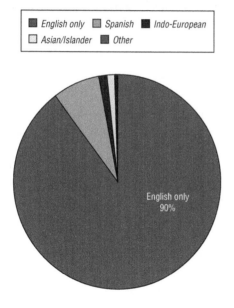

The Winston-Salem Metropolitan Statistical Area is comprised of more than 676,000 people spread over more than 2,000 square miles, as of July 2018. The median home value is $161,148 and the median income is $50,622. Ten percent of the population is Hispanic or Latino, with 68 percent of the foreign-born population coming from Latin America.

Place of birth for foreign-born population

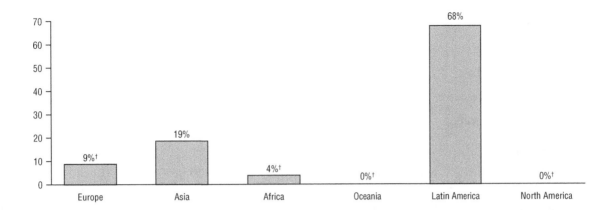

The largest industry in the Winston-Salem, North Carolina Metro Area is manufacturing, employing 46,501, or 15.3 percent of the total population. The total value of manufacturing shipments was more than $4 billion in 2012, roughly equivalent to retail sales at the same time.

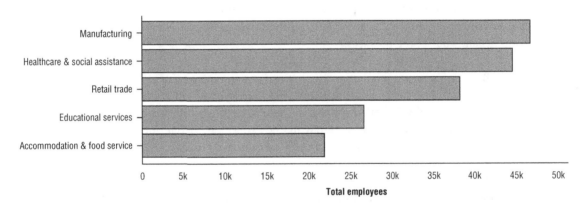

SERVICES

Businesses in all industries rely on having documents such as emails, policy manuals, advertising campaigns, and proposals translated. CB Lane Translation Services specializes in providing accurate, high-quality Spanish language translation services to the manufacturing industry. Our expertise in country-specific regulations, global compliance, and technical experience helps corporations communicate and succeed in the global marketplace and sets us apart from other translation companies.

CB Lane's primary focus is on document translation and electronic communications. As a specialist in the manufacturing industry, CB Lane understands the industry and can accurately address the context and nuances necessary for document translation in this situation. We can help clients meet the challenges of a changing employee and customer demographic as well as foreign markets to capitalize on new opportunities in the global marketplace.

Our accurate and localized translations are completed within the designated timeline and produced in any format that is required. We ensure that all translated content fully complies with local requirements and is easily understood by the end-user. Years of experience in manufacturing translation services has given us in-depth knowledge of the industry's needs and helped us create customized language solutions for each project.

Our specific areas of concentration include:

- Technical
- Websites
- eLearning
- Multimedia
- Human Resources
- Communications

Technical

CB Lane Translation Services prepares accurate, precise translations of technical documents, manuals, and specifications for the manufacturing industry. Our technical translation services help customers make the most of their technical publications and ensure that they are clearly understood by the target audience. Documents include: user guides, operating manuals, and engineering specifications.

Websites

Translation services can translate and localize websites to make your business more globally accessible. Localization is an important component of web translation to ensure your message is being accurately conveyed to your targeted cultural market. It is the single most cost-effective way to reach global consumers and expand your brand overseas.

eLearning

Online learning and training platforms deliver instruction and content to employees, end users, and customers around the globe. Whether the focus is educating and orienting a global workforce or delivering on-demand research and collaboration, having the expert knowledge and proven experience to help you make your training materials easily understood is essential to success.

Multimedia

Multimedia content is one of the most effective means of communicating in the global marketplace. From social media to eLearning, companies increasingly rely on video, audio, and interactive media to reach customers and employees alike. If the content is only in English, though, you may not effectively reach your target audience. Getting your message across in international markets requires localized multimedia content that is every bit as informative and impactful as the original. The final multimedia product must be seamlessly integrated and utilize the latest technology—with the target audience in mind. Precision, accuracy, and cultural sensitivity are essential.

Human Resources

Whether a company is multinational with offices overseas or a local business with non-English speaking employees, CB Lane Translation Services provides cost-effective solutions to meet all human resources translation needs. We specialize in translating employee manuals, policy procedure documents, benefits information, training documents, and newsletters. When it comes to translation of human resources materials, there's no room for error since employee handbooks and codes of conduct must be translated accurately to protect both your company and its employees.

Communications

Successful internal and external corporate communications are essential to a company's favorable standing, reputation, and success. Whether we are translating a press release, a shareholder letter, an annual report, or a corporate brochure, each translation will sound as if it were originally written in the target language.

Process

No matter what we are translating, CB Lane Translation Services will employ terminology management and glossary tools to build and manage client-specific glossaries, including abbreviations and branded terms for products and services.

We will also utilize a web-based client platform that enables clients to initiate a new request for translation services at any time and from any place in the world. This client platform lets clients request and approve quotes, track the status of ongoing projects, and download completed translations. Encryption is used to keep all client documents private and secure.

While most translations will be done directly by owner Lucia Reyes, machine translations may be employed in some instances. Human translation is preferred as it is more accurate and accounts for nuances and cultural context. However, for large or extremely time-sensitive projects that require only literal translations without exact cultural fluency, it may be more beneficial to begin with a machine translation, utilizing personal translating for reviewing and proofreading.

SPANISH LANGUAGE

The Spanish language has evolved over thousands of years across many continents, so many variations and dialects of the Spanish language have emerged and are in use across the globe. Indeed, in Latin America alone you can find different variants of Spanish including Amazonian, Bolivian, Caribbean, Central American, Andean, Chilean, Colombian, Ecuadorian, Mexican, Northern Mexican, Paraguayan, Peruvian, Puerto Rican, and Argentine Spanish.

This presents an interesting situation for anyone who wants to target all or part of the Spanish-speaking market. It provides an opportunity to tailor a particular translation to target a very specific group, making your communication more effective. However, if your intention is to target a broader audience of Spanish speakers, you will need to use a neutral Spanish that will be accepted and understood by the entire Spanish-speaking population.

Neutral Spanish, commonly referred to as Standard Spanish, Global Spanish, or Universal Spanish, is a variation of the Spanish language used to allow the greatest number of Spanish speakers to understand the message without the use of local terminology and certain verb tenses.

CB Lane Translation Services will help clients determine the best choice of Spanish depending on the nature of the project, objective, budget, communication needs, and the audience being addressed.

OPERATIONS

Location

CB Lane Translation Services will operate from the home office of owner Lucia Reyes. The office is outfitted with a large desk, a laptop with docking station, three monitors, a multiuse printer/copier/scanner/fax machine, and dedicated phone line. The laptop configuration allows Lucia the flexibility to continue to work even when she is traveling or not at home.

Hours

Having your own business means being available to clients 24 hours a day, 7 days a week to provide urgent estimates for any document translation service or to take on new projects. We understand that in certain situations, documents may require immediate attention and an expedited turnaround time. Some translations need to be done quickly, while others are not as urgent. A good mix of both types of projects will ensure a steady workflow, and successfully helping clients in pressing situations will encourage them to utilize our services in less stressful times as well.

Pricing

Translations are priced differently depending on length, complexity, and turnaround time. Discounts may be given for large or ongoing projects, or for repeat customers. As a general rule, projects are costed based on word count with a base rate of $0.15 per word, with a minimum charge of $50.00. This cost includes initial translation as well as proofreading and editing. Also, this is based on the English word count, not the final translated word count. As a general rule, text translated from English to Spanish will have about 20 percent more words. The basic reason for this expansion is related to the linguistic rules of the Spanish language. It often takes more words to say the same thing in Spanish.

Confidentiality

CB Lane Translation Services takes confidentiality and security issues very seriously. We are sensitive to the nature of this industry and fully respect the confidential documentation provided in connection with each project.

PERSONNEL

Owner Lucia Reyes is proficient in English and Spanish, having grown up in the southwestern United States in a household where Spanish was the only language spoken. She was also fortunate to travel to visit family and travel abroad for extended periods, giving her the opportunity to practice her skills and experience various cultures. Upon graduation from college, Lucia was employed as a project manager in the manufacturing industry for more than ten years. While there, she was able to utilize her Spanish skills by working with employees and suppliers in their native tongue. Her translation and interpretation skills have also been utilized in a volunteer capacity while working with various community organizations.

In addition to her Spanish skills and manufacturing experience, Lucia possesses many other skills that will ensure the success of the business, including:

- *Business skills.* Lucia possesses general business skills that will allow her to manage the company finances, from setting prices for work, billing customers, keeping records, and marketing company services in order to build the client base.

- *Concentration skills.* Lucia is able to concentrate while others are speaking or moving around her.

- *Cultural sensitivity.* Lucia is sensitive to cultural differences and expectations among the people with whom she is helping to communicate.

- *Interpersonal skills.* Lucia gets along with those who hire or use her services in order to retain clients and attract new business.

- *Listening skills.* Lucia listens carefully when interpreting for audiences to ensure that she hears and interprets correctly.

- *Reading skills.* Lucia can read Spanish fluently.

- *Speaking skills.* Lucia can speak Spanish clearly.

- *Writing skills.* Lucia can write in Spanish both clearly and effectively.

ASSOCIATIONS

Lucia is a member of the American Translators Association (ATA) (https://www.atanet.org/). The association was established to advance the translation and interpreting professions and foster the professional development of individual translators and interpreters. With more than 10,000 members, one of ATA's primary missions is to promote the professional development of translators and interpreters, including a certification exam that allows translators to demonstrate that they meet certain standards of the translation profession. A professional services directory, networking and support services, an annual conference, and various discounts are all benefits of membership in the association.

Lucia earned ATA certification by passing a challenging three-hour exam. The exam assessed her language skills to see if they were acceptable to be a professional translator: comprehension of the source-language text, translation techniques, and writing in the target language. The certification provides Lucia with a distinction that can set her apart and open doors to career advancement and higher compensation.

The cost of membership in ATA is $199 per year, while the cost of certification was $525.

BUSINESS STRATEGY

At the outset of business operations, Lucia will submit her resume and translation samples to different translation and interpreting companies who will match her skills with various jobs. Her reputation and referrals from former colleagues and clients will also lead to work as she builds up her clientele base. If the time comes when she is not able to handle additional jobs, Lucia will explore the possibility of hiring additional translators to work for CB Lane Translation Services.

FINANCIAL ANALYSIS

The startup cost for CB Lane Translation Services is minimal, requiring only the costs to set up the office and obtain certification. The specific breakdown includes:

Start-Up Costs

ATA Membership, $200

Certification, $525

Office furniture, $750

Office electronics, $3,600

Website, $150

Logo creation, $500

Marketing materials, $275

TOTAL, $6,000

Vacation Planning

Orlando Vacation Planning

24847 Walt Disney Way
Orlando, Florida 32803

Fran Fletcher

Orlando Vacation Planning is a vacation planning business located in the number one vacation spot, sunny Orlando, Florida.

BUSINESS OVERVIEW

Orlando Vacation Planning is an online vacation planning business based in Orlando, Florida. Its purpose is to help customers plan trips to Orlando, the top vacation spot in the United States. Orlando is home to several major theme parks and attractions, so planning a trip can be overwhelming. Orlando Vacation Planning will help potential tourists from all over the world determine what to see and what to skip based on their personal preferences.

Paul Gavin is the owner of Orlando Vacation Planning. Mr. Gavin is a world traveler and enjoys finding great deals that allow him to travel extensively without breaking the bank. He has even backpacked through Europe for six months with only $200 in his pocket! He blogs about his travels, and often helps friends and family find affordable travel deals. He is passionate about traveling and wants to build a business based on this passion.

Orlando Vacation Planning will conduct business through its website. The business will help tailor vacations using a questionnaire that seeks out the customer's preferences. Questions include:

- Number of vacation days
- Number of people in the group
- Ages of people in the group
- Amenities desired
- Cuisine likes and dislikes
- Entertainment likes and dislikes
- Budget

For a fee, Mr. Gavin will send customers a customized travel plan within 48 hours. The travel plan will include attractions that best align with the customer's interests.

Orlando, Florida, is a vacation hot spot. It welcomed more than 72 million visitors last year. Disney World has been and will remain the main attraction, but there are many other places in Orlando that are worth a visit.

The owner of Orlando Vacation Planning thinks he has found a niche market by specializing only in planning trips to Orlando. There are currently no competitors in the area offering the exact same service. Of course, online sites such as TripPlanner.com could be considered competition. However, as an Orlando insider and former concierge at a major resort, he has many contacts and connections that will make his business thrive. He also has the advantage of living in the city and can easily try out new restaurants and attractions and place first-hand information on his website and blog.

Mr. Gavin conservatively estimates that it will take a month or two to establish a solid web and social media presence. He expects profit increases as the website gets more traffic and his blog gets more attention.

The owner is seeking financing in the form of a loan in the amount of $3,500. This will cover start-up expenses. The loan will be paid back in one year.

COMPANY DESCRIPTION

Location
Mr. Gavin will operate Orlando Vacation Planning from his home office in Orlando, Florida.

Hours of Operations
Monday–Friday 8 a.m.–5 p.m., Saturday 2 p.m.–7 p.m.

Services
Orlando Vacation Planning will help customers plan trips to Orlando. Orlando Vacation Planning will conduct business through its website. The website will include reviews of Orlando businesses that Orlando Vacation Planning endorses through its blog.

Using an online questionnaire, the business will match customers with lodging, restaurants, and area attractions that most closely line up with their preferences and budget.

The questionnaire will ask a series of questions including the following:

- Number of vacation days
- Number of people in the group
- Ages of people in the group
- Amenities desired
- Cuisine likes and dislikes
- Entertainment likes and dislikes
- Budget

Orlando Vacation Planning will also work with local stores, restaurants, and attractions to get promotions and discounts that can be passed on to the customer, including:

- Disney World
- Sea World
- Animal Kingdom
- Discovery Cove
- GatoLand
- Epcot Center

- LegoLand
- The Holy Land Experience
- Safari Wilderness Ranch
- Orlando Aquarium
- Universal Studios

Personnel

Paul Gavin (owner)

Mr. Gavin received an MBA from The University of Florida. He has traveled extensively around the globe and has a knack for finding good travel deals. He served as a concierge at a popular Orlando resort for three years and made many business connections during that time.

MARKET ANALYSIS

Industry Overview

According to the Bureau of Labor Statistics, the vacation planning industry is expected to increase by three percent over the next decade. According to InternetTrends.com, there are thousands of Internet keyword searches each day for Orlando vacations. Florida's moderate weather makes any month of the year a good time to visit. Orlando welcomed 72 million tourists last year from all around the globe.

Target Market

Orlando Vacation Planning will target both domestic and international customers who would like help planning an Orlando vacation.

The primary target market will be online product sales to homeschool families. Local customers will be targeted mainly during the summer months.

Competition

There are travel agencies both on the Internet and locally in Orlando, but none are similar to Orlando Vacation Planning. Mr. Gavin thinks he has found a niche in vacation planning by specializing only in Orlando vacations. Additionally, using a questionnaire is a unique but effective way to suggest restaurants, resorts, attractions, and shopping tailored to the customers likes and dislikes.

As an Orlando insider and former concierge at a major resort, Mr. Gavin has many contacts and connections that will make his business thrive. He also has the advantage of living in the city and can easily try out new restaurants and attractions and place first-hand information on his website and blog.

GROWTH STRATEGY

The overall growth strategy of Orlando Vacation Planning is to create and maintain a website and blog that will adequately promote the business. The owner will review local resorts, theme parks, attractions, and restaurants so that he can offer the latest information. Each month, one superb establishment will be featured on the website. Mr. Gavin will market the fact that he is an Orlando insider and knows all of the places to go, both day and night, for endless fun and entertainment.

Sales and Marketing

The owner will use search engine optimization (SEO) to make his website and blog easier for customers to find. He will also maintain a social media presence on several different platforms.

Advertising and marketing will include:

- Orlando Vacation Planning website

- Orlando Vacation Planning blog

- Coupon and discount giveaways

FINANCIAL ANALYSIS

Estimated Start–up Costs

Business license	$ 500
Advertising	$1,000
Website design	$1,000
Software	$1,000
Total	**$3,500**

Estimated Monthly Expenses

Bank loan	$ 300
Phone, Internet	$ 100
Wages	$3,200
Website hosting, payment processing fees	$ 300
Total	**$3,900**

Estimated Monthly Income

Monthly income will largely depend on the demand for Orlando Vacation Planning's services. Income is projected to steadily increase during the first year of operation as the website gets more visitors and the blog expands. Even though the business will be operated by one person, the software that is used to match questionnaire results with Orlando businesses will make this possible. Expenses are expected to remain constant.

Price Schedule

5 day vacation plan	$15
7 day vacation plan	$20
Expedited plan (24 hours)	+$20

Profit/Loss

The owner conservatively estimates that he will gain twenty clients per week in the first month of operation. The number of clients is expected to steadily increase each month and then level out. Profits for the second year are expected to be more in line with the last six months of the first year, since the website and blog will be well established.

Monthly Profit/Loss

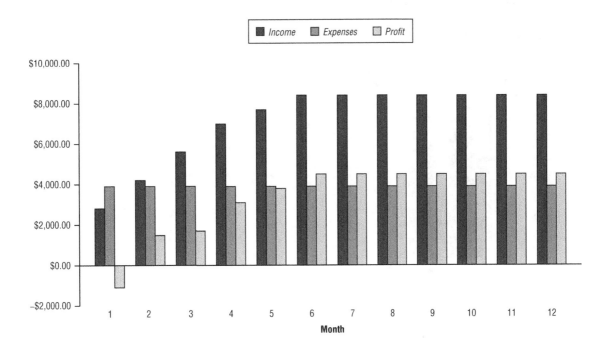

2-Year Profit Projections

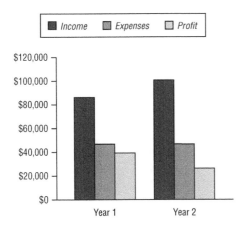

Financing

The owner of Orlando Vacation Planning wishes to obtain financing in the form of a business line of credit for $3,500. This amount will cover the start-up costs.

Repayment Plan

Loan payments are set at $300 per month. Orlando Vacation Planning will pay back the loan in 12 months.

Loan Repayment Plan

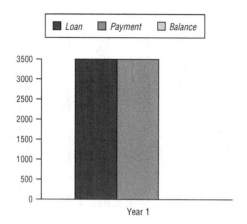

Virtual Assistant

Executive Office Solutions LLC

PO Box 87663
Troy, MI 48084

Zuzu Enterprises

Executive Office Solutions LLC is a company that provides virtual assistant services on a project or recurring basis. We provide a wide range of services from inbox management to arranging travel to researching and creating PowerPoint presentations.

EXECUTIVE SUMMARY

Virtual assistants (VAs) are independent contractors who support multiple clients in a variety of industries by providing administrative, creative, and technical services from a remote location. They perform various administrative tasks, including answering emails, scheduling meetings, and making travel arrangements. In today's fast paced corporate world, executives' time is stretched thin. They can greatly benefit from having help in completing tasks that are essential to the successful running of the business but do not require their specialized knowledge or expertise. At the same time, they may not require someone to help them on a full–time basis. Hiring a virtual assistant is the perfect solution—they will have the help they need without the overhead and costs of hiring a full–time staff member.

Executive Office Solutions LLC is a company that provides virtual assistant services on a project or recurring basis. We provide a wide range of services from inbox management to arranging travel to researching and creating PowerPoint presentations.

INDUSTRY ANALYSIS

There were an estimated 3.9 million secretaries and administrative assistants in the United States in 2016, according to the Bureau of Labor Statistics. However, this figure does not distinguish between assistants who work in an office, and the growing number of those who work online. Indeed, virtual assistants are quickly replacing traditional secretaries and in–office personal or administrative assistants. While the International Virtual Assistants Association, Virtual Assistant Networking Forum, and other organizations say that the number of VAs is increasing, it's hard to find verified statistics for this industry.

But we do know that the virtual assistant industry has grown significantly. It is no longer a profession that is frowned upon in the business industry, but rather a much–needed solution in the ever–growing and ever–changing work landscape. Many of those are virtual assistants that offer a wide range of services for almost every aspect of the business, services that are necessary to run an organization efficiently and successfully.

Indeed, virtual work in general has become increasingly popular among employees and employers. From 2005 to 2012, the number of telecommunicating employees in the United States grew by 79.7 percent. And the number of self-employed workers was growing too—freelancers now account for over 34 percent of the total U.S. workforce.

The main reason for the sharp increase in independent contractors, freelancers, or virtual workers is the cost savings. It has been estimated that hiring a virtual assistant over a full-time employee can save up to 78 percent in operating costs per year. This is because it is not necessary for you to find them a place to do their job. Most virtual assistants work from home where they have their own equipment, their own internet connection, and a designated working space. Companies also save money on taxes by hiring freelance staff.

And in terms of productivity, research shows that remote workers are more productive because they have better control of their time and spend less time traveling to the office. They also benefit from fewer office distractions and the ability to work longer hours at home. In fact, a study analyzed by the Harvard Business Review reveals that staff who worked from home finished 13.5 percent more work compared to staff who worked in the office. Remote workers know this to be true as well; a study from TINYpulse found that 91 percent of remote workers feel they're more productive at home.

Despite this, there is a common misconception that virtual assistants are a luxury only affordable by big companies. However, that is the opposite of the truth. Virtual assistants are valuable employees that can be utilized to save time and money to companies of all sizes and budgets.

MARKET ANALYSIS

The market for virtual assistants is limitless. They can be helpful to companies of all sizes and in all industries. Because they are not dependent on physical space, they can be located anywhere in the world to help companies across the globe. Virtual assistants are valuable employees that can be utilized to save time and money to companies of all sizes and budgets.

The reasons for hiring a virtual assistant include:

1. You don't need a full-time employee.

2. You can't afford a full-time employee.

3. You're having trouble completing your most important tasks.

4. You need work done that doesn't require an office presence.

5. You travel a lot and need someone who likes working virtually.

6. You spend more time organizing rather than executing.

7. You know what tasks need to be done but you don't have the manpower.

As you can see from this list, virtual assistants are valuable to just about every company.

SERVICES

Executive Office Solutions LLC offers a wide line of services to fit every company's specific needs and budget. Clients can choose from a comprehensive list of a la carte services billed at an hourly rate, or we can create a custom package of services. They may choose a recurring monthly block of time to do whatever is needed or service that is limited to a specific timeframe or project.

A la Carte Services

A la carte services includes tasks that are performed for a set hourly rate. These tasks include:

- Answer and direct phone calls
- Arrange payments for vendors, travel, and sales expenses
- Arrange travel itineraries, flights, and rooms
- Calendar management
- Create purchase orders and track and manage payments
- Follow up with clients/customers by sending thank you and other reminder emails
- Handle client inquiries by phone or e-mail
- Handle confidential employer and client information
- Inbox management—organize correspondence and answer emails, filtering messages
- Manage blog (Basic WordPress Skills), including publishing posts and filtering and replying to comments
- Manage contact lists
- Manage filing systems, update records, and organize documentation
- Personal errands, such as procuring presents and ordering flowers
- Prepare and create PowerPoint presentations and materials as needed
- Prepare and organize databases and reports
- Prepare and send out e-mail newsletters
- Prepare customer spreadsheets
- Prepare, collate, and ship proposals and meeting materials
- Research materials and sources for presentations, newsletters, and blog posts
- Schedule meetings, including scheduling meeting spaces and conference rooms
- Send out requested information to customers
- Set up and manage social media accounts and replies (Facebook, Twitter, Instagram, LinkedIn, Youtube)
- Set up Autoresponders (Aweber, Mailchimp)
- Take notes or transcribe meetings, voicemails, podcasts, etc.
- Track and manage expenses and payments
- Website updating and maintenance

Service Packages

In addition to a la carte services, clients may design a package of services that fits their specific needs. Packages can be based on time, where companies purchase a block on time on a weekly or monthly basis, or they can be project–based. They can be long–term in place of traditional employees, or short–term to cover things such as extended medical or maternity leaves. We will work with each client to determine the best solution for their situation and budget.

Pricing

The general rate for services is $40 per hour. Extended contracts and repeat customers may receive a bulk discount rate of $35–37 per hour, as negotiated.

OPERATIONS

Location

Executive Office Solutions LLC is run from the home office of owner Patricia Bruce. A dedicated room has been set up with all the needed office furniture and equipment. It is also outfitted with a small sitting area from which to take video calls and meetings.

Equipment

The needed equipment is minimal, including:

- Computer
- Internet connection
- Phone with voice mail
- Wifi hotspot
- All-in-one copier, scanner, fax machine
- Business and communications software, including instant messenger
- Antivirus software
- Desk and ergonomic chair
- Loveseat and coffee table

Hours

Executive Office Solutions LLC is available to clients 24 hours a day, seven days a week. Scheduled work is done primarily between the hours of 8 a.m. and 3 p.m., with additional work being done throughout the day and night as needed.

PERSONNEL

Owner-operator Patricia Bruce has extensive experience as an administrative assistant. She was attracted to the profession for the constant variety where every day is different, and a new challenge is just around the corner. She is transitioning from a full-time position at a local corporation to start her own virtual assistant business to save time commuting (1.5–2 hours a day) and design a more flexible schedule to fit her family's needs. Her resume includes:

- Associate in Business Administration degree from Oakland Community College
- Seven years' previous experience handling assistant and administrative responsibilities for the vice president of a prominent corporation
- Knowledge of online calendars and scheduling (e.g. Google Calendar)
- Excellent phone, email, and instant messaging communication skills
- Proficient computer skills, including Microsoft Office Suite (Word, PowerPoint, and Excel)
- Experience with Google Docs, cloud services, and other technology tools
- Knowledgeable in technology to communicate via computer, smartphone, or text
- Highly organized and works well with fast-paced directions and instructions
- Demonstrates excellent time management
- Able to organize and manage large amounts of files, tasks, schedules, and information
- Self-directed and able to work without supervision

- Excellent verbal and written communication skills

- Strong customer–service and presentation skills

- Ability to work as part of a team

- Excellent customer service skills

- Able to work nights, weekends, extended hours, and holidays as needed

KEYS TO SUCCESS

Executive Office Solutions LLC recognizes the following keys to success:

Planning and Strategizing

Executive Office Solutions LLC must be able to spot new opportunities and potential hazards well in advance. It may be easy to get caught up in the work that's in front of us right now, but we can't lose sight of the medium– and long–term future. The ability to plan and strategize is one of the most crucial and prized virtual assistant skills we can develop, which means we need to look at three, six and twelve months down the road to anticipate challenges and opportunities that deserve our attention.

Prioritizing Revenue–Generating Tasks

Another important key to success is the ability to prioritize revenue–generating tasks. There will always be a million things on our to–do list as a virtual assistant and business owner, but not all these items deserve the same level of attention. We must place an emphasis on tasks that generate revenue, or our bottom line will suffer immeasurably.

Batching Work Tasks

On top of this, it is imperative that Executive Office Solutions stops multi–tasking and starts batching work. Very little good comes from multitasking—it almost always results in lost productivity and more frequent mistakes. Learning to focus on one thing at a time is one of the most valuable virtual assistant skills we can develop. Batching is simple: instead of switching between various tasks on a macro level, we will try to complete many instances of the same task in one sitting. Email is the perfect example; instead of constantly checking email, we will set aside two specific times each day where we check and reply to emails, once in the morning and once in the afternoon. By reducing the number of times that you switch between tasks, we will save time while improving concentration and productivity.

Communicating More Effectively

Communication is an essential skill for any virtual assistant. Perhaps the most important thing to remember about improving our ability to communicate is that 50 percent of communication involves listening. Listening will make us better at sales, better at conflict resolution, and better at meeting the needs of our clients.

Developing Our Sales Skills

Ultimately, we're in the business of sales. We will succeed only if we can convince our clients and prospective clients that we're offering a service that will make their life or business better in some way. To sell ourselves, we will communicate our value and be true to ourselves.

Acquiring Basic Accounting Knowledge

There are several benefits to developing basic accounting knowledge and maintaining the books for our business. It will help us become more aware of what's happening in the business and help us to:

- Determine which clients and projects are most profitable.

- Know which clients pay their bills late and which ones are reliable.

- Understand which parts of the business generate the most revenue and in which quarter most of that revenue is earned.

- See when our expenses are getting out of hand or impacting profitability.

- Figure out which clients are due for a rate increase.

The more insight we have into the numbers behind the business, the greater our chance of success.

Committing to Personal and Professional Development

A commitment to personal and professional development has the potential to impact the business more than anything else. The never-ending pursuit of knowledge and the desire to continually improve is the desire to seek perfection of our craft, to become a better salesperson, a better communicator, and to understand more about the numbers behind the business. It's figuring out how we can provide more value and solve problems more efficiently for our clients. Commitment to personal and professional development means being a better virtual assistant and business owner today than we were yesterday.

ASSOCIATIONS

Executive Office Solutions LLC is a member of two associations dedicated to the advancement of virtual assistants. These associations include:

International Virtual Assistants Association (https://ivaa.org/)

The IVAA provides continuing education and networking opportunities, as well as providing a member directory and Request for Proposal (RFP) system for parties interested in utilizing the services of member virtual assistants. Membership costs $137 per year.

Global Alliance of Virtual Assistants (https://globalava.org/)

The mission of GAVA is to connect VAs and clients globally by providing a venue for VAs to network, share knowledge and skills, plan events, and obtain valuable support from other VAs in various stages of business development. Benefits of membership include a business listing in the membership directory, access to Requests for Proposals, webinars and chats, and a monthly newsletter. Membership costs $97 per year.

ETHICS PLEDGE

One concern companies have in hiring virtual assistants or freelance employees is the perception that they will be less invested in the company and thus not as loyal. Confidentiality of sensitive data and communications is seen to be at risk.

Executive Office Solutions LLC strives to be ethical and fair in all its dealings and will protect its clients and their integrity at all costs. To demonstrate this commitment to principled behavior, we will provide each client with our ethics pledge.

- We will maintain the highest ethics and honesty in all dealings with clients, colleagues, and the general public.

- We will seek to deal with colleagues, suppliers, and employees in a fair and equitable manner, and maintain the highest standards of personal conduct to bring credit our profession.

- We will only take on projects that are within our abilities.

- Client information will be held in the strictest of confidence and will not be shared with others or used for personal gain.

- We highly value each client relationship and will not place one client above another.

- We will make a commitment to possess and increase the required knowledge, skills, and training to be proficient and relevant in the provision of services.

- We will be honest about our intentions and never misrepresent our skills, peers, or profession, whether to networks or to prospects, clients, and the community at large.

- We will not knowingly be a part of any illegal or unethical activity.

- We will exhibit the utmost professionalism.

SWOT ANALYSIS

The success or failure of Executive Office Solutions LLC is dependent on many factors. Below is an analysis of these issues.

Strengths

- Work can be done from anywhere in the world and at any time of the day.

- Clients can be based anywhere in the world, so there is no dependency on physical location.

- The workload can be flexible depending on my availability.

- Virtual assistant services offer clients lower operational costs because they are not required to offer benefits, equipment, paid training, bonuses, or physical space. They also save money on taxes.

- Research shows that remote workers are more productive because they have better control of their time and spend less time traveling to the office. They also benefit from fewer office distractions and the ability to work longer hours at home.

- We have the flexibility of adapting our schedule to fit our own preferences and needs, ensuring we are able to work when we are most productive.

- Our experience in the industry has produced a large network of contacts familiar with our level of expertise and professionalism.

Weaknesses

- There is a need to constantly learn and evolve to meet changing demands.

- Some view virtual assistant services as a luxury.

- There are many competitors in the industry.

- In addition to client work, we will be responsible for accounting, billing, tax payments, marketing, and sales pitches, all of which are relatively new to us.

Opportunities

- Because clients can be based anywhere in the world, the market for potential clients is limitless.

- Word–of–mouth advertising from satisfied clients can lead to new contracts.

Threats

- An economic downturn may prompt businesses to look for ways to save money, and our services may be viewed as superfluous.

MARKETING

Fortunately, Executive Office Solutions LLC has already secured one client with a recurring monthly contract. Marketing for additional clients will initially include:

1. Letting our network of contacts know about the creation of our business and educating them on the benefits of our service.

2. Creating a social media presence including a website, Facebook page, and LinkedIn profile where people can learn about our available services and benefits.

3. Advertising through virtual assistant associations.

4. Responding to RFPs and bidding on new jobs to further build our client base.

FINANCIAL ANALYSIS

The startup costs for starting a virtual assistant business are relatively low. Office furniture and equipment is necessary, as are the creation of a social media presence and promotional materials.

Computer, $2,500

Internet service, $800

Phone with voice mail, $150

Wifi hotspot, $600

All–in–one copier, scanner, fax machine, $400

Business and communications software, including instant messenger, $400

Antivirus software, $150

Desk and ergonomic chair, $750

Promotional materials, $500

Website and social media creation with branding, $500

Association dues, $250

TOTAL, $7,000

Web Site Improvement Business

Optimal Web Technologies LLC

4 Devondale Ave.
Rochester, NY 14611

Paul Greenland

Optimal Web Technologies LLC is a boutique Web development service that specializes in making improvements to existing Web sites.

EXECUTIVE SUMMARY

According to the U.S. Small Business Administration, there are approximately 30.2 million small businesses in the United States. Many of these are non-employer businesses (one-person operations with no paid employees) led by entrepreneurs. With many responsibilities vying for their attention, small business owners invariably will need a hand making sure their Web site is as successful as possible. For example, small businesses without mobile-friendly sites risk losing customers to competitors. Sites that are not optimized for easy sharing/recommending on social media results in lost word-of-mouth marketing opportunities. Established by two experienced developers, Optimal Web Technologies LLC is a boutique Web development service that specializes in making improvements to existing sites. Small businesses have limited resources, but their money is well spent with Optimal Web Technologies. In most cases, significant improvements can be made to a Web site in just a few hours, producing long-term results that attract customers and benefit the bottom line.

INDUSTRY ANALYSIS

According to the U.S. Bureau of Labor Statistics (BLS), in 2016 nationwide employment of Web developers totaled 162,900. By 2026 this figure is projected to increase 15 percent (24,400 additional jobs), much faster than the average for all occupations. In 2017 Web developers generated a median annual salary of $67,990. The BLS reported that approximately 16 percent of developers were self-employed.

Some Web developers are represented by the non-profit professional association, WebProfessionals.org (http://www.webprofessionals.org). According to the organization, which offers education, training, and certification, it is "dedicated to the support of individuals and organizations who create, manage or market web sites." These include Web Designers, Web Administrators, Web Consultants, e-Commerce Managers, and Webmasters.

The non-profit National Center for Women & Information Technology (https://www.ncwit.org) is another prominent industry organization. NCWIT was established in 2004 by the National Science Foundation and bills itself as "the only national non-profit focused on women's participation in computing across the entire ecosystem." The organization's members include 1,100 different companies, nonprofits, government organizations, and universities "working to increase girls' and women's meaningful participation in computing."

MARKET ANALYSIS

Optimal Web Technologies will specialize in optimizing Web sites for small businesses throughout the continental United States. The owners believe that these types of businesses are most likely to need help improving an existing Web presence but lack the expertise to do so on their own. A 2018 U.S. Small Business Administration (SBA) report revealed that there are approximately 30.2 million small businesses in the United States. Collectively, they employ 58.9 million people, or 47.5 percent of all U.S. workers. Self-employed individuals working for incorporated businesses generated median incomes of $50,347 in 2016, while self-employed workers at unincorporated businesses earned $23,060.

Non-employer businesses (those with no paid employees) account for approximately four of every five businesses, according to the SBA, which claims that non-employer operations tend to be more diverse and younger than employer firms. Additionally, the SBA indicates that several industry categories top the list for small business employment. Collectively, these categories will comprise Optimal Web Technologies' primary target market:

- Health Care and Social Assistance (8.69 million)
- Accommodation and Food Services (8.00 million)
- Retail Trade (5.51 million)
- Manufacturing (5.16 million)
- Professional, Scientific, and Technical Services (5.08 million)
- Construction (4.94 million)

Other leading categories, which will comprise Optimal Web Technologies' secondary target market include:

- Other Services (except Public Administration) (4.63 million)
- Administrative, Support, and Waste Management (3.63 Million)
- Wholesale Trade (3.49 Million)
- Finance and Insurance (1.92 Million)
- Transportation and Warehousing (1.65 Million)

SERVICES

Optimal Web Technologies is a boutique Web development service that specializes in making improvements to existing Web sites. The business works with clients whose sites have been created on popular site builder platforms, as well as those created by developers. The company's owners will fix and enhance sites created in the following categories, or involving the following development languages:

Web Site Builders
- GoDaddy
- Shopify

- Squarespace

- Wix

- WordPress.com

- WordPress.org

Development Languages

- PHP

- Flash

- SQL

- HTML

- JavaScript

- .Net

Process

Optimal Web Technologies will begin all relationships by determining a client's objectives for improving their site. For example, one client may wish to optimize their site so that it not only works well on a regular computer screen, but also on tablets and smartphones. Another may wish to add social media sharing options throughout their site content. In some cases, a client may be unsatisfied with many different aspects of their Web site. Although starting from scratch and developing an entirely new site may be the best option, in some cases they simply may need assistance identifying key objectives and then prioritizing them based on level of importance and budget. Optimal Web Technologies will perform a free site analysis for all potential clients, offering several recommendations that can serve as a starting point.

Once objectives have been determined, Optimal Web Technologies will develop a detailed time and cost estimate to perform the recommended work. Depending on the client's needs, projects may involve:

- Adding call-to-action buttons

- Adding motion/animation

- Adding video

- Fixing broken links

- Improving design (color, photography, illustrations, branding, etc.)

- Improving page speed

- Maximizing whitespace

- Mobile optimization/responsiveness

- SEO content optimization

- Simplifying navigation

- Social media optimization (adding follow/share buttons)

Rates & Fees

Web developer rates range anywhere from $25–$200 per hour, based on the level of skill and experience and the market in which they operate. Optimal Web Technologies will base its fees on an hourly rate of $95, putting its services within reach of most small business customers.

OPERATIONS

Location & Communications

Initially, Optimal Web Technologies will operate virtually (e.g., from the owners' respective home offices) to keep expenses low. The owners will use designated spaces within their homes exclusively for business operations and have subscribed to business class Internet service, allowing them to upload and download large files when needed. Additionally a toll-free phone number has been secured for the business, along with an answering service that will field calls based on the owners' availability status.

Tools & Equipment

Optimal Web Technologies' owners already have the tools needed to begin operations, including laptop computers (PC and Mac) and office furniture. Examples of other tools needed for daily operations include:

- Adobe Creative Cloud + Adobe Stock Photos ($109.98/month per license) (2)

- Wordpress (free)

- Dropbox for Business (Advanced) ($20/month)

- Text Editor (free)

Business Structure

Optimal Web Technologies is structured as an S corporation, which provides its owners with certain tax and liability advantages. The S corporation was formed cost-effectively by using a popular online legal document service.

Liability

In conjunction with a reputable insurance agency, the owners of Optimal Web Technologies have secured an appropriate level of liability coverage for the business.

PERSONNEL

Louis Santos

After earning an associate's degree in Web design from Greenview Community College, Louis Santos pursued a career in back-end Web development. Working for several noteworthy companies, he focused on developing the technical framework for many successful Web sites and ensuring their optimal functionality. In this role, Santos developed procedures needed for making major site changes and adding new pages. In addition to his skills as a Web developer, Santos is a highly skilled project manager.

Jill Treadway

Jill Treadway earned a graphic design degree from Central State University and began working as a front-end Web designer. Her creative skills significantly improved the overall look and feel of Web sites for her employers, which included a leading metropolitan museum, healthcare system, and paper company. In her role, she integrated stunning graphics with various applications and plug-ins.

Together, Santos and Treadway possess the skills and attributes needed for success as Web developers, including:

- Project Management

- Customer Service

- Creativity

- Written Communication

- Oral Communication

- Attention to Detail

Independent Contractors

When necessary, Optimal Web Technologies will rely upon freelance independent programmers and developers. This will give the owners the ability to scale up capacity when additional resources are required and enable the business to offer customers highly specialized technical expertise when needed. Santos and Treadway have developed a short list of independent contractors who are available for project work.

Professional & Advisory Support

The owners of Optimal Web Technologies established a business checking account with Bank of America, along with a merchant account for accepting credit card payments. Tax advisory services are provided by Smith & Howell Accounting Services.

MARKETING & SALES

Optimal Web Technologies has developed a marketing plan that focuses heavily on its own Web site and blog. The owners will employ a content marketing strategy by making checklists, tip sheets, and guides available to small business owners willing to follow their blog and opt into their e-mail list. As their list grows, the owners will market to these prospects by providing them with valuable DIY content, Web strategies, and special offers for their services.

In addition to leveraging social media platforms such as YouTube, Facebook, and LinkedIn, Optimal Web Technologies' owners well rely heavily upon word-of-mouth marketing (e.g., referrals from satisfied customers).

Finally, the following freelance marketplaces will factor prominently into the business' marketing activities:

- 99designs

- Behance

- Clarity

- Creative Market

- Damongo

- Demand Media

- Fiverr

- Folyo

- Freelancer

- Gigster

- Guru

- iFreelance

- PeoplePerHour

- Smashing Jobs

- Toptal

- Upwork

- Zirtual

GROWTH STRATEGY

Optimal Web Technologies' owners will begin operations on a part-time basis, gradually building capacity until they have enough work to part ways with their existing employers. Independent contractors will be used as needed, should the owners' availability be limited by their existing employment commitments. Based on conversations with other developers, the owners have established realistic targets for Optimal Web Technologies' first three years of operations:

- **2020:** Achieve 1,600 billable hours ($152,000). Focus on establishing Optimal Web Technologies on leading freelance marketplaces and generating word-of-mouth referrals.

- **2021:** Achieve 1,800 billable hours ($171,000). Begin operating the business as a full-time operation. Focus on building awareness and generating referrals on freelance marketplaces, mainly among the business' primary target market.

- **2022:** Achieve 2,000 billable hours ($190,000). Begin expanding awareness-building activities to secondary target market prospects. Explore options for adding a third developer to the business.

FINANCIAL ANALYSIS

The owners anticipate that Optimal Web Technologies will be profitable during its first year of operation. Higher profits are anticipated during years one and two as the owners draw smaller salaries. Projected revenue, expenses, and net profit for the first three years of operations are detailed in the following table:

	2020	2021	2022
Revenue	**$152,000**	**$171,000**	**$190,000**
Expenses			
Salaries	$100,000	$120,000	$140,000
Payroll taxes	$ 15,000	$ 18,000	$ 21,000
Accounting & legal	$ 1,850	$ 1,850	$ 1,850
Marketing	$ 7,500	$ 8,500	$ 9,500
Business insurance	$ 750	$ 1,000	$ 1,250
Subscriptions & licenses	$ 3,000	$ 3,000	$ 3,000
Equipment	$ 1,000	$ 3,500	$ 3,500
Internet/telecommunications	$ 1,500	$ 1,750	$ 2,000
Miscellaneous	$ 500	$ 550	$ 500
Total	**$131,100**	**$158,100**	**$182,600**
Net profit	**$ 20,900**	**$ 12,900**	**$ 7,400**

The following bar graph shows a visual depiction of the business' projected revenue and net profit for the first three years:

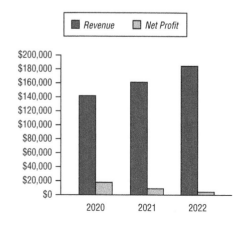

Youth Outreach Center

Havenwood Center Inc.

17798 Summit St.
Norwich, MO 62209

Paul Greenland

Havenwood Center Inc. is a nonprofit organization that provides meals, homework help, life skills training, and moral instruction on weekday evenings for inner-city kids.

EXECUTIVE SUMMARY

Linda Johnson has been a resident of Norwich, Missouri, her entire life. Over more than four decades, she has watched it decline. Once a proud manufacturing town, many of the factory jobs that provided a good living for residents have disappeared. Coupled with declining municipal and corporate investments, Norwich's population decreased significantly as residents left for better opportunities elsewhere. Those who remain face unemployment and fewer economic opportunities. Although Norwich's story has started to change for the better, significant challenges remain. Most children in the Norwich School District live below the poverty level. Only 16 percent of its students meet or exceed state standards in English language arts, and only 12 percent meet standards in math. The district's four-year high school graduation rate is 59 percent.

For many of Norwich's children, the only meals they receive are breakfast and lunch provided by the school district. Most do not receive help with school work at home. Convinced that more needed to be done to give Norwich's children a fighting chance, Johnson established Havenwood Center with the assistance of other like-minded community partners. The organization, whose mission is to provide a safe, supportive environment for children between the ages of 6 and 18, provides meals, homework help, life skills training, and moral instruction during the evening hours, Monday through Thursday. Havenwood Center was established as an afterschool program at a local church in 2016. The following plan describes the organization's next phase as it relocates to permanent quarters in Norwich's Midtown neighborhood.

History

Havenwood Center's origins date back three years, when Linda Johnson began a simple after-school tutoring and meal program operating from Norwich Baptist Church. Although attendance was sporadic at first, the program quickly became popular with children in the surrounding neighborhoods. At first, almost all funding and volunteer service was provided by the church. However, as word circulated throughout the community, like-minded people began volunteering, providing much-needed help with tutoring, food preparation, and coordination. Attendance and volunteers increased gradually throughout the first year, and it soon became apparent that more funding and a formal structure was needed.

This prompted Linda Johnson to establish a steering committee that led to the formation of Havenwood Center as a nonprofit corporation. The steering committee provided the nucleus of a board of directors.

Local businesses began providing monetary donations and hosting fundraising drives to purchase needed items (e.g., backpacks, school supplies, etc.). With the assistance of its board members, Linda Johnson also began securing grant funding, mainly from community foundations and organizations like United Way.

As its fourth year begins, Havenwood Center has grown to the point where Norwich Baptist Church is having difficulty accommodating its programming. Although the church remains a key source of financial and volunteer support, its facilities are not large enough to meet the needs of the children, which now number 85 (up from an average of 15 in year one, 23 in year two, and 55 in year three). When the local school district announced that the former Westview School would be put up for sale following the end of 2018–2019 school year, Havenwood Center's board of directors immediately began evaluating the feasibility of purchasing the building and gaining a permanent home in the Midtown neighborhood. Negotiations followed, and an agreeable price was soon reached.

Havenwood Center plans to relocate to the former Westview School building during the summer of 2019, where it will operate a summer day camp program and make preparations to continue its regular afterschool programming during the 2019–2020 school year. Havenwood Center will generate revenue for its programming by leasing office and storage space in the building and in an adjacent structure, and by renting classrooms to Norwich Community Center, which is in need of additional instructional space for its programs.

MARKET ANALYSIS

Havenwood Center is located in Norwich, Missouri. In 2018 the community had a population of 8,500 people (3,300 households). About 14 percent of residents are children ages 6–12, while 7.3 percent are 13–18. Approximately 79.7 percent of Norwich's housing units are occupied, and 20.3 percent are vacant.

In terms of race and ethnicity, the community's residents fall into the following categories:

- Black (74.6%)
- White (21.1%)
- Multi-Race (2.9%)
- Hispanic (1.4%)

Norwich's ratio of income to poverty level is as follows:

- Less Than .50 (1,013)
- .50–.99 (1,904)
- 1.00–1.24 (968)
- 1.25–1.49 (905)
- 1.50–1.84 (688)
- 1.85–1.99 (167)
- 2.00+ (2,876)

The median household income in Norwich was $25,200 in 2018. Residents fell into the following income brackets:

- $0–$9,999 (18.6%)
- $10,000–$14,999 (9.0%)
- $15,000–$24,999 (22.0%)

- $25,000–$34,999 (11.8%)
- $35,000–$49,999 (14.2%)
- $50,000–$74,999 (10.8%)
- $75,000–$99,999 (7.7%)
- $100,000–$124,999 (3.5%)
- $125,000–$149,999 (1.0%)
- $150,000+ (1.4%)

Havenwood Center has identified the following target markets for its fundraising and donation solicitation efforts:

- Individuals
- Businesses
- Service Agencies
- Community Foundations
- Civic Groups
- Churches

SERVICES

Havenwood Center provides the following core services to children in Norwich between the ages of 6 and 18 (grades 1–12):

- Tutoring/Homework Help
- Moral Instruction
- Leadership Training
- Hot Meals
- Snack Packs
- Seasonal Gifts (winter coats, school backpacks, school supplies, used bicycles, personal care supplies)
- Social Activities
- Bible Study

Weeknight Programming

Weeknight school year programming, offered Monday through Thursday, is a core offering of the Havenwood Center. On weekdays, the center opens its doors at 4 p.m., providing opportunities for recreation and play in a safe, supervised setting. An outdoor playground area is available, as well as an indoor gymnasium with basketball hoops. At 5 p.m., children receive a hot meal, which is preceded by a blessing. Beginning at 5:30 p.m., attendees are divided into age-based groups with their volunteer team leader, who begins each session with a brief discussion where children have the opportunity to share things about their day and discuss problems or challenges they are facing. The team leader is asked to lead each group in a brief prayer. At about 6 p.m., the team leader, in conjunction with other volunteers, provides tutoring and homework help. Group time concludes at 7 p.m., and children are dismissed at 7:30 p.m.. As children leave, they are provided with a small snack bag to take home.

Summer Program

Havenwood Center is excited to introduce its first summer program in 2019. Six churches in the Midtown neighborhood, which historically have offered their own summer programming (Bible schools, summer camps, etc.), have agreed to partner with the organization to offer a summer day camp program from 10 a.m.-2 p.m., Monday through Friday, during the months of June, July, and August. Each week, the camp will feature different themes, providing students with opportunities to engage in a mix of indoor and outdoor activities. Havenwood Center will partner with businesspeople and professionals throughout the community to host unique experiences for students, allowing them to learn new skills and have fun at the same time. Examples include:

- Building with Legos
- Cooking & Baking
- Making Movies
- Cheerleading & Dance
- Backyard Sports

Special Events

Throughout the year, Havenwood Center will host a series of special events for children and their families, including:

- Easter Egg Hunt
- Summer Picnic
- Back-to-School Kickoff
- Trunk-or-Treat
- Happy Thanksgiving Dinner
- Breakfast with Santa

Havenwood Center will rely on the generosity of area businesses, individual donors, and partner churches to support its special events through the donation of food, prizes, games, and volunteer help.

Transportation

Havenwood Center will focus on serving children in the city's Midtown neighborhood. Many of the children accessing the program live near, and can walk safely to and from, the facility. To help children for whom walking to and from the center would be difficult or unsafe, the organization provides transportation using 16-passenger van that was donated by a local car dealer. Additionally, the Baptist Church also provides a volunteer driver and a small bus to assist with transportation.

OPERATIONS

Facility & Location

Havenwood Center has agreed to purchase a 22,122-square-foot building, which once housed an elementary school, from the Norwich School District. The building includes a gymnasium, kitchen, cafeteria, fenced playground area, 19 classrooms, and several offices. Located in the heart of the impoverished Midtown neighborhood, the building was constructed in 1965 and has been well-maintained. The property also includes a smaller building with offices and six classrooms, which Havenwood Center will lease to a commercial or nonprofit organization.

Havenwood Center has secured a 20-year mortgage (3.92% interest) on the property from a small commercial mortgage broker that works with nonprofits. Following a 20-percent down payment ($57,000) on the property, which cost $285,000, Havenwood Center will make monthly payments of $1,372. Insurance will cost approximately $150 per month. As a nonprofit, Havenwood Center will be exempt from paying property taxes.

Hours of Operation

Havenwood Center maintains regular office hours from 9 a.m. to 3 p.m., Monday through Friday. Programming is provided from 4 p.m. to 7:30 p.m., Monday through Thursday. Dates and times for special events are variable.

Equipment & Supplies

Havenwood Center has obtained the following items for operations, some of which have been donated by individuals or community partners:

Office Equipment

- 2 Phones with Voicemail
- 2 Computers
- Productivity Software (for Word Processing and Database Management)
- Multifunction Device (Print/Fax/Copy)
- 3 Desks
- 2 Filing Cabinets

Office Supplies

- Plain Paper
- Forms
- Stationary
- Pens
- Pencils
- Markers

PERSONNEL

Staff

Havenwood Center was established by Linda Johnson. A lifelong resident of Norwich, Johnson has worked as a social worker in both private and school settings for 25 years. Over the years, she has watched her community decline. Once a proud manufacturing town, many of the factory jobs that provided a good living for residents have disappeared. Coupled with declining investments, Norwich's population has decreased significantly as residents left for better opportunities elsewhere. Those who remained faced unemployment and fewer economic opportunities. After establishing the organization as a simple after-school program, Johnson has overseen its growth into a much larger entity that has made a meaningful impact on many children and families throughout the area. Johnson serves as the executive director of the Havenwood Center. She oversees a small staff that includes a volunteer and operations coordinator and an administrative assistant.

Board of Directors

Havenwood Center's board of directors is responsible for establishing policies and making all major decisions for the organization in conjunction with Executive Director Linda Johnson. The board's members, several of whom were part of a steering committee responsible for its establishment, have been carefully chosen. Each member possesses specific knowledge, skills, and expertise that will be of great benefit to Havenwood Center. In 2019 the organization's board members included:

Annie Davis—a member of the Norwich Board of Education and a local business owner.

Terry Hanley—owner of Norwich Tax Service.

Crystal Potts—executive director of the Norwich Food Bank.

Esther Field—owner of Fields Grocery.

Mandy Denny—Public Relations director for the Norwich Park District.

Lamar Gentry—a local attorney.

Rev. Clifton Parks—pastor of Norwich Baptist Church.

MARKETING & SALES

Havenwood Center has developed a marketing plan that includes the following tactics:

1. **Public Meetings:** Havenwood Center will host two public meetings annually to garner public support, attract volunteers, and generate media coverage for its programs.

2. **Media Relations:** The organization will issue press releases on a regular basis to announce special events, promote the impact of its programming, and appeal to prospective donors.

3. **Newsletter:** An e-newsletter (e-mail and mobile-friendly format) will be developed to keep potential supporters, volunteers, partners, and community members informed of programmatic developments, success stories, progress, special events, and fundraising opportunities.

4. **Volunteer Drives:** Havenwood Center will host quarterly volunteer drives throughout Norwich.

5. **Public Service Announcements:** The organization will solicit public service announcements from local radio and television outlets to stay visible with community members and potential fundraising sources.

6. **Web Site:** A Web site will be developed for Havenwood Center that offers key information regarding its location, nonprofit status, programming, hours of operations, donation needs, volunteer opportunities, as well as a calendar of events, press releases, social media links, and contact information.

7. **Social Media:** The organization will maintain a presence on Facebook.

8. **Fundraising Event:** Each year, a fashion show luncheon will be held at a local conference center, with local government officials and members of the news media volunteering as models.

GROWTH STRATEGY

The following growth strategy has been developed for Havenwood Center' first three years of operations in its new facility:

1. **2019:** Establish permanent operations in the former Westview School. Secure tenants for available office space within the school, with a focus on attracting other nonprofit agencies. Work with a local

real estate agent to secure one or more tenants for the additional office/classroom building on the Westview School property. In conjunction with board members and the school district, develop a basic operations plan for the building and campus, including recommended maintenance tasks (HVAC, groundskeeping, etc.). Establish a committee to develop summer programming, including volunteer training, communications/promotion, and donations. Serve approximately 125 children. Generate revenue of $161,575.

2. **2020:** Using the services of a freelance grant writer, focus on pursuing additional grant funding, supporting an increase in revenues to $184,242. Establish a leadership program for high school students, providing participants with opportunities to serve younger children during both the after-school and summer camp programs. Explore the possibility of offering an on-site GED program. Serve approximately 175 children.

3. **2021:** Expand the high school leadership program to include opportunities for career exploration, including job shadowing assistance and help with college admission and scholarship applications. Launch a major public relations campaign focused on telling success stories from the first two years of operations in the former Westview School building. Generate revenue of $206,954 and serve approximately 225 children.

LEGAL

With the assistance of local attorney and Havenwood Center board member Lamar Gentry, Havenwood Center has been organized as a nonprofit corporation in the state of Missouri and is a tax-exempt 501(C)(3) organization. A Federal Employer Identification Number (FEIN) has been obtained. The corporation's bylaws have been reviewed by its legal counsel to ensure they adhere to state law. Liability insurance, property insurance, and vehicle insurance coverage has been obtained. Related policies are available for review upon request. Additionally, Lamar Johnson has assisted Havenwood Center with the development of safety and security policies for its facility. All volunteers must subject to criminal background checks. Additionally, children are not allowed to be alone with any adult volunteer; another adult volunteer must always be present away from group settings. These policies are available for review upon request.

FINANCIAL ANALYSIS

Havenwood Center has raised $74,986 over the past three years that can be used for operations. The following table provides a summary of Havenwood Center's projected income and expenses for 2019–2021. A more detailed breakdown is available upon request.

Projected Annual Income & Expenses, 2019–2021

	2019	2020	2021
Revenue			
Contributions, grants, gifts	$125,000	$145,000	$165,000
Special events	$ 18,325	$ 19,242	$ 20,204
Rental income	$ 18,250	$ 20,000	$ 21,750
Total revenue	**$161,575**	**$184,242**	**$206,954**
Expenses			
Program services	$ 75,000	$ 90,000	$108,000
Administration	$ 80,000	$ 82,400	$ 84,872
Fundraising	$ 2,500	$ 3,000	$ 3,500
Other expenses	$ 0	$ 0	$ 0
Total expenses	**$157,500**	**$175,400**	**$196,372**
Operating profit	**$ 4,075**	**$ 8,842**	**$ 10,582**

Business Plan Template

USING THIS TEMPLATE

A business plan carefully spells out a company's projected course of action over a period of time, usually the first two to three years after the start-up. In addition, banks, lenders, and other investors examine the information and financial documentation before deciding whether or not to finance a new business venture. Therefore, a business plan is an essential tool in obtaining financing and should describe the business itself in detail as well as all important factors influencing the company, including the market, industry, competition, operations and management policies, problem solving strategies, financial resources and needs, and other vital information. The plan enables the business owner to anticipate costs, plan for difficulties, and take advantage of opportunities, as well as design and implement strategies that keep the company running as smoothly as possible.

This template has been provided as a model to help you construct your own business plan. Please keep in mind that there is no single acceptable format for a business plan, and that this template is in no way comprehensive, but serves as an example.

The business plans provided in this section are fictional and have been used by small business agencies as models for clients to use in compiling their own business plans.

GENERIC BUSINESS PLAN

Main headings included below are topics that should be covered in a comprehensive business plan. They include:

Business Summary

Purpose
Provides a brief overview of your business, succinctly highlighting the main ideas of your plan.

Includes
- Topic Headings and Subheadings
- Page Number References

Table of Contents

Purpose
Organized in an Outline Format, the Table of Contents illustrates the selection and arrangement of information contained in your plan.

Includes
- Name and Type of Business
- Description of Product/Service
- Business History and Development
- Location

- Market
- Competition
- Management

- Financial Information
- Business Strengths and Weaknesses
- Business Growth

Business History and Industry Outlook

Purpose

Examines the conception and subsequent development of your business within an industry specific context.

Includes

- Start-up Information
- Owner/Key Personnel Experience
- Location
- Development Problems and Solutions
- Investment/Funding Information

- Future Plans and Goals
- Market Trends and Statistics
- Major Competitors
- Product/Service Advantages
- National, Regional, and Local Economic Impact

Product/Service

Purpose

Introduces, defines, and details the product and/or service that inspired the information of your business.

Includes

- Unique Features
- Niche Served
- Market Comparison
- Stage of Product/Service Development

- Production
- Facilities, Equipment, and Labor
- Financial Requirements
- Product/Service Life Cycle
- Future Growth

Market Examination

Purpose

Assessment of product/service applications in relation to consumer buying cycles.

Includes

- Target Market
- Consumer Buying Habits
- Product/Service Applications
- Consumer Reactions
- Market Factors and Trends

- Penetration of the Market
- Market Share
- Research and Studies
- Cost
- Sales Volume and Goals

Competition

Purpose

Analysis of Competitors in the Marketplace.

Includes

- Competitor Information
- Product/Service Comparison
- Market Niche

- Product/Service Strengths and Weaknesses
- Future Product/Service Development

Marketing

Purpose

Identifies promotion and sales strategies for your product/service.

Includes

- Product/Service Sales Appeal
- Special and Unique Features
- Identification of Customers
- Sales and Marketing Staff
- Sales Cycles

- Type of Advertising/ Promotion
- Pricing
- Competition
- Customer Services

Operations

Purpose

Traces product/service development from production/inception to the market environment.

Includes

- Cost Effective Production Methods
- Facility
- Location

- Equipment
- Labor
- Future Expansion

Administration and Management

Purpose

Offers a statement of your management philosophy with an in-depth focus on processes and procedures.

Includes

- Management Philosophy
- Structure of Organization
- Reporting System
- Methods of Communication
- Employee Skills and Training

- Employee Needs and Compensation
- Work Environment
- Management Policies and Procedures
- Roles and Responsibilities

Key Personnel

Purpose

Describes the unique backgrounds of principle employees involved in business.

Includes

- Owner(s)/Employee Education and Experience
- Positions and Roles

- Benefits and Salary
- Duties and Responsibilities
- Objectives and Goals

Potential Problems and Solutions

Purpose

Discussion of problem solving strategies that change issues into opportunities.

Includes

- Risks
- Litigation
- Future Competition

- Economic Impact
- Problem Solving Skills

Financial Information

Purpose

Secures needed funding and assistance through worksheets and projections detailing financial plans, methods of repayment, and future growth opportunities.

Includes

- Financial Statements
- Bank Loans
- Methods of Repayment
- Tax Returns

- Start-up Costs
- Projected Income (3 years)
- Projected Cash Flow (3 Years)
- Projected Balance Statements (3 years)

Appendices

Purpose

Supporting documents used to enhance your business proposal.

Includes

- Photographs of product, equipment, facilities, etc.
- Copyright/Trademark Documents
- Legal Agreements
- Marketing Materials
- Research and or Studies

- Operation Schedules
- Organizational Charts
- Job Descriptions
- Resumes
- Additional Financial Documentation

Fictional Food Distributor

Commercial Foods, Inc.

3003 Avondale Ave.
Knoxville, TN 37920

This plan demonstrates how a partnership can have a positive impact on a new business. It demonstrates how two individuals can carve a niche in the specialty foods market by offering gourmet foods to upscale restaurants and fine hotels. This plan is fictional and has not been used to gain funding from a bank or other lending institution.

STATEMENT OF PURPOSE

Commercial Foods, Inc. seeks a loan of $75,000 to establish a new business. This sum, together with $5,000 equity investment by the principals, will be used as follows:

- Merchandise inventory $25,000

- Office fixture/equipment $12,000

- Warehouse equipment $14,000

- One delivery truck $10,000

- Working capital $39,000

- Total $100,000

DESCRIPTION OF THE BUSINESS

Commercial Foods, Inc. will be a distributor of specialty food service products to hotels and upscale restaurants in the geographical area of a 50 mile radius of Knoxville. Richard Roberts will direct the sales effort and John Williams will manage the warehouse operation and the office. One delivery truck will be used initially with a second truck added in the third year. We expect to begin operation of the business within 30 days after securing the requested financing.

MANAGEMENT

A. Richard Roberts is a native of Memphis, Tennessee. He is a graduate of Memphis State University with a Bachelor's degree from the School of Business. After graduation, he worked for a major manufacturer of specialty food service products as a detail sales person for five years, and, for the past three years, he has served as a product sales manager for this firm.

167

B. John Williams is a native of Nashville, Tennessee. He holds a B.S. Degree in Food Technology from the University of Tennessee. His career includes five years as a product development chemist in gourmet food products and five years as operations manager for a food service distributor.

Both men are healthy and energetic. Their backgrounds complement each other, which will ensure the success of Commercial Foods, Inc. They will set policies together and personnel decisions will be made jointly. Initial salaries for the owners will be $1,000 per month for the first few years. The spouses of both principals are successful in the business world and earn enough to support the families.

They have engaged the services of Foster Jones, CPA, and William Hale, Attorney, to assist them in an advisory capacity.

PERSONNEL

The firm will employ one delivery truck driver at a wage of $8.00 per hour. One office worker will be employed at $7.50 per hour. One part-time employee will be used in the office at $5.00 per hour. The driver will load and unload his own trucks. Mr. Williams will assist in the warehouse operation as needed to assist one stock person at $7.00 per hour. An additional delivery truck and driver will be added the third year.

LOCATION

The firm will lease a 20,000 square foot building at 3003 Avondale Ave., in Knoxville, which contains warehouse and office areas equipped with two-door truck docks. The annual rental is $9,000. The building was previously used as a food service warehouse and very little modification to the building will be required.

PRODUCTS AND SERVICES

The firm will offer specialty food service products such as soup bases, dessert mixes, sauce bases, pastry mixes, spices, and flavors, normally used by upscale restaurants and nice hotels. We are going after a niche in the market with high quality gourmet products. There is much less competition in this market than in standard run of the mill food service products. Through their work experiences, the principals have contacts with supply sources and with local chefs.

THE MARKET

We know from our market survey that there are over 200 hotels and upscale restaurants in the area we plan to serve. Customers will be attracted by a direct sales approach. We will offer samples of our products and product application data on use of our products in the finished prepared foods. We will cultivate the chefs in these establishments. The technical background of John Williams will be especially useful here.

COMPETITION

We find that we will be only distributor in the area offering a full line of gourmet food service products. Other foodservice distributors offer only a few such items in conjunction with their standard product line. Our survey shows that many of the chefs are ordering products from Atlanta and Memphis because of a lack of adequate local supply.

SUMMARY

Commercial Foods, Inc. will be established as a foodservice distributor of specialty food in Knoxville. The principals, with excellent experience in the industry, are seeking a $75,000 loan to establish the business. The principals are investing $25,000 as equity capital.

The business will be set up as an S Corporation with each principal owning 50% of the common stock in the corporation.

Fictional Hardware Store

Oshkosh Hardware, Inc.

123 Main St.
Oshkosh, WI 54901

The following plan outlines how a small hardware store can survive competition from large discount chains by offering products and providing expert advice in the use of any product it sells. This plan is fictional and has not been used to gain funding from a bank or other lending institution.

EXECUTIVE SUMMARY

Oshkosh Hardware, Inc. is a new corporation that is going to establish a retail hardware store in a strip mall in Oshkosh, Wisconsin. The store will sell hardware of all kinds, quality tools, paint, and housewares. The business will make revenue and a profit by servicing its customers not only with needed hardware but also with expert advice in the use of any product it sells.

Oshkosh Hardware, Inc. will be operated by its sole shareholder, James Smith. The company will have a total of four employees. It will sell its products in the local market. Customers will buy our products because we will provide free advice on the use of all of our products and will also furnish a full refund warranty.

Oshkosh Hardware, Inc. will sell its products in the Oshkosh store staffed by three sales representatives. No additional employees will be needed to achieve its short and long range goals. The primary short range goal is to open the store by October 1, 1994. In order to achieve this goal a lease must be signed by July 1, 1994 and the complete inventory ordered by August 1, 1994.

Mr. James Smith will invest $30,000 in the business. In addition, the company will have to borrow $150,000 during the first year to cover the investment in inventory, accounts receivable, and furniture and equipment. The company will be profitable after six months of operation and should be able to start repayment of the loan in the second year.

THE BUSINESS

The business will sell hardware of all kinds, quality tools, paint, and housewares. We will purchase our products from three large wholesale buying groups.

In general our customers are homeowners who do their own repair and maintenance, hobbyists, and housewives. Our business is unique in that we will have a complete line of all hardware items and will be able to get special orders by overnight delivery. The business makes revenue and profits by servicing our customers not only with needed hardware but also with expert advice in the use of any product we sell. Our major costs for bringing our products to market are cost of merchandise of 36%, salaries of $45,000, and occupancy costs of $60,000.

Oshkosh Hardware, Inc.'s retail outlet will be located at 1524 Frontage Road, which is in a newly developed retail center of Oshkosh. Our location helps facilitate accessibility from all parts of town and reduces our delivery costs. The store will occupy 7500 square feet of space. The major equipment involved in our business is counters and shelving, a computer, a paint mixing machine, and a truck.

THE MARKET

Oshkosh Hardware, Inc. will operate in the local market. There are 15,000 potential customers in this market area. We have three competitors who control approximately 98% of the market at present. We feel we can capture 25% of the market within the next four years. Our major reason for believing this is that our staff is technically competent to advise our customers in the correct use of all products we sell.

After a careful market analysis, we have determined that approximately 60% of our customers are men and 40% are women. The percentage of customers that fall into the following age categories are:

Under 16: 0%
17-21: 5%
22-30: 30%
31-40: 30%
41-50: 20%
51-60: 10%
61-70: 5%
Over 70: 0%

The reasons our customers prefer our products is our complete knowledge of their use and our full refund warranty.

We get our information about what products our customers want by talking to existing customers. There seems to be an increasing demand for our product. The demand for our product is increasing in size based on the change in population characteristics.

SALES

At Oshkosh Hardware, Inc. we will employ three sales people and will not need any additional personnel to achieve our sales goals. These salespeople will need several years experience in home repair and power tool usage. We expect to attract 30% of our customers from newspaper ads, 5% of our customers from local directories, 5% of our customers from the yellow pages, 10% of our customers from family and friends, and 50% of our customers from current customers. The most cost effect source will be current customers. In general our industry is growing.

MANAGEMENT

We would evaluate the quality of our management staff as being excellent. Our manager is experienced and very motivated to achieve the various sales and quality assurance objectives we have set. We will use a management information system that produces key inventory, quality assurance, and sales data on a weekly basis. All data is compared to previously established goals for that week, and deviations are the primary focus of the management staff.

GOALS IMPLEMENTATION

The short term goals of our business are:

1. Open the store by October 1, 1994
2. Reach our breakeven point in two months
3. Have sales of $100,000 in the first six months

In order to achieve our first short term goal we must:

1. Sign the lease by July 1, 1994
2. Order a complete inventory by August 1, 1994

In order to achieve our second short term goal we must:

1. Advertise extensively in Sept. and Oct.
2. Keep expenses to a minimum

In order to achieve our third short term goal we must:

1. Promote power tool sales for the Christmas season
2. Keep good customer traffic in Jan. and Feb.

The long term goals for our business are:

1. Obtain sales volume of $600,000 in three years
2. Become the largest hardware dealer in the city
3. Open a second store in Fond du Lac

The most important thing we must do in order to achieve the long term goals for our business is to develop a highly profitable business with excellent cash flow.

FINANCE

Oshkosh Hardware, Inc. Faces some potential threats or risks to our business. They are discount house competition. We believe we can avoid or compensate for this by providing quality products complimented by quality advice on the use of every product we sell. The financial projections we have prepared are located at the end of this document.

JOB DESCRIPTION-GENERAL MANAGER

The General Manager of the business of the corporation will be the president of the corporation. He will be responsible for the complete operation of the retail hardware store which is owned by the corporation. A detailed description of his duties and responsibilities is as follows.

Sales

Train and supervise the three sales people. Develop programs to motivate and compensate these employees. Coordinate advertising and sales promotion effects to achieve sales totals as outlined in budget. Oversee purchasing function and inventory control procedures to insure adequate merchandise at all times at a reasonable cost.

Finance

Prepare monthly and annual budgets. Secure adequate line of credit from local banks. Supervise office personnel to insure timely preparation of records, statements, all government reports, control of receivables and payables, and monthly financial statements.

Administration

Perform duties as required in the areas of personnel, building leasing and maintenance, licenses and permits, and public relations.

Organizations, Agencies, & Consultants

A listing of Associations and Consultants of interest to entrepreneurs, followed by the Small Business Administration Regional Offices, Small Business Development Centers, Service Corps of Retired Executives offices, and Venture Capital and Finance Companies.

Associations

This section contains a listing of associations and other agencies of interest to the small business owner. Entries are listed alphabetically by organization name.

American Business Women's Association
9820 Metcalf Ave., Ste. 110
Overland Park, MO 66212
(800)228-0007
Fax: (913)660-0101
E-mail: webmail@abwa.org
Website: http://www.abwa.org
Rene Street, Exec. Dir.

American Franchisee Association
53 W Jackson Blvd., Ste. 1256
Chicago, IL 60604
(312)431-0545
Fax: (312)431-1469
E-mail: spkezios@franchisee.org
Website: http://www.franchisee.org
Susan P. Kezios, Pres.

American Independent Business Alliance
222 S Black Ave.
Bozeman, MT 59715
(406)582-1255
Website: http://www.amiba.net
Jennifer Rockne, Co-Dir.
Jeff Milchen, Co-Dir.

American Small Business Coalition
PO Box 2786
Columbia, MD 21045
(410)381-7378
Website: https://www.theasbc.org
Margaret H. Timberlake, Pres.

American Small Business League
3910 Cypress Dr., Ste. B
Petaluma, CA 94954
(707)789-9575
Fax: (707)789-9580
E-mail: jspatola@asbl.com
Website: http://www.asbl.com
Lloyd Chapman, Founder

American Small Business Travelers Alliance
3112 Bent Oak Cir.
Flower Mound, TX 75022
(972)836-8064
E-mail: info@asbta.com
Website: http://www.asbta.com/
Chuck Sharp, Pres./CEO

America's Small Business Development Center
8990 Burke Lake Rd., 2nd Fl.
Burke, VA 22015
(703)764-9850
Fax: (703)764-1234
E-mail: info@americassbdc.org
Website: http://americassbdc.org
Charles Rowe, Pres./CEO

Association for Enterprise Opportunity
1310 L St NW, Ste. 830
Washington, DC 22209
(202)650-5580
E-mail: cevans@aeoworks.org
Website: http://www.aeoworks.org
Connie Evans, Pres./CEO

Association of Printing and Data Solutions Professionals
PO Box 2249
Oak Park, IL 60303
(708)218-7755
E-mail: ed.avis@irga.com
Website: http://www.apdsp.org
Ed Avis, Mng. Dir.

Association of Publishers for Special Sales
PO Box 9725
Colorado Springs, CO 80932-0725
(719)924-5534
Fax: (719)213-2602
E-mail: BrianJud@bookapss.org
Website: http://community.bookapss.org
Brian Jud, Exec. Dir.

BEST Association
17701 Mitchell N
Irvine, CA 92614-6028
866-706-2225
Website: http://www.beassoc.org

Business Planning Institute, LLC
580 Village Blvd., Ste. 150
West Palm Beach, FL 33409
(561)236-5533
Fax: (561)689-5546
E-mail: info@bpiplans.com
Website: http://www.bpiplans.com

Coalition for Government Procurement
1990 M St. NW, Ste. 450
Washington, DC 20036
(202)331-0975
Fax: (202)521-3533
E-mail: rwaldron@thecgp.org
Website: http://thecgp.org
Roger Waldron, Pres.

Ewing Marion Kauffman Foundation
4801 Rockhill Rd.
Kansas City, MO 64110
(816)932-1000
Website: http://www.kauffman.org
Wendy Guillies, Pres./CEO

Family Business Coalition
PO Box 722
Washington, DC 20044
(202)393-8959

E-mail: info@familybusinesscoalition.org
Website: http://familybusinesscoalition
.org
Palmer Schoening, Chm.

Family Firm Institute, Inc.
200 Lincoln St., Ste. 201
Boston, MA 02111
(617)482-3045
Fax: (617)482-3049
E-mail: ffi@ffi.org
Website: http://www.ffi.org
Judy Green, Pres.

Film Independent
9911 W Pico Blvd., 11th Fl.
Los Angeles, CA 90035
(310)432-1200
Fax: (310)432-1203
E-mail: jwelsh@filmindependent.org
Website: http://www.filmindependent.org
Josh Welsh, Pres.

HR People and Strategy
1800 Duke St.
Alexandria, VA 223142
(703)535-6056
Fax: (703)535-6490
E-mail: info@hrps.org
Website: http://www.hrps.org
Lisa Connell, Exec. Dir.

**Independent Visually Impaired
Entrepreneurs**
2121 Scott Rd., No. 105
Burbank, CA 91504-1228
(818)238-9321
E-mail: abazyn@bazyncommunications
.com
Website: http://www.ivie-acb.org
Ardis Bazyn, Pres.

**International Council for Small
Business**
Funger Hall, Ste. 315
2201 G St. NW
Washington, DC 20052
(202)994-0704
Fax: (202)994-4930
E-mail: icsb@gwu.edu
Website: http://www.icsb.org
Dr. Ayman El Tarabishy, Exec. Dir.

LearnServe International
PO Box 6203
Washington, DC 20015
(202)370-1865
Fax: (202)355-0993
E-mail: info@learn-serve.org
Website: http://learn-serve.org
Scott Rechler, Dir./CEO

**National Association for the
Self-Employed**
PO Box 241
Annapolis Junction, MD 20701-0241
800-232-6273
800-649-6273 (Alaska and Hawaii only)
E-mail: media@nase.org
Website: http://www.nase.org
Keith R. Hall, CPA, Pres./CEO

**National Association of Business
Owners**
1509 Green Mountain Dr.
Little Rock, AR 72211
(501)227-8423
Website: http://nabo.org

**National Association of Small Business
Contractors**
700 12th St. NW, Ste. 700
Washington, DC 20005
Free: 888-861-9290
Website: http://www.nasbc.org
Cris Young, Pres.

National Business Association
15305 Dallas Pkwy., Ste. 300
Addison, TX 75001
800-456-0440
Fax: (972)960-9149
E-mail: database@nationalbusiness.org
Website: http://www.nationalbusiness
.org

**National Federation of Independent
Business**
1201 F St. NW
Washington, DC 20004
(615)872-5800
800-NFIBNOW
Fax: (615)872-5353
Website: http://www.nfib.org
Juanita Duggan, Pres./CEO

National Small Business Association
1156 15th St. NW, Ste. 502
Washington, DC 20005
800-345-6728
E-mail: info@nsba.biz
Website: http://www.nsba.biz
Todd McCracken, Pres.

**Professional Association of Small
Business Accountants**
6405 Metcalf Ave., Ste. 503
Shawnee Mission, KS 66202
866-296-0001
E-mail: director@pasba.org
Website: http://community.pasba.org/
home
Jordan Bennett, Exec. Dir.

Rainbow PUSH Wall Street Project
1441 Broadway, Ste. 5051
New York, NY 10018
(646)569-5889
(212)425-7874
E-mail: info@rainbowpush.org
Website: http://www.rainbow
push.org
Chee Chee Williams, Exec. Dir.

Root Cause
11 Avenue de Lafayette
Boston, MA 02111
(617)492-2300
E-mail: info@rootcause.org
Website: http://www.rootcause.org
Andrew Wolk, Founder/CEO

Sales Professionals USA
1400 W 122nd Ave., No. 101
Westminster, CO 80234
(303)578-2020
E-mail: support@dmdude.com
Website: http://www.salesprofessionals-
usa.com
Peter Brissette, Pres.

Score Association
1175 Herndon Pkwy., Ste. 900
Herndon, VA 20170
(202)205-6762
800-634-0245
E-mail: help@score.org
Website: http://www.score.org
W. Kenneth Yancey, Jr., CEO

Seedco
22 Cortlandt St., 33rd Fl.
New York, NY 10007
(212)473-0255
E-mail: info@seedco.org
Website: http://www.seedco.org
Barbara Dwyer Gunn, Pres./CEO

**Small Business and Entrepreneurship
Council**
301 Maple Ave. W, Ste. 690
Vienna, VA 22180
(703)242-5840
Website: http://www.sbecouncil.org
Karen Kerrigan, Pres./CEO

**Small Business Council
of America**
Brandywine East
1523 Concord Pike, Ste. 300
Wilmington, DE 19803
(302)691-SBCA
E-mail: lredstone@shanlaw.com
Website: http://sbca.net
Leanne Redstone, Exec. Dir.

Small Business Exporters Association of the United States
1156 15th St. NW, Ste. 502
Washington, DC 20005
(202)552-2903
800-345-6728
E-mail: info@sbea.org
Website: http://www.sbea.org
Jody Milanese, VP, Government Affairs

Small Business Investor Alliance
1100 H St. NW, Ste. 1200
Washington, DC 20005
(202)628-5055
E-mail: info@sbia.org
Website: http://www.sbia.org
Brett Palmer, Pres.

Small Business Legislative Council
4800 Hampden Ln., 6th Fl.
Bethesda, MD 20814
(301)652-8302
Website: http://www.sblc.org
Paula Calimafde, Pres.

Small Business Service Bureau, Inc.
554 Main St.
PO Box 15014
Worcester, MA 01615-0014
800-343-0939
E-mail: info@sbsb.com
Website: http://www.sbsb.com
Lisa M. Carroll, MS, MPH, RN, Pres.

Support Services Alliance
165 Main St.
Oneida, NY 13421
(315)363-65842
Website: http://www.oneidachamberny.org/supportservices.html
Michele Hummel, Contact

United States Association for Small Business and Entrepreneurship
University of Wisconsin
Whitewater College of Business and Economics
Hyland Hall
809 W Starin Rd.
Whitewater, WI 53190
(262)472-1449
E-mail: psnyder@usasbe.org
Website: http://www.usasbe.org
Patrick Snyder, Exec. Dir.

Consultants

This section contains a listing of consultants specializing in small business development. It is arranged alphabetically by country, then by state or province, then by city, then by firm name.

Canada

Alberta

Dark Horse Strategies
20 Coachway Rd. SW, Ste. 262
Calgary, AB, Canada T3H 1E6
(403)605-3881
E-mail: info@darkhorsestrategies.com
Website: http://www.darkhorsestrategies.com

Kenway Mack Slusarchuk Stewart L.L.P.
333 11th Ave. SW, Ste. 1500
Calgary, AB, Canada T2R 1L9
(403)233-7750
Fax: (403)266-5267
E-mail: info@kmss.ca
Website: http://www.kmss.ca

Kenway Mack Slusarchuk Stewart L.L.P.
714 10 St., Ste. 3
Canmore , AB, Canada T1W 2A6
(403)675-1010
Fax: (403)675-6789
Website: http://kmss.ca/about-us/canmore-office/

Tenato Strategy Inc.
1229A 9th Ave. SE
Calgary, AB, Canada T2G 0S9
(403)242-1127
E-mail: info@tenato.com
Website: http://www.tenato.com

Nichols Applied Management Inc.
10104 103rd Ave. NW, Ste. 2401
Edmonton, AB, Canada T5J 0H8
(780)424-0091
Fax: (780)428-7644
E-mail: info@nicholsapplied
management.com
Website: http://nicholsconsulting.com/WP

Abonar Business Consultants Ltd.
240-222 Baseline Rd., Ste. 212
Sherwood Park, AB, Canada T8H 1S8
(780)862-0282
Fax: (866)405-4510
E-mail: info@abonarconsultants.com
Website: http://www.abonarconsultants.com/index.html

AJL Consulting
52312 Range Rd. 225, Ste. 145
Sherwood Park, AB, Canada T8C 1E1
(780)467-6040
Fax: (780)449-2993
Website: http://www.ajlconsulting.ca

Taylor Warwick Consulting Ltd.
121 Courtenay Terr.
Sherwood Park, AB, Canada T8A 5S6
(780)669-1605
E-mail: info@taylorwarwick.ca
Website: http://www.taylor
warwick.ca

British Columbia

Stevenson Community Consultants
138 Pritchard Rd.
Comox, BC, Canada V9M 2T2
(250)890-0297
Fax: (250)890-0296
E-mail: dagit@island.net

Andrew R. De Boda Consulting
1523 Milford Ave.
Coquitlam, BC, Canada V3J 2V9
(604)936-4527
Fax: (604)936-4527
E-mail: deboda@intergate.bc.ca

Reality Marketing Associates
3049 Sienna Ct.
Coquitlam, BC, Canada V3E 3N7
(604)944-8603
Fax: (604)944-4708
E-mail: info@realityassociates.com
Website: http://www.realityassociates.com

Landmark Sq. II, 1708 Dolphin Ave., Ste. 806
Kelowna, BC, Canada V1Y 9S4
(250)763-4716
Fax: (877)353-8608
Free: 877-763-4022
E-mail: steve@burnsinnovation.com
Website: http://www.burnsinnovation.com

Kuber Business Consultants Ltd.
3003 Saint John's St., Ste. 202
Port Moody, BC, Canada V3H 2C4
(604)568-3055
Fax: (604)608-2903
E-mail: info@kuberbiz.ca
Website: http://www.kuberbiz.ca

Seajay Consulting Ltd.
800-15355 24th Ave., Ste. 527
Surrey, BC, Canada V4A 2H9
(604)541-0148
E-mail: chris@seajayconsulting.ca
Website: http://www.seajayconsulting.ca

Einblau and Associates Ltd.
999 W Broadway, Ste. 720
Vancouver, BC, Canada V5Z 1K5
(604)684-7164
Fax: (604)873-8256
E-mail: office@einblau.com
Website: http://www.einblau.com

Pinpoint Tactics Business Consulting
5525 West Blvd., Ste. 330
Vancouver, BC, Canada V6M 3W6
(604)263-4698
Fax: (604)909-4916
E-mail: info@pinpointtactics.com
Website: http://www.pinpointtactics.com

Synergy Complete Management Consulting
1489 Marine Dr., Ste. 317
West Vancouver, BC, Canada V7T 1B8
(604)260-5477
Free: 866-866-8755
E-mail: info@synergy-cmc.com
Website: http://www.synergy-cmc.com

Nova Scotia

The Marketing Clinic
1384 Bedford Hwy.
Bedford, NS, Canada B4A 1E2
(902)835-4122
Fax: (902)832-9389
Free: 877-401-9398
E-mail: office@themarketingclinic.ca
Website: http://www.themarketing clinic.ca

Thyagrissen Consulting Ltd.
35 Talon Ct.
Bible Hill, NS, Canada B2N 7B4
(902)895-1414
Fax: (902)895-5188
E-mail: yvonne@thyagrissenconsulting.ca
Website: http://www.thyagrissen consulting.ca

Coburg Consultants Ltd.
6100 University Ave.
Halifax, NS, Canada B3H 3J5
E-mail: info@coburgconsultants.ca
Website: http://www.coburgconsultants.ca

MacDonnell Group Consulting Ltd.
1505 Barrington St., Ste. 1100
Halifax, NS, Canada B3J 3K5
(902)425-3980
Fax: (902)423-7593
Website: http://www.macdonnell.com

Ontario

The Cynton Co.
17 Massey St.

Brampton, ON, Canada L6S 2V6
(905)792-7769
Fax: (905)792-8116
E-mail: cynton@cynton.com
Website: http://www.cynton.com

Fresh Insights Consulting
901 Guelph Line
Burlington, ON, Canada L7R 3N8
(905)634-6500
E-mail: info@freshinsightsconsulting.ca
Website: http://freshinsightsconsulting.ca

Globe Consult Corp.
34 Willow Shore Way
Carleton Place, ON, Canada K7C 0B1
(613)257-8265
Fax: (613)253-2436
E-mail: infoid@globeconsult.ca
Website: http://www.globeconsult.ca

KLynn Inc.
4421 Hwy. 45
Cobourg, ON K9A 4J9
(905)373-4909
Free: 888-717-2220
E-mail: info@klynnbusinessconsulting
.com
Website: www.klynnbusinessconsulting
.com

Heaslip Associates
50 West St., Unit 2
Collingwood, ON, Canada L9Y 3T1
(613)537-8900
E-mail: info@heaslipassociates.com
Website: http://www.heaslipassociates
.com

JThomson & Co. CPA
645 Upper James St. S
Hamilton, ON, Canada L9C 2Y9
(905)388-7229
Fax: (905)388-3134
Website: http://www.jthomsonco.com

Queen's Business Consulting
Queen's University
Stephen J.R. Smith School of Business
Goodes Hall, Rm. LL201
Kingston, ON, Canada K7L 3N6
(613)533-2309
Fax: (613)533-2744
E-mail: qbc@business.queensu.ca
Website: http://smith.queensu.ca/centres/
business-consulting/index.php

Fronchak Corporate Development Inc.
23-500 Fairway Rd. S, Ste. 209
Kitchener, ON, Canada N2C 1X3
(519)896-9950

E-mail: mike@fronchak.com
Website: http://www.fronchak.com

Eigenmacht Crackower
345 Renfrew Dr., Ste. 202
Markham, ON, Canada L3R 9S9
(905)305-9722
(905)607-6468
Fax: (905)305-9502
E-mail: jack@eigenmachtcrackower.com
Website: http://www.eigenmachtcrack
ower.com

JPL Consulting
236 Millard Ave.
Newmarket, ON, Canada L3Y 1Z2
(416)606-9124
E-mail: jplbiz1984@gmail.com
Website: http://www.jplbiz.ca

Roger Hay & Associates Ltd.
1272 Elgin Cres.
Oakville, ON, Canada L6H 2J7
(416)848-0997
E-mail: info@rogerhay.ca
Website: http://www.rogerhay.ca

Comgate Engineering Ltd.
236 1st Ave.
Ottawa, ON, Canada K1S 2G6
(613)235-4778
Fax: (613)248-4644
E-mail: info_eng@comgate.com
Website: http://www.comgate.com

PMC Training
858 Bank St., Ste. 109
Ottawa, ON, Canada K1S 3W3
(613)234-2020
Fax: (613)569-1333
E-mail: info@pmctraining.com
Website: http://pmctraining.com/

Arbex Forest Resource Consultants Ltd.
1555 Scotch Line Rd. E
Oxford Mills, ON, Canada K0G 1S0
(613)798-3099
Website: http://www.arbex.ca

G.R. Eagleson Consulting Inc.
69436 Mollard Line
RR3
Parkhill, ON, Canada N0M 2K0
(519)238-2676
Fax: (519)238-1224
E-mail: eagleson@hay.net
Website: http://www.eagleson.com/
consulting

Mark H. Goldberg & Associates Inc.
91 Forest Lane Dr.
Thornhill, ON, Canada L4J 3P2

(905)882-0417
Fax: (905)882-2219
E-mail: info@mhgoldberg.com
Website: http://www.mhgoldberg.com

Petersen Consulting
136 Cedar St. S
Timmons, ON, Canada P4N 2G8
(705)264-5323
E-mail: pcmanage@nt.net
Website: http://www.petersenconsulting.ca

Care Concepts & Communications
21 Spruce Hill Rd.
Toronto, ON, Canada M4E 3G2
(416)420-8840
E-mail: info@cccbizconsultants.com
Website: http://www.cccbizconsultants
.com

FHG International Inc.
99 Crown's Ln., 1st Fl.
Toronto, ON, Canada M5R 3P4
(416)402-8000
E-mail: info@fhgi.com
Website: http://www.fhgi.com

KLynn Inc.
6 Bartlett Ave., Ste. 8
Toronto, ON M6H 3E6
Free: 888-717-2220
E-mail: info@klynnbusinessconsulting.com
Website: www.klynnbusinessconsulting
.com

PWR Health Consultants, Inc.
720 Spadina Ave., Ste. 303
Toronto, ON, Canada M5S 2T9
(416)467-1844
Fax: (416)467-5600
Fax: (416)323-3166
E-mail: ldoupe@pwr.ca
Website: http://www.pwr.ca

Ryerson Consulting Group
575 Bay St., Ste. 2-005
Toronto, ON, Canada M5G 2C5
(416)979-5059
E-mail: info@rcginsight.com
Website: http://www.rcginsight.com

David Trahair CPA, CA
15 Coldwater Rd., Ste. 101
Toronto, ON, Canada M3B 1Y8
(416)420-8840
Fax: (416)385-3813
Website: http://www.trahair.com

Quebec

PGP Consulting
17 Linton

Dollard-des-Ormeaux, QC, Canada
H9B 1P2
(514)796-7613
(514)862-5837
Fax: (866)750-0947
E-mail: pierre@pgpconsulting.com
Website: http://www.pgpconsulting.com

Conseil Saint-Paul
400 Blvd. Saint-Martin Ouest, Bureau 121
Laval, QC, Canada H7M 3Y8
(450)664-4442
Fax: (450)664-3631
E-mail: info@spaul.ca
Website: http://spaul.ca

KLynn Inc.
2025 Rue de la Visitation
Montreal, QC H2L 3C8
Free: 888-717-2220
E-mail: info@klynnbusinessconsulting
.com
Website: www.klynnbusinessconsulting
.com

Komand Consulting Inc.
1250 Rene Levesque Blvd. W, Ste. 2200
Montreal, QC, Canada H3B 4W8
(514)934-9281
E-mail: info@komand.ca
Website: http://www.komand.ca

Lemay-Yates Associates Inc.
2015 Peel St., Ste. 425
Montreal, QC, Canada H3A 1T8
(514)288-6555
E-mail: lya@lya.com
Website: http://www.lya.com

Groupe Dancause Inc.
3175 Chemin des Quatre-Bourgeois,
Ste. 375
Quebec, QC, Canada G1W 2K7
(418)681-0268
E-mail: groupe@dancause.net
Website: http://www.dancause.net

Saskatchewan

Abonar Business Consultants Ltd.
3110 8th St. E, Ste. 8B-376
Saskatoon, SK, Canada S7H 0W2
Fax: (866)405-4510
Free: 866-405-4510
E-mail: info@abonarconsultants.com
Website: http://www.abonarconsultants
.com/index.html

Banda Marketing Group
3-1124 8th St. E
Saskatoon, SK, Canada S7H 0S4

(306)343-6100
E-mail: brent.banda@bandagroup.com
Website: http://www.bandagroup.com

Hoggard International
435 McKercher Dr.
Saskatoon, SK, Canada S7H 4G3
(306)374-6747
Fax: (306)653-7252
E-mail: bhoggard@shaw.ca
Website: http://hoggardinternational.com

United States

Alabama

Accounting & Business Consultants Inc.
1711 9th Ave. N
Bessemer, AL 35020
E-mail: tclay@abcconsultants.com
Website:http://www.abcconsultants.com

Accounting & Business Consultants Inc.
4120 2nd Ave. S
Birmingham, AL 35222
(205)425-9000
E-mail: tclay@abcconsultants.com
Website: http://www.abcconsultants.com

MILBO, LLC
2214 3rd Ave. N, Ste. 204
Birmingham, AL 35203
(205)543-0645
Website: http://www.milbollc.com

Jackson Thorton Dothan Office
304 Jamestown Blvd.
Dothan, AL 36301
(334)793-7001
Fax: (334)793-7004
Website: http://www.jacksonthornton.com

Mason, Bearden & Diehl, Inc.
4100 Bob Wallace Ave.
Huntsville, AL 35805
(256)533-0806
Fax: (256)533-7742 fax
E-mail: mbd@mbdaccounting.com
Website: http://www.mbdaccounting.com

SEL & Associates
103 Cabot Circ., Ste. 201
Madison, AL 35758
(256)325-9809
Fax: (256)325-9809
E-mail: steven@stevenlevyassociates.com
Website: http://www.stevenlevyassociates
.com

Jackson Thorton Montgomery Office
200 Commerce St.

Montgomery, AL 36104
(334)834-7660
Fax: (334)956-5090
Website: http://www.jacksonthornton
.com

Jackson Thorton Auburn/Opelka Office
100 N 9th St.
Opelika, AL 36801
(334)749-8191
Fax: (334)749-9358
Website: http://www.jacksonthornton
.com

Jackson Thorton Prattville Office
310 S Washington St.
Prattville, AL 36067
(334)365-1445
Fax: (334)956-5066
Website: http://www.jacksonthornton.com

Jackson Thorton Wetumpka Office
194 Fort Toulouse
Wetumpka, AL 36092
(334)567-3400
Fax: (334)956-5005
Website: http://www.jacksonthornton
.com

Alaska

Agnew::Beck Consulting
441 W 5th Ave., Ste. 202
Anchorage, AK 99501
(907)222-5424
Fax: (907)222-5426
E-mail: admin@agnewbeck.com
Website: http://agnewbeck.com

McDowell Group
1400 W Benson Blvd., Ste. 510
Anchorage, AK 99503
(907)274-3200
Fax: (907)274-3201
E-mail: info@mcdowellgroup.net
Website: http://www.mcdowellgroup.net

The Foraker Group
161 Klevin St., Ste. 101
Anchorage AK 99508
(907)743-1200
Fax: (907)276-5014
Free: 877-834-5003
Website: http://www.forakergroup.org

Consulting Professionals of Alaska
17137 Park Place St.
Eagle River, AK, 99577
(907)694-0105
Fax: (907)694-0107
Website: http://www.cpalaska.com

McDowell Group
9360 Glacier Hwy., Ste. 201
Juneau, AK 99801
(907)586-6126
Fax: (907)586-2673
E-mail: info@mcdowellgroup.net
Website: http://www.mcdowellgroup.net

Sheinberg Associates
1107 W 8th St., Ste. 4
Juneau, AK 99801
(907)586-3141
Fax: (907)586-2331
Website: http://www.sheinbergassociates
.com

Arizona

Comgate Telemanagement Ltd.
428 E Thunderbird Rd., Ste. 133
Phoenix, AZ 85022
(602)485-5708
Fax: (602)485-5709
E-mail: info_telemgmt@comgate.com
Website: http://www.comgate.com

Kalil & Associates, LLC
245 S Plumer Ave., Ste. 16
Tucson, AZ 85719
(520)628-4264
Fax: (520)903-0347
E-mail: info@kalilassociates.com
Website: https://www.kalilassociates.com

California

Cayenne Consulting, LLC
155 N Riverview Dr.
Anaheim Hills, CA 92808
Website: https://www.caycon.com

Fessel International, Inc.
20 E Foothill Blvd., Ste. 128
Arcadia, CA 91006
(626)566-3500
Fax: (626)566-3875
Free: 877-432-8380
Website: http://www.fessel.com/
default.asp

Streamline Planning Consultants
1062 G St. Suite I
Arcata, CA 95521
(707)822-5785
Fax: (707)822-5786
Website: http://streamlineplanning.net

The One Page Business Plan Co.
1798 Fifth St.
Berkeley, CA 94710
(510)705-8400

Fax: (510)705-8403
E-mail: info@onepagebusinessplan.com
Website: http://www.onepagebusiness
plan.com

Business Consulting Group
30 Landing Cir. 300
Chico, CA 95973
(530)864-5980
E-mail: info@bcgca.com
Website: http://www.bcgca.com

Go Jade Solutions
9808 Valgrande Way
Elk Grove, CA 95757
(916)538-7561
E-mail: info@gojadesolutions.com
Website: http://gojadesolutions.com

La Piana Consulting
5858 Horton St., Ste. 272
Emeryville, CA 94608-2007
(510)601-9056
Fax: (510)420-0478
E-mail: info@lapiana.org
Website: http://lapiana.org

Norris Bernstein, CMC
9309 Marina Pacifica Dr. N
Long Beach, CA 90803
(562)493-5458
Fax: (562)493-5459
E-mail: norris@norrisbernstein.com
Website: http://www.norrisbernstein.com

Blue Garnet Associates L.L.C.
8055 W Manchester Ave., Ste. 430
Los Angeles, CA 90293
(310)439-1930
E-mail: hello@bluegarnet.net
Website: http://www.bluegarnet.net

Edeska LLC (dba Go Business Plans)
Bldg. D, Fl. 3
12777 W Jefferson Blvd., Ste. 3119
Los Angeles, CA 90066
Free: 855-546-0037
Website: http://edeska.com

Growthink Inc.
12655 W Jefferson Blvd.
Los Angeles, CA 90045
Free: 800-647-6983
E-mail: services@growthink.com
Website: http://www.growthink.com

Paul Yelder Consulting
3964 Hubert Ave.
Los Angeles, CA 90008-2620
(323)295-7652
E-mail: email: consulting@yelder.com
Website: http://www.yelder.com

BizplanSource
1048 Irvine Ave., Ste. 621
Newport Beach, CA 92660
Free: 888-253-0974
Fax: (800)859-8254
E-mail: info@bizplansource.com
Website: http://www.bizplansource.com

MakeGreenGo!
240 3rd St., Ste. 2A
Oakland, CA 94607
(510)250-9890
Website: http://makegreengo.com

Accessible Business, LLC
18325 Keswick St.
Reseda, CA 91335
(818)264-7830
Free: 800-490-8362
Fax: (818)264-7833
E-mail: info@accessiblebusiness.com
Website: https://www.accessiblebusiness.com

International Business Partners
8045 Darby Pl.
Reseda, CA 91335
(714)875-3604
E-mail: admin@IBPconsultants.com
Website: http://www.ibpconsultants.com/home.html

Jackson Law Firm, P.C.
979 Golf Course Dr., Ste. 300
Rohnert Park, CA 94928
(707)584-4529
(707)584-9033
E-mail: shawnjackson@businessdevelopmentattorney.com
Website: http://jacksonlawfirm.net/

Business Performance Consultants
9777 Caminito Joven
San Diego, CA 92131
(858)583-4159
E-mail: larrymiller@businessperformanceconsultants.com
Website: http://businessperformanceconsultants.com/

The Startup Garage
San Diego, CA 92109
(858)876-4597
E-mail: info@thestartupgarage.com
Website: https://thestartupgarage.com

Venture Builder, Inc.
1286 University Ave., Ste. 315
San Diego, CA 92103
(619)563-1841
Website: http://www.venturebuilderinc.com

Growthink Inc.
55 2nd St., Ste. 570
San Francisco, CA 94105
Free: 800-647-6983
E-mail: services@growthink.com
Website: http://www.growthink.com

San Francisco Management Group
1048 Union St., Ste. 7
San Francisco, CA 94133
(415)775-3405
E-mail: info@sfmanagementgroup.com
Website: http://www.sfmanagementgroup.com/

The Wright Consultants
835 Market St.
San Francisco, CA 94105
(415)928-2071
Website: http://www.thewrightconsultants.com

Business Group
369-B 3rd St., Ste. 387
San Rafael, CA 94901
(415)491-1896
Fax: (415)459-6472
E-mail: mvh@businessgroup.biz
Website: http://www.businessownerstoolbox.com

Manex Inc.
2010 Crow Canyon Pl., Ste. 320
San Ramon, CA 94583
(925)807-5100
Free: 877-336-2639
Website: http://www.manexconsulting.com

Bargain Business Plan, Inc.
12400 Ventura Blvd., Ste. 658
Studio City, CA 91604
Free: 800-866-9971
Fax: (800)866-9971
E-mail: info@bargainbusinessplan.com
Website: http://www.bargainbusinessplan.com

Out of Your Mind … and Into the Marketplace
13381 White Sands Dr.
Tustin, CA 92780-4565
(714)544-0248
Fax: (714)730-1414
Free: 800-419-1513
E-mail: lpinson@aol.com
Website: http://www.business-plan.com

Colorado

Comer & Associates, LLC
5255 Holmes Pl.
Boulder, CO 80303
(303)786-7986
E-mail: info@comerassociates.com
Website: http://www.comerassociates.com

McCord Consulting Group
2525 Arapahoe Ave., Ste. 515
Boulder, CO 80302
(720)443-0894
E-mail: nikki@mcconsultgroup.com
Website: http://mcconsultgroup.com/

The Startup Expert
661 Eldorado Blvd. Ste. 623
Broomfield, CO 80021
(303)534-1019
Website: http://thestartupexpert.com/

Ameriwest Business Consultants, Inc.
PO Box 26266
Colorado Springs, CO 80936
(719)380-7096
Fax: (719)380-7096
E-mail: email@abchelp.com
Website: http://www.abchelp.com

GVNW Consulting Inc.
2270 La Montana Way, Ste. 200
Colorado Springs, CO 80918
(719)594-5800
E-mail: jushio@gvnw.com
Website: http://www.gvnw.com

Wilson Hughes Consulting LLC
2100 Humboldt St., Ste. 302
Denver, CO 80205
(303)680-7889
E-mail: bhughescnm@gmail.com
Website: http://wilsonhughesconsulting.com/

Extelligent Inc.
8400 E Crescent Pky., Ste. 600
Greenwood Village, CO 80111
(720)201-5672
E-mail: clientrelations@extelligent.com
Website: http://www.extelligent.com

The Schallert Group, Inc.
321 Main St.
Longmont, CO 80501
(303)774-6522
Website: http://jonschallert.com/

Vaughn CPA
210 E 29th St.
Loveland, CO 80538
(970)667-2123
E-mail: vaughn@vaughncpa.com
Website: http://vaughncpa.com/loveland-cpa-firm

Connecticut

Alltis Corp.
PO Box 1292
Farmington, CT 06034-1292
(860)255-7610
Fax: (860)674-8168
E-mail: info@alltis.com
Website: http://www.alltis.com

Christiansen Consulting
56 Scarborough St.
Hartford, CT 06105
(860)586-8265
Fax: (860)233-3420
E-mail: Francine@Christiansen
Consulting.com
Website: http://www.christiansen
consulting.com/

Musevue360
555 Millbrook Rd.
Middletown, CT 06457
(860)463-7722
Fax: (860)346-3013
E-mail: jennifer.eifrig@musevue360.com
Website: http://www.musevue360.com

Kalba International Inc.
116 McKinley Ave.
New Haven, CT 06515
(203)397-2199
Fax: (781)240-2657
E-mail: kas.kalba@kalbainternational
.com
Website: http://www.kalbainternational
.com

Delaware

Doherty & Associates
Stoney Batter Office Bldg.
5301 Limestone Rd., Ste. 100
Wilmington, DE 19808
(302)239-3500
Fax: (302)239-3600
E-mail: info@dohertyandassociates.com
Website: http://www.dohertyand
associates.com

Gunnip & Co. LLP
Little Falls Centre 2
2751 Centerville Rd., Ste. 300
Wilmington, DE 19808-1627
(302)225-5000
Fax: (302)225-5100
E-mail: info@gunnip.com
Website: http://www.gunnip.com

Master, Sidlow & Associates, P.A.
2002 W 14th St.

Wilmington, DE 19806
(302)652-3480
Fax: (302)656-8778
E-mail: imail@mastersidlow.com
Website: http://www.mastersidlow.com

Florida

BackBone, Inc.
20404 Hacienda Ct.
Boca Raton, FL 33498
(561)470-0965
Fax: (561)908-4038
E-mail: che@backboneinc.com
Website: http://www.backboneinc.com

Dr. Eric H. Shaw & Associates
500 S Ocean Blvd., Ste. 2105
Boca Raton, FL 33432
(561)338-5151
E-mail: ericshaw@bellsouth.net
Website: http://www.ericshaw.com

Professional Planning Associates, Inc.
1440 NE 35th St.
Oakland Park, FL 33334
(954)829-2523
Fax:(954)537-7945
E-mail: mgoldstein@proplana.com
Website: http://proplana.com

Alfred Endeio LLC
8700 Maitland Summit Blvd., Ste. 214
Orlando, FL 32810
Website: http://www.alfredeconsulting.
com

Hughes Consulting Services LLC
522 Alternate 19
Palm Harbor, FL 34683
(727)631-2536
Fax: (727)474-9818
Website: http://consultinghughes.com

Strategic Business Planning Co.
PO Box 821006
South Florida, FL 33082
(954)704-9100
Fax: (888)704-3290
Free: 888-704-9100
E-mail: info@SBPlan.com
Website: http://www.ipplan.com

Cohen & Grieb, P.A.
500 N Westshore Blvd., Ste. 700
Tampa, FL 33609
(813)739-7200
Fax: (813)282-7225
E-mail: info@cohengrieb.com
Website: http://www.cohengrieb.com/
contact

Dufresne Consulting Group, Inc.
13014 N Dale Mabry, Ste. 175
Tampa, FL 33618-2808
(813)264-4775
E-mail: info@dcgconsult.com
Website: http://www.dcgconsult.com

Reliance Consulting, LLC
13940 N Dale Mabry Hwy.
Tampa, FL, 33618
(813)931-7258
Fax: (813)931-5555
Website: http://www.reliancecpa.com

Tunstall Consulting LLC
13153 N Dale Mabry Hwy., Ste. 200
Tampa, FL 33618
(813)968-4461
Fax: (813)961-2315
E-mail: info@tunstallconsulting.com
Website: http://www.tunstallconsulting.
com

The Business Planning Institute, LLC.
580 Village Blvd., Ste. 150
West Palm Beach, FL 33409
(561)236-5533
Fax: (561)689-5546
E-mail: info@bpiplans.com
Website: http://www.bpiplans.com

Georgia

CHScottEnterprises
227 Sandy Springs Pl. NE, Ste. 720702
Atlanta, GA 30358-9032
(770)356-4808
E-mail: info@chscottenterprises.com
Website: http://www.chscottenterprises.
com

Fountainhead Consulting Group, Inc.
3970 Old Milton Pkwy, Ste. 210
Atlanta, GA 30005
(770)642-4220
Website: http://www.fountainhead
consultinggroup.com

PSMJ Resources Inc.
2746 Rangewood Dr.
Atlanta, GA 30345
(770)723-9651
Fax: (815)461-7478
Free: 800-537-7765
Website: http://www.psmj.com

Scullyworks, LLC
PO Box 8641
Atlanta, GA 31106-0641
(404)310-9499
Website: http://www.scullyworks.com

Theisen Consulting LLC
865 Waddington Ct.
Atlanta, GA 30350
(770)396-7344
Fax: (404)393-3527
E-mail: terri@theisenconsulting.com
Website: http://www.theisenconsulting.com

Sterling Rose Consulting Corp.
722 Collins Hill Rd., Ste. H-307
Lawrenceville, GA 30046
(678)892-8528
E-mail: info@sterlingroseconsultingcorp.
com
Website: http://www.sterlingroseconsult
ingcorp.com

Lemongrass Consulting, Inc.
951 Gettysburg Way
Locust Grove, GA 30248
(678)235-5901
E-mail: chamilton@lemongrassplanning.
com
Website: http://lemongrassplanning.com

Samet Consulting
4672 Oxford Cir.
Macon, GA 31210
(478)757-1070
Fax:(478)757-1984
Website: http://sametconsulting.com/

Hawaii

Maui Venture Consulting LLC
PO Box 81515
Haiku, HI 96708
(808)269-1031
E-mail: df@mauiventure.net
Website: http://www.mauiventure.net

Business Plans Hawaii
3059 Maigret St.
Honolulu, HI 96816
(808)735-5597
E-mail: valerie@ businessplanshawaii.com
Website: http://www.businessplanshawaii
.com

**John V. McCoy Communications
Consultant**
425 Ena Rd., Apt. 1204-B
Honolulu, HI 96815
(510)219-2276
E-mail: mccoy.jv@gmail.com
Website: http://www.busplan.com

Idaho

Agnew::Beck Consulting
802 W Bannock St., Ste. 803

Boise, ID 83702
(208)342-3976
E-mail: admin@agnewbeck.com
Website: http://agnewbeck.com

Kairosys
16645 Plum Rd.
Caldwell, ID 83607
(208)454-0086
E-mail: support@kairosys.net
Website: http://kairosys.net

Illinois

Midwest Business Consulting, LLC
Midway Corporate Ctr.
6640 S Cicero Ave., Ste. 204
Bedford Park, IL 60638
(708)571-3401
Fax: (708)571-3409
E-mail: inquiries@mbconsultingco.com
Website: https://www.mbconsultingco.
com

Anchor Advisors, Ltd.
5366 N Elston Ave., Ste. 203
Chicago, IL 60630
(773)282-7677
Website: http://anchoradvisors.com

Brighton Windsor Group, LLC
Chicago, IL 60602
Free: 888-781-1304
E-mail: hello@brightonwindsor.com
Website: http://brightonwindsor.com

Ground Floor Partners, Inc.
150 N Michigan Ave., Ste. 2800
Chicago, IL 60601
(312)726-1981
Website: http://groundfloorpartners.com

Midwest Business Consulting, LLC
Chicago Temple Bldg.
77 W Washington, Ste. 718
Chicago, IL 60602
(312)415-0340
Fax: (312)994-8554
E-mail: inquiries@mbconsultingco.com
Website: https://www.mbconsultingco.
com

Gold Consulting, Inc.
18 Exmoor Ct.
Highwood, IL 60040
(847)433-8141
Fax: (847)433-2446
E-mail: ron@goldconsultinginc.com
Website: http://goldconsultinginc.com

Francorp
20200 Governors Dr.

Olympia Fields, IL 60461
(708)481-2900
Free: 800-372-6244
E-mail: francorp@aol.com
Website: http://www.francorp.com

MD Consultants of America, Inc.
6738 N Frostwood Pkwy.
Peoria, IL 61615
Free: 877-272-1631
Fax: (309)414-0298
E-mail: info@mdconsultantus.com
Website: http://www.mdconsultantus.com

Quiet Storm Enterprises Ltd.
3701 Trilling Ave., Ste. 201
Rockford IL 61103-2157
(815)315-0146
Free: 877-958-0160
E-mail: info@qsenterprisesltd.net
Website: http://www.qsenterprisesltd.net

Public Sector Consulting
5718 Barlow Rd.
Sherman, IL 62684
(217)629-9869
Fax: (217)629-9732
E-mail: mail@gotopsc.com
Website: http://www.gotopsc.com

GVNW Illinois
3220 Pleasant Run, Ste. A
Springfield, IL 62711
(217)698-2700
E-mail: jushio@gvnw.com
Website: http://www.gvnw.com

Indiana

Compass CPA Group
435 Ann St.
Fort Wayne, IN 46774
(260)749-2200
Free: 866-788-9789
E-mail: information@compasscpagroup
.com
Website: http://www.compasscpagroup
.com

Cox and Co.
3930 Mezzanine Dr. Ste A
Lafayette, IN, 47905
(765)449-4495
Fax: (765)449-1218
E-mail: stan@coxpa.com
Website: http://coxcpa.com

Kimmel Consulting LLC
136 S 9th St Ste 320
Noblesville, IN 46060
(317)773-3810

Fax: (317)770-8787
E-mail: info@kimmelconsultingllc.com
Website: http://www.kimmelconsulting
llc.com

Iowa

TD&T CPAs and Advisors, P.C. Burlington Office
323 Jefferson St.
Burlington, IA 52601
(319)753-9877
Fax: (319)753-1156
E-mail: briani@tdtpc.com
Website: http://www.tdtpc.com/index.php

TD&T CPAs and Advisors, P.C. Cedar Rapids Office
1700 42nd St. NE
Cedar Rapids, IA 52402
(319)393-2374
Fax: (319)393-2375
E-mail: amandal@tdtpc.com
Website: http://www.tdtpc.com/index.
php

Terry, Lockridge and Dunn
210 2nd St. SE
Cedar Rapids, IA 52407
(319)364-2945
Fax: (319)362-4487
E-mail: info@tld-inc.com
Website: http://www.tld-inc.com

TD&T CPAs and Advisors, P.C. Centerville Office
101 W Van Buren St.
Centerville, IA 52544
(641)437-4296
Fax: (641)437-1574
E-mail: markl@tdtpc.com
Website: http://www.tdtpc.com/index
.php

TD&T CPAs and Advisors, P.C. Fairfield Office
2109 W Jefferson Ave.
Fairfield, IA 52556
(641)472-6171
Fax: (641)472-6632
E-mail: jodik@tdtpc.com
Website: http://www.tdtpc.com/
index.php

Steve Meyer Consulting LLC
304 E Maple
Garrison, IA 52229
(319)477-5041
E-mail: gfdchief@netins.net
Website: http://www.stevemeyer
consulting.com/

Terry, Lockridge and Dunn
2225 Mormon Trek Blvd.
Iowa City, IA 52246
(319)339-4884
Fax: (319)358-9113
E-mail: info@tld-inc.com
Website: http://www.tld-inc.com

TD&T CPAs and Advisors, P.C. Mount Pleasant Office
204 N Main
Mount Pleasant, IA 52641
(319)385-9718
Fax: (319)385-2612
E-mail: tomh@tdtpc.com
Website: http://www.tdtpc.com/index
.php

TD&T CPAs and Advisors, P.C. Muscatine Office
500 Cedar St.
Muscatine, IA 52761
(563)264-2727
Fax: (563)263-7777
E-mail: vickib@tdtpc.com; dennyt@tdtpc
.com
Website: http://www.tdtpc.com/index.
php

TD&T CPAs and Advisors, P.C. Oskaloosa Office
317 High Ave. E
Oskaloosa, IA 52577
(641)672-2523
Fax: (641)673-7453
E-mail: joshb@tdtpc.com
Website: http://www.tdtpc.com/index.php

TD&T CPAs and Advisors, P.C. Ottumwa Office
117 S Court
Ottumwa, IA 52501
(641)683-1823
Fax: (641)683-1868
E-mail: dougm@tdtpc.com
Website: http://www.tdtpc.com/index.php

TD&T CPAs and Advisors, P.C. Pella Office
1108 Washington St.
Pella, IA 50219
(641)628-9411
Fax: (641)628-1321
E-mail: justinp@tdtpc.com
Website: http://www.tdtpc.com/index.php

Murk-n-T, Inc.
209 Rose Ave. SW
Swisher, IA 52338
(319)857-4638
Fax: (319)857-4648

E-mail: info@murknt.com
Website: http://www.murknt.com/index
.php

TD&T CPAs and Advisors, P.C. West Des Moines Office
1240 Office Plaza Dr.
West Des Moines, IA 50266
(515)657-5800
Fax: (515)657-5801
E-mail: davef@tdtpc.com
Website: http://www.tdtpc.com/index.php

Kansas

Nail CPA Firm, LLC
4901 W 136th St.
Leawood, KS 66224
(913)663-2500
E-mail: info@nailcpafirm.com
Website: http://www.nailcpafirm.com

Shockey Consulting Services, LLC
12351 W 96th Ter., Ste. 107
Lenexa, KS 66215
(913)248-9585
E-mail: solutions@shockeyconsulting.com
Website: http://www.shockeyconsulting
.com/

Aspire Business Development
10955 Lowell Ave., Ste. 400
Overland Park, KS 66210
(913)660-9400
Free: 888-548-1504
Website: http://www.aspirekc.com

Wichita Technology Corp.
7829 E Rockhill Rd., Ste. 307
Wichita, KS 67206
(316)651-5900
Free: 866-810-6671
E-mail: wtc@wichitatechnology.com
Website: http://www.wichitatechnology
.com

Kentucky

BizFixes
277 E High St.
Lexington, KY 40507
(859)552-5151
Website: http://bizfixes.com

Louisiana

Cathy Denison, PhD & Associates Professional Services, Inc.
9655 Perkins Rd., Ste. C-123
Baton Rouge, LA 70810
(337)502-1911

E-mail: cdenison@denisonassociates.com
Website: http://www.denisonassociates
.com

Rabalais Business Consulting
209 Rue Louis XIV, Ste. B
Lafayette, LA 70508
(337)981-2577
Fax: (337)981-2579
Website: http://rabbiz.com

Terk Consulting Business Plans
3819A Magazine St.
New Orleans, LA 70115
(504)237-0480
E-mail: info@terkconsulting.com
Website: https://terkconsulting.com

Maine

PFBF CPAs Bath Office
259 Front St.
Bath, ME 04530
(207)371-8002
Fax: (207)877-7407
E-mail: mail@pfbf.com
Website: http://www.pfbf.com

John Rust Consulting
PO Box 459
Hampden, ME 04444
(207)337-5858
E-mail: john@johnrustconsulting.com
Website: http://www.johnrustconsulting.
com

PFBF CPAs Oakland Office
46 First Park Dr.
Oakland, ME 04963
(207)873-1603
Fax: (207)877-7407
E-mail: mail@pfbf.com
Website: http://www.pfbf.com

Maryland

**Maryland Capital Enterprises, Inc.
Baltimore Area Office**
333 N Charles St.
Baltimore, MD 21201
(410)546-1900
Fax: (410)546-9718
E-mail: info@marylandcapital.org
Website: http://www.marylandcapital.org

Burdeshaw Associates Ltd.
4701 Sangamore Rd.
Bethesda, MD 20816
(301)229-5800
E-mail: jstacy@burdeshaw.com
Website: http://www.burdeshaw.com

Jacoby
2304 Frederick Rd.
Catonsville, MD 21228
(410)744-3900
Fax: (410)747-7850
Free: 877-799-GROW
E-mail: info@artjacoby.com

Black Rock Accounting & Consulting
13424 Burnt Woods Pl.
Germantown, MD 20874
(301)928-7600
Fax: (301)515-1840
E-mail: mike@blackrockaccounting.com
Website: http://www.blackrock
accounting.com

L&H Business Consulting
1212 York Rd., Ste. C-300
Lutherville, MD 21093
(410)828-4177
Fax: (410)321-1588
E-mail: info@lhbusinessconsulting.com
Website: http://www.lhbusiness
consulting.com

**Maryland Capital Enterprises, Inc.
Eastern Shore Office**
144 E Main St.
Salisbury, MD 21801
(410)546-1900
Fax: (410)546-9718
E-mail: info@marylandcapital.org
Website: http://www.marylandcapital.org

Massachusetts

The Carrot Project
89 South St.
Boston, MA 02111
(617)674-2371
E-mail: info@thecarrotproject.org
Website: http://www.thecarrotproject.
org/home

Julia Shanks Food Consulting
37 Tremont St.
Cambridge, MA 02139
(617)945-8718
E-mail: info@juliashanks.com
Website: http://www.juliashanks.com

CYTO Consulting
363 N Emerson Rd.
Lexington, MA 02420
(339)707-0767
E-mail: info@cytoconsulting.com
Website: http://www.cytoconsulting.com

Foxboro Consulting Group Inc.
36 Lancashire Dr.

Mansfield, MA 02048
(774)719-2236
E-mail: moreinfo@foxboro-consulting.
com
Website: http://www.foxboro-consulting
.com

Dahn Consulting Group
Newburyport, MA 01950
(978)314-1722
E-mail: info@dahnconsulting.com
Website: http://www.dahnconsulting.com

PSMJ Resources Inc.
10 Midland Ave.
Newton, MA 02458
(617)965-0055
Fax: (617)965-5152
Free: 800-537-7765
Website: http://www.psmj.com

Spark Business Consulting
167 Washington St.
Norwell, MA 02061
(781)871-1003
Website: http://sparkbusinessconsulting
.com

Bruno P.C.
57 Obery St., Ste. 4
Plymouth, MA 02360
(508)830-0800
Fax: (508)830-0801
E-mail: info@BrunoAccountants.com
Website: https://www.brunoaccountants
.com

Non Profit Capital Management
41 Main St.
Sterling, MA 01564
(781)933-6726
Fax: (978)563-1007
E-mail: info@npcm.com
Website: http://www.npcm.com/

Michigan

Aimattech Consulting LLC
568 Woodway Ct., Ste. 1
Bloomfield Hills, MI 48302-1572
(248)540-3758
Fax: (775)305-4755
E-mail: dweaver@aimattech.com
Website: http://www.aimattech.com

**BBC Entrepreneurial Training &
Consulting LLC**
12671 E Old U.S. 12
Chelsea, MI 48118
(734)930-9741
Fax: (734)930-6629

E-mail: info@bbcetc.com
Website: http://www.bioconsultants.com

LifeLine Business Consulting
1400 Woodbridge St., 4th Fl.
Detroit, MI 48207
(313)965-3155
E-mail: hello@thelifelinenetwork.com
Website: https://thelifelinenetwork.com

TL Cramer Associates LLC
1788 Broadstone Rd.
Grosse Pointe Woods, MI 48236
(313)332-0182
E-mail: info@tlcramerassociates.com
Website: http://www.tlcramerassociates
.com

Jackson Small Business Support Center
950 W Monroe St., Ste. G-100
Jackson, MI 49202
(517)796-8151
Website: http://www.smallbusiness
supportcenter.com

Tedder Whitlock Consulting
17199 N Laurel Park Dr.
Livonia, MI 48152
(734)542-4200
Fax: (734)542-4201
E-mail: info@tedderwhitlock.com
Website: http://www.tedderwhitlock.com

MarketingHelp Inc.
6647 Riverwoods Ct. NE
Rockford, MI 49341
(616)856-0148
Website: http://www.mktghelp.com

Lucid Business Strategies
8187 Rhode Dr., Ste. D
Shelby Township, MI 48317
(586)254-0095
E-mail: results@lucidbusiness.com
Website: http://www.lucidbusiness
.com

QT Business Solution
24901 Northwestern Hwy., Ste. 305
Southfield, MI 48075
(248)416-1755
Free: 877-859-6768
E-mail: info@qtbizsolutions.com
Website: http://qtbizsolutions.com

Cool & Associates Inc.
921 Village Green Ln., Ste. 1068
Waterford, MI 48328
(248)683-1130
E-mail: info@cool-associates.com
Website: http://www.cool-associates.com

Griffioen Consulting Group, Inc.
6689 Orchard Lake Rd., Ste. 295
West Bloomfield, MI 48322
Free: 888-262-5850
Fax: (248)855-4084
Website: http://www.griffioenconsulting
.com

NooJoom Immigration Services & Business Plan
35253 Warren Rd.
Westland, MI 48185
(734)728-5755
E-mail: wadak@noojoom.org
Website: http://www.noojoomimmigra
tionservices.com

Minnesota

Devoted Business Development
2434 E 117th St., Ste. 100
Burnsville, Minnesota
(952) 582-4669
E-mail: info@devoted-business.com
Website: http://devoted-business.com

Community & Economic Development Associates (CEDA)
1500 S Hwy. 52
Chatfield, MN 55923
(507)867-3164
E-mail: ron.zeigler@cedausa.com
Website: https://www.cedausa.com

Metropolitan Consortium of Community Developers (MCCD)
Open to Business Program
3137 Chicago Ave.
Minneapolis, MN 55407
(612)789-7337
Fax: (612)822-1489
E-mail: info@opentobusinessmn.org
Website: http://www.opentobusinessmn
.org

Metropolitan Economic Development Association (MEDA)
250 2nd Ave. S, Ste. 106
Minneapolis, MN 55401
(612)332-6332
E-mail: info@meda.net
Website: http://meda.net

WomenVenture
2021 E Hennepin Ave., Ste. 200
Minneapolis, MN 55413
(612)224-9540
Fax: (612)200-8369
E-mail: info@womenventure.org
Website: https://www.womenventure.org/
index.html

Mississippi

The IRON Network, LLC
1636 Popps Ferry Rd., Ste. 201
Biloxi, MS 39532
(412)336-8807
E-mail: sales@theironcom.com
Website: http://theironcom.com/services/
business-consulting

Richardson's Writing Service
3285 Squirrel Lake Rd.
Sledge, MS 38670
(662)326-3996
Website: http://www.richws.com

Missouri

Taylor Management Group, LLC (TMG)
PO Box 50155
Clayton, MO 63015
(314)488-1566
Website: http://taymg.com

Stuff
316 W 63rd St.
Kansas City, MO 64113
(816)361-8222
E-mail: sloaneandcasey@pursuegood
stuff.com
Website: http://www.pursuegoodstuff.com

Westphal-Kelpe Consulting Inc.
4050 Broadway, Ste. 201
Kansas City, MO 64111
(816)931-7141
Fax: (816)931-7180
E-mail: info@wkcrestaurants.com
Website: http://www.westphal-kelpe.com

Shockey Consulting Services, LLC
441 Alice Ave.
Kirkwood, MO 66122
(314)497-3126
E-mail: solutions@shockeyconsulting.com
Website: http://www.shockeyconsulting
.com/

Sanford, Lea & Associates
1655 S Enterprise Ave., Ste. B-4
Springfield, MO 65804
(417)886-2220
Fax: (417)886-3979
E-mail: david@adifferentcpa.com
Website: https://www.adifferentcpa.com

EMD Consulting
11111 Conway Rd.
Saint Louis, MO 63131
(314)692-7551
E-mail: info@emdconsulting.com
Website: http://www.emdconsulting.com

M.A. Birsinger & Company, LLC
2464 Taylor Rd., Ste. 106
Wildwood, MO 63040
(314)249-7076
E-mail: brook@mabirsinger.com
Website: http://www.mabirsinger.com

Nebraska

McDermott & Miller, P.C.
2722 S Locust St.
Grand Island, NE 68802
(308)382-7850
Fax: (308)382-7240
E-mail: nsaale@mmcpas.com
Website: http://www.mmcpas.com

McDermott & Miller, P.C.
747 N Burlington Ave., Ste. 401
Hastings, NE 68902
(402)462-4154
Fax: (402)462-5057
E-mail: nsaale@mmcpas.com
Website: http://www.mmcpas.com

McDermott & Miller, P.C.
404 E 25th St.
Kearney, NE 68848
(308)234-5565
Fax: (308)234-2990
E-mail: nsaale@mmcpas.com
Website: http://www.mmcpas.com

Lincoln Partnership for Economic Development (LPED)
3 Landmark Centre
1128 Lincoln Mall, Ste. 100
Lincoln, NE 68508
(402)436-2350
E-mail: info@selectlincoln.org
Website: http://www.selectlincoln.org

Farm Credit Services of America
5015 S 118th St.
Omaha, NE 68137
Free: 800-884-FARM
Website: https://www.fcsamerica.com

McDermott & Miller, P.C.
11602 W Center Rd., Ste. 125
Omaha, NE 68144
(402)391-1207
Fax: (402)391-3424
E-mail: nsaale@mmcpas.com
Website: http://www.mmcpas.com

Nebraska Credit Union League (NCUL)
4885 S 118th St., Ste. 150
Omaha, NE 68137
(402)333-9331
Fax: (402)333-9431

Free: 800-950-4455
E-mail: ssullivan@nebrcul.org
Website: http://www.nebrcul.org

Steier & Prchal, Ltd.
1015 N 98th St., Ste. 100
Omaha, NE 68114
(402)390-9090
Fax: (402)505-5044
E-mail: info@steiertax.com
Website: http://www.steiertax.com/
bizplan.php

Nevada

Anderson Business Advisors, PLLC
3225 McLeod Dr., Ste. 100
Las Vegas, NV 89121
Free: 800-706-4741
Fax: (702)664-0545
E-mail: info@andersonadvisors.com
Website: https://andersonadvisors.com

Stone Law Offices, Ltd.
3295 N Fort Apache Rd., Ste. 150
Las Vegas, NV 89129
Free: 877-800-3424
Fax: (702)998-0443
Website: http://nvestateplan.com

Wise Business Plans
7251 W Lake Mead Blvd., Ste. 300
Las Vegas, NV 89128
Free: 800-496-1056 (United States)
Free: 702-562-4247 (International)
E-mail: info@wisebusinessplans.com
Website: https://wisebusinessplans.com

Drew Aguilar, CPA
1663 Hwy. 395, Ste. 201
Minden, NV 89423
(775)782-7874
Fax: (775)782-8374
E-mail: drew@carsonvalleyaccounting.com
Website: http://www.carsonvalleyaccounting.com

Thunder Vick & Co.
1325 Airmotive Way, Ste. 125
Reno, NV 89502
(775)323-4440
Fax: (775)323-8977
E-mail: admin@thunderrandcpa.com
Website: http://www.thundervickcpa.com

New Hampshire

HJ Marshall Associates
136 Sewalls Falls Rd.
Concord, NH 03301

(603)224-7073
E-mail: franmarshall@comcast.net
Website: http://www.hjmarshall
associates.com

Rodger O. Howells, LLC
6 Loudon Rd., Ste. 205
Concord, New Hampshire 03301
(603)224-3224
Free: 877-224-3224
E-mail: info@rhowellsconsulting.com
Website: http://www.rhowellsconsulting
.com

Nathan Wechsler & Co.
70 Commercial St., 4th Fl.
Concord, NH 03301
(603)224-5357
Fax: (603)224-3792
Website: http://www.nathanwechsler.com

Kieschnick Consulting Services
9 Woodland Rd.
Dover, NH 03820
(603)749-2922
E-mail: peggy@kieschnickconsulting.com
Website: http://www.kieschnick
consulting.com

Trojan Consulting Group LLC
PO Box 27
Dover, NH 03821
(603)343-1707
E-mail: MNT@TrojanConsultingGroup
.com
Website: http://trojanconsultinggroup
.com

Executive Service Corps (ESC)
80 Locke Rd.
Hampton, NH 03842
(603)926-0752
Website: http://www.nonprofit-
consultants.org

Hannah Grimes Center for Entrepreneurship
25 Roxbury St.
Keene, NH 03431
(603)352-5063
Fax: (603)352-5538
E-mail: info@hannahgrimes.com
Website: https://www.hannahgrimes
.com/

Nathan Wechsler & Co.
59 Emerald St.
Keene, NH 03431
(603)357-7665
Fax: (603)358-6800
Website: http://www.nathanwechsler.com

Nathan Wechsler & Co.
44 School St.
Lebanon, NH 03766
(603)448-2650
Fax: (603)448-2476
Website: http://www.nathanwechsler.com

Blue Ribbon Consulting, LDO, LLC
PO Box 435
New Ipswich, NH 03071
(603)878-1694
E-mail: lisa@blueribbonconsulting.com
Website: www.blueribbonconsultingllc.com

Dare Mighty Things, LLC
1 New Hampshire Ave., Ste. 125
Portsmouth, NH 03801
(603)431-4331
Fax: (603)431-4332
E-mail: info@daremightythings.com
Website: http://www.daremightythings
.com

New Jersey

Huffman & Huffman LLC
Changebridge Plaza
2 Changebridge Rd., Ste. 204
Montville, NJ 07045
(973)334-2600
Fax: (973)334-2627
E-mail: jhuffman@huffmancompany.com
Website: http://www.huffmancompany
.com

New Venture Design
Sperro Corporate Ctr.
2 Skyline Dr.
Montville, NJ 07045
(973)331-0022
Fax: (973)335-2656
Free: 866-639-3527
E-mail: info@newventuredesign.com
Website: http://www.newventuredesign
.com

Patterson & Associates LLC
Glendale Executive Campus
1000 White Horse Rd., Ste. 304
Voorhees, NJ 08043-4409
(856)435-2700
Fax: (856)435-1190
E-mail: info@pattersonassociatesllc.com
Website: http://www.patterson
associatesllc.com

New Mexico

Hinkle + Landers, P.C.
2500 9th St. NW
Albuquerque, NM 87102

(505)883-8788
Fax: (505)883-8797
E-mail: info@HL-cpas.com
Website: http://www.hl-cpas.com

Vaughn CPA
6605 Uptown Blvd., Ste. 370
Albuquerque, NM 87110
(505)828-0900
E-mail: vaughn@vaughncpa.com
Website: http://vaughncpa.com

WESST
WESST Enterprise Center
609 Broadway Blvd. NE
Albuquerque, NM 87102
(505)246-6900
Fax: (505)243-3035
Free: 800-GO-WESST
Website: https://www.wesst.org

WESST Farmington
San Juan College Quality Center for
Business
5101 College Blvd., Ste. 5060
Farmington, NM 87402
(505)566-3715
Fax: (505)566-3698
Website: https://www.wesst.org/
farmington

WESST Las Cruces
221 N Main St., #104a
Las Cruces, NM 88001
(575)541-1583
Website: https://www.wesst.org/
las-cruces

WESST Rio Rancho
New Mexico Bank & Trust Bldg.
4001 Southern Blvd. SE, Ste. B
Rio Rancho, NM 87124-2069
(505)892-1238
Fax: (505)892-6157
Website: https://www.wesst.org/rio-rancho

WESST Roswell
Bank of America Bldg.
500 N Main St., Ste. 700
Roswell, NM 88201
Fax: (575)624-9850
Free: 575-624-9845
Website: https://www.wesst.org/roswell

Hinkle + Landers, P.C.
404 Brunn School Rd., Bldg. B
Santa Fe, NM 87505
(505)883-8788
Fax: (505)883-8797
E-mail: info@HL-cpas.com
Website: http://www.hl-cpas.com

WESST Santa Fe
Santa Fe Business Incubator
3900 Paseo del Sol, Ste. 351
Santa Fe, NM 87507
(505)474-6556
Fax: (505)474-6687
Website: https://www.wesst.org/santa-fe

New York

Key Accounting of New York
2488 Grand Concourse, Ste. 320B
Bronx, NY 10458
(718)584-8097
Fax: (866)496-5624
E-mail: info@keyaccnewyork.com
Website: http://keyaccnewyork.com

Soundview Business Consulting
53 Prospect Park W, Ste. 4A
Brooklyn, NY 11215
(718)499-0809
Fax: (718)499-0829
E-mail: brendan@soundviewfirm.com
Website: http://www.soundviewfirm.com

Addenda Solutions
5297 Parkside Dr., Ste. 412
Canandaigua, NY 14424
(585)394-4950
Free: 888-851-0414
Website: http://addendasolutions.com

Aspire Consulting, Ltd.
1 Horseshoe Dr.
Hyde Park, NY 12538
(845)803-0438
Fax: (845)229-8262
E-mail: info@AspireAdvantage.com
Website: http://www.aspireadvantage.
com/index.html

Capacity Business Consulting
3 Wallkill Ave.
Montgomery, NY 12549
(845)764-9484
E-mail: info@capacityconsultinginc.com
Website: http://www.capacitybusiness-
consulting.com

Growthink Inc.
27 Radio Circle Dr., Ste. 202
Mount Kisco, NY 10549
Free: 800-647-6983
E-mail: services@growthink.com
Website: http://www.growthink.com

Gershon Consulting
833 Broadway, 2nd Fl.
New York, NY 10003
Free: 800-701-0176

E-mail: info@gershonconsulting.com
Website: http://www.gershonconsulting
.com

New York Business Consultants LLC
Chrysler Bldg.
405 Lexington Ave.
New York, NY 10174
(315)572-1938
Fax: (888)201-9524
Free: 800-481-2707
E-mail: info@newyorkbusinessconsult
ants.com
Website: http://www.newyorkbusiness
consultants.com/index.html

The Wright Consultants
394 Broadway
New York, NY 10013
(415)928-2071
Website: http://www.thewrightconsult
ants.com

Addenda Solutions
1100 University Ave., Ste. 122
Rochester, NY 14607
(585)461-2654
Free: 888-851-0414
Website: http://addendasolutions.com

Addenda Solutions
126 Kiwassa Rd.
Saranac Lake, NY 12983
(518)891-1681
Free: 888-851-0414
Website: http://addendasolutions.com

North Carolina

Birds Eye Business Planning & Adventures
153 S Lexington Ave.
Asheville, NC 28801
(828)367-7248
E-mail: info@birdseye.info
Website: http://www.birdseye.info

Mountain BizWorks
153 S Lexington Ave.
Asheville, NC 28801
(828)253-2834
Free: 855-296-0048
E-mail: info@mountainbizworks.org
Website: https://www.mountainbizworks
.org

Allied Tax & Accounting Consultants, LLC
5550 77 Center Dr., Ste. 245
Charlotte, NC 28217
(704)676-1882

Fax: (704)676-1884
Free: 888-849-5119
E-mail: help@alliedtaxaccounting.com
Website: http://www.alliedtaxaccounting.
com/services/business-consulting

Brewery Business Plan
9205 Cub Run Dr.
Concord, NC 28027
(704)960-4032
Website: https://brewerybusinessplan
.com

EMD Consulting
140 Foothills Dr.
Hendersonville, NC 28792
E-mail: info@emdconsulting.com
Website: http://www.emdconsulting.com

Anagard Business Consulting, LLC
9360 Falls of Neuse Rd., Ste. 205
Raleigh, NC 27615
(919)876-1314
E-mail: info@ANAGARD.com
Website: http://www.anagard.com/index
.html

Davis Group, PA, CPAs
640 Statesville Blvd., Ste. 1
Salisbury, NC 28145-1307
(704)636-1040
Fax: (704)637-3084
E-mail: gary@dgcpa.com
Website: https://www.dgcpa.com/
business-advisory

North Dakota

Center for Innovation
Ina Mae Rude Entrepreneur Ctr.
4200 James Ray Dr.
Grand Forks, ND 58203
(701)777-3132
Fax: (701)777-2339
E-mail: info@innovators.net
Website: http://www.innovators.net

Ohio

Brown Consulting Group LLC
7965 North High St., Ste. 130
Columbus, OH 43235
(614)205-5323
E-mail: keith@browngroupcpa.com
Website: http://browngroupcpa.com

Oklahoma

Wymer Brownlee
3650 SE Camelot Dr.
Bartlesville, OK 74006

(918)333-7291
Fax: (918)333-7295
E-mail: info@wymerbrownlee.com
Website: http://www.wymerbrownlee
.com

Wymer Brownlee
201 N Grand, Ste. 100
Enid, OK 73701
(580)237-0060
Fax: (580)237-0092
E-mail: info@wymerbrownlee.com
Website: http://www.wymerbrownlee
.com

Wymer Brownlee
126 S Main
Fairview, OK 73737
(580)227-4709
Fax: (580)227-2166
E-mail: info@wymerbrownlee.com
Website: http://www.wymerbrownlee
.com

Entrepot
5711 E 72nd Ct.
Tulsa, Oklahoma 74136
(918)497-1748
Website: http://www.entrepotusa.com

Wymer Brownlee
7645 E 63rd St., Ste. 120
Tulsa, OK 74133
(918)392-8600
Fax: (918)392-8601
E-mail: info@wymerbrownlee.com
Website: http://www.wymerbrownlee
.com

Wymer Brownlee
10936 NW Expressway
Yukon, OK 73099
(405)283-0100
Fax: (405)283-0200
E-mail: info@wymerbrownlee.com
Website: http://www.wymerbrownlee
.com

Oregon

Timothy J. Berry
44 W Broadway Ste. 500
Eugene, OR, 97401
(541)683-6162
Website: http://timberry.com/business-
plan-expert

Advanced Trainers & Consultants, LLC (ATAC)
116 SE Hood
Gresham, OR 97080

(503)661-4013
Fax: (503)665-0775
E-mail: info@advancedtrainers.com
Website: http://www.advancedtrainers
.com

Alten Sakai & Company LLP
10260 SW Greenburg Rd., Ste. 300
Portland, OR 97223
(503)297-1072
Fax: (503)297-6634
E-mail: info@altensakai.com
Website: http://www.altensakai.com

Pointman Consulting, LLC
1130 SW Morrison
Portland, OR 97205
(503)804-2074
E-mail: noah@pointmanconsulting.com
Website: http://www.pointmanconsult
ing.com/index.htm

GVNW Oregon
8050 SW Warm Springs St.
Tualatin, OR 97062
(503)612-4400
E-mail: jrennard@gvnw.com
Website: http://www.gvnw.com

Pennsylvania

Main Line Rail Management, Inc.
116 N Bellevue Ave., Ste. 206
Langhorne, PA 19047
(215)741-6007
Fax: (215)741-6009
E-mail: dsg@voicenet.com
Website: http://www.mlrail.com

Fairmount Ventures, Inc.
2 Penn Ctr.
1500 JFK Blvd., Ste. 1150
Philadelphia, PA 19102
(215)717-2299
E-mail: info@fairmountinc.com
Website: http://fairmountinc.com

RINK Consulting
1420 Locust St., Ste. 31N
Philadelphia, PA 19102
(215)546-5863
Website: http://www.lindarink.com

FlagShip Business Plans and Consulting
2 Gateway Ctr.
?603 Stanwix St., Ste. 1626
Pittsburgh, PA 15222
(412)219-8157
E-mail: info@flagshipbusinessplans.com
Website: http://www.flagshipbusiness
plans.com/page.html

Puerto Rico

Manuel L. Porrata & Associates
898 Muñoz Rivera Ave., Ste. 300
San Juan, PR 00927
(787)765-2140
Fax: (787)754-3285
E-mail: mporrata@manuelporrata.com
Website: http://www.manuelporrata.com/
home.html

Rhode Island

Ledoux, Petruska & Co., Inc.
1006 Charles St.
North Providence, RI 02904
(401)727-8100
Fax: (401)727-8181
E-mail: beancounter@lpcpari.com
Website: http://www.lpcpari.com/services/
business-consulting-and-solutions

South Carolina

Fluent Decisions, LLC
701 Gervais St., Ste. 150-157
Columbia, SC 29201
(803)748-2933
Website: https://www.fluentdecisions
.com

South Dakota

South Dakota Enterprise Institute
Research Park at South Dakota State
University
2301 Research Park Way, Ste. 114
Brookings, SD 57006
(605)697-5015
E-mail: info@sdei.org
Website: http://www.sdei.org

Tennessee

Jackson Thorton Nashville Office
333 Commerce St., Ste. 1050
Nashville, TN 37201
(615)869-2050
Website: http://www.jacksonthornton
.com

Texas

Zaetric Business Solutions LLC
27350 Blueberry Hill, Ste. 14
Conroe, TX 77385
(281)298-1878
Fax: (713)621-4885
E-mail: inquiries@zaetric.com
Website: http://www.zaetric.com

Optimus Business Plans
13355 Noel Rd., Ste. 1100
Dallas, TX 75240
(844)760-0903
Website: http://optimusbusinessplans
.com

GVNW Texas
1001 Water St., Ste. A-100
Kerrville, TX 78028
(830)896-5200
E-mail: sgatto@gvnw.com
Website: http://www.gvnw.com

Butler Consultants
555 Republic Dr., Ste. 200
Plano, TX 75074
(214)491-4001
E-mail: Info@Financial-Projections.com
Website: http://contact.financial-
projections.com

**Central Texas Business Consultants
(CTBC)**
PO Box 2213
Wimberley, TX 78676
(512)626-2938
Fax: (512)847-5541
E-mail: info@centraltexasbusiness
consulting.com
Website: http://www.centraltexas
businessconsulting.com

Utah

Vector Resources
7651 S Main St., Ste. 106
Midvale, UT 84047-7158
(801)352-8500
Fax: (801)352-8506
E-mail: info@vectorresources.com
Website: http://www.vectorresources
.com

Ron Woodbury Consulting, Inc.
2899 E 3240 South St.
Saint George, UT 84790
(435)275-2978
E-mail: ron@ronwoodburyconsulting.
com
Website: http://ronwoodburyconsulting.
com

Vermont

CDS Consulting Co-op
659 Old Codding Rd.
Putney, VT 05346
(802)387-6013
Website: http://www.cdsconsulting.
coop

Virginia

The Profit Partner, LLC
3900 Jermantown Rd., Ste. 300
Fairfax, VA 22030
(703)934-4630
Website: http://www.theprofitpartner.
com

Dare Mighty Things, LLC
805 Park Ave.
Herndon, VA 20170
(703)424-3119
Fax: (603)431-4332
E-mail: info@daremightythings.com
Website: http://www.daremightythings.
com

Washington

ECG Management Consultants Inc.
1111 3rd Ave., Ste. 2700
Seattle, WA 98101-3201
(206)689-2200
Fax: (206)689-2209
E-mail: ecg@ecgmc.com
Website: http://www.ecgmc.com

West Virginia

Cava & Banko, PLLC
117 E Main St.
Bridgeport, WV 26330
(304)842-4499
Fax: (304)842-4585
Website: http://cavabankocpa.com

Wisconsin

Virtual Management Solutions
959 Primrose Center Rd.
Belleville, WI 53508-9376
(608)832-8003
E-mail: davelind@chorus.net
Website: http://www.virtualmanagement-
solutions.com

Wyoming

CPA Consulting Group, LLP
300 Country Club Rd., Ste. 302
Casper, WY 82609
(307)577-4040
E-mail: taxes@cpawyo.com
Website: http://www.cpacasper.com

CA Boner Business Plans
3218 Rock Springs St.
Cheyenne, WY 82001
(307)214-2043
Website: http://caboner.biz

CPA Group of Laramie, LLC
1273 N 15th St., Ste. 121
Laramie, WY 82072
(307)745-7241
Fax: (307)745-7292
Website: http://www.cpalaramie.com/
index.php

Small Business Administration Regional Offices

This section contains a listing of Small Business Administration offices arranged numerically by region. Service areas are provided. Contact the appropriate office for a referral to the nearest field office, or visit the Small Business Administration online at www.sba.gov.

Region I

U.S. Small Business Administration New England Office
10 Causeway St., Ste. 265A
Boston, MA 02222
Phone: (617)565-8416
Fax: (617)565-8420
Website: http://www.sba.gov/offices/
regional/i
Serves Connecticut, Maine, Massachusetts, New Hampshire, Rhode Island, and Vermont.

Region II

U.S. Small Business Administration Atlantic Office
26 Federal Plaza, Ste. 3108
New York, NY 10278
Phone: (212)264-1450
Website: http://www.sba.gov/offices/
regional/ii
Serves New Jersey, New York, Puerto Rico, and the U.S. Virgin Islands.

Region III

U.S. Small Business Administration Mid-Atlantic Office
1150 1st Ave., Ste. 1001
King of Prussia, PA 19406
(610)382-3092
Website: http://www.sba.gov/offices/
regional/iii
Serves Delaware, Maryland, Pennsylvania, Virginia, Washington, DC, and West Virginia.

Region IV

U.S. Small Business Administration Southeast Office
233 Peachtree St. NE, Ste. 1800
Atlanta, GA 30303
Phone: (404)331-4999
Fax: (404)331-2354
Website: http://www.sba.gov/offices/
regional/iv
Serves Alabama, Florida, Georgia, Kentucky, Mississippi, North Carolina, South Carolina, and Tennessee.

Region V

U.S. Small Business Administration Great Lakes Office
500 W Madison St., Ste. 1150
Chicago, IL 60661
Phone: (312)353-0357
Fax: (312)353-3426
Website: http://www.sba.gov/offices/
regional/v
Serves Illinois, Indiana, Michigan, Minnesota, Ohio, and Wisconsin.

Region VI

U.S. Small Business Administration South Central Office
4300 Amon Carter Blvd., Ste. 108
Fort Worth, TX 76155
Phone: (817)684-5581
Fax: (817)684-5588
TTY/TDD: (817)684-5552
Website: http://www.sba.gov/offices/
regional/vi
Serves Arkansas, Louisiana, New Mexico, Oklahoma, and Texas.

Region VII

U.S. Small Business Administration Great Plains Office
1000 Walnut, Ste. 530
Kansas City, MO 64106
Phone: (816)426-4840
Fax: (816)426-4848
Website: http://www.sba.gov/offices/
regional/vii
Serves Iowa, Kansas, Missouri, and Nebraska.

Region VIII

U.S. Small Business Administration Rocky Mountains Office
721 19th St., Ste. 400
Denver, CO 80202

Fax: (303)844-0506
Website: http://www.sba.gov/offices/
regional/viii
Serves Colorado, Montana, North Dakota,
South Dakota, Utah, and Wyoming.

Region IX

**U.S. Small Business Administration
Pacific Office**
330 N Brand Blvd., Ste. 1200
Glendale, CA 91203
Phone: (818)552-3437
Fax: (202)481-0344
Website: http://www.sba.gov/offices/
regional/ix
Serves Arizona, California, Guam,
Hawaii, and Nevada.

Region X

**U.S. Small Business Administration
Pacific Northwest Office**
2401 4th Ave., Ste. 400
Seattle, WA 98121
Phone: (206)553-5676
Fax: (206)553-4155
Website: http://www.sba.gov/offices/
regional/x
Serves Alaska, Idaho, Oregon, and
Washington.

Small Business Development Centers

*This section contains a listing of all Small
Business Development Centers, organized
alphabetically by state/U.S. territory, then
by city, then by agency name.*

Alabama

Alabama SBDC

UNIVERSITY OF ALABAMA
2800 Milan Court Suite 124
Birmingham, AL 35211-6908
Phone: 205-943-6750
Fax: 205-943-6752
E-Mail: wcampbell@provost.uab.edu
Website: http://www.asbdc.org
Mr. William Campbell Jr, State Director

Alaska

Alaska SBDC

**UNIVERSITY OF ALASKA -
ANCHORAGE**
430 West Seventh Avenue, Suite 110

Anchorage, AK 99501
Phone: 907-274 -7232
Fax: 907-272-0565
E-Mail: Isaac.Vanderburg@aksbdc.org
Website: http://www.aksbdc.org
Isaac Vanderburg, State Director

American Samoa

American Samoa SBDC

**AMERICAN SAMOA COMMUNITY
COLLEGE**
P.O. Box 2609
Pago Pago, American Samoa 96799
Phone: 011-684-699-4830
Fax: 011-684-699-6132
E-Mail: hthweatt.sbdc@hotmail.com
Website: www.as-sbdc.org
Mr. Herbert Thweatt, Director

Arizona

Arizona SBDC

**MARICOPA COUNTY COMMUNITY
COLLEGE**
2411 West 14th Street, Suite 114
Tempe, AZ 85281
Phone: (480)731-8720
Fax: (480)731-8729
E-Mail: janice.washington@domail.
maricopa.edu
Website: http://www.azsbdc.net
Janice Washington, State Director

Arkansas

Arkansas SBDC

UNIVERSITY OF ARKANSAS
2801 South University Avenue
Little Rock, AR 72204
Phone: 501-683-7700
Fax: 501-683-7720
E-Mail: jmroderick@ualr.edu
Website: http://asbtdc.org
Ms. Janet M. Roderick, State Director

California

**California - Northern California
Regional SBDC**

Northern California SBDC

HUMBOLDT STATE UNIVERSITY
1 Harpst Street 2006A, 209 Siemens Hall
Arcata, CA, 95521
Phone: 707-826-3920
Fax: 707-826-3912

E-Mail: Kristin.Johnson@humboldt.edu
Website: https://www.norcalsbdc.org
Kristin Johnson, Regional Director

California - Northern California SBDC

**CALIFORNIA STATE UNIVERSITY -
CHICO**
35 Main St., Rm 203rr
Chico, CA 95929-0765
Phone: 530-898-5443
Fax: 530-898-4734
E-Mail: dripke@csuchico.edu
Website: https://www.necsbdc.org
Mr. Dan Ripke, Interim Regional
Director

**California - San Diego and Imperial
SBDC**

**SOUTHWESTERN COMMUNITY
COLLEGE**
880 National City Boulevard,
Suite 103
National City, CA 91950
Phone: 619-216-6721
Fax: 619-216-6692
E-Mail: awilson@swccd.edu
Website: http://www.SBDCRegional
Network.org
Aleta Wilson, Regional Director

California - UC Merced SBDC

UC Merced Lead Center

**UNIVERSITY OF CALIFORNIA -
MERCED**
550 East Shaw, Suite 105A
Fresno, CA 93710
Phone: 559-241-6590
Fax: 559-241-7422
E-Mail: dhowerton@ucmerced.edu
Website: http://sbdc.ucmerced.edu
Diane Howerton, State Director

**California - Orange County/Inland
Empire SBDC**

Tri-County Lead SBDC

**CALIFORNIA STATE UNIVERSITY -
FULLERTON**
800 North State College Boulevard,
SGMH 5313
Fullerton, CA 92834
Phone: 714-278-5168
Fax: 714-278-7101
E-Mail: kmpayne@fullerton.edu
Website: http://www.leadsbdc.org
Katrina Payne Smith, Lead Center
Director

California - Los Angeles Region SBDC

LONG BEACH CITY COLLEGE
4900 E Conant Street, Building 2
Long Beach, CA 90808
Phone: 562-938-5006
Fax: 562-938-5030
E-Mail: jtorres@lbcc.edu
Website: http://www.smallbizla.org
Jesse Torres, Lead Center Director

Colorado

Colorado SBDC

COLORADO SBDC
1625 Broadway, Suite 2700
Denver, CO 80202
Phone: 303-892-3864
Fax: 303-892-3848
E-Mail: Kelly.Manning@state.co.us
Website: http://www.www.coloradosbdc
.org
Ms. Kelly Manning, State Director

Connecticut

Connecticut SBDC

UNIVERSITY OF CONNECTICUT
2100 Hillside Road, Unit 1044
Storrs, CT 06269
Phone: 855-428-7232
E-Mail: ecarter@uconn.edu
Website: www.ctsbdc.com
Emily Carter, State Director

Delaware

Delaware SBDC

DELAWARE TECHNOLOGY PARK
1 Innovation Way, Suite 301
Newark, DE 19711
Phone: 302-831-4283
Fax: 302-831-1423
E-Mail: jmbowman@udel.edu
Website: http://www.delawaresbdc.org
Mike Bowman, State Director

District of Columbia

District of Columbia SBDC

HOWARD UNIVERSITY
2600 6th Street, NW Room 128
Washington, DC 20059
Phone: 202-806-1550
Fax: 202-806-1777
E-Mail: darrell.brown@howard.edu
Website: http://www.dcsbdc.com
Darrell Brown, Executive Director

Florida

Florida SBDC

UNIVERSITY OF WEST FLORIDA
11000 University Parkway, Building 38
Pensacola, FL 32514
Phone: 850-473-7800
Fax: 850-473-7813
E-Mail: mmyhre@uwf.edu
Website: http://www.floridasbdc.com
Michael Myhre, State Director

Georgia

Georgia SBDC

UNIVERSITY OF GEORGIA
1180 East Broad Street
Athens, GA 30602
Phone: 706-542-6762
Fax: 706-542-7935
E-mail: aadams@georgiasbdc.org
Website: http://www.georgiasbdc
.org
Mr. Allan Adams, State Director

Guam

Guam Small Business Development Center

UNIVERSITY OF GUAM
Pacific Islands SBDC
P.O. Box 5014 - U.O.G. Station
Mangilao, GU 96923
Phone: 671-735-2590
Fax: 671-734-2002
E-mail: casey@pacificsbdc.com
Website: http://www.uog.edu/sbdc
Mr. Casey Jeszenka, Director

Hawaii

Hawaii SBDC

UNIVERSITY OF HAWAII - HILO
200 W Kawili Street, Suite 107
Hilo, HI 96720
Phone: 808-974-7515
Fax: 808-974-7683
E-Mail: cathy.wiltse@hisbdc.org
Website: http://www.hisbdc.org
Cathy Wiltse, State Director

Idaho

Idaho SBDC

BOISE STATE UNIVERSITY
1910 University Drive
Boise, ID 83725

Phone: 208-426-3838
Fax: 208-426-3877
E-mail: ksewell@boisestate.edu
Website: http://www.idahosbdc.org
Katie Sewell, State Director

Illinois

Illinois SBDC

DEPARTMENT OF COMMERCE AND ECONOMIC OPPORTUNITY
500 E Monroe
Springfield, IL 62701
Phone: 217-524-5700
Fax: 217-524-0171
E-mail: mark.petrilli@illinois.gov
Website: http://www.ilsbdc.biz
Mr. Mark Petrilli, State Director

Indiana

Indiana SBDC

INDIANA ECONOMIC DEVELOPMENT CORPORATION
One North Capitol, Suite 700
Indianapolis, IN 46204
Phone: 317-232-8805
Fax: 317-232-8872
E-mail: JSchpok@iedc.in.gov
Website: http://www.isbdc.org
Jacob Schpok, State Director

Iowa

Iowa SBDC

IOWA STATE UNIVERSITY
2321 North Loop Drive, Suite 202
Ames, IA 50010
Phone: 515-294-2030
Fax: 515-294-6522
E-mail: lshimkat@iastate.edu
Website: http://www.iowasbdc.org
Lisa Shimkat, State Director

Kansas

Kansas SBDC

FORT HAYS STATE UNIVERSITY
214 SW Sixth Street, Suite 301
Topeka, KS 66603
Phone: 785-296-6514
Fax: 785-291-3261
E-mail: panichello@ksbdc.net
Website: http://www.fhsu.edu/
ksbdc
Greg Panichello, State Director

Kentucky

Kentucky SBDC

UNIVERSITY OF KENTUCKY
One Quality Street
Lexington, KY 40507
Phone: 859-257-7668
Fax: 859-323-1907
E-mail: lrnaug0@uky.edu
Website: http://www.ksbdc.org
Becky Naugle, State Director

Louisiana

Louisiana SBDC

**UNIVERSITY OF LOUISIANA -
MONROE**

College of Business Administration
700 University Avenue
Monroe, LA 71209
Phone: 318-342-5507
Fax: 318-342-5510
E-mail: rkessler@lsbdc.org
Website: http://www.lsbdc.org
Rande Kessler, State Director

Maine

Maine SBDC

UNIVERSITY OF SOUTHERN MAINE
96 Falmouth Street P.O. Box 9300
Portland, ME 04104
Phone: 207-780-4420
Fax: 207-780-4810
E-mail: mark.delisle@maine.edu
Website: http://www.mainesbdc.org
Mark Delisle, State Director

Maryland

Maryland SBDC

UNIVERSITY OF MARYLAND
7100 Baltimore Avenue, Suite 401
College Park, MD 20742
Phone: 301-403-8300
Fax: 301-403-8303
E-mail: rsprow@mdsbdc.umd.edu
Website: http://www.mdsbdc.umd.edu
Renee Sprow, State Director

Massachusetts

Massachusetts SBDC

UNIVERSITY OF MASSACHUSETTS
23 Tillson Farm Road
Amherst, MA 01003
Phone: 413-545-6301

Fax: 413-545-1273
E-mail: gparkin@msbdc.umass.edu
Website: http://www.www.msbdc.org
Georgianna Parkin, State Director

Michigan

Michigan SBTDC

**GRAND VALLEY STATE
UNIVERSITY**
510 West Fulton Avenue
Grand Rapids, MI 49504
Phone: 616-331-7480
Fax: 616-331-7485
E-mail: boesen@gvsu.edu
Website: http://www.misbtdc.org
Nancy Boese, State Director

Minnesota

Minnesota SBDC

**MINNESOTA SMALL BUSINESS
DEVELOPMENT CENTER**
1st National Bank Building
332 Minnesota Street, Suite E200
Saint Paul, MN 55101-1349
Phone: 651-259-7420
Fax: 651-296-5287
E-mail: Bruce.Strong@state.mn.us
Website: http://www.mnsbdc.com
Bruce H. Strong, State Director

Mississippi

Mississippi SBDC

UNIVERSITY OF MISSISSIPPI
122 Jeanette Phillips Drive
P.O. Box 1848
University, MS 38677
Phone: 662-915-5001
Fax: 662-915-5650
E-mail: wgurley@olemiss.edu
Website: http://www.mssbdc.org
Doug Gurley, Jr., State Director

Missouri

Missouri SBDC

UNIVERSITY OF MISSOURI
410 South 6th Street, ?200 Engineering
North
Columbia, MO 65211
Phone: 573-882-9206
Fax: 573-884-4297
E-mail: bouchardc@missouri.edu
Website: http://www.missouribusiness
.net
Chris Bouchard, State Director

Montana

Montana SBDC

DEPARTMENT OF COMMERCE
301 S Park Avenue, Room 114
Helena, MT 59601
Phone: 406-841-2746
Fax: 406-841-2728
E-mail: adesch@mt.gov
Website: http://www.sbdc.mt.gov
Ms. Ann Desch, State Director

Nebraska

Nebraska SBDC

**UNIVERSITY OF NEBRASKA -
OMAHA**
200 Mammel Hall, 67th & Pine Streets
Omaha, NE 68182
Phone: 402-554-2521
Fax: 402-554-3473
E-mail: rbernier@unomaha.edu
Website: http://nbdc.unomaha.edu
Robert Bernier, State Director

Nevada

Nevada SBDC

UNIVERSITY OF NEVADA - RENO
Reno College of Business, Room 411
Reno, NV 89557-0100
Phone: 775-784-1717
Fax: 775-784-4337
E-mail: males@unr.edu
Website: http://www.nsbdc.org
Sam Males, State Director

New Hampshire

New Hampshire SBDC

UNIVERSITY OF NEW HAMPSHIRE
10 Garrison Avenue
Durham, NH 03824-3593
Phone: 603-862-2200
Fax: 603-862-4876
E-mail: Mary.Collins@unh.edu
Website: http://www.nhsbdc.org
Mary Collins, State Director

New Jersey

New Jersey SBDC

RUTGERS UNIVERSITY
1 Washington Park, 3rd Floor
Newark, NJ 07102
Phone: 973-353-1927
Fax: 973-353-1110
E-mail: bhopper@njsbdc.com

Website: http://www.njsbdc.com
Brenda Hopper, State Director

New Mexico

New Mexico SBDC

SANTA FE COMMUNITY COLLEGE
6401 Richards Avenue
Santa Fe, NM 87508
Phone: 505-428-1362
Fax: 505-428-1469
E-mail: russell.wyrick@sfcc.edu
Website: http://www.nmsbdc.org
Russell Wyrick, State Director

New York

New York SBDC

STATE UNIVERSITY OF NEW YORK
22 Corporate Woods, 3rd Floor
Albany, NY 12246
Phone: 518-443-5398
Fax: 518-443-5275
E-mail: j.king@nyssbdc.org
Website: http://www.nyssbdc.org
Jim King, State Director

North Carolina

North Carolina SBDTC

UNIVERSITY OF NORTH CAROLINA
5 West Hargett Street, Suite 600
Raleigh, NC 27601
Phone: 919-715-7272
Fax: 919-715-7777
E-mail: sdaugherty@sbtdc.org
Website: http://www.sbtdc.org
Scott Daugherty, State Director

North Dakota

North Dakota SBDC

UNIVERSITY OF NORTH DAKOTA
1200 Memorial Highway, PO Box 5509
Bismarck, ND 58506
Phone: 701-328-5375
Fax: 701-250-4304
E-mail: dkmartin@ndsbdc.org
Website: http://www.ndsbdc.org
David Martin, State Director

Ohio

Ohio SBDC

OHIO DEPARTMENT OF DEVELOPMENT
77 South High Street, 28th Floor
Columbus, OH 43216

Phone: 614-466-2711
Fax: 614-466-1789
E-mail: ezra.escudero@development.ohio.gov
Website: http://www.ohiosbdc.org
Ezra Escudero, State Director

Oklahoma

Oklahoma SBDC

SOUTHEAST OKLAHOMA STATE UNIVERSITY
1405 N. 4th Avenue, PMB 2584
Durant, OK 74701
Phone: 580-745-2955
Fax: 580-745-7471
E-mail: wcarter@se.edu
Website: http://www.osbdc.org
Grady Pennington, State Director

Oregon

Oregon SBDC

LANE COMMUNITY COLLEGE
1445 Willamette Street, Suite 5
Eugene, OR 97401
Phone: 541-463-5250
Fax: 541-345-6006
E-mail: gregorym@lanecc.edu
Website: http://www.bizcenter.org
Mark Gregory, State Director

Pennsylvania

Pennsylvania SBDC

UNIVERSITY OF PENNSYLVANIA

The Wharton School
3819-33 Chestnut Street, Suite 325
Philadelphia, PA 19104
Phone: 215-898-1219
Fax: 215-573-2135
E-mail: cconroy@wharton.upenn.edu
Website: http://pasbdc.org
Christian Conroy, State Director

Puerto Rico

Puerto Rico SBDC

INTER-AMERICAN UNIVERSITY OF PUERTO RICO
416 Ponce de Leon Avenue, Union Plaza, Tenth Floor
Hato Rey, PR 00918
Phone: 787-763-6811
Fax: 787-763-6875
E-mail: cmarti@prsbdc.org
Website: http://www.prsbdc.org
Carmen Marti, Executive Director

Rhode Island

Rhode Island SBDC

UNIVERSITY OF RHODE ISLAND
75 Lower College Road, 2nd Floor
Kingston, RI 02881
Phone: 401-874-4576
E-mail: gsonnenfeld@uri.edu
Website: http://www.risbdc.org
Gerald Sonnenfeld, State Director

South Carolina

South Carolina SBDC

UNIVERSITY OF SOUTH CAROLINA

Moore School of Business
1014 Greene Street
Columbia, SC 29208
Phone: 803-777-0749
Fax: 803-777-6876
E-mail: michele.abraham@moore.sc.edu
Website: http://www.scsbdc.com
Michele Abraham, State Director

South Dakota

South Dakota SBDC

UNIVERSITY OF SOUTH DAKOTA
414 East Clark Street, Patterson Hall
Vermillion, SD 57069
Phone: 605-677-5103
Fax: 605-677-5427
E-mail: jeff.eckhoff@usd.edu
Website: http://www.usd.edu/sbdc
Jeff Eckhoff, State Director

Tennessee

Tennessee SBDC

MIDDLE TENNESSEE STATE UNIVERSITY
3050 Medical Center Parkway, Ste. 200
Nashville, TN 37129
Phone: 615-849-9999
Fax: 615-893-7089
E-mail: pgeho@tsbdc.org
Website: http://www.tsbdc.org
Patrick Geho, State Director

Texas

Texas-North SBDC

DALLAS COUNTY COMMUNITY COLLEGE
1402 Corinth Street
Dallas, TX 75215

Phone: 214-860-5832
Fax: 214-860-5813
E-mail: m.langford@dcccd.edu
Website: http://www.ntsbdc.org
Mark Langford, Region Director

Texas Gulf Coast SBDC

UNIVERSITY OF HOUSTON
2302 Fannin, Suite 200
Houston, TX 77002
Phone: 713-752-8444
Fax: 713-756-1500
E-mail: fyoung@uh.edu
Website: http://sbdcnetwork.uh.edu
Mike Young, Executive Director

Texas-NW SBDC

TEXAS TECH UNIVERSITY
2579 South Loop 289, Suite 114
Lubbock, TX 79423
Phone: 806-745-3973
Fax: 806-745-6207
E-mail: c.bean@nwtsbdc.org
Website: http://www.nwtsbdc.org
Craig Bean, Executive Director

Texas-South-West Texas Border Region SBDC

UNIVERSITY OF TEXAS - SAN ANTONIO
501 West Durango Boulevard
San Antonio, TX 78207-4415
Phone: 210-458-2480
Fax: 210-458-2425
E-mail: albert.salgado@utsa.edu
Website: https://www.txsbdc.org
Alberto Salgado, Region Director

Utah

Utah SBDC

SALT LAKE COMMUNITY COLLEGE
9750 South 300 West
Salt Lake City, UT 84070
Phone: 801-957-5384
Fax: 801-985-5300
E-mail: Sherm.Wilkinson@slcc.edu
Website: http://www.utahsbdc.org
Sherm Wilkinson, State Director

Vermont

Vermont SBDC

VERMONT TECHNICAL COLLEGE
PO Box 188, 1 Main Street
Randolph Center, VT 05061-0188

Phone: 802-728-9101
Fax: 802-728-3026
E-mail: lrossi@vtsbdc.org
Website: http://www.vtsbdc.org
Linda Rossi, State Director

Virgin Islands

Virgin Islands SBDC

UNIVERSITY OF THE VIRGIN ISLANDS
8000 Nisky Center, Suite 720
Saint Thomas, VI 00802
Phone: 340-776-3206
Fax: 340-775-3756
E-mail: ldottin@uvi.edu
Website: http://www.sbdcvi.org
Leonor Dottin, State Director

Virginia

Virginia SBDC

GEORGE MASON UNIVERSITY
4031 University Drive, Suite100
Fairfax, VA 22030
Phone: 703-277-7727
Fax: 703-352-8518
E-mail: jkeenan@gmu.edu
Website: http://www.virginiasbdc.org
Jody Keenan, Director

Washington

Washington SBDC

WASHINGTON STATE UNIVERSITY
1235 N. Post Street, Suite 201
Spokane, WA 99201
Phone: 509-358-7765
Fax: 509-358-7764
E-mail: duane.fladland@wsbdc.org
Website: http://www.wsbdc.org
Duane Fladland, State Director

West Virginia

West Virginia SBDC

WEST VIRGINIA DEVELOPMENT OFFICE
Capital Complex, Building 6, Room 652
1900 Kanawha Boulevard
Charleston, WV 25305
Phone: 304-957-2087
Fax: 304-558-0127
E-mail: Kristina.J.Oliver@wv.gov
Website: http://www.wvsbdc.org
Mr. Conley Salyor, State Director

Wisconsin

Wisconsin SBDC

UNIVERSITY OF WISCONSIN
432 North Lake Street, Room 423
Madison, WI 53706
Phone: 608-263-7794
Fax: 608-263-7830
E-mail: bon.wikenheiser@uwex.edu
Website: http://www.uwex.edu/sbdc
Bon Wikenheiser, State Director

Wyoming

Wyoming SBDC

UNIVERSITY OF WYOMING
1000 E University Ave., Dept. 3922
Laramie, WY 82071-3922
Phone: (307)766-3405
Fax: (307)766-3406
E-mail: jkline@uwyo.edu
Website: http://www.wyomingentre
preneur.biz
Jill Kline, Acting State Director

Service Corps of Retired Executives (Score) Offices

This section contains a listing of all SCORE offices organized alphabetically by state/U.S. territory, then by city, then by agency name.

Alabama

SCORE Office (Northeast Alabama)
1400 Commerce Blvd., Northeast
Anniston, AL 36207
(256)241-6111

SCORE Office (North Alabama)
1731 1st Ave. North, Ste. 200
Birmingham, AL 35203
(205)264-8425
Fax: (205)934-0538

SCORE Office (Baldwin County)
327 Fairhope Avenue
Fairhope, AL 36532
(251)928-6387

SCORE Office (Mobile)
451 Government Street
Mobile, AL 36652
(251)431-8614
Fax: (251)431-8646

SCORE Office (Alabama Capitol City)
600 S Court St.
Montgomery, AL 36104
(334)240-6868
Fax: (334)240-6869

SCORE Office (Tuscaloosa)
2200 University Blvd.
Tuscaloosa, AL 35402
(205)758-7588

Alaska

SCORE Office (Anchorage)
420 L St., Ste. 300
Anchorage, AK 99501
(907)271-4022
Fax: (907)271-4545

Arizona

SCORE Office (Greater Phoenix)
2828 N. Central Ave., Ste. 800
Phoenix, AZ 85004
(602)745-7250
Fax: (602)745-7210
E-mail: e-mail@SCORE-phoenix.org
Website: http://www.greaterphoenix
.score.org

SCORE Office (Northern Arizona)
1228 Willow Creek Rd., Ste. 2
Prescott, AZ 86301
(928)778-7438
Fax: (928)778-0812
Website: http://www.northernarizona
.score.org

SCORE Office (Southern Arizona)
1400 W Speedway Blvd.
Tucson, AZ 85745
(520)505-3636
Fax: (520)670-5011
Website: http://www.southernarizona
.score.org

Arkansas

SCORE Office (South Central)
201 N. Jackson Ave.
El Dorado, AR 71730-5803
(870)863-6113
Fax: (870)863-6115

SCORE Office (Northwest Arkansas)
614 E Emma St., Room M412
Springdale, AR 72764
(479)725-1809
Website: http://www.northwestarkansas
.score.org

SCORE Office (Little Rock)
2120 Riverfront Dr., Ste. 250

Little Rock, AR 72202-1747
(501)324-7379
Fax: (501)324-5199
Website: http://www.littlerock.score.org

SCORE Office (Southeast Arkansas)
P.O. Box 5069
Pine Bluff, AR 71611-5069
(870)535-0110
Fax: (870)535-1643

California

SCORE Office (Bakersfield)
P.O. Box 2426
Bakersfield, CA 93303
(661)861-9249
Fax: (661)395-4134
Website: http://www.bakersfield.score.org

SCORE Office (Santa Cruz County)
716 G Capitola Ave.
Capitola, CA 95010
(831)621-3735
Fax: (831)475-6530
Website: http://santacruzcounty.score.org

SCORE Office (Greater Chico Area)
1324 Mangrove St., Ste. 114
Chico, CA 95926
(530)342-8932
Fax: (530)342-8932
Website: http://www.greaterchicoarea
.score.org

SCORE Office (El Centro)
1850 W Main St, Ste. C
El Centro, CA 92243
(760)337-2692
Website: http://www.sandiego.score.org

SCORE Office (Central Valley)
801 R St., Ste. 201
Fresno, CA 93721
(559)487-5605
Fax: (559)487-5636
Website: http://www.centralvalley.
score.org

SCORE Office (Los Angeles)
330 N. Brand Blvd., Ste. 190
Glendale, CA 91203-2304
(818)552-3206
Fax: (818)552-3323
Website: http://www.greaterlosangeles
.score.org

SCORE Office (Modesto Merced)
1880 W Wardrobe Ave.
Merced, CA 95340
(209)725-2033
Fax: (209)577-2673

Website: http://www.modestomerced
.score.org

SCORE Office (Monterey Bay)
Monterey Chamber of Commerce
30 Ragsdale Dr.
Monterey, CA 93940
(831)648-5360
Website: http://www.montereybay
.score.org

SCORE Office (East Bay)
492 9th St., Ste. 350
Oakland, CA 94607
(510)273-6611
Fax: (510)273-6015
E-mail: webmaster@eastbayscore.org
Website: http://www.eastbay.score.org

SCORE Office (Ventura County)
400 E Esplanade Dr., Ste. 301
Oxnard, CA 93036
(805)204-6022
Fax: (805)650-1414
Website: http://www.ventura.score.org

SCORE Office (Coachella)
43100 Cook St., Ste. 104
Palm Desert, CA 92211
(760)773-6507
Fax: (760)773-6514
Website: http://www.coachellavalley
.score.org

SCORE Office (Antelope Valley)
1212 E Avenue, S Ste. A3
Palmdale, CA 93550
(661)947-7679
Website: http://www.antelopevalley
.score.org

SCORE Office (Inland Empire)
11801 Pierce St., 2nd Fl.
Riverside, CA 92505
(951)-652-4390
Fax: (951)929-8543
Website: http://www.inlandempire
.score.org

SCORE Office (Sacramento)
4990 Stockton Blvd.
Sacramento, CA 95820
(916)635-9085
Fax: (916)635-9089
Website: http://www.sacramento
.score.org

SCORE Office (San Diego)
550 West C. St., Ste. 550
San Diego, CA 92101-3540
(619)557-7272
Website: http://www.sandiego.score.org

SCORE Office (San Francisco)
455 Market St., 6th Fl.
San Francisco, CA 94105
(415)744-6827
Fax: (415)744-6750
E-mail: sfscore@sfscore.
Website: http://www.sanfrancisco
.score.org

SCORE Office (Silicon Valley)
234 E Gish Rd., Ste. 100
San Jose, CA 95112
(408)453-6237
Fax: (408)494-0214
E-mail: info@svscore.org
Website: http://www.siliconvalley
.score.org

SCORE Office (San Luis Obispo)
711 Tank Farm Rd., Ste. 210
San Luis Obispo, CA 93401
(805)547-0779
Website: http://www.sanluisobispo
.score.org

SCORE Office (Orange County)
200 W Santa Anna Blvd., Ste. 700
Santa Ana, CA 92701
(714)550-7369
Fax: (714)550-0191
Website: http://www.orangecounty
.score.org

SCORE Office (Santa Barbara)
924 Anacapa St.
Santa Barbara, CA 93101
(805)563-0084
Website: http://www.santabarbara
.score.org

SCORE Office (North Coast)
777 Sonoma Ave., Rm. 115E
Santa Rosa, CA 95404
(707)571-8342
Fax: (707)541-0331
Website: http://www.northcoast.score.org

SCORE Office (Tuolumne County)
222 S Shepherd St.
Sonora, CA 95370
(209)532-4316
Fax: (209)588-0673
Website: http://www.tuolumnecounty
.score.org

Colorado

SCORE Office (Colorado Springs)
3595 E Fountain Blvd., Ste. E-1
Colorado Springs, CO 80910
(719)636-3074

Fax: (719)635-1571
Website: http://www.coloradosprings.
score.org

SCORE Office (Denver)
US Custom's House, 4th Fl.
721 19th St.
Denver, CO 80202
(303)844-3985
Fax: (303)844-6490
Website: http://www.denver.score.org

SCORE Office (Tri-River)
1102 Grand Ave.
Glenwood Springs, CO 81601
(970)945-6589

SCORE Office (Grand Junction)
2591 B & 3/4 Rd.
Grand Junction, CO 81503
(970)243-5242

SCORE Office (Gunnison)
608 N. 11th
Gunnison, CO 81230
(303)641-4422

SCORE Office (Montrose)
1214 Peppertree Dr.
Montrose, CO 81401
(970)249-6080

SCORE Office (Pagosa Springs)
PO Box 4381
Pagosa Springs, CO 81157
(970)731-4890

SCORE Office (Rifle)
0854 W Battlement Pky., Apt. C106
Parachute, CO 81635
(970)285-9390

SCORE Office (Pueblo)
302 N. Santa Fe
Pueblo, CO 81003
(719)542-1704
Fax: (719)542-1624
Website: http://www.pueblo.score.org

SCORE Office (Ridgway)
143 Poplar Pl.
Ridgway, CO 81432

SCORE Office (Silverton)
PO Box 480
Silverton, CO 81433
(303)387-5430

SCORE Office (Minturn)
PO Box 2066
Vail, CO 81658
(970)476-1224

Connecticut

SCORE Office (Greater Bridgeport)
230 Park Ave.
Bridgeport, CT 06604
(203)450-9484
Fax: (203)576-4388

SCORE Office (Western Connecticut)
155 Deer Hill Ave.
Danbury, CT 06010
(203)794-1404
Website: http://www.westernconnecticut
.score.org

SCORE Office (Greater Hartford County)
330 Main St., 2nd Fl.
Hartford, CT 06106
(860)240-4700
Fax: (860)240-4659
Website: http://www.greaterhartford
.score.org

SCORE Office (Manchester)
20 Hartford Rd.
Manchester, CT 06040
(203)646-2223
Fax: (203)646-5871

SCORE Office (New Britain)
185 Main St., Ste. 431
New Britain, CT 06051
(203)827-4492
Fax: (203)827-4480

SCORE Office (New Haven)
60 Sargent Dr.
New Haven, CT 06511
(203)865-7645
Website: http://www.newhaven.score.org

SCORE Office (Fairfield County)
111 East Ave.
Norwalk, CT 06851
(203)847-7348
Fax: (203)849-9308
Website: http://www.fairfieldcounty.
score.org

SCORE Office (Southeastern Connecticut)
665 Boston Post Rd.
Old Saybrook, CT 06475
(860)388-9508
Website: http://www.southeastern
connecticut.score.org

SCORE Office (Northwest Connecticut)
333 Kennedy Dr.
Torrington, CT 06790
(560)482-6586

Website: http://www.northwest
connecticut.score.org

Delaware

SCORE Office (Dover)
Treadway Towers
PO Box 576
Dover, DE 19903
(302)678-0892
Fax: (302)678-0189

SCORE Office (Lewes)
PO Box 1
Lewes, DE 19958
(302)645-8073
Fax: (302)645-8412

SCORE Office (Milford)
204 NE Front St.
Milford, DE 19963
(302)422-3301

SCORE Office (Wilmington)
824 Market St., Ste. 610
Wilmington, DE 19801
(302)573-6652
Fax: (302)573-6092
Website: http://www.scoredelaware
.com

District of Columbia

**SCORE Office (George Mason
University)**
409 3rd St. SW, 4th Fl.
Washington, DC 20024
800-634-0245

SCORE Office (Washington DC)
1110 Vermont Ave. NW, 9th Fl.
Washington, DC 20043
(202)606-4000
Fax: (202)606-4225
E-mail: dcscore@hotmail.com
Website: http://www.scoredc.org

Florida

**SCORE Office (Desota County
Chamber of Commerce)**
16 South Velucia Ave.
Arcadia, FL 34266
(941)494-4033

SCORE Office (Suncoast/Pinellas)
Airport Business Ctr.
4707 - 140th Ave. N, No. 311
Clearwater, FL 33755
(813)532-6800
Fax: (813)532-6800

SCORE Office (DeLand)
336 N. Woodland Blvd.
DeLand, FL 32720
(904)734-4331
Fax: (904)734-4333

SCORE Office (South Palm Beach)
1050 S Federal Hwy., Ste. 132
Delray Beach, FL 33483
(561)278-7752
Fax: (561)278-0288

SCORE Office (Fort Lauderdale)
Federal Bldg., Ste. 123
299 E Broward Blvd.
Fort Lauderdale, FL 33301
(954)356-7263
Fax: (954)356-7145

SCORE Office (Southwest Florida)
The Renaissance
8695 College Pky., Ste. 345 & 346
Fort Myers, FL 33919
(941)489-2935
Fax: (941)489-1170

SCORE Office (Treasure Coast)
Professional Center, Ste. 2
3220 S US, No. 1
Fort Pierce, FL 34982
(561)489-0548

SCORE Office (Gainesville)
101 SE 2nd Pl., Ste. 104
Gainesville, FL 32601
(904)375-8278

SCORE Office (Hialeah Dade Chamber)
59 W 5th St.
Hialeah, FL 33010
(305)887-1515
Fax: (305)887-2453

SCORE Office (Daytona Beach)
921 Nova Rd., Ste. A
Holly Hills, FL 32117
(904)255-6889
Fax: (904)255-0229
E-mail: score87@dbeach.com

SCORE Office (South Broward)
3475 Sheridian St., Ste. 203
Hollywood, FL 33021
(305)966-8415

SCORE Office (Citrus County)
5 Poplar Ct.
Homosassa, FL 34446
(352)382-1037

SCORE Office (Jacksonville)
7825 Baymeadows Way, Ste. 100-B

Jacksonville, FL 32256
(904)443-1911
Fax: (904)443-1980
E-mail: scorejax@juno.com
Website: http://www.scorejax.org

SCORE Office (Jacksonville Satellite)
3 Independent Dr.
Jacksonville, FL 32256
(904)366-6600
Fax: (904)632-0617

SCORE Office (Central Florida)
5410 S Florida Ave., No. 3
Lakeland, FL 33801
(941)687-5783
Fax: (941)687-6225

SCORE Office (Lakeland)
100 Lake Morton Dr.
Lakeland, FL 33801
(941)686-2168

SCORE Office (Saint Petersburg)
800 W Bay Dr., Ste. 505
Largo, FL 33712
(813)585-4571

SCORE Office (Leesburg)
9501 US Hwy. 441
Leesburg, FL 34788-8751
(352)365-3556
Fax: (352)365-3501

SCORE Office (Cocoa)
1600 Farno Rd., Unit 205
Melbourne, FL 32935
(407)254-2288

SCORE Office (Melbourne)
Melbourne Professional Complex
1600 Sarno, Ste. 205
Melbourne, FL 32935
(407)254-2288
Fax: (407)245-2288

SCORE Office (Merritt Island)
1600 Sarno Rd., Ste. 205
Melbourne, FL 32935
(407)254-2288
Fax: (407)254-2288

SCORE Office (Space Coast)
Melbourn Professional Complex
1600 Sarno, Ste. 205
Melbourne, FL 32935
(407)254-2288
Fax: (407)254-2288

SCORE Office (Dade)
49 NW 5th St.
Miami, FL 33128

(305)371-6889
Fax: (305)374-1882
E-mail: score@netrox.net
Website: http://www.netrox.net/~score

SCORE Office (Naples of Collier)
International College
2654 Tamiami Trl. E
Naples, FL 34112
(941)417-1280
Fax: (941)417-1281
E-mail: score@naples.net
Website: http://www.naples.net/clubs/
score/index.htm

SCORE Office (Pasco County)
6014 US Hwy. 19, Ste. 302
New Port Richey, FL 34652
(813)842-4638

SCORE Office (Southeast Volusia)
115 Canal St.
New Smyrna Beach, FL 32168
(904)428-2449
Fax: (904)423-3512

SCORE Office (Ocala)
110 E Silver Springs Blvd.
Ocala, FL 34470
(352)629-5959

Clay County SCORE Office
Clay County Chamber of Commerce
1734 Kingsdey Ave.
PO Box 1441
Orange Park, FL 32073
(904)264-2651
Fax: (904)269-0363

SCORE Office (Orlando)
80 N. Hughey Ave.
Rm. 445 Federal Bldg.
Orlando, FL 32801
(407)648-6476
Fax: (407)648-6425

SCORE Office (Emerald Coast)
19 W Garden St., No. 325
Pensacola, FL 32501
(904)444-2060
Fax: (904)444-2070

SCORE Office (Charlotte County)
201 W Marion Ave., Ste. 211
Punta Gorda, FL 33950
(941)575-1818
E-mail: score@gls3c.com
Website: http://www.charlotte-florida.
com/business/scorepg01.htm

SCORE Office (Saint Augustine)
1 Riberia St.

Saint Augustine, FL 32084
(904)829-5681
Fax: (904)829-6477

SCORE Office (Bradenton)
2801 Fruitville, Ste. 280
Sarasota, FL 34237
(813)955-1029

SCORE Office (Manasota)
2801 Fruitville Rd., Ste. 280
Sarasota, FL 34237
(941)955-1029
Fax: (941)955-5581
E-mail: score116@gte.net
Website: http://www.score-suncoast.org

SCORE Office (Tallahassee)
200 W Park Ave.
Tallahassee, FL 32302
(850)487-2665

SCORE Office (Hillsborough)
4732 Dale Mabry Hwy. N, Ste. 400
Tampa, FL 33614-6509
(813)870-0125

SCORE Office (Lake Sumter)
122 E Main St.
Tavares, FL 32778-3810
(352)365-3556

SCORE Office (Titusville)
2000 S Washington Ave.
Titusville, FL 32780
(407)267-3036
Fax: (407)264-0127

SCORE Office (Venice)
257 N. Tamiami Trl.
Venice, FL 34285
(941)488-2236
Fax: (941)484-5903

SCORE Office (Palm Beach)
500 Australian Ave. S, Ste. 100
West Palm Beach, FL 33401
(561)833-1672
Fax: (561)833-1712

SCORE Office (Wildwood)
103 N. Webster St.
Wildwood, FL 34785

Georgia

SCORE Office (Atlanta)
Harris Tower, Suite 1900
233 Peachtree Rd., NE
Atlanta, GA 30309
(404)347-2442
Fax: (404)347-1227

SCORE Office (Augusta)
3126 Oxford Rd.
Augusta, GA 30909
(706)869-9100

SCORE Office (Columbus)
School Bldg.
PO Box 40
Columbus, GA 31901
(706)327-3654

SCORE Office (Dalton-Whitfield)
305 S Thorton Ave.
Dalton, GA 30720
(706)279-3383

SCORE Office (Gainesville)
PO Box 374
Gainesville, GA 30503
(770)532-6206
Fax: (770)535-8419

SCORE Office (Macon)
711 Grand Bldg.
Macon, GA 31201
(912)751-6160

SCORE Office (Brunswick)
4 Glen Ave.
Saint Simons Island, GA 31520
(912)265-0620
Fax: (912)265-0629

SCORE Office (Savannah)
111 E Liberty St., Ste. 103
Savannah, GA 31401
(912)652-4335
Fax: (912)652-4184
E-mail: info@scoresav.org
Website: http://www.coastalempire.com/
score/index.htm

Guam

SCORE Office (Guam)
Pacific News Bldg., Rm. 103
238 Archbishop Flores St.
Agana, GU 96910-5100
(671)472-7308

Hawaii

SCORE Office (Hawaii, Inc.)
1111 Bishop St., Ste. 204
PO Box 50207
Honolulu, HI 96813
(808)522-8132
Fax: (808)522-8135
E-mail: hnlscore@juno.com

SCORE Office (Kahului)
250 Alamaha, Unit N16A

Kahului, HI 96732
(808)871-7711

SCORE Office (Maui, Inc.)
590 E Lipoa Pkwy., Ste. 227
Kihei, HI 96753
(808)875-2380

Idaho

SCORE Office (Treasure Valley)
1020 Main St., No. 290
Boise, ID 83702
(208)334-1696
Fax: (208)334-9353

SCORE Office (Eastern Idaho)
2300 N. Yellowstone, Ste. 119
Idaho Falls, ID 83401
(208)523-1022
Fax: (208)528-7127

Illinois

SCORE Office (Fox Valley)
40 W Downer Pl.
PO Box 277
Aurora, IL 60506
(630)897-9214
Fax: (630)897-7002

SCORE Office (Greater Belvidere)
419 S State St.
Belvidere, IL 61008
(815)544-4357
Fax: (815)547-7654

SCORE Office (Bensenville)
1050 Busse Hwy. Suite 100
Bensenville, IL 60106
(708)350-2944
Fax: (708)350-2979

SCORE Office (Central Illinois)
402 N. Hershey Rd.
Bloomington, IL 61704
(309)644-0549
Fax: (309)663-8270
E-mail: webmaster@central-illinois-score.org
Website: http://www.central-illinois-score.org

SCORE Office (Southern Illinois)
150 E Pleasant Hill Rd.
Box 1
Carbondale, IL 62901
(618)453-6654
Fax: (618)453-5040

SCORE Chicago
500 W Madison St., Ste. 1150

Chicago, IL 60661
(312)353-7724
Fax: (312)886-4879
E-mail: info@scorechicago.org
Website: http://scorechicago.org

SCORE Office (Danville)
28 W N. Street
Danville, IL 61832
(217)442-7232
Fax: (217)442-6228

SCORE Office (Decatur)
Milliken University
1184 W Main St.
Decatur, IL 62522
(217)424-6297
Fax: (217)424-3993
E-mail: charding@mail.millikin.edu
Website: http://www.millikin.edu/academics/Tabor/score.html

SCORE Office (Downers Grove)
925 Curtis
Downers Grove, IL 60515
(708)968-4050
Fax: (708)968-8368

SCORE Office (Elgin)
24 E Chicago, 3rd Fl.
PO Box 648
Elgin, IL 60120
(847)741-5660
Fax: (847)741-5677

SCORE Office (Freeport Area)
26 S Galena Ave.
Freeport, IL 61032
(815)233-1350
Fax: (815)235-4038

SCORE Office (Galesburg)
292 E Simmons St.
PO Box 749
Galesburg, IL 61401
(309)343-1194
Fax: (309)343-1195

SCORE Office (Glen Ellyn)
500 Pennsylvania
Glen Ellyn, IL 60137
(708)469-0907
Fax: (708)469-0426

SCORE Office (Greater Alton)
Alden Hall
5800 Godfrey Rd.
Godfrey, IL 62035-2466
(618)467-2280
Fax: (618)466-8289
Website: http://www.altonweb.com/score

SCORE Office (Grayslake)
19351 W Washington St.
Grayslake, IL 60030
(708)223-3633
Fax: (708)223-9371

SCORE Office (Harrisburg)
303 S Commercial
Harrisburg, IL 62946-1528
(618)252-8528
Fax: (618)252-0210

SCORE Office (Joliet)
100 N. Chicago
Joliet, IL 60432
(815)727-5371
Fax: (815)727-5374

SCORE Office (Kankakee)
101 S Schuyler Ave.
Kankakee, IL 60901
(815)933-0376
Fax: (815)933-0380

SCORE Office (Macomb)
216 Seal Hall, Rm. 214
Macomb, IL 61455
(309)298-1128
Fax: (309)298-2520

SCORE Office (Matteson)
210 Lincoln Mall
Matteson, IL 60443
(708)709-3750
Fax: (708)503-9322

SCORE Office (Mattoon)
1701 Wabash Ave.
Mattoon, IL 61938
(217)235-5661
Fax: (217)234-6544

SCORE Office (Quad Cities)
622 19th St.
Moline, IL 61265
(309)797-0082
Fax: (309)757-5435
E-mail: score@qconline.com
Website: http://www.qconline.com/business/score

SCORE Office (Naperville)
131 W Jefferson Ave.
Naperville, IL 60540
(708)355-4141
Fax: (708)355-8355

SCORE Office (Northbrook)
2002 Walters Ave.
Northbrook, IL 60062
(847)498-5555
Fax: (847)498-5510

SCORE Office (Palos Hills)
10900 S 88th Ave.
Palos Hills, IL 60465
(847)974-5468
Fax: (847)974-0078

SCORE Office (Peoria)
124 SW Adams, Ste. 300
Peoria, IL 61602
(309)676-0755
Fax: (309)676-7534

SCORE Office (Prospect Heights)
1375 Wolf Rd.
Prospect Heights, IL 60070
(847)537-8660
Fax: (847)537-7138

SCORE Office (Quincy Tri-State)
300 Civic Center Plz., Ste. 245
Quincy, IL 62301
(217)222-8093
Fax: (217)222-3033

SCORE Office (River Grove)
2000 5th Ave.
River Grove, IL 60171
(708)456-0300
Fax: (708)583-3121

SCORE Office (Northern Illinois)
515 N. Court St.
Rockford, IL 61103
(815)962-0122
Fax: (815)962-0122

SCORE Office (Saint Charles)
103 N. 1st Ave.
Saint Charles, IL 60174-1982
(847)584-8384
Fax: (847)584-6065

SCORE Office (Springfield)
511 W Capitol Ave., Ste. 302
Springfield, IL 62704
(217)492-4416
Fax: (217)492-4867

SCORE Office (Sycamore)
112 Somunak St.
Sycamore, IL 60178
(815)895-3456
Fax: (815)895-0125

SCORE Office (University)
Hwy. 50 & Stuenkel Rd. Ste. C3305
University Park, IL 60466
(708)534-5000
Fax: (708)534-8457

Indiana

SCORE Office (Anderson)
205 W 11th St.

Anderson, IN 46015
(317)642-0264

SCORE Office (Bloomington)
Star Center
216 W Allen
Bloomington, IN 47403
(812)335-7334
E-mail: wtfische@indiana.edu
Website: http://www.brainfreezemedia.
com/score527

SCORE Office (South East Indiana)
500 Franklin St.
Box 29
Columbus, IN 47201
(812)379-4457

SCORE Office (Corydon)
310 N. Elm St.
Corydon, IN 47112
(812)738-2137
Fax: (812)738-6438

SCORE Office (Crown Point)
Old Courthouse Sq. Ste. 206
PO Box 43
Crown Point, IN 46307
(219)663-1800

SCORE Office (Elkhart)
418 S Main St.
Elkhart, IN 46515
(219)293-1531
Fax: (219)294-1859

SCORE Office (Evansville)
1100 W Lloyd Expy., Ste. 105
Evansville, IN 47708
(812)426-6144

SCORE Office (Fort Wayne)
1300 S Harrison St.
Fort Wayne, IN 46802
(219)422-2601
Fax: (219)422-2601

SCORE Office (Gary)
973 W 6th Ave., Rm. 326
Gary, IN 46402
(219)882-3918

SCORE Office (Hammond)
7034 Indianapolis Blvd.
Hammond, IN 46324
(219)931-1000
Fax: (219)845-9548

SCORE Office (Indianapolis)
429 N. Pennsylvania St., Ste. 100
Indianapolis, IN 46204-1873
(317)226-7264

Fax: (317)226-7259
E-mail: inscore@indy.net
Website: http://www.score-indianapolis.org

SCORE Office (Jasper)
PO Box 307
Jasper, IN 47547-0307
(812)482-6866

**SCORE Office (Kokomo/Howard
Counties)**
106 N. Washington St.
Kokomo, IN 46901
(765)457-5301
Fax: (765)452-4564

SCORE Office (Logansport)
300 E Broadway, Ste. 103
Logansport, IN 46947
(219)753-6388

SCORE Office (Madison)
301 E Main St.
Madison, IN 47250
(812)265-3135
Fax: (812)265-2923

SCORE Office (Marengo)
Rt. 1 Box 224D
Marengo, IN 47140
Fax: (812)365-2793

SCORE Office (Marion/Grant Counties)
215 S Adams
Marion, IN 46952
(765)664-5107

SCORE Office (Merrillville)
255 W 80th Pl.
Merrillville, IN 46410
(219)769-8180
Fax: (219)736-6223

SCORE Office (Michigan City)
200 E Michigan Blvd.
Michigan City, IN 46360
(219)874-6221
Fax: (219)873-1204

SCORE Office (South Central Indiana)
4100 Charleston Rd.
New Albany, IN 47150-9538
(812)945-0066

SCORE Office (Rensselaer)
104 W Washington
Rensselaer, IN 47978

SCORE Office (Salem)
210 N. Main St.
Salem, IN 47167
(812)883-4303
Fax: (812)883-1467

SCORE Office (South Bend)
300 N. Michigan St.
South Bend, IN 46601
(219)282-4350
E-mail: chair@southbend-score.org
Website: http://www.southbend-score.org

SCORE Office (Valparaiso)
150 Lincolnway
Valparaiso, IN 46383
(219)462-1105
Fax: (219)469-5710

SCORE Office (Vincennes)
27 N. 3rd
PO Box 553
Vincennes, IN 47591
(812)882-6440
Fax: (812)882-6441

SCORE Office (Wabash)
PO Box 371
Wabash, IN 46992
(219)563-1168
Fax: (219)563-6920

Iowa

SCORE Office (Burlington)
Federal Bldg.
300 N. Main St.
Burlington, IA 52601
(319)752-2967

SCORE Office (Cedar Rapids)
2750 1st Ave. NE, Ste 350
Cedar Rapids, IA 52401-1806
(319)362-6405
Fax: (319)362-7861
E:mail: score@scorecr.org
Website: http://www.scorecr.org

SCORE Office (Illowa)
333 4th Ave. S
Clinton, IA 52732
(319)242-5702

SCORE Office (Council Bluffs)
7 N. 6th St.
Council Bluffs, IA 51502
(712)325-1000

SCORE Office (Northeast Iowa)
3404 285th St.
Cresco, IA 52136
(319)547-3377

SCORE Office (Des Moines)
Federal Bldg., Rm. 749
210 Walnut St.
Des Moines, IA 50309-2186
(515)284-4760

SCORE Office (Fort Dodge)
Federal Bldg., Rm. 436
205 S 8th St.
Fort Dodge, IA 50501
(515)955-2622

SCORE Office (Independence)
110 1st. St. E
Independence, IA 50644
(319)334-7178
Fax: (319)334-7179

SCORE Office (Iowa City)
210 Federal Bldg.
PO Box 1853
Iowa City, IA 52240-1853
(319)338-1662

SCORE Office (Keokuk)
401 Main St.
Pierce Bldg., No. 1
Keokuk, IA 52632
(319)524-5055

SCORE Office (Central Iowa)
Fisher Community College
709 S Center
Marshalltown, IA 50158
(515)753-6645

SCORE Office (River City)
15 West State St.
Mason City, IA 50401
(515)423-5724

SCORE Office (South Central)
SBDC, Indian Hills Community
College
525 Grandview Ave.
Ottumwa, IA 52501
(515)683-5127
Fax: (515)683-5263

SCORE Office (Dubuque)
10250 Sundown Rd.
Peosta, IA 52068
(319)556-5110

SCORE Office (Southwest Iowa)
614 W Sheridan
Shenandoah, IA 51601
(712)246-3260

SCORE Office (Sioux City)
Federal Bldg.
320 6th St.
Sioux City, IA 51101
(712)277-2324
Fax: (712)277-2325

SCORE Office (Iowa Lakes)
122 W 5th St.

Spencer, IA 51301
(712)262-3059

SCORE Office (Vista)
119 W 6th St.
Storm Lake, IA 50588
(712)732-3780

SCORE Office (Waterloo)
215 E 4th
Waterloo, IA 50703
(319)233-8431

Kansas

SCORE Office (Southwest Kansas)
501 W Spruce
Dodge City, KS 67801
(316)227-3119

SCORE Office (Emporia)
811 Homewood
Emporia, KS 66801
(316)342-1600

SCORE Office (Golden Belt)
1307 Williams
Great Bend, KS 67530
(316)792-2401

SCORE Office (Hays)
PO Box 400
Hays, KS 67601
(913)625-6595

SCORE Office (Hutchinson)
1 E 9th St.
Hutchinson, KS 67501
(316)665-8468
Fax: (316)665-7619

SCORE Office (Southeast Kansas)
404 Westminster Pl.
PO Box 886
Independence, KS 67301
(316)331-4741

SCORE Office (McPherson)
306 N. Main
PO Box 616
McPherson, KS 67460
(316)241-3303

SCORE Office (Salina)
120 Ash St.
Salina, KS 67401
(785)243-4290
Fax: (785)243-1833

SCORE Office (Topeka)
1700 College
Topeka, KS 66621
(785)231-1010

SCORE Office (Wichita)
100 E English, Ste. 510
Wichita, KS 67202
(316)269-6273
Fax: (316)269-6499

SCORE Office (Ark Valley)
205 E 9th St.
Winfield, KS 67156
(316)221-1617

Kentucky

SCORE Office (Ashland)
PO Box 830
Ashland, KY 41105
(606)329-8011
Fax: (606)325-4607

SCORE Office (Bowling Green)
812 State St.
PO Box 51
Bowling Green, KY 42101
(502)781-3200
Fax: (502)843-0458

SCORE Office (Tri-Lakes)
508 Barbee Way
Danville, KY 40422-1548
(606)231-9902

SCORE Office (Glasgow)
301 W Main St.
Glasgow, KY 42141
(502)651-3161
Fax: (502)651-3122

SCORE Office (Hazard)
B & I Technical Center
100 Airport Gardens Rd.
Hazard, KY 41701
(606)439-5856
Fax: (606)439-1808

SCORE Office (Lexington)
410 W Vine St., Ste. 290, Civic C
Lexington, KY 40507
(606)231-9902
Fax: (606)253-3190
E-mail: scorelex@uky.campus.mci.net

SCORE Office (Louisville)
188 Federal Office Bldg.
600 Dr. Martin L. King Jr. Pl.
Louisville, KY 40202
(502)582-5976

SCORE Office (Madisonville)
257 N. Main
Madisonville, KY 42431
(502)825-1399
Fax: (502)825-1396

SCORE Office (Paducah)
Federal Office Bldg.
501 Broadway, Rm. B-36
Paducah, KY 42001
(502)442-5685

Louisiana

SCORE Office (Central Louisiana)
802 3rd St.
Alexandria, LA 71309
(318)442-6671

SCORE Office (Baton Rouge)
564 Laurel St.
PO Box 3217
Baton Rouge, LA 70801
(504)381-7130
Fax: (504)336-4306

SCORE Office (North Shore)
2 W Thomas
Hammond, LA 70401
(504)345-4457
Fax: (504)345-4749

SCORE Office (Lafayette)
804 St. Mary Blvd.
Lafayette, LA 70505-1307
(318)233-2705
Fax: (318)234-8671
E-mail: score302@aol.com

SCORE Office (Lake Charles)
120 W Pujo St.
Lake Charles, LA 70601
(318)433-3632

SCORE Office (New Orleans)
365 Canal St., Ste. 3100
New Orleans, LA 70130
(504)589-2356
Fax: (504)589-2339

SCORE Office (Shreveport)
400 Edwards St.
Shreveport, LA 71101
(318)677-2536
Fax: (318)677-2541

Maine

SCORE Office (Augusta)
40 Western Ave.
Augusta, ME 04330
(207)622-8509

SCORE Office (Bangor)
Peabody Hall, Rm. 229
One College Cir.
Bangor, ME 04401
(207)941-9707

SCORE Office (Central & Northern Arroostock)
111 High St.
Caribou, ME 04736
(207)492-8010
Fax: (207)492-8010

SCORE Office (Penquis)
South St.
Dover Foxcroft, ME 04426
(207)564-7021

SCORE Office (Maine Coastal)
Mill Mall
Box 1105
Ellsworth, ME 04605-1105
(207)667-5800
E-mail: score@arcadia.net

SCORE Office (Lewiston-Auburn)
BIC of Maine-Bates Mill Complex
35 Canal St.
Lewiston, ME 04240-7764
(207)782-3708
Fax: (207)783-7745

SCORE Office (Portland)
66 Pearl St., Rm. 210
Portland, ME 04101
(207)772-1147
Fax: (207)772-5581
E-mail: Score53@score.maine.org
Website: http://www.score.maine.org/
chapter53

SCORE Office (Western Mountains)
255 River St.
PO Box 252
Rumford, ME 04257-0252
(207)369-9976

SCORE Office (Oxford Hills)
166 Main St.
South Paris, ME 04281
(207)743-0499

Maryland

SCORE Office (Southern Maryland)
2525 Riva Rd., Ste. 110
Annapolis, MD 21401
(410)266-9553
Fax: (410)573-0981
E-mail: score390@aol.com
Website: http://members.aol.com/
score390/index.htm

SCORE Office (Baltimore)
The City Crescent Bldg., 6th Fl.
10 S Howard St.
Baltimore, MD 21201
(410)962-2233
Fax: (410)962-1805

SCORE Office (Bel Air)
108 S Bond St.
Bel Air, MD 21014
(410)838-2020
Fax: (410)893-4715

SCORE Office (Bethesda)
7910 Woodmont Ave., Ste. 1204
Bethesda, MD 20814
(301)652-4900
Fax: (301)657-1973

SCORE Office (Bowie)
6670 Race Track Rd.
Bowie, MD 20715
(301)262-0920
Fax: (301)262-0921

SCORE Office (Dorchester County)
203 Sunburst Hwy.
Cambridge, MD 21613
(410)228-3575

SCORE Office (Upper Shore)
210 Marlboro Ave.
Easton, MD 21601
(410)822-4606
Fax: (410)822-7922

SCORE Office (Frederick County)
43A S Market St.
Frederick, MD 21701
(301)662-8723
Fax: (301)846-4427

SCORE Office (Gaithersburg)
9 Park Ave.
Gaithersburg, MD 20877
(301)840-1400
Fax: (301)963-3918

SCORE Office (Glen Burnie)
103 Crain Hwy. SE
Glen Burnie, MD 21061
(410)766-8282
Fax: (410)766-9722

SCORE Office (Hagerstown)
111 W Washington St.
Hagerstown, MD 21740
(301)739-2015
Fax: (301)739-1278

SCORE Office (Laurel)
7901 Sandy Spring Rd. Ste. 501
Laurel, MD 20707
(301)725-4000
Fax: (301)725-0776

SCORE Office (Salisbury)
300 E Main St.
Salisbury, MD 21801

(410)749-0185
Fax: (410)860-9925

Massachusetts

SCORE Office (NE Massachusetts)
100 Cummings Ctr., Ste. 101 K
Beverly, MA 01923
(978)922-9441
Website: http://www1.shore.net/~score

SCORE Office (Boston)
10 Causeway St., Rm. 265
Boston, MA 02222-1093
(617)565-5591
Fax: (617)565-5598
E-mail: boston-score-20@worldnet
.att.net
Website: http://www.scoreboston.org

SCORE office (Bristol/Plymouth County)
53 N. 6th St., Federal Bldg.
Bristol, MA 02740
(508)994-5093

SCORE Office (SE Massachusetts)
60 School St.
Brockton, MA 02401
(508)587-2673
Fax: (508)587-1340
Website: http://www.metrosouthchamber
.com/score.html

SCORE Office (North Adams)
820 N. State Rd.
Cheshire, MA 01225
(413)743-5100

SCORE Office (Clinton Satellite)
1 Green St.
Clinton, MA 01510
Fax: (508)368-7689

SCORE Office (Greenfield)
PO Box 898
Greenfield, MA 01302
(413)773-5463
Fax: (413)773-7008

SCORE Office (Haverhill)
87 Winter St.
Haverhill, MA 01830
(508)373-5663
Fax: (508)373-8060

SCORE Office (Hudson Satellite)
PO Box 578
Hudson, MA 01749
(508)568-0360
Fax: (508)568-0360

SCORE Office (Cape Cod)
Independence Pk., Ste. 5B
270 Communications Way
Hyannis, MA 02601
(508)775-4884
Fax: (508)790-2540

SCORE Office (Lawrence)
264 Essex St.
Lawrence, MA 01840
(508)686-0900
Fax: (508)794-9953

SCORE Office (Leominster Satellite)
110 Erdman Way
Leominster, MA 01453
(508)840-4300
Fax: (508)840-4896

SCORE Office (Bristol/Plymouth Counties)
53 N. 6th St., Federal Bldg.
New Bedford, MA 02740
(508)994-5093

SCORE Office (Newburyport)
29 State St.
Newburyport, MA 01950
(617)462-6680

SCORE Office (Pittsfield)
66 West St.
Pittsfield, MA 01201
(413)499-2485

SCORE Office (Haverhill-Salem)
32 Derby Sq.
Salem, MA 01970
(508)745-0330
Fax: (508)745-3855

SCORE Office (Springfield)
1350 Main St.
Federal Bldg.
Springfield, MA 01103
(413)785-0314

SCORE Office (Carver)
12 Taunton Green, Ste. 201
Taunton, MA 02780
(508)824-4068
Fax: (508)824-4069

SCORE Office (Worcester)
33 Waldo St.
Worcester, MA 01608
(508)753-2929
Fax: (508)754-8560

Michigan

SCORE Office (Allegan)
PO Box 338

Allegan, MI 49010
(616)673-2479

SCORE Office (Ann Arbor)
425 S Main St., Ste. 103
Ann Arbor, MI 48104
(313)665-4433

SCORE Office (Battle Creek)
34 W Jackson Ste. 4A
Battle Creek, MI 49017-3505
(616)962-4076
Fax: (616)962-6309

SCORE Office (Cadillac)
222 Lake St.
Cadillac, MI 49601
(616)775-9776
Fax: (616)768-4255

SCORE Office (Detroit)
477 Michigan Ave., Rm. 515
Detroit, MI 48226
(313)226-7947
Fax: (313)226-3448

SCORE Office (Flint)
708 Root Rd., Rm. 308
Flint, MI 48503
(810)233-6846

SCORE Office (Grand Rapids)
111 Pearl St. NW
Grand Rapids, MI 49503-2831
(616)771-0305
Fax: (616)771-0328
E-mail: scoreone@iserv.net
Website: http://www.iserv.net/~scoreone

SCORE Office (Holland)
480 State St.
Holland, MI 49423
(616)396-9472

SCORE Office (Jackson)
209 East Washington
PO Box 80
Jackson, MI 49204
(517)782-8221
Fax: (517)782-0061

SCORE Office (Kalamazoo)
345 W Michigan Ave.
Kalamazoo, MI 49007
(616)381-5382
Fax: (616)384-0096
E-mail: score@nucleus.net

SCORE Office (Lansing)
117 E Allegan
PO Box 14030
Lansing, MI 48901

(517)487-6340
Fax: (517)484-6910

SCORE Office (Livonia)
15401 Farmington Rd.
Livonia, MI 48154
(313)427-2122
Fax: (313)427-6055

SCORE Office (Madison Heights)
26345 John R
Madison Heights, MI 48071
(810)542-5010
Fax: (810)542-6821

SCORE Office (Monroe)
111 E 1st
Monroe, MI 48161
(313)242-3366
Fax: (313)242-7253

SCORE Office (Mount Clemens)
58 S/B Gratiot
Mount Clemens, MI 48043
(810)463-1528
Fax: (810)463-6541

SCORE Office (Muskegon)
PO Box 1087
230 Terrace Plz.
Muskegon, MI 49443
(616)722-3751
Fax: (616)728-7251

SCORE Office (Petoskey)
401 E Mitchell St.
Petoskey, MI 49770
(616)347-4150

SCORE Office (Pontiac)
Executive Office Bldg.
1200 N. Telegraph Rd.
Pontiac, MI 48341
(810)975-9555

SCORE Office (Pontiac)
PO Box 430025
Pontiac, MI 48343
(810)335-9600

SCORE Office (Port Huron)
920 Pinegrove Ave.
Port Huron, MI 48060
(810)985-7101

SCORE Office (Rochester)
71 Walnut Ste. 110
Rochester, MI 48307
(810)651-6700
Fax: (810)651-5270

SCORE Office (Saginaw)
901 S Washington Ave.

Saginaw, MI 48601
(517)752-7161
Fax: (517)752-9055

SCORE Office (Upper Peninsula)
2581 I-75 Business Spur
Sault Ste. Marie, MI 49783
(906)632-3301

SCORE Office (Southfield)
21000 W 10 Mile Rd.
Southfield, MI 48075
(810)204-3050
Fax: (810)204-3099

SCORE Office (Traverse City)
202 E Grandview Pkwy.
PO Box 387
Traverse City, MI 49685
(616)947-5075
Fax: (616)946-2565

SCORE Office (Warren)
30500 Van Dyke, Ste. 118
Warren, MI 48093
(810)751-3939

Minnesota

SCORE Office (Aitkin)
Aitkin, MN 56431
(218)741-3906

SCORE Office (Albert Lea)
202 N. Broadway Ave.
Albert Lea, MN 56007
(507)373-7487

SCORE Office (Austin)
PO Box 864
Austin, MN 55912
(507)437-4561
Fax: (507)437-4869

SCORE Office (South Metro)
Ames Business Ctr.
2500 W County Rd., No. 42
Burnsville, MN 55337
(612)898-5645
Fax: (612)435-6972
E-mail: southmetro@scoreminn.org
Website: http://www.scoreminn.org/
southmetro

SCORE Office (Duluth)
1717 Minnesota Ave.
Duluth, MN 55802
(218)727-8286
Fax: (218)727-3113
E-mail: duluth@scoreminn.org
Website: http://www.scoreminn.org

SCORE Office (Fairmont)
PO Box 826
Fairmont, MN 56031
(507)235-5547
Fax: (507)235-8411

SCORE Office (Southwest Minnesota)
112 Riverfront St.
Box 999
Mankato, MN 56001
(507)345-4519
Fax: (507)345-4451
Website: http://www.scoreminn.org

SCORE Office (Minneapolis)
North Plaza Bldg., Ste. 51
5217 Wayzata Blvd.
Minneapolis, MN 55416
(612)591-0539
Fax: (612)544-0436
Website: http://www.scoreminn.org

SCORE Office (Owatonna)
PO Box 331
Owatonna, MN 55060
(507)451-7970
Fax: (507)451-7972

SCORE Office (Red Wing)
2000 W Main St., Ste. 324
Red Wing, MN 55066
(612)388-4079

SCORE Office (Southeastern Minnesota)
220 S Broadway, Ste. 100
Rochester, MN 55901
(507)288-1122
Fax: (507)282-8960
Website: http://www.scoreminn.org

SCORE Office (Brainerd)
Saint Cloud, MN 56301

SCORE Office (Central Area)
1527 Northway Dr.
Saint Cloud, MN 56301
(320)240-1332
Fax: (320)255-9050
Website: http://www.scoreminn.org

SCORE Office (Saint Paul)
350 St. Peter St., No. 295
Lowry Professional Bldg.
Saint Paul, MN 55102
(651)223-5010
Fax: (651)223-5048
Website: http://www.scoreminn.org

SCORE Office (Winona)
Box 870
Winona, MN 55987

(507)452-2272
Fax: (507)454-8814

SCORE Office (Worthington)
1121 3rd Ave.
Worthington, MN 56187
(507)372-2919
Fax: (507)372-2827

Mississippi

SCORE Office (Delta)
915 Washington Ave.
PO Box 933
Greenville, MS 38701
(601)378-3141

SCORE Office (Gulfcoast)
1 Government Plaza
2909 13th St., Ste. 203
Gulfport, MS 39501
(228)863-0054

SCORE Office (Jackson)
1st Jackson Center, Ste. 400
101 W Capitol St.
Jackson, MS 39201
(601)965-5533

SCORE Office (Meridian)
5220 16th Ave.
Meridian, MS 39305
(601)482-4412

Missouri

SCORE Office (Lake of the Ozark)
University Extension
113 Kansas St.
PO Box 1405
Camdenton, MO 65020
(573)346-2644
Fax: (573)346-2694
E-mail: score@cdoc.net
Website: http://sites.cdoc.net/score

Chamber of Commerce (Cape Girardeau)
PO Box 98
Cape Girardeau, MO 63702-0098
(314)335-3312

SCORE Office (Mid-Missouri)
1705 Halstead Ct.
Columbia, MO 65203
(573)874-1132

SCORE Office (Ozark-Gateway)
1486 Glassy Rd.
Cuba, MO 65453-1640
(573)885-4954

SCORE Office (Kansas City)
323 W 8th St., Ste. 104
Kansas City, MO 64105
(816)374-6675
Fax: (816)374-6692
E-mail: SCOREBIC@AOL.COM
Website: http://www.crn.org/score

SCORE Office (Sedalia)
Lucas Place
323 W 8th St., Ste.104
Kansas City, MO 64105
(816)374-6675

SCORE office (Tri-Lakes)
PO Box 1148
Kimberling, MO 65686
(417)739-3041

SCORE Office (Tri-Lakes)
HCRI Box 85
Lampe, MO 65681
(417)858-6798

SCORE Office (Mexico)
111 N. Washington St.
Mexico, MO 65265
(314)581-2765

SCORE Office (Southeast Missouri)
Rte. 1, Box 280
Neelyville, MO 63954
(573)989-3577

SCORE office (Poplar Bluff Area)
806 Emma St.
Poplar Bluff, MO 63901
(573)686-8892

SCORE Office (Saint Joseph)
3003 Frederick Ave.
Saint Joseph, MO 64506
(816)232-4461

SCORE Office (Saint Louis)
815 Olive St., Rm. 242
Saint Louis, MO 63101-1569
(314)539-6970
Fax: (314)539-3785
E-mail: info@stlscore.org
Website: http://www.stlscore.org

SCORE Office (Lewis & Clark)
425 Spencer Rd.
Saint Peters, MO 63376
(314)928-2900
Fax: (314)928-2900
E-mail: score01@mail.win.org

SCORE Office (Springfield)
620 S Glenstone, Ste. 110
Springfield, MO 65802-3200

(417)864-7670
Fax: (417)864-4108

SCORE office (Southeast Kansas)
1206 W First St.
Webb City, MO 64870
(417)673-3984

Montana

SCORE Office (Billings)
815 S 27th St.
Billings, MT 59101
(406)245-4111

SCORE Office (Bozeman)
1205 E Main St.
Bozeman, MT 59715
(406)586-5421

SCORE Office (Butte)
1000 George St.
Butte, MT 59701
(406)723-3177

SCORE Office (Great Falls)
710 First Ave. N
Great Falls, MT 59401
(406)761-4434
E-mail: scoregtf@in.tch.com

SCORE Office (Havre, Montana)
518 First St.
Havre, MT 59501
(406)265-4383

SCORE Office (Helena)
Federal Bldg.
301 S Park
Helena, MT 59626-0054
(406)441-1081

SCORE Office (Kalispell)
2 Main St.
Kalispell, MT 59901
(406)756-5271
Fax: (406)752-6665

SCORE Office (Missoula)
723 Ronan
Missoula, MT 59806
(406)327-8806
E-mail: score@safeshop.com
Website: http://missoula.bigsky.net/score

Nebraska

SCORE Office (Columbus)
Columbus, NE 68601
(402)564-2769

SCORE Office (Fremont)
92 W 5th St.

Fremont, NE 68025
(402)721-2641

SCORE Office (Hastings)
Hastings, NE 68901
(402)463-3447

SCORE Office (Lincoln)
8800 O St.
Lincoln, NE 68520
(402)437-2409

SCORE Office (Panhandle)
150549 CR 30
Minatare, NE 69356
(308)632-2133
Website: http://www.tandt.com/SCORE

SCORE Office (Norfolk)
3209 S 48th Ave.
Norfolk, NE 68106
(402)564-2769

SCORE Office (North Platte)
3301 W 2nd St.
North Platte, NE 69101
(308)532-4466

SCORE Office (Omaha)
11145 Mill Valley Rd.
Omaha, NE 68154
(402)221-3606
Fax: (402)221-3680
E-mail: infoctr@ne.uswest.net
Website: http://www.tandt.com/score

Nevada

SCORE Office (Incline Village)
969 Tahoe Blvd.
Incline Village, NV 89451
(702)831-7327
Fax: (702)832-1605

SCORE Office (Carson City)
301 E Stewart
PO Box 7527
Las Vegas, NV 89125
(702)388-6104

SCORE Office (Las Vegas)
300 Las Vegas Blvd. S, Ste. 1100
Las Vegas, NV 89101
(702)388-6104

SCORE Office (Northern Nevada)
SBDC, College of Business
Administration
Univ. of Nevada
Reno, NV 89557-0100
(702)784-4436
Fax: (702)784-4337

New Hampshire

SCORE Office (North Country)
PO Box 34
Berlin, NH 03570
(603)752-1090

SCORE Office (Concord)
143 N. Main St., Rm. 202A
PO Box 1258
Concord, NH 03301
(603)225-1400
Fax: (603)225-1409

SCORE Office (Dover)
299 Central Ave.
Dover, NH 03820
(603)742-2218
Fax: (603)749-6317

SCORE Office (Monadnock)
34 Mechanic St.
Keene, NH 03431-3421
(603)352-0320

SCORE Office (Lakes Region)
67 Water St., Ste. 105
Laconia, NH 03246
(603)524-9168

SCORE Office (Upper Valley)
Citizens Bank Bldg., Rm. 310
20 W Park St.
Lebanon, NH 03766
(603)448-3491
Fax: (603)448-1908
E-mail: billt@valley.net
Website: http://www.valley.net/~score

SCORE Office (Merrimack Valley)
275 Chestnut St., Rm. 618
Manchester, NH 03103
(603)666-7561
Fax: (603)666-7925

SCORE Office (Mount Washington Valley)
PO Box 1066
North Conway, NH 03818
(603)383-0800

SCORE Office (Seacoast)
195 Commerce Way, Unit-A
Portsmouth, NH 03801-3251
(603)433-0575

New Jersey

SCORE Office (Somerset)
Paritan Valley Community College,
Rte. 28
Branchburg, NJ 08807

(908)218-8874
E-mail: nj-score@grizbiz.com.
Website: http://www.nj-score.org

SCORE Office (Chester)
5 Old Mill Rd.
Chester, NJ 07930
(908)879-7080

SCORE Office (Greater Princeton)
4 A George Washington Dr.
Cranbury, NJ 08512
(609)520-1776

SCORE Office (Freehold)
36 W Main St.
Freehold, NJ 07728
(908)462-3030
Fax: (908)462-2123

SCORE Office (North West)
Picantinny Innovation Ctr.
3159 Schrader Rd.
Hamburg, NJ 07419
(973)209-8525
Fax: (973)209-7252
E-mail: nj-score@grizbiz.com
Website: http://www.nj-score.org

SCORE Office (Monmouth)
765 Newman Springs Rd.
Lincroft, NJ 07738
(908)224-2573
E-mail: nj-score@grizbiz.com
Website: http://www.nj-score.org

SCORE Office (Manalapan)
125 Symmes Dr.
Manalapan, NJ 07726
(908)431-7220

SCORE Office (Jersey City)
2 Gateway Ctr., 4th Fl.
Newark, NJ 07102
(973)645-3982
Fax: (973)645-2375

SCORE Office (Newark)
2 Gateway Center, 15th Fl.
Newark, NJ 07102-5553
(973)645-3982
Fax: (973)645-2375
E-mail: nj-score@grizbiz.com
Website: http://www.nj-score.org

SCORE Office (Bergen County)
327 E Ridgewood Ave.
Paramus, NJ 07652
(201)599-6090
E-mail: nj-score@grizbiz.com
Website: http://www.nj-score.org

SCORE Office (Pennsauken)
4900 Rte. 70
Pennsauken, NJ 08109
(609)486-3421

SCORE Office (Southern New Jersey)
4900 Rte. 70
Pennsauken, NJ 08109
(609)486-3421
E-mail: nj-score@grizbiz.com
Website: http://www.nj-score.org

SCORE Office (Greater Princeton)
216 Rockingham Row
Princeton Forrestal Village
Princeton, NJ 08540
(609)520-1776
Fax: (609)520-9107
E-mail: nj-score@grizbiz.com
Website: http://www.nj-score.org

SCORE Office (Shrewsbury)
Hwy. 35
Shrewsbury, NJ 07702
(908)842-5995
Fax: (908)219-6140

SCORE Office (Ocean County)
33 Washington St.
Toms River, NJ 08754
(732)505-6033
E-mail: nj-score@grizbiz.com
Website: http://www.nj-score.org

SCORE Office (Wall)
2700 Allaire Rd.
Wall, NJ 07719
(908)449-8877

SCORE Office (Wayne)
2055 Hamburg Tpke.
Wayne, NJ 07470
(201)831-7788
Fax: (201)831-9112

New Mexico

SCORE Office (Albuquerque)
525 Buena Vista, SE
Albuquerque, NM 87106
(505)272-7999
Fax: (505)272-7963

SCORE Office (Las Cruces)
Loretto Towne Center
505 S Main St., Ste. 125
Las Cruces, NM 88001
(505)523-5627
Fax: (505)524-2101
E-mail: score.397@zianet.com

SCORE Office (Roswell)
Federal Bldg., Rm. 237
Roswell, NM 88201
(505)625-2112
Fax: (505)623-2545

SCORE Office (Santa Fe)
Montoya Federal Bldg.
120 Federal Place, Rm. 307
Santa Fe, NM 87501
(505)988-6302
Fax: (505)988-6300

New York

SCORE Office (Northeast)
1 Computer Dr. S
Albany, NY 12205
(518)446-1118
Fax: (518)446-1228

SCORE Office (Auburn)
30 South St.
PO Box 675
Auburn, NY 13021
(315)252-7291

SCORE Office (South Tier Binghamton)
Metro Center, 2nd Fl.
49 Court St.
PO Box 995
Binghamton, NY 13902
(607)772-8860

SCORE Office (Queens County City)
12055 Queens Blvd., Rm. 333
Borough Hall, NY 11424
(718)263-8961

SCORE Office (Buffalo)
Federal Bldg., Rm. 1311
111 W Huron St.
Buffalo, NY 14202
(716)551-4301
Website: http://www2.pcom.net/score/
buf45.html

SCORE Office (Canandaigua)
Chamber of Commerce Bldg.
113 S Main St.
Canandaigua, NY 14424
(716)394-4400
Fax: (716)394-4546

SCORE Office (Chemung)
333 E Water St., 4th Fl.
Elmira, NY 14901
(607)734-3358

SCORE Office (Geneva)
Chamber of Commerce Bldg.
PO Box 587

Geneva, NY 14456
(315)789-1776
Fax: (315)789-3993

SCORE Office (Glens Falls)
84 Broad St.
Glens Falls, NY 12801
(518)798-8463
Fax: (518)745-1433

SCORE Office (Orange County)
40 Matthews St.
Goshen, NY 10924
(914)294-8080
Fax: (914)294-6121

SCORE Office (Huntington Area)
151 W Carver St.
Huntington, NY 11743
(516)423-6100

SCORE Office (Tompkins County)
904 E Shore Dr.
Ithaca, NY 14850
(607)273-7080

SCORE Office (Long Island City)
120-55 Queens Blvd.
Jamaica, NY 11424
(718)263-8961
Fax: (718)263-9032

SCORE Office (Chatauqua)
101 W 5th St.
Jamestown, NY 14701
(716)484-1103

SCORE Office (Westchester)
2 Caradon Ln.
Katonah, NY 10536
(914)948-3907
Fax: (914)948-4645
E-mail: score@w-w-w.com
Website: http://w-w-w.com/score

SCORE Office (Queens County)
Queens Borough Hall
120-55 Queens Blvd. Rm. 333
Kew Gardens, NY 11424
(718)263-8961
Fax: (718)263-9032

SCORE Office (Brookhaven)
3233 Rte. 112
Medford, NY 11763
(516)451-6563
Fax: (516)451-6925

SCORE Office (Melville)
35 Pinelawn Rd., Rm. 207-W
Melville, NY 11747
(516)454-0771

SCORE Office (Nassau County)
400 County Seat Dr., No. 140
Mineola, NY 11501
(516)571-3303
E-mail: Counse1998@aol.com
Website: http://members.aol.com/
Counse1998/Default.htm

SCORE Office (Mount Vernon)
4 N. 7th Ave.
Mount Vernon, NY 10550
(914)667-7500

SCORE Office (New York)
26 Federal Plz., Rm. 3100
New York, NY 10278
(212)264-4507
Fax: (212)264-4963
E-mail: score1000@erols.com
Website: http://users.erols.com/score-nyc

SCORE Office (Newburgh)
47 Grand St.
Newburgh, NY 12550
(914)562-5100

SCORE Office (Owego)
188 Front St.
Owego, NY 13827
(607)687-2020

SCORE Office (Peekskill)
1 S Division St.
Peekskill, NY 10566
(914)737-3600
Fax: (914)737-0541

SCORE Office (Penn Yan)
2375 Rte. 14A
Penn Yan, NY 14527
(315)536-3111

SCORE Office (Dutchess)
110 Main St.
Poughkeepsie, NY 12601
(914)454-1700

SCORE Office (Rochester)
601 Keating Federal Bldg., Rm. 410
100 State St.
Rochester, NY 14614
(716)263-6473
Fax: (716)263-3146
Website: http://www.ggw.org/score

SCORE Office (Saranac Lake)
30 Main St.
Saranac Lake, NY 12983
(315)448-0415

SCORE Office (Suffolk)
286 Main St.

Setauket, NY 11733
(516)751-3886

SCORE Office (Staten Island)
130 Bay St.
Staten Island, NY 10301
(718)727-1221

SCORE Office (Ulster)
Clinton Bldg., Rm. 107
Stone Ridge, NY 12484
(914)687-5035
Fax: (914)687-5015
Website: http://www.scoreulster.org

SCORE Office (Syracuse)
401 S Salina, 5th Fl.
Syracuse, NY 13202
(315)471-9393

SCORE Office (Utica)
SUNY Institute of Technology, Route 12
Utica, NY 13504-3050
(315)792-7553

SCORE Office (Watertown)
518 Davidson St.
Watertown, NY 13601
(315)788-1200
Fax: (315)788-8251

North Carolina

SCORE office (Asheboro)
317 E Dixie Dr.
Asheboro, NC 27203
(336)626-2626
Fax: (336)626-7077

SCORE Office (Asheville)
Federal Bldg., Rm. 259
151 Patton
Asheville, NC 28801-5770
(828)271-4786
Fax: (828)271-4009

SCORE Office (Chapel Hill)
104 S Estes Dr.
PO Box 2897
Chapel Hill, NC 27514
(919)967-7075

SCORE Office (Coastal Plains)
PO Box 2897
Chapel Hill, NC 27515
(919)967-7075
Fax: (919)968-6874

SCORE Office (Charlotte)
200 N. College St., Ste. A-2015
Charlotte, NC 28202
(704)344-6576

Fax: (704)344-6769
E-mail: CharlotteSCORE47@AOL.com
Website: http://www.charweb.org/
business/score

SCORE Office (Durham)
411 W Chapel Hill St.
Durham, NC 27707
(919)541-2171

SCORE Office (Gastonia)
PO Box 2168
Gastonia, NC 28053
(704)864-2621
Fax: (704)854-8723

SCORE Office (Greensboro)
400 W Market St., Ste. 103
Greensboro, NC 27401-2241
(910)333-5399

SCORE Office (Henderson)
PO Box 917
Henderson, NC 27536
(919)492-2061
Fax: (919)430-0460

SCORE Office (Hendersonville)
Federal Bldg., Rm. 108
W 4th Ave. & Church St.
Hendersonville, NC 28792
(828)693-8702
E-mail: score@circle.net
Website: http://www.wncguide.com/
score/Welcome.html

SCORE Office (Unifour)
PO Box 1828
Hickory, NC 28603
(704)328-6111

SCORE Office (High Point)
1101 N. Main St.
High Point, NC 27262
(336)882-8625
Fax: (336)889-9499

SCORE Office (Outer Banks)
Collington Rd. and Mustain
Kill Devil Hills, NC 27948
(252)441-8144

SCORE Office (Down East)
312 S Front St., Ste. 6
New Bern, NC 28560
(252)633-6688
Fax: (252)633-9608

SCORE Office (Kinston)
PO Box 95
New Bern, NC 28561
(919)633-6688

SCORE Office (Raleigh)
Century Post Office Bldg., Ste. 306
300 Federal St. Mall
Raleigh, NC 27601
(919)856-4739
E-mail: jendres@ibm.net
Website: http://www.intrex.net/score96/
score96.htm

SCORE Office (Sanford)
1801 Nash St.
Sanford, NC 27330
(919)774-6442
Fax: (919)776-8739

SCORE Office (Sandhills Area)
1480 Hwy. 15-501
PO Box 458
Southern Pines, NC 28387
(910)692-3926

SCORE Office (Wilmington)
Corps of Engineers Bldg.
96 Darlington Ave., Ste. 207
Wilmington, NC 28403
(910)815-4576
Fax: (910)815-4658

North Dakota

SCORE Office (Bismarck-Mandan)
700 E Main Ave., 2nd Fl.
PO Box 5509
Bismarck, ND 58506-5509
(701)250-4303

SCORE Office (Fargo)
657 2nd Ave., Rm. 225
Fargo, ND 58108-3083
(701)239-5677

SCORE Office (Upper Red River)
4275 Technology Dr., Rm. 156
Grand Forks, ND 58202-8372
(701)777-3051

SCORE Office (Minot)
100 1st St. SW
Minot, ND 58701-3846
(701)852-6883
Fax: (701)852-6905

Ohio

SCORE Office (Akron)
1 Cascade Plz., 7th Fl.
Akron, OH 44308
(330)379-3163
Fax: (330)379-3164

SCORE Office (Ashland)
Gill Center

47 W Main St.
Ashland, OH 44805
(419)281-4584

SCORE Office (Canton)
116 Cleveland Ave. NW, Ste. 601
Canton, OH 44702-1720
(330)453-6047

SCORE Office (Chillicothe)
165 S Paint St.
Chillicothe, OH 45601
(614)772-4530

SCORE Office (Cincinnati)
Ameritrust Bldg., Rm. 850
525 Vine St.
Cincinnati, OH 45202
(513)684-2812
Fax: (513)684-3251
Website: http://www.score.chapter34.org

SCORE Office (Cleveland)
Eaton Center, Ste. 620
1100 Superior Ave.
Cleveland, OH 44114-2507
(216)522-4194
Fax: (216)522-4844

SCORE Office (Columbus)
2 Nationwide Plz., Ste. 1400
Columbus, OH 43215-2542
(614)469-2357
Fax: (614)469-2391
E-mail: info@scorecolumbus.org
Website: http://www.scorecolumbus.org

SCORE Office (Dayton)
Dayton Federal Bldg., Rm. 505
200 W Second St.
Dayton, OH 45402-1430
(513)225-2887
Fax: (513)225-7667

SCORE Office (Defiance)
615 W 3rd St.
PO Box 130
Defiance, OH 43512
(419)782-7946

SCORE Office (Findlay)
123 E Main Cross St.
PO Box 923
Findlay, OH 45840
(419)422-3314

SCORE Office (Lima)
147 N. Main St.
Lima, OH 45801
(419)222-6045
Fax: (419)229-0266

SCORE Office (Mansfield)
55 N. Mulberry St.
Mansfield, OH 44902
(419)522-3211

SCORE Office (Marietta)
Thomas Hall
Marietta, OH 45750
(614)373-0268

SCORE Office (Medina)
County Administrative Bldg.
144 N. Broadway
Medina, OH 44256
(216)764-8650

SCORE Office (Licking County)
50 W Locust St.
Newark, OH 43055
(614)345-7458

SCORE Office (Salem)
2491 State Rte. 45 S
Salem, OH 44460
(216)332-0361

SCORE Office (Tiffin)
62 S Washington St.
Tiffin, OH 44883
(419)447-4141
Fax: (419)447-5141

SCORE Office (Toledo)
608 Madison Ave, Ste. 910
Toledo, OH 43624
(419)259-7598
Fax: (419)259-6460

SCORE Office (Heart of Ohio)
377 W Liberty St.
Wooster, OH 44691
(330)262-5735
Fax: (330)262-5745

SCORE Office (Youngstown)
306 Williamson Hall
Youngstown, OH 44555
(330)746-2687

Oklahoma

SCORE Office (Anadarko)
PO Box 366
Anadarko, OK 73005
(405)247-6651

SCORE Office (Ardmore)
410 W Main
Ardmore, OK 73401
(580)226-2620

SCORE Office (Northeast Oklahoma)
210 S Main

Grove, OK 74344
(918)787-2796
Fax: (918)787-2796
E-mail: Score595@greencis.net

SCORE Office (Lawton)
4500 W Lee Blvd., Bldg. 100, Ste. 107
Lawton, OK 73505
(580)353-8727
Fax: (580)250-5677

SCORE Office (Oklahoma City)
210 Park Ave., No. 1300
Oklahoma City, OK 73102
(405)231-5163
Fax: (405)231-4876
E-mail: score212@usa.net

SCORE Office (Stillwater)
439 S Main
Stillwater, OK 74074
(405)372-5573
Fax: (405)372-4316

SCORE Office (Tulsa)
616 S Boston, Ste. 406
Tulsa, OK 74119
(918)581-7462
Fax: (918)581-6908
Website: http://www.ionet.net/~tulscore

Oregon

SCORE Office (Bend)
63085 N. Hwy. 97
Bend, OR 97701
(541)923-2849
Fax: (541)330-6900

SCORE Office (Willamette)
1401 Willamette St.
PO Box 1107
Eugene, OR 97401-4003
(541)465-6600
Fax: (541)484-4942

SCORE Office (Florence)
3149 Oak St.
Florence, OR 97439
(503)997-8444
Fax: (503)997-8448

SCORE Office (Southern Oregon)
33 N. Central Ave., Ste. 216
Medford, OR 97501
(541)776-4220
E-mail: pgr134f@prodigy.com

SCORE Office (Portland)
1515 SW 5th Ave., Ste. 1050
Portland, OR 97201
(503)326-3441

Fax: (503)326-2808
E-mail: gr134@prodigy.com

SCORE Office (Salem)
416 State St. (corner of Liberty)
Salem, OR 97301
(503)370-2896

Pennsylvania

SCORE Office (Altoona-Blair)
1212 12th Ave.
Altoona, PA 16601-3493
(814)943-8151

SCORE Office (Lehigh Valley)
Rauch Bldg. 37
Lehigh University
621 Taylor St.
Bethlehem, PA 18015
(610)758-4496
Fax: (610)758-5205

SCORE Office (Butler County)
100 N. Main St.
PO Box 1082
Butler, PA 16003
(412)283-2222
Fax: (412)283-0224

SCORE Office (Harrisburg)
4211 Trindle Rd.
Camp Hill, PA 17011
(717)761-4304
Fax: (717)761-4315

SCORE Office (Cumberland Valley)
75 S 2nd St.
Chambersburg, PA 17201
(717)264-2935

SCORE Office (Monroe County-Stroudsburg)
556 Main St.
East Stroudsburg, PA 18301
(717)421-4433

SCORE Office (Erie)
120 W 9th St.
Erie, PA 16501
(814)871-5650
Fax: (814)871-7530

SCORE Office (Bucks County)
409 Hood Blvd.
Fairless Hills, PA 19030
(215)943-8850
Fax: (215)943-7404

SCORE Office (Hanover)
146 Broadway
Hanover, PA 17331

(717)637-6130
Fax: (717)637-9127

SCORE Office (Harrisburg)
100 Chestnut, Ste. 309
Harrisburg, PA 17101
(717)782-3874

SCORE Office (East Montgomery County)
Baederwood Shopping Center
1653 The Fairways, Ste. 204
Jenkintown, PA 19046
(215)885-3027

SCORE Office (Kittanning)
2 Butler Rd.
Kittanning, PA 16201
(412)543-1305
Fax: (412)543-6206

SCORE Office (Lancaster)
118 W Chestnut St.
Lancaster, PA 17603
(717)397-3092

SCORE Office (Westmoreland County)
300 Fraser Purchase Rd.
Latrobe, PA 15650-2690
(412)539-7505
Fax: (412)539-1850

SCORE Office (Lebanon)
252 N. 8th St.
PO Box 899
Lebanon, PA 17042-0899
(717)273-3727
Fax: (717)273-7940

SCORE Office (Lewistown)
3 W Monument Sq., Ste. 204
Lewistown, PA 17044
(717)248-6713
Fax: (717)248-6714

SCORE Office (Delaware County)
602 E Baltimore Pike
Media, PA 19063
(610)565-3677
Fax: (610)565-1606

SCORE Office (Milton Area)
112 S Front St.
Milton, PA 17847
(717)742-7341
Fax: (717)792-2008

SCORE Office (Mon-Valley)
435 Donner Ave.
Monessen, PA 15062
(412)684-4277
Fax: (412)684-7688

SCORE Office (Monroeville)
William Penn Plaza
2790 Mosside Blvd., Ste. 295
Monroeville, PA 15146
(412)856-0622
Fax: (412)856-1030

SCORE Office (Airport Area)
986 Brodhead Rd.
Moon Township, PA 15108-2398
(412)264-6270
Fax: (412)264-1575

SCORE Office (Northeast)
8601 E Roosevelt Blvd.
Philadelphia, PA 19152
(215)332-3400
Fax: (215)332-6050

SCORE Office (Philadelphia)
1315 Walnut St., Ste. 500
Philadelphia, PA 19107
(215)790-5050
Fax: (215)790-5057
E-mail: score46@bellatlantic.net
Website: http://www.pgweb.net/score46

SCORE Office (Pittsburgh)
1000 Liberty Ave., Rm. 1122
Pittsburgh, PA 15222
(412)395-6560
Fax: (412)395-6562

SCORE Office (Tri-County)
801 N. Charlotte St.
Pottstown, PA 19464
(610)327-2673

SCORE Office (Reading)
601 Penn St.
Reading, PA 19601
(610)376-3497

SCORE Office (Scranton)
Oppenheim Bldg.
116 N. Washington Ave., Ste. 650
Scranton, PA 18503
(717)347-4611
Fax: (717)347-4611

SCORE Office (Central Pennsylvania)
200 Innovation Blvd., Ste. 242-B
State College, PA 16803
(814)234-9415
Fax: (814)238-9686
Website: http://countrystore.org/
business/score.htm

SCORE Office (Monroe-Stroudsburg)
556 Main St.
Stroudsburg, PA 18360
(717)421-4433

SCORE Office (Uniontown)
Federal Bldg.
Pittsburg St.
PO Box 2065 DTS
Uniontown, PA 15401
(412)437-4222
E-mail: uniontownscore@lcsys.net

SCORE Office (Warren County)
315 2nd Ave.
Warren, PA 16365
(814)723-9017

SCORE Office (Waynesboro)
323 E Main St.
Waynesboro, PA 17268
(717)762-7123
Fax: (717)962-7124

SCORE Office (Chester County)
Government Service Center, Ste. 281
601 Westtown Rd.
West Chester, PA 19382-4538
(610)344-6910
Fax: (610)344-6919
E-mail: score@locke.ccil.org

SCORE Office (Wilkes-Barre)
7 N. Wilkes-Barre Blvd.
Wilkes Barre, PA 18702-5241
(717)826-6502
Fax: (717)826-6287

SCORE Office (North Central Pennsylvania)
240 W 3rd St., Rm. 227
PO Box 725
Williamsport, PA 17703
(717)322-3720
Fax: (717)322-1607
E-mail: score234@mail.csrlink.net
Website: http://www.lycoming.org/score

SCORE Office (York)
Cyber Center
2101 Pennsylvania Ave.
York, PA 17404
(717)845-8830
Fax: (717)854-9333

Puerto Rico

SCORE Office (Puerto Rico & Virgin Islands)
PO Box 12383-96
San Juan, PR 00914-0383
(787)726-8040
Fax: (787)726-8135

Rhode Island

SCORE Office (Barrington)
281 County Rd.

Barrington, RI 02806
(401)247-1920
Fax: (401)247-3763

SCORE Office (Woonsocket)
640 Washington Hwy.
Lincoln, RI 02865
(401)334-1000
Fax: (401)334-1009

SCORE Office (Wickford)
8045 Post Rd.
North Kingstown, RI 02852
(401)295-5566
Fax: (401)295-8987

SCORE Office (J.G.E. Knight)
380 Westminster St.
Providence, RI 02903
(401)528-4571
Fax: (401)528-4539
Website: http://www.riscore.org

SCORE Office (Warwick)
3288 Post Rd.
Warwick, RI 02886
(401)732-1100
Fax: (401)732-1101

SCORE Office (Westerly)
74 Post Rd.
Westerly, RI 02891
(401)596-7761
800-732-7636
Fax: (401)596-2190

South Carolina

SCORE Office (Aiken)
PO Box 892
Aiken, SC 29802
(803)641-1111
800-542-4536
Fax: (803)641-4174

SCORE Office (Anderson)
Anderson Mall
3130 N. Main St.
Anderson, SC 29621
(864)224-0453

SCORE Office (Coastal)
284 King St.
Charleston, SC 29401
(803)727-4778
Fax: (803)853-2529

SCORE Office (Midlands)
Strom Thurmond Bldg., Rm. 358
1835 Assembly St., Rm 358
Columbia, SC 29201
(803)765-5131

Fax: (803)765-5962
Website: http://www.scoremidlands.org

SCORE Office (Piedmont)
Federal Bldg., Rm. B-02
300 E Washington St.
Greenville, SC 29601
(864)271-3638

SCORE Office (Greenwood)
PO Drawer 1467
Greenwood, SC 29648
(864)223-8357

SCORE Office (Hilton Head Island)
52 Savannah Trail
Hilton Head, SC 29926
(803)785-7107
Fax: (803)785-7110

SCORE Office (Grand Strand)
937 Broadway
Myrtle Beach, SC 29577
(803)918-1079
Fax: (803)918-1083
E-mail: score381@aol.com

SCORE Office (Spartanburg)
PO Box 1636
Spartanburg, SC 29304
(864)594-5000
Fax: (864)594-5055

South Dakota

SCORE Office (West River)
Rushmore Plz. Civic Ctr.
444 Mount Rushmore Rd., No. 209
Rapid City, SD 57701
(605)394-5311
E-mail: score@gwtc.net

SCORE Office (Sioux Falls)
First Financial Center
110 S Phillips Ave., Ste. 200
Sioux Falls, SD 57104-6727
(605)330-4231
Fax: (605)330-4231

Tennessee

SCORE Office (Chattanooga)
Federal Bldg., Rm. 26
900 Georgia Ave.
Chattanooga, TN 37402
(423)752-5190
Fax: (423)752-5335

SCORE Office (Cleveland)
PO Box 2275
Cleveland, TN 37320
(423)472-6587
Fax: (423)472-2019

SCORE Office (Upper Cumberland Center)
1225 S Willow Ave.
Cookeville, TN 38501
(615)432-4111
Fax: (615)432-6010

SCORE Office (Unicoi County)
PO Box 713
Erwin, TN 37650
(423)743-3000
Fax: (423)743-0942

SCORE Office (Greeneville)
115 Academy St.
Greeneville, TN 37743
(423)638-4111
Fax: (423)638-5345

SCORE Office (Jackson)
194 Auditorium St.
Jackson, TN 38301
(901)423-2200

SCORE Office (Northeast Tennessee)
1st Tennessee Bank Bldg.
2710 S Roan St., Ste. 584
Johnson City, TN 37601
(423)929-7686
Fax: (423)461-8052

SCORE Office (Kingsport)
151 E Main St.
Kingsport, TN 37662
(423)392-8805

SCORE Office (Greater Knoxville)
Farragot Bldg., Ste. 224
530 S Gay St.
Knoxville, TN 37902
(423)545-4203
E-mail: scoreknox@ntown.com
Website: http://www.scoreknox.org

SCORE Office (Maryville)
201 S Washington St.
Maryville, TN 37804-5728
(423)983-2241
800-525-6834
Fax: (423)984-1386

SCORE Office (Memphis)
Federal Bldg., Ste. 390
167 N. Main St.
Memphis, TN 38103
(901)544-3588

SCORE Office (Nashville)
50 Vantage Way, Ste. 201
Nashville, TN 37228-1500
(615)736-7621

Texas

SCORE Office (Abilene)
2106 Federal Post Office and Court Bldg.
Abilene, TX 79601
(915)677-1857

SCORE Office (Austin)
2501 S Congress
Austin, TX 78701
(512)442-7235
Fax: (512)442-7528

SCORE Office (Golden Triangle)
450 Boyd St.
Beaumont, TX 77704
(409)838-6581
Fax: (409)833-6718

SCORE Office (Brownsville)
3505 Boca Chica Blvd., Ste. 305
Brownsville, TX 78521
(210)541-4508

SCORE Office (Brazos Valley)
3000 Briarcrest, Ste. 302
Bryan, TX 77802
(409)776-8876
E-mail: 102633.2612@compuserve.com

SCORE Office (Cleburne)
Watergarden Pl., 9th Fl., Ste. 400
Cleburne, TX 76031
(817)871-6002

SCORE Office (Corpus Christi)
651 Upper North Broadway,
Ste. 654
Corpus Christi, TX 78477
(512)888-4322
Fax: (512)888-3418

SCORE Office (Dallas)
6260 E Mockingbird
Dallas, TX 75214-2619
(214)828-2471
Fax: (214)821-8033

SCORE Office (El Paso)
10 Civic Center Plaza
El Paso, TX 79901
(915)534-0541
Fax: (915)534-0513

SCORE Office (Bedford)
100 E 15th St., Ste. 400
Fort Worth, TX 76102
(817)871-6002

SCORE Office (Fort Worth)
100 E 15th St., No. 24
Fort Worth, TX 76102
(817)871-6002

Fax: (817)871-6031
E-mail: fwbac@onramp.net

SCORE Office (Garland)
2734 W Kingsley Rd.
Garland, TX 75041
(214)271-9224

SCORE Office (Granbury Chamber of Commerce)
416 S Morgan
Granbury, TX 76048
(817)573-1622
Fax: (817)573-0805

SCORE Office (Lower Rio Grande Valley)
222 E Van Buren, Ste. 500
Harlingen, TX 78550
(956)427-8533
Fax: (956)427-8537

SCORE Office (Houston)
9301 Southwest Fwy., Ste. 550
Houston, TX 77074
(713)773-6565
Fax: (713)773-6550

SCORE Office (Irving)
3333 N. MacArthur Blvd., Ste. 100
Irving, TX 75062
(214)252-8484
Fax: (214)252-6710

SCORE Office (Lubbock)
1205 Texas Ave., Rm. 411D
Lubbock, TX 79401
(806)472-7462
Fax: (806)472-7487

SCORE Office (Midland)
Post Office Annex
200 E Wall St., Rm. P121
Midland, TX 79701
(915)687-2649

SCORE Office (Orange)
1012 Green Ave.
Orange, TX 77630-5620
(409)883-3536
800-528-4906
Fax: (409)886-3247

SCORE Office (Plano)
1200 E 15th St.
PO Drawer 940287
Plano, TX 75094-0287
(214)424-7547
Fax: (214)422-5182

SCORE Office (Port Arthur)
4749 Twin City Hwy., Ste. 300
Port Arthur, TX 77642

(409)963-1107
Fax: (409)963-3322

SCORE Office (Richardson)
411 Belle Grove
Richardson, TX 75080
(214)234-4141
800-777-8001
Fax: (214)680-9103

SCORE Office (San Antonio)
Federal Bldg., Rm. A527
727 E Durango
San Antonio, TX 78206
(210)472-5931
Fax: (210)472-5935

SCORE Office (Texarkana State College)
819 State Line Ave.
Texarkana, TX 75501
(903)792-7191
Fax: (903)793-4304

SCORE Office (East Texas)
RTDC
1530 SSW Loop 323, Ste. 100
Tyler, TX 75701
(903)510-2975
Fax: (903)510-2978

SCORE Office (Waco)
401 Franklin Ave.
Waco, TX 76701
(817)754-8898
Fax: (817)756-0776
Website: http://www.brc-waco.com

SCORE Office (Wichita Falls)
Hamilton Bldg.
900 8th St.
Wichita Falls, TX 76307
(940)723-2741
Fax: (940)723-8773

Utah

SCORE Office (Northern Utah)
160 N. Main
Logan, UT 84321
(435)746-2269

SCORE Office (Ogden)
1701 E Windsor Dr.
Ogden, UT 84604
(801)629-8613
E-mail: score158@netscape.net

SCORE Office (Central Utah)
1071 E Windsor Dr.
Provo, UT 84604
(801)373-8660

SCORE Office (Southern Utah)
225 South 700 East
Saint George, UT 84770
(435)652-7751

SCORE Office (Salt Lake)
310 S Main St.
Salt Lake City, UT 84101
(801)746-2269
Fax: (801)746-2273

Vermont

SCORE Office (Champlain Valley)
Winston Prouty Federal Bldg.
11 Lincoln St., Rm. 106
Essex Junction, VT 05452
(802)951-6762

SCORE Office (Montpelier)
87 State St., Rm. 205
PO Box 605
Montpelier, VT 05601
(802)828-4422
Fax: (802)828-4485

SCORE Office (Marble Valley)
256 N. Main St.
Rutland, VT 05701-2413
(802)773-9147

SCORE Office (Northeast Kingdom)
20 Main St.
PO Box 904
Saint Johnsbury, VT 05819
(802)748-5101

Virgin Islands

SCORE Office (Saint Croix)
United Plaza Shopping Center
PO Box 4010, Christiansted
Saint Croix, VI 00822
(809)778-5380

SCORE Office (Saint Thomas-Saint John)
Federal Bldg., Rm. 21
Veterans Dr.
Saint Thomas, VI 00801
(809)774-8530

Virginia

SCORE Office (Arlington)
2009 N. 14th St., Ste. 111
Arlington, VA 22201
(703)525-2400

SCORE Office (Blacksburg)
141 Jackson St.
Blacksburg, VA 24060
(540)552-4061

SCORE Office (Bristol)
20 Volunteer Pkwy.
Bristol, VA 24203
(540)989-4850

SCORE Office (Central Virginia)
1001 E Market St., Ste. 101
Charlottesville, VA 22902
(804)295-6712
Fax: (804)295-7066

SCORE Office (Alleghany Satellite)
241 W Main St.
Covington, VA 24426
(540)962-2178
Fax: (540)962-2179

SCORE Office (Central Fairfax)
3975 University Dr., Ste. 350
Fairfax, VA 22030
(703)591-2450

SCORE Office (Falls Church)
PO Box 491
Falls Church, VA 22040
(703)532-1050
Fax: (703)237-7904

SCORE Office (Glenns)
Glenns Campus
Box 287
Glenns, VA 23149
(804)693-9650

SCORE Office (Peninsula)
6 Manhattan Sq.
PO Box 7269
Hampton, VA 23666
(757)766-2000
Fax: (757)865-0339
E-mail: score100@seva.net

SCORE Office (Tri-Cities)
108 N. Main St.
Hopewell, VA 23860
(804)458-5536

SCORE Office (Lynchburg)
Federal Bldg.
1100 Main St.
Lynchburg, VA 24504-1714
(804)846-3235

SCORE Office (Greater Prince William)
8963 Center St
Manassas, VA 20110
(703)368-4813
Fax: (703)368-4733

SCORE Office (Martinsvile)
115 Broad St.
Martinsville, VA 24112-0709

(540)632-6401
Fax: (540)632-5059

SCORE Office (Hampton Roads)
Federal Bldg., Rm. 737
200 Grandby St.
Norfolk, VA 23510
(757)441-3733
Fax: (757)441-3733
E-mail: scorehr60@juno.com

SCORE Office (Norfolk)
Federal Bldg., Rm. 737
200 Granby St.
Norfolk, VA 23510
(757)441-3733
Fax: (757)441-3733

SCORE Office (Virginia Beach)
Chamber of Commerce
200 Grandby St., Rm 737
Norfolk, VA 23510
(804)441-3733

SCORE Office (Radford)
1126 Norwood St.
Radford, VA 24141
(540)639-2202

SCORE Office (Richmond)
Federal Bldg.
400 N. 8th St., Ste. 1150
PO Box 10126
Richmond, VA 23240-0126
(804)771-2400
Fax: (804)771-8018
E-mail: scorechapter12@yahoo.com
Website: http://www.cvco.org/score

SCORE Office (Roanoke)
Federal Bldg., Rm. 716
250 Franklin Rd.
Roanoke, VA 24011
(540)857-2834
Fax: (540)857-2043
E-mail: scorerva@juno.com
Website: http://hometown.aol.com/
scorerv/Index.html

SCORE Office (Fairfax)
8391 Old Courthouse Rd., Ste. 300
Vienna, VA 22182
(703)749-0400

SCORE Office (Greater Vienna)
513 Maple Ave. West
Vienna, VA 22180
(703)281-1333
Fax: (703)242-1482

SCORE Office (Shenandoah Valley)
301 W Main St.

Waynesboro, VA 22980
(540)949-8203
Fax: (540)949-7740
E-mail: score427@intelos.net

SCORE Office (Williamsburg)
201 Penniman Rd.
Williamsburg, VA 23185
(757)229-6511
E-mail: wacc@williamsburgcc.com

SCORE Office (Northern Virginia)
1360 S Pleasant Valley Rd.
Winchester, VA 22601
(540)662-4118

Washington

SCORE Office (Gray's Harbor)
506 Duffy St.
Aberdeen, WA 98520
(360)532-1924
Fax: (360)533-7945

SCORE Office (Bellingham)
101 E Holly St.
Bellingham, WA 98225
(360)676-3307

SCORE Office (Everett)
2702 Hoyt Ave.
Everett, WA 98201-3556
(206)259-8000

SCORE Office (Gig Harbor)
3125 Judson St.
Gig Harbor, WA 98335
(206)851-6865

SCORE Office (Kennewick)
PO Box 6986
Kennewick, WA 99336
(509)736-0510

SCORE Office (Puyallup)
322 2nd St. SW
PO Box 1298
Puyallup, WA 98371
(206)845-6755
Fax: (206)848-6164

SCORE Office (Seattle)
1200 6th Ave., Ste. 1700
Seattle, WA 98101
(206)553-7320
Fax: (206)553-7044
E-mail: score55@aol.com
Website: http://www.scn.org/civic/
score-online/index55.html

SCORE Office (Spokane)
801 W Riverside Ave., No. 240
Spokane, WA 99201

(509)353-2820
Fax: (509)353-2600
E-mail: score@dmi.net
Website: http://www.dmi.net/score

SCORE Office (Clover Park)
PO Box 1933
Tacoma, WA 98401-1933
(206)627-2175

SCORE Office (Tacoma)
1101 Pacific Ave.
Tacoma, WA 98402
(253)274-1288
Fax: (253)274-1289

SCORE Office (Fort Vancouver)
1701 Broadway, S-1
Vancouver, WA 98663
(360)699-1079

SCORE Office (Walla Walla)
500 Tausick Way
Walla Walla, WA 99362
(509)527-4681

SCORE Office (Mid-Columbia)
1113 S 14th Ave.
Yakima, WA 98907
(509)574-4944
Fax: (509)574-2943
Website: http://www.ellensburg
.com/~score

West Virginia

SCORE Office (Charleston)
1116 Smith St.
Charleston, WV 25301
(304)347-5463
E-mail: score256@juno.com

SCORE Office (Virginia Street)
1116 Smith St., Ste. 302
Charleston, WV 25301
(304)347-5463

SCORE Office (Marion County)
PO Box 208
Fairmont, WV 26555-0208
(304)363-0486

**SCORE Office (Upper Monongahela
Valley)**
1000 Technology Dr., Ste. 1111
Fairmont, WV 26555
(304)363-0486
E-mail: score537@hotmail.com

SCORE Office (Huntington)
1101 6th Ave., Ste. 220
Huntington, WV 25701-2309
(304)523-4092

SCORE Office (Wheeling)
1310 Market St.
Wheeling, WV 26003
(304)233-2575
Fax: (304)233-1320

Wisconsin

SCORE Office (Fox Cities)
227 S Walnut St.
Appleton, WI 54913
(920)734-7101
Fax: (920)734-7161

SCORE Office (Beloit)
136 W Grand Ave., Ste. 100
PO Box 717
Beloit, WI 53511
(608)365-8835
Fax: (608)365-9170

SCORE Office (Eau Claire)
Federal Bldg., Rm. B11
510 S Barstow St.
Eau Claire, WI 54701
(715)834-1573
E-mail: score@ecol.net
Website: http://www.ecol.net/~score

SCORE Office (Fond du Lac)
207 N. Main St.
Fond du Lac, WI 54935
(414)921-9500
Fax: (414)921-9559

SCORE Office (Green Bay)
835 Potts Ave.
Green Bay, WI 54304
(414)496-8930
Fax: (414)496-6009

SCORE Office (Janesville)
20 S Main St., Ste. 11
PO Box 8008
Janesville, WI 53547
(608)757-3160
Fax: (608)757-3170

SCORE Office (La Crosse)
712 Main St.
La Crosse, WI 54602-0219
(608)784-4880

SCORE Office (Madison)
505 S Rosa Rd.
Madison, WI 53719
(608)441-2820

SCORE Office (Manitowoc)
1515 Memorial Dr.
PO Box 903
Manitowoc, WI 54221-0903

(414)684-5575
Fax: (414)684-1915

SCORE Office (Milwaukee)
310 W Wisconsin Ave., Ste. 425
Milwaukee, WI 53203
(414)297-3942
Fax: (414)297-1377

SCORE Office (Central Wisconsin)
1224 Lindbergh Ave.
Stevens Point, WI 54481
(715)344-7729

SCORE Office (Superior)
Superior Business Center Inc.
1423 N. 8th St.
Superior, WI 54880
(715)394-7388
Fax: (715)393-7414

SCORE Office (Waukesha)
223 Wisconsin Ave.
Waukesha, WI 53186-4926
(414)542-4249

SCORE Office (Wausau)
300 3rd St., Ste. 200
Wausau, WI 54402-6190
(715)845-6231

SCORE Office (Wisconsin Rapids)
2240 Kingston Rd.
Wisconsin Rapids, WI 54494
(715)423-1830

Wyoming

SCORE Office (Casper)
Federal Bldg., No. 2215
100 East B St.
Casper, WY 82602
(307)261-6529
Fax: (307)261-6530

Venture Capital & Financing Companies

This section contains a listing of financing and loan companies in the United States and Canada. These listing are arranged alphabetically by country, then by state or province, then by city, then by organization name.

Canada

Alberta

Launchworks Inc.
1902J 11th St., SE

Calgary, AB, Canada T2G 3G2
(403)269-1119
Fax: (403)269-1141
Website: http://www.launchworks.com

Native Venture Capital Company, Inc.
21 Artist View Point, Box 7
Site 25, RR 12
Calgary, AB, Canada T3E 6W3
(903)208-5380

Miralta Capital Inc.
4445 Calgary Trail South
888 Terrace Plaza Alberta
Edmonton, AB, Canada T6H 5R7
(780)438-3535
Fax: (780)438-3129

Vencap Equities Alberta Ltd.
10180-101st St., Ste. 1980
Edmonton, AB, Canada T5J 3S4
(403)420-1171
Fax: (403)429-2541

British Columbia

Discovery Capital
5th Fl., 1199 West Hastings
Vancouver, BC, Canada V6E 3T5
(604)683-3000
Fax: (604)662-3457
E-mail: info@discoverycapital.com
Website: http://www.discoverycapital
.com

Greenstone Venture Partners
1177 West Hastings St.
Ste. 400
Vancouver, BC, Canada V6E 2K3
(604)717-1977
Fax: (604)717-1976
Website: http://www.greenstonevc.com

Growthworks Capital
2600-1055 West Georgia St.
Box 11170 Royal Centre
Vancouver, BC, Canada V6E 3R5
(604)895-7259
Fax: (604)669-7605
Website: http://www.wofund.com

MDS Discovery Venture Management, Inc.
555 W Eighth Ave., Ste. 305
Vancouver, BC, Canada V5Z 1C6
(604)872-8464
Fax: (604)872-2977
E-mail: info@mds-ventures.com

Ventures West Management Inc.
1285 W Pender St., Ste. 280
Vancouver, BC, Canada V6E 4B1

(604)688-9495
Fax: (604)687-2145
Website: http://www.ventureswest.com

Nova Scotia

ACF Equity Atlantic Inc.
Purdy's Wharf Tower II
Ste. 2106
Halifax, NS, Canada B3J 3R7
(902)421-1965
Fax: (902)421-1808

Montgomerie, Huck & Co.
146 Bluenose Dr.
PO Box 538
Lunenburg, NS, Canada B0J 2C0
(902)634-7125
Fax: (902)634-7130

Ontario

IPS Industrial Promotion Services Ltd.
60 Columbia Way, Ste. 720
Markham, ON, Canada L3R 0C9
(905)475-9400
Fax: (905)475-5003

Betwin Investments Inc.
Box 23110
Sault Ste. Marie, ON, Canada P6A 6W6
(705)253-0744
Fax: (705)253-0744

Bailey & Company, Inc.
594 Spadina Ave.
Toronto, ON, Canada M5S 2H4
(416)921-6930
Fax: (416)925-4670

BCE Capital
200 Bay St.
South Tower, Ste. 3120
Toronto, ON, Canada M5J 2J2
(416)815-0078
Fax: (416)941-1073
Website: http://www.bcecapital.com

Castlehill Ventures
55 University Ave., Ste. 500
Toronto, ON, Canada M5J 2H7
(416)862-8574
Fax: (416)862-8875

CCFL Mezzanine Partners of Canada
70 University Ave.
Ste. 1450
Toronto, ON, Canada M5J 2M4
(416)977-1450
Fax: (416)977-6764
E-mail: info@ccfl.com
Website: http://www.ccfl.com

Celtic House International
100 Simcoe St., Ste. 100
Toronto, ON, Canada M5H 3G2
(416)542-2436
Fax: (416)542-2435
Website: http://www.celtic-house.com

Clairvest Group Inc.
22 St. Clair Ave. East
Ste. 1700
Toronto, ON, Canada M4T 2S3
(416)925-9270
Fax: (416)925-5753

Crosbie & Co., Inc.
One First Canadian Place
9th Fl.
PO Box 116
Toronto, ON, Canada M5X 1A4
(416)362-7726
Fax: (416)362-3447
E-mail: info@crosbieco.com
Website: http://www.crosbieco.com

Drug Royalty Corp.
Eight King St. East
Ste. 202
Toronto, ON, Canada M5C 1B5
(416)863-1865
Fax: (416)863-5161

Grieve, Horner, Brown & Asculai
8 King St. E, Ste. 1704
Toronto, ON, Canada M5C 1B5
(416)362-7668
Fax: (416)362-7660

Jefferson Partners
77 King St. West
Ste. 4010
PO Box 136
Toronto, ON, Canada M5K 1H1
(416)367-1533
Fax: (416)367-5827
Website: http://www.jefferson.com

J.L. Albright Venture Partners
Canada Trust Tower, 161 Bay St.
Ste. 4440
PO Box 215
Toronto, ON, Canada M5J 2S1
(416)367-2440
Fax: (416)367-4604
Website: http://www.jlaventures.com

McLean Watson Capital Inc.
One First Canadian Place
Ste. 1410
PO Box 129
Toronto, ON, Canada M5X 1A4
(416)363-2000

Fax: (416)363-2010
Website: http://www.mcleanwatson.com

Middlefield Capital Fund
One First Canadian Place
85th Fl.
PO Box 192
Toronto, ON, Canada M5X 1A6
(416)362-0714
Fax: (416)362-7925
Website: http://www.middlefield.com

Mosaic Venture Partners
24 Duncan St.
Ste. 300
Toronto, ON, Canada M5V 3M6
(416)597-8889
Fax: (416)597-2345

Onex Corp.
161 Bay St.
PO Box 700
Toronto, ON, Canada M5J 2S1
(416)362-7711
Fax: (416)362-5765

Penfund Partners Inc.
145 King St. West
Ste. 1920
Toronto, ON, Canada M5H 1J8
(416)865-0300
Fax: (416)364-6912
Website: http://www.penfund.com

Primaxis Technology Ventures Inc.
1 Richmond St. West, 8th Fl.
Toronto, ON, Canada M5H 3W4
(416)313-5210
Fax: (416)313-5218
Website: http://www.primaxis.com

Priveq Capital Funds
240 Duncan Mill Rd., Ste. 602
Toronto, ON, Canada M3B 3P1
(416)447-3330
Fax: (416)447-3331
E-mail: priveq@sympatico.ca

Roynat Ventures
40 King St. West, 26th Fl.
Toronto, ON, Canada M5H 1H1
(416)933-2667
Fax: (416)933-2783
Website: http://www.roynatcapital.com

Tera Capital Corp.
366 Adelaide St. East, Ste. 337
Toronto, ON, Canada M5A 3X9
(416)368-1024
Fax: (416)368-1427

Working Ventures Canadian Fund Inc.
250 Bloor St. East, Ste. 1600

Toronto, ON, Canada M4W 1E6
(416)934-7718
Fax: (416)929-0901
Website: http://www.workingventures.ca

Quebec

Altamira Capital Corp.
202 University
Niveau de Maisoneuve, Bur. 201
Montreal, QC, Canada H3A 2A5
(514)499-1656
Fax: (514)499-9570

Federal Business Development Bank
Venture Capital Division
Five Place Ville Marie, Ste. 600
Montreal, QC, Canada H3B 5E7
(514)283-1896
Fax: (514)283-5455

Hydro-Quebec Capitech Inc.
75 Boul, Rene Levesque Quest
Montreal, QC, Canada H2Z 1A4
(514)289-4783
Fax: (514)289-5420
Website: http://www.hqcapitech.com

Investissement Desjardins
2 complexe Desjardins
C.P. 760
Montreal, QC, Canada H5B 1B8
(514)281-7131
Fax: (514)281-7808
Website: http://www.desjardins.com/id

Marleau Lemire Inc.
One Place Ville-Marie, Ste. 3601
Montreal, QC, Canada H3B 3P2
(514)877-3800
Fax: (514)875-6415

Speirs Consultants Inc.
365 Stanstead
Montreal, QC, Canada H3R 1X5
(514)342-3858
Fax: (514)342-1977

Tecnocap Inc.
4028 Marlowe
Montreal, QC, Canada H4A 3M2
(514)483-6009
Fax: (514)483-6045
Website: http://www.technocap.com

Telsoft Ventures
1000, Rue de la Gauchetiere
Quest, 25eme Etage
Montreal, QC, Canada H3B 4W5
(514)397-8450
Fax: (514)397-8451

Saskatchewan

Saskatchewan Government Growth Fund
1801 Hamilton St., Ste. 1210
Canada Trust Tower
Regina, SK, Canada S4P 4B4
(306)787-2994
Fax: (306)787-2086

United States

Alabama

FHL Capital Corp.
600 20th Street North
Suite 350
Birmingham, AL 35203
(205)328-3098
Fax: (205)323-0001

Harbert Management Corp.
One Riverchase Pkwy. South
Birmingham, AL 35244
(205)987-5500
Fax: (205)987-5707
Website: http://www.harbert.net

Jefferson Capital Fund
PO Box 13129
Birmingham, AL 35213
(205)324-7709

Private Capital Corp.
100 Brookwood Pl., 4th Fl.
Birmingham, AL 35209
(205)879-2722
Fax: (205)879-5121

21st Century Health Ventures
One Health South Pkwy.
Birmingham, AL 35243
(256)268-6250
Fax: (256)970-8928

FJC Growth Capital Corp.
200 Westside Sq., Ste. 340
Huntsville, AL 35801
(256)922-2918
Fax: (256)922-2909

Hickory Venture Capital Corp.
301 Washington St. NW
Suite 301
Huntsville, AL 35801
(256)539-1931
Fax: (256)539-5130
E-mail: hvcc@hvcc.com
Website: http://www.hvcc.com

Southeastern Technology Fund
7910 South Memorial Pkwy., Ste. F

Huntsville, AL 35802
(256)883-8711
Fax: (256)883-8558

Cordova Ventures
4121 Carmichael Rd., Ste. 301
Montgomery, AL 36106
(334)271-6011
Fax: (334)260-0120
Website: http://www.cordovaventures
.com

**Small Business Clinic of Alabama/
AG Bartholomew & Associates**
PO Box 231074
Montgomery, AL 36123-1074
(334)284-3640

Arizona

Miller Capital Corp.
4909 E McDowell Rd.
Phoenix, AZ 85008
(602)225-0504
Fax: (602)225-9024
Website: http://www.themillergroup.com

The Columbine Venture Funds
9449 North 90th St., Ste. 200
Scottsdale, AZ 85258
(602)661-9222
Fax: (602)661-6262

Koch Ventures
17767 N. Perimeter Dr., Ste. 101
Scottsdale, AZ 85255
(480)419-3600
Fax: (480)419-3606
Website: http://www.kochventures.com

McKee & Co.
7702 E Doubletree Ranch Rd.
Suite 230
Scottsdale, AZ 85258
(480)368-0333
Fax: (480)607-7446

Merita Capital Ltd.
7350 E Stetson Dr., Ste. 108-A
Scottsdale, AZ 85251
(480)947-8700
Fax: (480)947-8766

**Valley Ventures / Arizona Growth
Partners L.P.**
6720 N. Scottsdale Rd., Ste. 208
Scottsdale, AZ 85253
(480)661-6600
Fax: (480)661-6262

Estreetcapital.com
660 South Mill Ave., Ste. 315

Tempe, AZ 85281
(480)968-8400
Fax: (480)968-8480
Website: http://www.estreetcapital.com

Coronado Venture Fund
PO Box 65420
Tucson, AZ 85728-5420
(520)577-3764
Fax: (520)299-8491

Arkansas

Arkansas Capital Corp.
225 South Pulaski St.
Little Rock, AR 72201
(501)374-9247
Fax: (501)374-9425
Website: http://www.arcapital.com

California

Sundance Venture Partners, L.P.
100 Clocktower Place, Ste. 130
Carmel, CA 93923
(831)625-6500
Fax: (831)625-6590

Westar Capital (Costa Mesa)
949 South Coast Dr., Ste. 650
Costa Mesa, CA 92626
(714)481-5160
Fax: (714)481-5166
E-mail: mailbox@westarcapital.com
Website: http://www.westarcapital.com

Alpine Technology Ventures
20300 Stevens Creek Boulevard, Ste. 495
Cupertino, CA 95014
(408)725-1810
Fax: (408)725-1207
Website: http://www.alpineventures.com

Bay Partners
10600 N. De Anza Blvd.
Cupertino, CA 95014-2031
(408)725-2444
Fax: (408)446-4502
Website: http://www.baypartners.com

Novus Ventures
20111 Stevens Creek Blvd., Ste. 130
Cupertino, CA 95014
(408)252-3900
Fax: (408)252-1713
Website: http://www.novusventures.com

Triune Capital
19925 Stevens Creek Blvd., Ste. 200
Cupertino, CA 95014
(310)284-6800
Fax: (310)284-3290

Acorn Ventures
268 Bush St., Ste. 2829
Daly City, CA 94014
(650)994-7801
Fax: (650)994-3305
Website: http://www.acornventures.com

Digital Media Campus
2221 Park Place
El Segundo, CA 90245
(310)426-8000
Fax: (310)426-8010
E-mail: info@thecampus.com
Website: http://www.digitalmediacampus
.com

BankAmerica Ventures / BA Venture Partners
950 Tower Ln., Ste. 700
Foster City, CA 94404
(650)378-6000
Fax: (650)378-6040
Website: http://www.baventurepartners
.com

Starting Point Partners
666 Portofino Lane
Foster City, CA 94404
(650)722-1035
Website: http://www.startingpoint
partners.com

Opportunity Capital Partners
2201 Walnut Ave., Ste. 210
Fremont, CA 94538
(510)795-7000
Fax: (510)494-5439
Website: http://www.ocpcapital.com

Imperial Ventures Inc.
9920 S La Cienega Boulevar, 14th Fl.
Inglewood, CA 90301
(310)417-5409
Fax: (310)338-6115

Ventana Global (Irvine)
18881 Von Karman Ave., Ste. 1150
Irvine, CA 92612
(949)476-2204
Fax: (949)752-0223
Website: http://www.ventanaglobal.com

Integrated Consortium Inc.
50 Ridgecrest Rd.
Kentfield, CA 94904
(415)925-0386
Fax: (415)461-2726

Enterprise Partners
979 Ivanhoe Ave., Ste. 550
La Jolla, CA 92037
(858)454-8833

Fax: (858)454-2489
Website: http://www.epvc.com

Domain Associates
28202 Cabot Rd., Ste. 200
Laguna Niguel, CA 92677
(949)347-2446
Fax: (949)347-9720
Website: http://www.domainvc.com

Cascade Communications Ventures
60 E Sir Francis Drake Blvd., Ste. 300
Larkspur, CA 94939
(415)925-6500
Fax: (415)925-6501

Allegis Capital
One First St., Ste. Two
Los Altos, CA 94022
(650)917-5900
Fax: (650)917-5901
Website: http://www.allegiscapital.com

Aspen Ventures
1000 Fremont Ave., Ste. 200
Los Altos, CA 94024
(650)917-5670
Fax: (650)917-5677
Website: http://www.aspenventures.com

AVI Capital L.P.
1 First St., Ste. 2
Los Altos, CA 94022
(650)949-9862
Fax: (650)949-8510
Website: http://www.avicapital.com

Bastion Capital Corp.
1999 Avenue of the Stars, Ste. 2960
Los Angeles, CA 90067
(310)788-5700
Fax: (310)277-7582
E-mail: ga@bastioncapital.com
Website: http://www.bastioncapital.com

Davis Group
PO Box 69953
Los Angeles, CA 90069-0953
(310)659-6327
Fax: (310)659-6337

Developers Equity Corp.
1880 Century Park East, Ste. 211
Los Angeles, CA 90067
(213)277-0300

Far East Capital Corp.
350 S Grand Ave., Ste. 4100
Los Angeles, CA 90071
(213)687-1361
Fax: (213)617-7939
E-mail: free@fareastnationalbank.com

Kline Hawkes & Co.
11726 San Vicente Blvd., Ste. 300
Los Angeles, CA 90049
(310)442-4700
Fax: (310)442-4707
Website: http://www.klinehawkes.com

Lawrence Financial Group
701 Teakwood
PO Box 491773
Los Angeles, CA 90049
(310)471-4060
Fax: (310)472-3155

Riordan Lewis & Haden
300 S Grand Ave., 29th Fl.
Los Angeles, CA 90071
(213)229-8500
Fax: (213)229-8597

Union Venture Corp.
445 S Figueroa St., 9th Fl.
Los Angeles, CA 90071
(213)236-4092
Fax: (213)236-6329

Wedbush Capital Partners
1000 Wilshire Blvd.
Los Angeles, CA 90017
(213)688-4545
Fax: (213)688-6642
Website: http://www.wedbush.com

Advent International Corp.
2180 Sand Hill Rd., Ste. 420
Menlo Park, CA 94025
(650)233-7500
Fax: (650)233-7515
Website: http://www.adventinternational
.com

Altos Ventures
2882 Sand Hill Rd., Ste. 100
Menlo Park, CA 94025
(650)234-9771
Fax: (650)233-9821
Website: http://www.altosvc.com

Applied Technology
1010 El Camino Real, Ste. 300
Menlo Park, CA 94025
(415)326-8622
Fax: (415)326-8163

APV Technology Partners
535 Middlefield, Ste. 150
Menlo Park, CA 94025
(650)327-7871
Fax: (650)327-7631
Website: http://www.apvtp.com

August Capital Management
2480 Sand Hill Rd., Ste. 101

Menlo Park, CA 94025
(650)234-9900
Fax: (650)234-9910
Website: http://www.augustcap.com

Baccharis Capital Inc.
2420 Sand Hill Rd., Ste. 100
Menlo Park, CA 94025
(650)324-6844
Fax: (650)854-3025

Benchmark Capital
2480 Sand Hill Rd., Ste. 200
Menlo Park, CA 94025
(650)854-8180
Fax: (650)854-8183
E-mail: info@benchmark.com
Website: http://www.benchmark.com

Bessemer Venture Partners (Menlo Park)
535 Middlefield Rd., Ste. 245
Menlo Park, CA 94025
(650)853-7000
Fax: (650)853-7001
Website: http://www.bvp.com

The Cambria Group
1600 El Camino Real Rd., Ste. 155
Menlo Park, CA 94025
(650)329-8600
Fax: (650)329-8601
Website: http://www.cambriagroup.com

Canaan Partners
2884 Sand Hill Rd., Ste. 115
Menlo Park, CA 94025
(650)854-8092
Fax: (650)854-8127
Website: http://www.canaan.com

Capstone Ventures
3000 Sand Hill Rd., Bldg. One, Ste. 290
Menlo Park, CA 94025
(650)854-2523
Fax: (650)854-9010
Website: http://www.capstonevc.com

Comdisco Venture Group (Silicon Valley)
3000 Sand Hill Rd., Bldg. 1, Ste. 155
Menlo Park, CA 94025
(650)854-9484
Fax: (650)854-4026

Commtech International
535 Middlefield Rd., Ste. 200
Menlo Park, CA 94025
(650)328-0190
Fax: (650)328-6442

Compass Technology Partners
1550 El Camino Real, Ste. 275

Menlo Park, CA 94025-4111
(650)322-7595
Fax: (650)322-0588
Website: http://www.compasstech
partners.com

Convergence Partners
3000 Sand Hill Rd., Ste. 235
Menlo Park, CA 94025
(650)854-3010
Fax: (650)854-3015
Website: http://www.convergence
partners.com

The Dakota Group
PO Box 1025
Menlo Park, CA 94025
(650)853-0600
Fax: (650)851-4899
E-mail: info@dakota.com

Delphi Ventures
3000 Sand Hill Rd.
Bldg. One, Ste. 135
Menlo Park, CA 94025
(650)854-9650
Fax: (650)854-2961
Website: http://www.delphiventures.com

El Dorado Ventures
2884 Sand Hill Rd., Ste. 121
Menlo Park, CA 94025
(650)854-1200
Fax: (650)854-1202
Website: http://www.eldoradoventures.com

Glynn Ventures
3000 Sand Hill Rd., Bldg. 4, Ste. 235
Menlo Park, CA 94025
(650)854-2215

Indosuez Ventures
2180 Sand Hill Rd., Ste. 450
Menlo Park, CA 94025
(650)854-0587
Fax: (650)323-5561
Website: http://www.indosuezventures
.com

Institutional Venture Partners
3000 Sand Hill Rd., Bldg. 2, Ste. 290
Menlo Park, CA 94025
(650)854-0132
Fax: (650)854-5762
Website: http://www.ivp.com

Interwest Partners (Menlo Park)
3000 Sand Hill Rd., Bldg. 3, Ste. 255
Menlo Park, CA 94025-7112
(650)854-8585
Fax: (650)854-4706
Website: http://www.interwest.com

Kleiner Perkins Caufield & Byers (Menlo Park)
2750 Sand Hill Rd.
Menlo Park, CA 94025
(650)233-2750
Fax: (650)233-0300
Website: http://www.kpcb.com

Magic Venture Capital LLC
1010 El Camino Real, Ste. 300
Menlo Park, CA 94025
(650)325-4149

Matrix Partners
2500 Sand Hill Rd., Ste. 113
Menlo Park, CA 94025
(650)854-3131
Fax: (650)854-3296
Website: http://www.matrixpartners.com

Mayfield Fund
2800 Sand Hill Rd.
Menlo Park, CA 94025
(650)854-5560
Fax: (650)854-5712
Website: http://www.mayfield.com

McCown De Leeuw and Co. (Menlo Park)
3000 Sand Hill Rd., Bldg. 3, Ste. 290
Menlo Park, CA 94025-7111
(650)854-6000
Fax: (650)854-0853
Website: http://www.mdcpartners.com

Menlo Ventures
3000 Sand Hill Rd., Bldg. 4, Ste. 100
Menlo Park, CA 94025
(650)854-8540
Fax: (650)854-7059
Website: http://www.menloventures.com

Merrill Pickard Anderson & Eyre
2480 Sand Hill Rd., Ste. 200
Menlo Park, CA 94025
(650)854-8600
Fax: (650)854-0345

New Enterprise Associates (Menlo Park)
2490 Sand Hill Rd.
Menlo Park, CA 94025
(650)854-9499
Fax: (650)854-9397
Website: http://www.nea.com

Onset Ventures
2400 Sand Hill Rd., Ste. 150
Menlo Park, CA 94025
(650)529-0700
Fax: (650)529-0777
Website: http://www.onset.com

Paragon Venture Partners
3000 Sand Hill Rd., Bldg. 1, Ste. 275
Menlo Park, CA 94025
(650)854-8000
Fax: (650)854-7260

**Pathfinder Venture Capital Funds
(Menlo Park)**
3000 Sand Hill Rd., Bldg. 3, Ste. 255
Menlo Park, CA 94025
(650)854-0650
Fax: (650)854-4706

Rocket Ventures
3000 Sandhill Rd., Bldg. 1, Ste. 170
Menlo Park, CA 94025
(650)561-9100
Fax: (650)561-9183
Website: http://www.rocketventures.com

Sequoia Capital
3000 Sand Hill Rd., Bldg. 4, Ste. 280
Menlo Park, CA 94025
(650)854-3927
Fax: (650)854-2977
E-mail: sequoia@sequoiacap.com
Website: http://www.sequoiacap.com

Sierra Ventures
3000 Sand Hill Rd., Bldg. 4, Ste. 210
Menlo Park, CA 94025
(650)854-1000
Fax: (650)854-5593
Website: http://www.sierraventures.com

Sigma Partners
2884 Sand Hill Rd., Ste. 121
Menlo Park, CA 94025-7022
(650)853-1700
Fax: (650)853-1717
E-mail: info@sigmapartners.com
Website: http://www.sigmapartners.com

Sprout Group (Menlo Park)
3000 Sand Hill Rd.
Bldg. 3, Ste. 170
Menlo Park, CA 94025
(650)234-2700
Fax: (650)234-2779
Website: http://www.sproutgroup.com

TA Associates (Menlo Park)
70 Willow Rd., Ste. 100
Menlo Park, CA 94025
(650)328-1210
Fax: (650)326-4933
Website: http://www.ta.com

Thompson Clive & Partners Ltd.
3000 Sand Hill Rd., Bldg. 1, Ste. 185
Menlo Park, CA 94025-7102
(650)854-0314

Fax: (650)854-0670
E-mail: mail@tcvc.com
Website: http://www.tcvc.com

Trinity Ventures Ltd.
3000 Sand Hill Rd., Bldg. 1, Ste. 240
Menlo Park, CA 94025
(650)854-9500
Fax: (650)854-9501
Website: http://www.trinityventures.com

U.S. Venture Partners
2180 Sand Hill Rd., Ste. 300
Menlo Park, CA 94025
(650)854-9080
Fax: (650)854-3018
Website: http://www.usvp.com

USVP-Schlein Marketing Fund
2180 Sand Hill Rd., Ste. 300
Menlo Park, CA 94025
(415)854-9080
Fax: (415)854-3018
Website: http://www.usvp.com

Venrock Associates
2494 Sand Hill Rd., Ste. 200
Menlo Park, CA 94025
(650)561-9580
Fax: (650)561-9180
Website: http://www.venrock.com

Brad Peery Capital Inc.
145 Chapel Pkwy.
Mill Valley, CA 94941
(415)389-0625
Fax: (415)389-1336

Dot Edu Ventures
650 Castro St., Ste. 270
Mountain View, CA 94041
(650)575-5638
Fax: (650)325-5247
Website: http://www.doteduventures.com

Forrest, Binkley & Brown
840 Newport Ctr. Dr., Ste. 480
Newport Beach, CA 92660
(949)729-3222
Fax: (949)729-3226
Website: http://www.fbbvc.com

Marwit Capital LLC
180 Newport Center Dr., Ste. 200
Newport Beach, CA 92660
(949)640-6234
Fax: (949)720-8077
Website: http://www.marwit.com

**Kaiser Permanente / National Venture
Development**
1800 Harrison St., 22nd Fl.

Oakland, CA 94612
(510)267-4010
Fax: (510)267-4036
Website: http://www.kpventures.com

Nu Capital Access Group, Ltd.
7677 Oakport St., Ste. 105
Oakland, CA 94621
(510)635-7345
Fax: (510)635-7068

Inman and Bowman
4 Orinda Way, Bldg. D, Ste. 150
Orinda, CA 94563
(510)253-1611
Fax: (510)253-9037

Accel Partners (San Francisco)
428 University Ave.
Palo Alto, CA 94301
(650)614-4800
Fax: (650)614-4880
Website: http://www.accel.com

Advanced Technology Ventures
485 Ramona St., Ste. 200
Palo Alto, CA 94301
(650)321-8601
Fax: (650)321-0934
Website: http://www.atvcapital.com

Anila Fund
400 Channing Ave.
Palo Alto, CA 94301
(650)833-5790
Fax: (650)833-0590
Website: http://www.anila.com

**Asset Management Company
Venture Capital**
2275 E Bayshore, Ste. 150
Palo Alto, CA 94303
(650)494-7400
Fax: (650)856-1826
E-mail: postmaster@assetman.com
Website: http://www.assetman.com

**BancBoston Capital / BancBoston
Ventures**
435 Tasso St., Ste. 250
Palo Alto, CA 94305
(650)470-4100
Fax: (650)853-1425
Website: http://www.bancbostoncapital
.com

Charter Ventures
525 University Ave., Ste. 1400
Palo Alto, CA 94301
(650)325-6953
Fax: (650)325-4762
Website: http://www.charterventures.com

Communications Ventures
505 Hamilton Avenue, Ste. 305
Palo Alto, CA 94301
(650)325-9600
Fax: (650)325-9608
Website: http://www.comven.com

HMS Group
2468 Embarcadero Way
Palo Alto, CA 94303-3313
(650)856-9862
Fax: (650)856-9864

Jafco America Ventures, Inc.
505 Hamilton Ste. 310
Palto Alto, CA 94301
(650)463-8800
Fax: (650)463-8801
Website: http://www.jafco.com

New Vista Capital
540 Cowper St., Ste. 200
Palo Alto, CA 94301
(650)329-9333
Fax: (650)328-9434
E-mail: fgreene@nvcap.com
Website: http://www.nvcap.com

Norwest Equity Partners (Palo Alto)
245 Lytton Ave., Ste. 250
Palo Alto, CA 94301-1426
(650)321-8000
Fax: (650)321-8010
Website: http://www.norwestvp.com

Oak Investment Partners
525 University Ave., Ste. 1300
Palo Alto, CA 94301
(650)614-3700
Fax: (650)328-6345
Website: http://www.oakinv.com

Patricof & Co. Ventures, Inc. (Palo Alto)
2100 Geng Rd., Ste. 150
Palo Alto, CA 94303
(650)494-9944
Fax: (650)494-6751
Website: http://www.patricof.com

RWI Group
835 Page Mill Rd.
Palo Alto, CA 94304
(650)251-1800
Fax: (650)213-8660
Website: http://www.rwigroup.com

Summit Partners (Palo Alto)
499 Hamilton Ave., Ste. 200
Palo Alto, CA 94301
(650)321-1166
Fax: (650)321-1188

Website: http://www.summitpartners
.com

Sutter Hill Ventures
755 Page Mill Rd., Ste. A-200
Palo Alto, CA 94304
(650)493-5600
Fax: (650)858-1854
E-mail: shv@shv.com

Vanguard Venture Partners
525 University Ave., Ste. 600
Palo Alto, CA 94301
(650)321-2900
Fax: (650)321-2902
Website: http://www.vanguardventures
.com

Venture Growth Associates
2479 East Bayshore St., Ste. 710
Palo Alto, CA 94303
(650)855-9100
Fax: (650)855-9104

Worldview Technology Partners
435 Tasso St., Ste. 120
Palo Alto, CA 94301
(650)322-3800
Fax: (650)322-3880
Website: http://www.worldview.com

Draper, Fisher, Jurvetson / Draper Associates
400 Seaport Ct., Ste.250
Redwood City, CA 94063
(415)599-9000
Fax: (415)599-9726
Website: http://www.dfj.com

Gabriel Venture Partners
350 Marine Pkwy., Ste. 200
Redwood Shores, CA 94065
(650)551-5000
Fax: (650)551-5001
Website: http://www.gabrielvp.com

Hallador Venture Partners, L.L.C.
740 University Ave., Ste. 110
Sacramento, CA 95825-6710
(916)920-0191
Fax: (916)920-5188
E-mail: chris@hallador.com

Emerald Venture Group
12396 World Trade Dr., Ste. 116
San Diego, CA 92128
(858)451-1001
Fax: (858)451-1003
Website: http://www.emeraldventure.com

Forward Ventures
9255 Towne Centre Dr.

San Diego, CA 92121
(858)677-6077
Fax: (858)452-8799
E-mail: info@forwardventure.com
Website: http://www.forwardventure.com

Idanta Partners Ltd.
4660 La Jolla Village Dr., Ste. 850
San Diego, CA 92122
(619)452-9690
Fax: (619)452-2013
Website: http://www.idanta.com

Kingsbury Associates
3655 Nobel Dr., Ste. 490
San Diego, CA 92122
(858)677-0600
Fax: (858)677-0800

Kyocera International Inc.
Corporate Development
8611 Balboa Ave.
San Diego, CA 92123
(858)576-2600
Fax: (858)492-1456

Sorrento Associates, Inc.
4370 LaJolla Village Dr., Ste. 1040
San Diego, CA 92122
(619)452-3100
Fax: (619)452-7607
Website: http://www.sorrentoventures
.com

Western States Investment Group
9191 Towne Ctr. Dr., Ste. 310
San Diego, CA 92122
(619)678-0800
Fax: (619)678-0900

Aberdare Ventures
One Embarcadero Center, Ste. 4000
San Francisco, CA 94111
(415)392-7442
Fax: (415)392-4264
Website: http://www.aberdare.com

Acacia Venture Partners
101 California St., Ste. 3160
San Francisco, CA 94111
(415)433-4200
Fax: (415)433-4250
Website: http://www.acaciavp.com

Access Venture Partners
319 Laidley St.
San Francisco, CA 94131
(415)586-0132
Fax: (415)392-6310
Website: http://www.accessventure
partners.com

Alta Partners
One Embarcadero Center, Ste. 4050
San Francisco, CA 94111
(415)362-4022
Fax: (415)362-6178
E-mail: alta@altapartners.com
Website: http://www.altapartners.com

Bangert Dawes Reade Davis & Thom
220 Montgomery St., Ste. 424
San Francisco, CA 94104
(415)954-9900
Fax: (415)954-9901
E-mail: bdrdt@pacbell.net

Berkeley International Capital Corp.
650 California St., Ste. 2800
San Francisco, CA 94108-2609
(415)249-0450
Fax: (415)392-3929
Website: http://www.berkeleyvc.com

Blueprint Ventures LLC
456 Montgomery St., 22nd Fl.
San Francisco, CA 94104
(415)901-4000
Fax: (415)901-4035
Website: http://www.blueprintventures
.com

Blumberg Capital Ventures
580 Howard St., Ste. 401
San Francisco, CA 94105
(415)905-5007
Fax: (415)357-5027
Website: http://www.blumberg-capital
.com

Burr, Egan, Deleage, and Co. (San Francisco)
1 Embarcadero Center, Ste. 4050
San Francisco, CA 94111
(415)362-4022
Fax: (415)362-6178

Burrill & Company
120 Montgomery St., Ste. 1370
San Francisco, CA 94104
(415)743-3160
Fax: (415)743-3161
Website: http://www.burrillandco.com

CMEA Ventures
235 Montgomery St., Ste. 920
San Francisco, CA 94401
(415)352-1520
Fax: (415)352-1524
Website: http://www.cmeaventures.com

Crocker Capital
1 Post St., Ste. 2500
San Francisco, CA 94101

(415)956-5250
Fax: (415)959-5710

Dominion Ventures, Inc.
44 Montgomery St., Ste. 4200
San Francisco, CA 94104
(415)362-4890
Fax: (415)394-9245

Dorset Capital
Pier 1
Bay 2
San Francisco, CA 94111
(415)398-7101
Fax: (415)398-7141
Website: http://www.dorsetcapital.com

Gatx Capital
Four Embarcadero Center, Ste. 2200
San Francisco, CA 94904
(415)955-3200
Fax: (415)955-3449

IMinds
135 Main St., Ste. 1350
San Francisco, CA 94105
(415)547-0000
Fax: (415)227-0300
Website: http://www.iminds.com

LF International Inc.
360 Post St., Ste. 705
San Francisco, CA 94108
(415)399-0110
Fax: (415)399-9222
Website: http://www.lfvc.com

Newbury Ventures
535 Pacific Ave., 2nd Fl.
San Francisco, CA 94133
(415)296-7408
Fax: (415)296-7416
Website: http://www.newburyven.com

Quest Ventures (San Francisco)
333 Bush St., Ste. 1750
San Francisco, CA 94104
(415)782-1414
Fax: (415)782-1415

Robertson-Stephens Co.
555 California St., Ste. 2600
San Francisco, CA 94104
(415)781-9700
Fax: (415)781-2556
Website: http://www.omegaadventures.
com

Rosewood Capital, L.P.
One Maritime Plaza, Ste. 1330
San Francisco, CA 94111-3503
(415)362-5526

Fax: (415)362-1192
Website: http://www.rosewoodvc.com

Ticonderoga Capital Inc.
555 California St., No. 4950
San Francisco, CA 94104
(415)296-7900
Fax: (415)296-8956

21st Century Internet Venture Partners
Two South Park
2nd Floor
San Francisco, CA 94107
(415)512-1221
Fax: (415)512-2650
Website: http://www.21vc.com

VK Ventures
600 California St., Ste.1700
San Francisco, CA 94111
(415)391-5600
Fax: (415)397-2744

Walden Group of Venture Capital Funds
750 Battery St., Seventh Floor
San Francisco, CA 94111
(415)391-7225
Fax: (415)391-7262

Acer Technology Ventures
2641 Orchard Pkwy.
San Jose, CA 95134
(408)433-4945
Fax: (408)433-5230

Authosis
226 Airport Pkwy., Ste. 405
San Jose, CA 95110
(650)814-3603
Website: http://www.authosis.com

Western Technology Investment
2010 N. First St., Ste. 310
San Jose, CA 95131
(408)436-8577
Fax: (408)436-8625
E-mail: mktg@westerntech.com

Drysdale Enterprises
177 Bovet Rd., Ste. 600
San Mateo, CA 94402
(650)341-6336
Fax: (650)341-1329
E-mail: drysdale@aol.com

Greylock
2929 Campus Dr., Ste. 400
San Mateo, CA 94401
(650)493-5525
Fax: (650)493-5575
Website: http://www.greylock.com

Technology Funding
2000 Alameda de las Pulgas, Ste. 250
San Mateo, CA 94403
(415)345-2200
Fax: (415)345-1797

2M Invest Inc.
1875 S Grant St.
Suite 750
San Mateo, CA 94402
(650)655-3765
Fax: (650)372-9107
E-mail: 2minfo@2minvest.com
Website: http://www.2minvest.com

Phoenix Growth Capital Corp.
2401 Kerner Blvd.
San Rafael, CA 94901
(415)485-4569
Fax: (415)485-4663

NextGen Partners LLC
1705 East Valley Rd.
Santa Barbara, CA 93108
(805)969-8540
Fax: (805)969-8542
Website: http://www.nextgenpartners
.com

Denali Venture Capital
1925 Woodland Ave.
Santa Clara, CA 95050
(408)690-4838
Fax: (408)247-6979
E-mail: wael@denaliventurecapital.com
Website: http://www.denaliventurecapital
.com

Dotcom Ventures LP
3945 Freedom Circle, Ste. 740
Santa Clara, CA 95045
(408)919-9855
Fax: (408)919-9857
Website: http://www.dotcomventuresatl
.com

Silicon Valley Bank
3003 Tasman
Santa Clara, CA 95054
(408)654-7400
Fax: (408)727-8728

Al Shugart International
920 41st Ave.
Santa Cruz, CA 95062
(831)479-7852
Fax: (831)479-7852
Website: http://www.alshugart.com

Leonard Mautner Associates
1434 Sixth St.
Santa Monica, CA 90401

(213)393-9788
Fax: (310)459-9918

Palomar Ventures
100 Wilshire Blvd., Ste. 450
Santa Monica, CA 90401
(310)260-6050
Fax: (310)656-4150
Website: http://www.palomarventures
.com

Medicus Venture Partners
12930 Saratoga Ave., Ste. D8
Saratoga, CA 95070
(408)447-8600
Fax: (408)447-8599
Website: http://www.medicusvc.com

Redleaf Venture Management
14395 Saratoga Ave., Ste. 130
Saratoga, CA 95070
(408)868-0800
Fax: (408)868-0810
E-mail: nancy@redleaf.com
Website: http://www.redleaf.com

Artemis Ventures
207 Second St., Ste. E
3rd Fl.
Sausalito, CA 94965
(415)289-2500
Fax: (415)289-1789
Website: http://www.artemisventures.com

Deucalion Venture Partners
19501 Brooklime
Sonoma, CA 95476
(707)938-4974
Fax: (707)938-8921

Windward Ventures
PO Box 7688
Thousand Oaks, CA 91359-7688
(805)497-3332
Fax: (805)497-9331

National Investment Management, Inc.
2601 Airport Dr., Ste.210
Torrance, CA 90505
(310)784-7600
Fax: (310)784-7605

Southern California Ventures
406 Amapola Ave. Ste. 125
Torrance, CA 90501
(310)787-4381
Fax: (310)787-4382

Sandton Financial Group
21550 Oxnard St., Ste. 300
Woodland Hills, CA 91367
(818)702-9283

Woodside Fund
850 Woodside Dr.
Woodside, CA 94062
(650)368-5545
Fax: (650)368-2416
Website: http://www.woodsidefund.com

Colorado

Colorado Venture Management
Ste. 300
Boulder, CO 80301
(303)440-4055
Fax: (303)440-4636

Dean & Associates
4362 Apple Way
Boulder, CO 80301
Fax: (303)473-9900

Roser Ventures LLC
1105 Spruce St.
Boulder, CO 80302
(303)443-6436
Fax: (303)443-1885
Website: http://www.roserventures.com

Sequel Venture Partners
4430 Arapahoe Ave., Ste. 220
Boulder, CO 80303
(303)546-0400
Fax: (303)546-9728
E-mail: tom@sequelvc.com
Website: http://www.sequelvc.com

New Venture Resources
445C E Cheyenne Mtn. Blvd.
Colorado Springs, CO 80906-4570
(719)598-9272
Fax: (719)598-9272

The Centennial Funds
1428 15th St.
Denver, CO 80202-1318
(303)405-7500
Fax: (303)405-7575
Website: http://www.centennial.com

Rocky Mountain Capital Partners
1125 17th St., Ste. 2260
Denver, CO 80202
(303)291-5200
Fax: (303)291-5327

Sandlot Capital LLC
600 South Cherry St., Ste. 525
Denver, CO 80246
(303)893-3400
Fax: (303)893-3403
Website: http://www.sandlotcapital.com

Wolf Ventures
50 South Steele St., Ste. 777

Denver, CO 80209
(303)321-4800
Fax: (303)321-4848
E-mail: businessplan@wolfventures.com
Website: http://www.wolfventures.com

The Columbine Venture Funds
5460 S Quebec St., Ste. 270
Englewood, CO 80111
(303)694-3222
Fax: (303)694-9007

Investment Securities of Colorado, Inc.
4605 Denice Dr.
Englewood, CO 80111
(303)796-9192

Kinship Partners
6300 S Syracuse Way, Ste. 484
Englewood, CO 80111
(303)694-0268
Fax: (303)694-1707
E-mail: block@vailsys.com

Boranco Management, L.L.C.
1528 Hillside Dr.
Fort Collins, CO 80524-1969
(970)221-2297
Fax: (970)221-4787

Aweida Ventures
890 West Cherry St., Ste. 220
Louisville, CO 80027
(303)664-9520
Fax: (303)664-9530
Website: http://www.aweida.com

Access Venture Partners
8787 Turnpike Dr., Ste. 260
Westminster, CO 80030
(303)426-8899
Fax: (303)426-8828

Connecticut

Medmax Ventures, LP
1 Northwestern Dr., Ste. 203
Bloomfield, CT 06002
(860)286-2960
Fax: (860)286-9960

James B. Kobak & Co.
Four Mansfield Place
Darien, CT 06820
(203)656-3471
Fax: (203)655-2905

Orien Ventures
1 Post Rd.
Fairfield, CT 06430
(203)259-9933
Fax: (203)259-5288

ABP Acquisition Corporation
115 Maple Ave.
Greenwich, CT 06830
(203)625-8287
Fax: (203)447-6187

Catterton Partners
9 Greenwich Office Park
Greenwich, CT 06830
(203)629-4901
Fax: (203)629-4903
Website: http://www.cpequity.com

Consumer Venture Partners
3 Pickwick Plz.
Greenwich, CT 06830
(203)629-8800
Fax: (203)629-2019

Insurance Venture Partners
31 Brookside Dr., Ste. 211
Greenwich, CT 06830
(203)861-0030
Fax: (203)861-2745

The NTC Group
Three Pickwick Plaza
Ste. 200
Greenwich, CT 06830
(203)862-2800
Fax: (203)622-6538

Regulus International Capital Co., Inc.
140 Greenwich Ave.
Greenwich, CT 06830
(203)625-9700
Fax: (203)625-9706

Axiom Venture Partners
City Place II
185 Asylum St., 17th Fl.
Hartford, CT 06103
(860)548-7799
Fax: (860)548-7797
Website: http://www.axiomventures.com

Conning Capital Partners
City Place II
185 Asylum St.
Hartford, CT 06103-4105
(860)520-1289
Fax: (860)520-1299
E-mail: pe@conning.com
Website: http://www.conning.com

First New England Capital L.P.
100 Pearl St.
Hartford, CT 06103
(860)293-3333
Fax: (860)293-3338
E-mail: info@firstnewenglandcapital.com
Website: http://www.firstnewengland
capital.com

Northeast Ventures
One State St., Ste. 1720
Hartford, CT 06103
(860)547-1414
Fax: (860)246-8755

Windward Holdings
38 Sylvan Rd.
Madison, CT 06443
(203)245-6870
Fax: (203)245-6865

Advanced Materials Partners, Inc.
45 Pine St.
PO Box 1022
New Canaan, CT 06840
(203)966-6415
Fax: (203)966-8448
E-mail: wkb@amplink.com

RFE Investment Partners
36 Grove St.
New Canaan, CT 06840
(203)966-2800
Fax: (203)966-3109
Website: http://www.rfeip.com

Connecticut Innovations, Inc.
999 West St.
Rocky Hill, CT 06067
(860)563-5851
Fax: (860)563-4877
E-mail: pamela.hartley@ctinnovations
.com
Website: http://www.ctinnovations.com

Canaan Partners
105 Rowayton Ave.
Rowayton, CT 06853
(203)855-0400
Fax: (203)854-9117
Website: http://www.canaan.com

Landmark Partners, Inc.
10 Mill Pond Ln.
Simsbury, CT 06070
(860)651-9760
Fax: (860)651-8890
Website: http://www.landmarkpartners
.com

Sweeney & Company
PO Box 567
Southport, CT 06490
(203)255-0220
Fax: (203)255-0220
E-mail: sweeney@connix.com

Baxter Associates, Inc.
PO Box 1333
Stamford, CT 06904
(203)323-3143
Fax: (203)348-0622

Beacon Partners Inc.
6 Landmark Sq., 4th Fl.
Stamford, CT 06901-2792
(203)359-5776
Fax: (203)359-5876

Collinson, Howe, and Lennox, LLC
1055 Washington Blvd., 5th Fl.
Stamford, CT 06901
(203)324-7700
Fax: (203)324-3636
E-mail: info@chlmedical.com
Website: http://www.chlmedical.com

Prime Capital Management Co.
550 West Ave.
Stamford, CT 06902
(203)964-0642
Fax: (203)964-0862

Saugatuck Capital Co.
1 Canterbury Green
Stamford, CT 06901
(203)348-6669
Fax: (203)324-6995
Website: http://www.saugatuckcapital
.com

Soundview Financial Group Inc.
22 Gatehouse Rd.
Stamford, CT 06902
(203)462-7200
Fax: (203)462-7350
Website: http://www.sndv.com

TSG Ventures, L.L.C.
177 Broad St., 12th Fl.
Stamford, CT 06901
(203)406-1500
Fax: (203)406-1590

Whitney & Company
177 Broad St.
Stamford, CT 06901
(203)973-1400
Fax: (203)973-1422
Website: http://www.jhwhitney.com

Cullinane & Donnelly Venture Partners L.P.
970 Farmington Ave.
West Hartford, CT 06107
(860)521-7811

The Crestview Investment and Financial Group
431 Post Rd. E, Ste. 1
Westport, CT 06880-4403
(203)222-0333
Fax: (203)222-0000

Marketcorp Venture Associates, L.P. (MCV)
274 Riverside Ave.
Westport, CT 06880
(203)222-3030
Fax: (203)222-3033

Oak Investment Partners (Westport)
1 Gorham Island
Westport, CT 06880
(203)226-8346
Fax: (203)227-0372
Website: http://www.oakinv.com

Oxford Bioscience Partners
315 Post Rd. W
Westport, CT 06880-5200
(203)341-3300
Fax: (203)341-3309
Website: http://www.oxbio.com

Prince Ventures (Westport)
25 Ford Rd.
Westport, CT 06880
(203)227-8332
Fax: (203)226-5302

LTI Venture Leasing Corp.
221 Danbury Rd.
Wilton, CT 06897
(203)563-1100
Fax: (203)563-1111
Website: http://www.ltileasing.com

Delaware

Blue Rock Capital
5803 Kennett Pike, Ste. A
Wilmington, DE 19807
(302)426-0981
Fax: (302)426-0982
Website: http://www.bluerockcapital.com

District of Columbia

Allied Capital Corp.
1919 Pennsylvania Ave. NW
Washington, DC 20006-3434
(202)331-2444
Fax: (202)659-2053
Website: http://www.alliedcapital.com

Atlantic Coastal Ventures, L.P.
3101 South St. NW
Washington, DC 20007
(202)293-1166
Fax: (202)293-1181
Website: http://www.atlanticcv.com

Columbia Capital Group, Inc.
1660 L St. NW, Ste. 308
Washington, DC 20036

(202)775-8815
Fax: (202)223-0544

Core Capital Partners
901 15th St., NW
9th Fl.
Washington, DC 20005
(202)589-0090
Fax: (202)589-0091
Website: http://www.core-capital.com

Next Point Partners
701 Pennsylvania Ave. NW, Ste. 900
Washington, DC 20004
(202)661-8703
Fax: (202)434-7400
E-mail: mf@nextpoint.vc
Website: http://www.nextpointvc.com

Telecommunications Development Fund
2020 K. St. NW
Ste. 375
Washington, DC 20006
(202)293-8840
Fax: (202)293-8850
Website: http://www.tdfund.com

Wachtel & Co., Inc.
1101 4th St. NW
Washington, DC 20005-5680
(202)898-1144

Winslow Partners LLC
1300 Connecticut Ave. NW
Washington, DC 20036-1703
(202)530-5000
Fax: (202)530-5010
E-mail: winslow@winslowpartners.com

Women's Growth Capital Fund
1054 31st St., NW
Ste. 110
Washington, DC 20007
(202)342-1431
Fax: (202)341-1203
Website: http://www.wgcf.com

Florida

Sigma Capital Corp.
22668 Caravelle Circle
Boca Raton, FL 33433
(561)368-9783

North American Business Development Co., L.L.C.
111 East Las Olas Blvd.
Fort Lauderdale, FL 33301
(305)463-0681
Fax: (305)527-0904

Website: http://www.northamericanfund
.com

Chartwell Capital Management Co. Inc.
1 Independent Dr., Ste. 3120
Jacksonville, FL 32202
(904)355-3519
Fax: (904)353-5833
E-mail: info@chartwellcap.com

CEO Advisors
1061 Maitland Center Commons
Ste. 209
Maitland, FL 32751
(407)660-9327
Fax: (407)660-2109

Henry & Co.
8201 Peters Rd., Ste. 1000
Plantation, FL 33324
(954)797-7400

Avery Business Development Services
2506 St. Michel Ct.
Ponte Vedra, FL 32082
(904)285-6033

New South Ventures
5053 Ocean Blvd.
Sarasota, FL 34242
(941)358-6000
Fax: (941)358-6078
Website: http://www.newsouthventures.
com

Venture Capital Management Corp.
PO Box 2626
Satellite Beach, FL 32937
(407)777-1969

Florida Capital Venture Ltd.
325 Florida Bank Plaza
100 W Kennedy Blvd.
Tampa, FL 33602
(813)229-2294
Fax: (813)229-2028

Quantum Capital Partners
339 South Plant Ave.
Tampa, FL 33606
(813)250-1999
Fax: (813)250-1998
Website: http://www.quantumcapital
partners.com

South Atlantic Venture Fund
614 W Bay St.
Tampa, FL 33606-2704
(813)253-2500
Fax: (813)253-2360
E-mail: venture@southatlantic.com
Website: http://www.southatlantic.com

LM Capital Corp.
120 S Olive, Ste. 400
West Palm Beach, FL 33401
(561)833-9700
Fax: (561)655-6587
Website: http://www.lmcapitalsecurities.
com

Georgia

Venture First Associates
4811 Thornwood Dr.
Acworth, GA 30102
(770)928-3733
Fax: (770)928-6455

Alliance Technology Ventures
8995 Westside Pkwy., Ste. 200
Alpharetta, GA 30004
(678)336-2000
Fax: (678)336-2001
E-mail: info@atv.com
Website: http://www.atv.com

Cordova Ventures
2500 North Winds Pkwy., Ste. 475
Alpharetta, GA 30004
(678)942-0300
Fax: (678)942-0301
Website: http://www.cordovaventures
.com

**Advanced Technology
Development Fund**
1000 Abernathy, Ste. 1420
Atlanta, GA 30328-5614
(404)668-2333
Fax: (404)668-2333

CGW Southeast Partners
12 Piedmont Center, Ste. 210
Atlanta, GA 30305
(404)816-3255
Fax: (404)816-3258
Website: http://www.cgwlp.com

Cyberstarts
1900 Emery St., NW
3rd Fl.
Atlanta, GA 30318
(404)267-5000
Fax: (404)267-5200
Website: http://www.cyberstarts.com

EGL Holdings, Inc.
10 Piedmont Center, Ste. 412
Atlanta, GA 30305
(404)949-8300
Fax: (404)949-8311

Equity South
1790 The Lenox Bldg.

3399 Peachtree Rd. NE
Atlanta, GA 30326
(404)237-6222
Fax: (404)261-1578

Five Paces
3400 Peachtree Rd., Ste. 200
Atlanta, GA 30326
(404)439-8300
Fax: (404)439-8301
Website: http://www.fivepaces.com

Frontline Capital, Inc.
3475 Lenox Rd., Ste. 400
Atlanta, GA 30326
(404)240-7280
Fax: (404)240-7281

Fuqua Ventures LLC
1201 W Peachtree St. NW, Ste. 5000
Atlanta, GA 30309
(404)815-4500
Fax: (404)815-4528
Website: http://www.fuquaventures.com

Noro-Moseley Partners
4200 Northside Pkwy., Bldg. 9
Atlanta, GA 30327
(404)233-1966
Fax: (404)239-9280
Website: http://www.noro-moseley.com

Renaissance Capital Corp.
34 Peachtree St. NW, Ste. 2230
Atlanta, GA 30303
(404)658-9061
Fax: (404)658-9064

River Capital, Inc.
Two Midtown Plaza
1360 Peachtree St. NE, Ste. 1430
Atlanta, GA 30309
(404)873-2166
Fax: (404)873-2158

State Street Bank & Trust Co.
3414 Peachtree Rd. NE, Ste. 1010
Atlanta, GA 30326
(404)364-9500
Fax: (404)261-4469

UPS Strategic Enterprise Fund
55 Glenlake Pkwy. NE
Atlanta, GA 30328
(404)828-8814
Fax: (404)828-8088
E-mail: jcacyce@ups.com
Website: http://www.ups.com/sef/
sef_home

Wachovia
191 Peachtree St. NE, 26th Fl.

Atlanta, GA 30303
(404)332-1000
Fax: (404)332-1392
Website: http://www.wachovia.com/wca

Brainworks Ventures
4243 Dunwoody Club Dr.
Chamblee, GA 30341
(770)239-7447

First Growth Capital Inc.
Best Western Plaza, Ste. 105
PO Box 815
Forsyth, GA 31029
(912)781-7131

Financial Capital Resources, Inc.
21 Eastbrook Bend, Ste. 116
Peachtree City, GA 30269
(404)487-6650

Hawaii

HMS Hawaii Management Partners
Davies Pacific Center
841 Bishop St., Ste. 860
Honolulu, HI 96813
(808)545-3755
Fax: (808)531-2611

Idaho

Sun Valley Ventures
160 Second St.
Ketchum, ID 83340
(208)726-5005
Fax: (208)726-5094

Illinois

Open Prairie Ventures
115 N. Neil St., Ste. 209
Champaign, IL 61820
(217)351-7000
Fax: (217)351-7051
E-mail: inquire@openprairie.com
Website: http://www.openprairie.com

ABN AMRO Private Equity
208 S La Salle St., 10th Fl.
Chicago, IL 60604
(312)855-7079
Fax: (312)553-6648
Website: http://www.abnequity.com

Alpha Capital Partners, Ltd.
122 S Michigan Ave., Ste. 1700
Chicago, IL 60603
(312)322-9800
Fax: (312)322-9808
E-mail: acp@alphacapital.com

Ameritech Development Corp.
30 S Wacker Dr., 37th Fl.
Chicago, IL 60606
(312)750-5083
Fax: (312)609-0244

Apex Investment Partners
225 W Washington, Ste. 1450
Chicago, IL 60606
(312)857-2800
Fax: (312)857-1800
E-mail: apex@apexvc.com
Website: http://www.apexvc.com

Arch Venture Partners
8725 W Higgins Rd., Ste. 290
Chicago, IL 60631
(773)380-6600
Fax: (773)380-6606
Website: http://www.archventure.com

The Bank Funds
208 South LaSalle St., Ste. 1680
Chicago, IL 60604
(312)855-6020
Fax: (312)855-8910

Batterson Venture Partners
303 W Madison St., Ste. 1110
Chicago, IL 60606-3309
(312)269-0300
Fax: (312)269-0021
Website: http://www.battersonvp.com

William Blair Capital Partners, L.L.C.
222 W Adams St., Ste. 1300
Chicago, IL 60606
(312)364-8250
Fax: (312)236-1042
E-mail: privateequity@wmblair.com
Website: http://www.wmblair.com

Bluestar Ventures
208 South LaSalle St., Ste. 1020
Chicago, IL 60604
(312)384-5000
Fax: (312)384-5005
Website: http://www.bluestarventures.com

The Capital Strategy Management Co.
233 S Wacker Dr.
Box 06334
Chicago, IL 60606
(312)444-1170

DN Partners
77 West Wacker Dr., Ste. 4550
Chicago, IL 60601
(312)332-7960
Fax: (312)332-7979

Dresner Capital Inc.
29 South LaSalle St., Ste. 310
Chicago, IL 60603
(312)726-3600
Fax: (312)726-7448

Eblast Ventures LLC
11 South LaSalle St., 5th Fl.
Chicago, IL 60603
(312)372-2600
Fax: (312)372-5621
Website: http://www.eblastventures
.com

Essex Woodlands Health Ventures, L.P.
190 S LaSalle St., Ste. 2800
Chicago, IL 60603
(312)444-6040
Fax: (312)444-6034
Website: http://www.essexwoodlands
.com

First Analysis Venture Capital
233 S Wacker Dr., Ste. 9500
Chicago, IL 60606
(312)258-1400
Fax: (312)258-0334
Website: http://www.firstanalysis.com

Frontenac Co.
135 S LaSalle St., Ste.3800
Chicago, IL 60603
(312)368-0044
Fax: (312)368-9520
Website: http://www.frontenac.com

GTCR Golder Rauner, LLC
6100 Sears Tower
Chicago, IL 60606
(312)382-2200
Fax: (312)382-2201
Website: http://www.gtcr.com

High Street Capital LLC
311 South Wacker Dr., Ste. 4550
Chicago, IL 60606
(312)697-4990
Fax: (312)697-4994
Website: http://www.highstr.com

IEG Venture Management, Inc.
70 West Madison
Chicago, IL 60602
(312)644-0890
Fax: (312)454-0369
Website: http://www.iegventure.com

JK&B Capital
180 North Stetson, Ste. 4500
Chicago, IL 60601
(312)946-1200
Fax: (312)946-1103

E-mail: gspencer@jkbcapital.com
Website: http://www.jkbcapital.com

Kettle Partners L.P.
350 W Hubbard, Ste. 350
Chicago, IL 60610
(312)329-9300
Fax: (312)527-4519
Website: http://www.kettlevc.com

Lake Shore Capital Partners
20 N. Wacker Dr., Ste. 2807
Chicago, IL 60606
(312)803-3536
Fax: (312)803-3534

LaSalle Capital Group Inc.
70 W Madison St., Ste. 5710
Chicago, IL 60602
(312)236-7041
Fax: (312)236-0720

Linc Capital, Inc.
303 E Wacker Pkwy., Ste. 1000
Chicago, IL 60601
(312)946-2670
Fax: (312)938-4290
E-mail: bdemars@linccap.com

Madison Dearborn Partners, Inc.
3 First National Plz., Ste. 3800
Chicago, IL 60602
(312)895-1000
Fax: (312)895-1001
E-mail: invest@mdcp.com
Website: http://www.mdcp.com

Mesirow Private Equity Investments Inc.
350 N. Clark St.
Chicago, IL 60610
(312)595-6950
Fax: (312)595-6211
Website: http://www.meisrowfinancial
.com

Mosaix Ventures LLC
1822 North Mohawk
Chicago, IL 60614
(312)274-0988
Fax: (312)274-0989
Website: http://www.mosaixventures.com

Nesbitt Burns
111 West Monroe St.
Chicago, IL 60603
(312)416-3855
Fax: (312)765-8000
Website: http://www.harrisbank.com

Polestar Capital, Inc.
180 N. Michigan Ave., Ste. 1905
Chicago, IL 60601
(312)984-9090

Fax: (312)984-9877
E-mail: wl@polestarvc.com
Website: http://www.polestarvc.com

Prince Ventures (Chicago)
10 S Wacker Dr., Ste. 2575
Chicago, IL 60606-7407
(312)454-1408
Fax: (312)454-9125

Prism Capital
444 N. Michigan Ave.
Chicago, IL 60611
(312)464-7900
Fax: (312)464-7915
Website: http://www.prismfund.com

Third Coast Capital
900 N. Franklin St., Ste. 700
Chicago, IL 60610
(312)337-3303
Fax: (312)337-2567
E-mail: manic@earthlink.com
Website: http://www.thirdcoastcapital
.com

Thoma Cressey Equity Partners
4460 Sears Tower, 92nd Fl.
233 S Wacker Dr.
Chicago, IL 60606
(312)777-4444
Fax: (312)777-4445
Website: http://www.thomacressey.com

Tribune Ventures
435 N. Michigan Ave., Ste. 600
Chicago, IL 60611
(312)527-8797
Fax: (312)222-5993
Website: http://www.tribuneventures.com

Wind Point Partners (Chicago)
676 N. Michigan Ave., Ste. 330
Chicago, IL 60611
(312)649-4000
Website: http://www.wppartners.com

Marquette Venture Partners
520 Lake Cook Rd., Ste. 450
Deerfield, IL 60015
(847)940-1700
Fax: (847)940-1724
Website: http://www.marquetteventures
.com

Duchossois Investments Limited, LLC
845 Larch Ave.
Elmhurst, IL 60126
(630)530-6105
Fax: (630)993-8644
Website: http://www.duchtec.com

Evanston Business Investment Corp.
1840 Oak Ave.
Evanston, IL 60201
(847)866-1840
Fax: (847)866-1808
E-mail: t-parkinson@nwu.com
Website: http://www.ebic.com

Inroads Capital Partners L.P.
1603 Orrington Ave., Ste. 2050
Evanston, IL 60201-3841
(847)864-2000
Fax: (847)864-9692

The Cerulean Fund/WGC Enterprises
1701 E Lake Ave., Ste. 170
Glenview, IL 60025
(847)657-8002
Fax: (847)657-8168

Ventana Financial Resources, Inc.
249 Market Sq.
Lake Forest, IL 60045
(847)234-3434

Beecken, Petty & Co.
901 Warrenville Rd., Ste. 205
Lisle, IL 60532
(630)435-0300
Fax: (630)435-0370
E-mail: hep@bpcompany.com
Website: http://www.bpcompany.com

Allstate Private Equity
3075 Sanders Rd., Ste. G5D
Northbrook, IL 60062-7127
(847)402-8247
Fax: (847)402-0880

KB Partners
1101 Skokie Blvd., Ste. 260
Northbrook, IL 60062-2856
(847)714-0444
Fax: (847)714-0445
E-mail: keith@kbpartners.com
Website: http://www.kbpartners.com

Transcap Associates Inc.
900 Skokie Blvd., Ste. 210
Northbrook, IL 60062
(847)753-9600
Fax: (847)753-9090

**Graystone Venture Partners, L.L.C. /
Portage Venture Partners**
One Northfield Plaza, Ste. 530
Northfield, IL 60093
(847)446-9460
Fax: (847)446-9470
Website: http://www.portageventures
.com

Motorola Inc.
1303 E Algonquin Rd.
Schaumburg, IL 60196-1065
(847)576-4929
Fax: (847)538-2250
Website: http://www.mot.com/mne

Indiana

Irwin Ventures LLC
500 Washington St.
Columbus, IN 47202
(812)373-1434
Fax: (812)376-1709
Website: http://www.irwinventures.com

Cambridge Venture Partners
4181 East 96th St., Ste. 200
Indianapolis, IN 46240
(317)814-6192
Fax: (317)944-9815

CID Equity Partners
One American Square, Ste. 2850
Box 82074
Indianapolis, IN 46282
(317)269-2350
Fax: (317)269-2355
Website: http://www.cidequity.com

Gazelle Techventures
6325 Digital Way, Ste. 460
Indianapolis, IN 46278
(317)275-6800
Fax: (317)275-1101
Website: http://www.gazellevc.com

Monument Advisors Inc.
Bank One Center/Circle
111 Monument Circle, Ste. 600
Indianapolis, IN 46204-5172
(317)656-5065
Fax: (317)656-5060
Website: http://www.monumentadv.com

MWV Capital Partners
201 N. Illinois St., Ste. 300
Indianapolis, IN 46204
(317)237-2323
Fax: (317)237-2325
Website: http://www.mwvcapital.com

First Source Capital Corp.
100 North Michigan St.
PO Box 1602
South Bend, IN 46601
(219)235-2180
Fax: (219)235-2227

Iowa

Allsop Venture Partners
118 Third Ave. SE, Ste. 837

Cedar Rapids, IA 52401
(319)368-6675
Fax: (319)363-9515

InvestAmerica Investment Advisors, Inc.
101 2nd St. SE, Ste. 800
Cedar Rapids, IA 52401
(319)363-8249
Fax: (319)363-9683

Pappajohn Capital Resources
2116 Financial Center
Des Moines, IA 50309
(515)244-5746
Fax: (515)244-2346
Website: http://www.pappajohn.com

Berthel Fisher & Company Planning Inc.
701 Tama St.
PO Box 609
Marion, IA 52302
(319)497-5700
Fax: (319)497-4244

Kansas

Enterprise Merchant Bank
7400 West 110th St., Ste. 560
Overland Park, KS 66210
(913)327-8500
Fax: (913)327-8505

Kansas Venture Capital, Inc. (Overland Park)
6700 Antioch Plz., Ste. 460
Overland Park, KS 66204
(913)262-7117
Fax: (913)262-3509
E-mail: jdalton@kvci.com

Child Health Investment Corp.
6803 W 64th St., Ste. 208
Shawnee Mission, KS 66202
(913)262-1436
Fax: (913)262-1575
Website: http://www.chca.com

Kansas Technology Enterprise Corp.
214 SW 6th, 1st Fl.
Topeka, KS 66603-3719
(785)296-5272
Fax: (785)296-1160
E-mail: ktec@ktec.com
Website: http://www.ktec.com

Kentucky

Kentucky Highlands Investment Corp.
362 Old Whitley Rd.
London, KY 40741

(606)864-5175
Fax: (606)864-5194
Website: http://www.khic.org

Chrysalis Ventures, L.L.C.
1850 National City Tower
Louisville, KY 40202
(502)583-7644
Fax: (502)583-7648
E-mail: bobsany@chrysalisventures.com
Website: http://www.chrysalisventures
.com

Humana Venture Capital
500 West Main St.
Louisville, KY 40202
(502)580-3922
Fax: (502)580-2051
E-mail: gemont@humana.com
George Emont, Director

Summit Capital Group, Inc.
6510 Glenridge Park Pl., Ste. 8
Louisville, KY 40222
(502)332-2700

Louisiana

Bank One Equity Investors, Inc.
451 Florida St.
Baton Rouge, LA 70801
(504)332-4421
Fax: (504)332-7377

Advantage Capital Partners
LLE Tower
909 Poydras St., Ste. 2230
New Orleans, LA 70112
(504)522-4850
Fax: (504)522-4950
Website: http://www.advantagecap.com

Maine

CEI Ventures / Coastal Ventures LP
2 Portland Fish Pier, Ste. 201
Portland, ME 04101
(207)772-5356
Fax: (207)772-5503
Website: http://www.ceiventures.com

Commwealth Bioventures, Inc.
4 Milk St.
Portland, ME 04101
(207)780-0904
Fax: (207)780-0913

Maryland

Annapolis Ventures LLC
151 West St., Ste. 302
Annapolis, MD 21401

(443)482-9555
Fax: (443)482-9565
Website: http://www.annapolisventures
.com

Delmag Ventures
220 Wardour Dr.
Annapolis, MD 21401
(410)267-8196
Fax: (410)267-8017
Website: http://www.delmagventures.com

Abell Venture Fund
111 S Calvert St., Ste. 2300
Baltimore, MD 21202
(410)547-1300
Fax: (410)539-6579
Website: http://www.abell.org

ABS Ventures (Baltimore)
1 South St., Ste. 2150
Baltimore, MD 21202
(410)895-3895
Fax: (410)895-3899
Website: http://www.absventures.com

Anthem Capital, L.P.
16 S Calvert St., Ste. 800
Baltimore, MD 21202-1305
(410)625-1510
Fax: (410)625-1735
Website: http://www.anthemcapital.com

Catalyst Ventures
1119 St. Paul St.
Baltimore, MD 21202
(410)244-0123
Fax: (410)752-7721

Maryland Venture Capital Trust
217 E Redwood St., Ste. 2200
Baltimore, MD 21202
(410)767-6361
Fax: (410)333-6931

New Enterprise Associates (Baltimore)
1119 St. Paul St.
Baltimore, MD 21202
(410)244-0115
Fax: (410)752-7721
Website: http://www.nea.com

T. Rowe Price Threshold Partnerships
100 E Pratt St., 8th Fl.
Baltimore, MD 21202
(410)345-2000
Fax: (410)345-2800

Spring Capital Partners
16 W Madison St.
Baltimore, MD 21201
(410)685-8000

Fax: (410)727-1436
E-mail: mailbox@springcap.com

Arete Corporation
3 Bethesda Metro Ctr., Ste. 770
Bethesda, MD 20814
(301)657-6268
Fax: (301)657-6254
Website: http://www.arete-microgen.com

Embryon Capital
7903 Sleaford Place
Bethesda, MD 20814
(301)656-6837
Fax: (301)656-8056

Potomac Ventures
7920 Norfolk Ave., Ste. 1100
Bethesda, MD 20814
(301)215-9240
Website: http://www.potomacventures
.com

Toucan Capital Corp.
3 Bethesda Metro Center, Ste. 700
Bethesda, MD 20814
(301)961-1970
Fax: (301)961-1969
Website: http://www.toucancapital.com

Kinetic Ventures LLC
2 Wisconsin Cir., Ste. 620
Chevy Chase, MD 20815
(301)652-8066
Fax: (301)652-8310
Website: http://www.kineticventures.com

Boulder Ventures Ltd.
4750 Owings Mills Blvd.
Owings Mills, MD 21117
(410)998-3114
Fax: (410)356-5492
Website: http://www.boulderventures.
com

Grotech Capital Group
9690 Deereco Rd., Ste. 800
Timonium, MD 21093
(410)560-2000
Fax: (410)560-1910
Website: http://www.grotech.com

Massachusetts

Adams, Harkness & Hill, Inc.
60 State St.
Boston, MA 02109
(617)371-3900

Advent International
75 State St., 29th Fl.
Boston, MA 02109

(617)951-9400
Fax: (617)951-0566
Website: http://www.adventinternational.
com

American Research and Development
30 Federal St.
Boston, MA 02110-2508
(617)423-7500
Fax: (617)423-9655

Ascent Venture Partners
255 State St., 5th Fl.
Boston, MA 02109
(617)270-9400
Fax: (617)270-9401
E-mail: info@ascentvp.com
Website: http://www.ascentvp.com

Atlas Venture
222 Berkeley St.
Boston, MA 02116
(617)488-2200
Fax: (617)859-9292
Website: http://www.atlasventure.com

Axxon Capital
28 State St., 37th Fl.
Boston, MA 02109
(617)722-0980
Fax: (617)557-6014
Website: http://www.axxoncapital.com

BancBoston Capital/BancBoston Ventures
175 Federal St., 10th Fl.
Boston, MA 02110
(617)434-2509
Fax: (617)434-6175
Website: http://www.bancbostoncapital
.com

Boston Capital Ventures
Old City Hall
45 School St.
Boston, MA 02108
(617)227-6550
Fax: (617)227-3847
E-mail: info@bcv.com
Website: http://www.bcv.com

Boston Financial & Equity Corp.
20 Overland St.
PO Box 15071
Boston, MA 02215
(617)267-2900
Fax: (617)437-7601
E-mail: debbie@bfec.com

Boston Millennia Partners
30 Rowes Wharf
Boston, MA 02110

(617)428-5150
Fax: (617)428-5160
Website: http://www.millenniapartners
.com

Bristol Investment Trust
842A Beacon St.
Boston, MA 02215-3199
(617)566-5212
Fax: (617)267-0932

Brook Venture Management LLC
50 Federal St., 5th Fl.
Boston, MA 02110
(617)451-8989
Fax: (617)451-2369
Website: http://www.brookventure.com

Burr, Egan, Deleage, and Co. (Boston)
200 Clarendon St., Ste. 3800
Boston, MA 02116
(617)262-7770
Fax: (617)262-9779

Cambridge/Samsung Partners
One Exeter Plaza
Ninth Fl.
Boston, MA 02116
(617)262-4440
Fax: (617)262-5562

Chestnut Street Partners, Inc.
75 State St., Ste. 2500
Boston, MA 02109
(617)345-7220
Fax: (617)345-7201
E-mail: chestnut@chestnutp.com

Claflin Capital Management, Inc.
10 Liberty Sq., Ste. 300
Boston, MA 02109
(617)426-6505
Fax: (617)482-0016
Website: http://www.claflincapital.com

Copley Venture Partners
99 Summer St., Ste. 1720
Boston, MA 02110
(617)737-1253
Fax: (617)439-0699

Corning Capital / Corning Technology Ventures
121 High Street, Ste. 400
Boston, MA 02110
(617)338-2656
Fax: (617)261-3864
Website: http://www.corningventures
.com

Downer & Co.
211 Congress St.

Boston, MA 02110
(617)482-6200
Fax: (617)482-6201
E-mail: cdowner@downer.com
Website: http://www.downer.com

Fidelity Ventures
82 Devonshire St.
Boston, MA 02109
(617)563-6370
Fax: (617)476-9023
Website: http://www.fidelityventures.com

Greylock Management Corp. (Boston)
1 Federal St.
Boston, MA 02110-2065
(617)423-5525
Fax: (617)482-0059

Gryphon Ventures
222 Berkeley St., Ste.1600
Boston, MA 02116
(617)267-9191
Fax: (617)267-4293
E-mail: all@gryphoninc.com

Halpern, Denny & Co.
500 Boylston St.
Boston, MA 02116
(617)536-6602
Fax: (617)536-8535

Harbourvest Partners, LLC
1 Financial Center, 44th Fl.
Boston, MA 02111
(617)348-3707
Fax: (617)350-0305
Website: http://www.hvpllc.com

Highland Capital Partners
2 International Pl.
Boston, MA 02110
(617)981-1500
Fax: (617)531-1550
E-mail: info@hcp.com
Website: http://www.hcp.com

Lee Munder Venture Partners
John Hancock Tower T-53
200 Clarendon St.
Boston, MA 02103
(617)380-5600
Fax: (617)380-5601
Website: http://www.leemunder.com

M/C Venture Partners
75 State St., Ste. 2500
Boston, MA 02109
(617)345-7200
Fax: (617)345-7201
Website: http://www.mcventurepartners
.com

Massachusetts Capital Resources Co.
420 Boylston St.
Boston, MA 02116
(617)536-3900
Fax: (617)536-7930

Massachusetts Technology Development Corp. (MTDC)
148 State St.
Boston, MA 02109
(617)723-4920
Fax: (617)723-5983
E-mail: jhodgman@mtdc.com
Website: http://www.mtdc.com

New England Partners
One Boston Place, Ste. 2100
Boston, MA 02108
(617)624-8400
Fax: (617)624-8999
Website: http://www.nepartners.com

North Hill Ventures
Ten Post Office Square
11th Fl.
Boston, MA 02109
(617)788-2112
Fax: (617)788-2152
Website: http://www.northhillventures
.com

OneLiberty Ventures
150 Cambridge Park Dr.
Boston, MA 02140
(617)492-7280
Fax: (617)492-7290
Website: http://www.oneliberty.com

Schroder Ventures
Life Sciences
60 State St., Ste. 3650
Boston, MA 02109
(617)367-8100
Fax: (617)367-1590
Website: http://www.shroderventures.com

Shawmut Capital Partners
75 Federal St., 18th Fl.
Boston, MA 02110
(617)368-4900
Fax: (617)368-4910
Website: http://www.shawmutcapital.com

Solstice Capital LLC
15 Broad St., 3rd Fl.
Boston, MA 02109
(617)523-7733
Fax: (617)523-5827
E-mail: solticecapital@solcap.com

Spectrum Equity Investors
One International Pl., 29th Fl.

Boston, MA 02110
(617)464-4600
Fax: (617)464-4601
Website: http://www.spectrumequity.com

Spray Venture Partners
One Walnut St.
Boston, MA 02108
(617)305-4140
Fax: (617)305-4144
Website: http://www.sprayventure.com

The Still River Fund
100 Federal St., 29th Fl.
Boston, MA 02110
(617)348-2327
Fax: (617)348-2371
Website: http://www.stillriverfund.com

Summit Partners
600 Atlantic Ave., Ste. 2800
Boston, MA 02210-2227
(617)824-1000
Fax: (617)824-1159
Website: http://www.summitpartners
.com

TA Associates, Inc. (Boston)
High Street Tower
125 High St., Ste. 2500
Boston, MA 02110
(617)574-6700
Fax: (617)574-6728
Website: http://www.ta.com

TVM Techno Venture Management
101 Arch St., Ste. 1950
Boston, MA 02110
(617)345-9320
Fax: (617)345-9377
E-mail: info@tvmvc.com
Website: http://www.tvmvc.com

UNC Ventures
64 Burough St.
Boston, MA 02130-4017
(617)482-7070
Fax: (617)522-2176

Venture Investment Management Company (VIMAC)
177 Milk St.
Boston, MA 02190-3410
(617)292-3300
Fax: (617)292-7979
E-mail: bzeisig@vimac.com
Website: http://www.vimac.com

MDT Advisers, Inc.
125 Cambridge Park Dr.
Cambridge, MA 02140-2314
(617)234-2200

Fax: (617)234-2210
Website: http://www.mdtai.com

TTC Ventures
One Main St., 6th Fl.
Cambridge, MA 02142
(617)528-3137
Fax: (617)577-1715
E-mail: info@ttcventures.com

Zero Stage Capital Co. Inc.
101 Main St., 17th Fl.
Cambridge, MA 02142
(617)876-5355
Fax: (617)876-1248
Website: http://www.zerostage.com

Atlantic Capital
164 Cushing Hwy.
Cohasset, MA 02025
(617)383-9449
Fax: (617)383-6040
E-mail: info@atlanticcap.com
Website: http://www.atlanticcap.com

Seacoast Capital Partners
55 Ferncroft Rd.
Danvers, MA 01923
(978)750-1300
Fax: (978)750-1301
E-mail: gdeli@seacoastcapital.com
Website: http://www.seacoastcapital.com

Sage Management Group
44 South Street
PO Box 2026
East Dennis, MA 02641
(508)385-7172
Fax: (508)385-7272
E-mail: sagemgt@capecod.net

Applied Technology
1 Cranberry Hill
Lexington, MA 02421-7397
(617)862-8622
Fax: (617)862-8367

Royalty Capital Management
5 Downing Rd.
Lexington, MA 02421-6918
(781)861-8490

Argo Global Capital
210 Broadway, Ste. 101
Lynnfield, MA 01940
(781)592-5250
Fax: (781)592-5230
Website: http://www.gsmcapital.com

Industry Ventures
6 Bayne Lane
Newburyport, MA 01950

(978)499-7606
Fax: (978)499-0686
Website: http://www.industryventures
.com

Softbank Capital Partners
10 Langley Rd., Ste. 202
Newton Center, MA 02459
(617)928-9300
Fax: (617)928-9305
E-mail: clax@bvc.com

Advanced Technology Ventures (Boston)
281 Winter St., Ste. 350
Waltham, MA 02451
(781)290-0707
Fax: (781)684-0045
E-mail: info@atvcapital.com
Website: http://www.atvcapital.com

Castile Ventures
890 Winter St., Ste. 140
Waltham, MA 02451
(781)890-0060
Fax: (781)890-0065
Website: http://www.castileventures.com

Charles River Ventures
1000 Winter St., Ste. 3300
Waltham, MA 02451
(781)487-7060
Fax: (781)487-7065
Website: http://www.crv.com

Comdisco Venture Group (Waltham)
Totton Pond Office Center
400-1 Totten Pond Rd.
Waltham, MA 02451
(617)672-0250
Fax: (617)398-8099

Marconi Ventures
890 Winter St., Ste. 310
Waltham, MA 02451
(781)839-7177
Fax: (781)522-7477
Website: http://www.marconi.com

Matrix Partners
Bay Colony Corporate Center
1000 Winter St., Ste.4500
Waltham, MA 02451
(781)890-2244
Fax: (781)890-2288
Website: http://www.matrixpartners.com

North Bridge Venture Partners
950 Winter St. Ste. 4600
Waltham, MA 02451
(781)290-0004
Fax: (781)290-0999
E-mail: eta@nbvp.com

Polaris Venture Partners
Bay Colony Corporate Ctr.
1000 Winter St., Ste. 3500
Waltham, MA 02451
(781)290-0770
Fax: (781)290-0880
E-mail: partners@polarisventures.com
Website: http://www.polarisventures.com

Seaflower Ventures
Bay Colony Corporate Ctr.
1000 Winter St. Ste. 1000
Waltham, MA 02451
(781)466-9552
Fax: (781)466-9553
E-mail: moot@seaflower.com
Website: http://www.seaflower.com

Ampersand Ventures
55 William St., Ste. 240
Wellesley, MA 02481
(617)239-0700
Fax: (617)239-0824
E-mail: info@ampersandventures.com
Website: http://www.ampersandventures
.com

Battery Ventures (Boston)
20 William St., Ste. 200
Wellesley, MA 02481
(781)577-1000
Fax: (781)577-1001
Website: http://www.battery.com

Commonwealth Capital Ventures, L.P.
20 William St., Ste.225
Wellesley, MA 02481
(781)237-7373
Fax: (781)235-8627
Website: http://www.ccvlp.com

Fowler, Anthony & Company
20 Walnut St.
Wellesley, MA 02481
(781)237-4201
Fax: (781)237-7718

Gemini Investors
20 William St.
Wellesley, MA 02481
(781)237-7001
Fax: (781)237-7233

Grove Street Advisors Inc.
20 William St., Ste. 230
Wellesley, MA 02481
(781)263-6100
Fax: (781)263-6101
Website: http://www.grovestreetadvisors
.com

Mees Pierson Investeringsmaat B.V.
20 William St., Ste. 210

Wellesley, MA 02482
(781)239-7600
Fax: (781)239-0377

Norwest Equity Partners
40 William St., Ste. 305
Wellesley, MA 02481-3902
(781)237-5870
Fax: (781)237-6270
Website: http://www.norwestvp.com

Bessemer Venture Partners (Wellesley Hills)
83 Walnut St.
Wellesley Hills, MA 02481
(781)237-6050
Fax: (781)235-7576
E-mail: travis@bvpny.com
Website: http://www.bvp.com

Venture Capital Fund of New England
20 Walnut St., Ste. 120
Wellesley Hills, MA 02481-2175
(781)239-8262
Fax: (781)239-8263

Prism Venture Partners
100 Lowder Brook Dr., Ste. 2500
Westwood, MA 02090
(781)302-4000
Fax: (781)302-4040
E-mail: dwbaum@prismventure.com

Palmer Partners LP
200 Unicorn Park Dr.
Woburn, MA 01801
(781)933-5445
Fax: (781)933-0698

Michigan

Arbor Partners, L.L.C.
130 South First St.
Ann Arbor, MI 48104
(734)668-9000
Fax: (734)669-4195
Website: http://www.arborpartners.com

EDF Ventures
425 N. Main St.
Ann Arbor, MI 48104
(734)663-3213
Fax: (734)663-7358
E-mail: edf@edfvc.com
Website: http://www.edfvc.com

White Pines Management, L.L.C.
2401 Plymouth Rd., Ste. B
Ann Arbor, MI 48105
(734)747-9401
Fax: (734)747-9704

E-mail: ibund@whitepines.com
Website: http://www.whitepines.com

Wellmax, Inc.
3541 Bendway Blvd., Ste. 100
Bloomfield Hills, MI 48301
(248)646-3554
Fax: (248)646-6220

Venture Funding, Ltd.
Fisher Bldg.
3011 West Grand Blvd., Ste. 321
Detroit, MI 48202
(313)871-3606
Fax: (313)873-4935

Investcare Partners L.P. / GMA Capital LLC
32330 W Twelve Mile Rd.
Farmington Hills, MI 48334
(248)489-9000
Fax: (248)489-8819
E-mail: gma@gmacapital.com
Website: http://www.gmacapital.com

Liberty Bidco Investment Corp.
30833 Northwestern Highway, Ste. 211
Farmington Hills, MI 48334
(248)626-6070
Fax: (248)626-6072

Seaflower Ventures
5170 Nicholson Rd.
PO Box 474
Fowlerville, MI 48836
(517)223-3335
Fax: (517)223-3337
E-mail: gibbons@seaflower.com
Website: http://www.seaflower.com

Ralph Wilson Equity Fund LLC
15400 E Jefferson Ave.
Gross Pointe Park, MI 48230
(313)821-9122
Fax: (313)821-9101
Website: http://www.RalphWilson
EquityFund.com
J. Skip Simms, President

Minnesota

Development Corp. of Austin
1900 Eighth Ave., NW
Austin, MN 55912
(507)433-0346
Fax: (507)433-0361
E-mail: dca@smig.net
Website: http://www.spamtownusa.com

Northeast Ventures Corp.
802 Alworth Bldg.
Duluth, MN 55802

(218)722-9915
Fax: (218)722-9871

Medical Innovation Partners, Inc.
6450 City West Pkwy.
Eden Prairie, MN 55344-3245
(612)828-9616
Fax: (612)828-9596

St. Paul Venture Capital, Inc.
10400 Vicking Dr., Ste. 550
Eden Prairie, MN 55344
(612)995-7474
Fax: (612)995-7475
Website: http://www.stpaulvc.com

Cherry Tree Investments, Inc.
7601 France Ave. S, Ste. 150
Edina, MN 55435
(612)893-9012
Fax: (612)893-9036
Website: http://www.cherrytree.com

Shared Ventures, Inc.
6550 York Ave. S
Edina, MN 55435
(612)925-3411

Sherpa Partners LLC
5050 Lincoln Dr., Ste. 490
Edina, MN 55436
(952)942-1070
Fax: (952)942-1071
Website: http://www.sherpapartners.com

Affinity Capital Management
901 Marquette Ave., Ste. 1810
Minneapolis, MN 55402
(612)252-9900
Fax: (612)252-9911
Website: http://www.affinitycapital.com

Artesian Capital
1700 Foshay Tower
821 Marquette Ave.
Minneapolis, MN 55402
(612)334-5600
Fax: (612)334-5601
E-mail: artesian@artesian.com

Coral Ventures
60 S 6th St., Ste. 3510
Minneapolis, MN 55402
(612)335-8666
Fax: (612)335-8668
Website: http://www.coralventures.com

Crescendo Venture Management, L.L.C.
800 LaSalle Ave., Ste. 2250
Minneapolis, MN 55402
(612)607-2800
Fax: (612)607-2801
Website: http://www.crescendoventures
.com

Gideon Hixon Venture
1900 Foshay Tower
821 Marquette Ave.
Minneapolis, MN 55402
(612)904-2314
Fax: (612)204-0913

Norwest Equity Partners
3600 IDS Center
80 S 8th St.
Minneapolis, MN 55402
(612)215-1600
Fax: (612)215-1601
Website: http://www.norwestvp.com

Oak Investment Partners (Minneapolis)
4550 Norwest Center
90 S 7th St.
Minneapolis, MN 55402
(612)339-9322
Fax: (612)337-8017
Website: http://www.oakinv.com

Pathfinder Venture Capital Funds (Minneapolis)
7300 Metro Blvd., Ste. 585
Minneapolis, MN 55439
(612)835-1121
Fax: (612)835-8389
E-mail: jahrens620@aol.com

U.S. Bancorp Piper Jaffray Ventures, Inc.
800 Nicollet Mall, Ste. 800
Minneapolis, MN 55402
(612)303-5686
Fax: (612)303-1350
Website: http://www.paperjaffrey
ventures.com

The Food Fund, Ltd. Partnership
5720 Smatana Dr., Ste. 300
Minnetonka, MN 55343
(612)939-3950
Fax: (612)939-8106

Mayo Medical Ventures
200 First St. SW
Rochester, MN 55905
(507)266-4586
Fax: (507)284-5410
Website: http://www.mayo.edu

Missouri

Bankers Capital Corp.
3100 Gillham Rd.
Kansas City, MO 64109
(816)531-1600
Fax: (816)531-1334

Capital for Business, Inc. (Kansas City)
1000 Walnut St., 18th Fl.

Kansas City, MO 64106
(816)234-2357
Fax: (816)234-2952
Website: http://www.capitalforbusiness
.com

De Vries & Co. Inc.
800 West 47th St.
Kansas City, MO 64112
(816)756-0055
Fax: (816)756-0061

InvestAmerica Venture Group Inc. (Kansas City)
Commerce Tower
911 Main St., Ste. 2424
Kansas City, MO 64105
(816)842-0114
Fax: (816)471-7339

Kansas City Equity Partners
233 W 47th St.
Kansas City, MO 64112
(816)960-1771
Fax: (816)960-1777
Website: http://www.kcep.com

Bome Investors, Inc.
8000 Maryland Ave., Ste. 1190
Saint Louis, MO 63105
(314)721-5707
Fax: (314)721-5135
Website: http://www.gatewayventures
.com

Capital for Business, Inc. (Saint Louis)
11 S Meramac St., Ste. 1430
Saint Louis, MO 63105
(314)746-7427
Fax: (314)746-8739
Website: http://www.capitalforbusiness
.com

Crown Capital Corp.
540 Maryville Centre Dr., Ste. 120
Saint Louis, MO 63141
(314)576-1201
Fax: (314)576-1525
Website: http://www.crown-cap.com

Gateway Associates L.P.
8000 Maryland Ave., Ste. 1190
Saint Louis, MO 63105
(314)721-5707
Fax: (314)721-5135

Harbison Corp.
8112 Maryland Ave., Ste. 250
Saint Louis, MO 63105
(314)727-8200
Fax: (314)727-0249

Nebraska

Heartland Capital Fund, Ltd.
PO Box 642117
Omaha, NE 68154
(402)778-5124
Fax: (402)445-2370
Website: http://www.heartlandcapital-fund.com

Odin Capital Group
1625 Farnam St., Ste. 700
Omaha, NE 68102
(402)346-6200
Fax: (402)342-9311
Website: http://www.odincapital.com

Nevada

Edge Capital Investment Co. LLC
1350 E Flamingo Rd., Ste. 3000
Las Vegas, NV 89119
(702)438-3343
E-mail: info@edgecapital.net
Website: http://www.edgecapital.net

The Benefit Capital Companies Inc.
PO Box 542
Logandale, NV 89021
(702)398-3222
Fax: (702)398-3700

Millennium Three Venture Group LLC
6880 South McCarran Blvd., Ste. A-11
Reno, NV 89509
(775)954-2020
Fax: (775)954-2023
Website: http://www.m3vg.com

New Jersey

Alan I. Goldman & Associates
497 Ridgewood Ave.
Glen Ridge, NJ 07028
(973)857-5680
Fax: (973)509-8856

CS Capital Partners LLC
328 Second St., Ste. 200
Lakewood, NJ 08701
(732)901-1111
Fax: (212)202-5071
Website: http://www.cs-capital.com

Edison Venture Fund
1009 Lenox Dr., Ste. 4
Lawrenceville, NJ 08648
(609)896-1900
Fax: (609)896-0066
E-mail: info@edisonventure.com
Website: http://www.edisonventure.com

Tappan Zee Capital Corp. (New Jersey)
201 Lower Notch Rd.
PO Box 416
Little Falls, NJ 07424
(973)256-8280
Fax: (973)256-2841

The CIT Group/Venture Capital, Inc.
650 CIT Dr.
Livingston, NJ 07039
(973)740-5429
Fax: (973)740-5555
Website: http://www.cit.com

Capital Express, L.L.C.
1100 Valleybrook Ave.
Lyndhurst, NJ 07071
(201)438-8228
Fax: (201)438-5131
E-mail: niles@capitalexpress.com
Website: http://www.capitalexpress.com

Westford Technology Ventures, L.P.
17 Academy St.
Newark, NJ 07102
(973)624-2131
Fax: (973)624-2008

Accel Partners
1 Palmer Sq.
Princeton, NJ 08542
(609)683-4500
Fax: (609)683-4880
Website: http://www.accel.com

Cardinal Partners
221 Nassau St.
Princeton, NJ 08542
(609)924-6452
Fax: (609)683-0174
Website: http://www.cardinalhealthpartners.com

Domain Associates L.L.C.
One Palmer Sq., Ste. 515
Princeton, NJ 08542
(609)683-5656
Fax: (609)683-9789
Website: http://www.domainvc.com

Johnston Associates, Inc.
181 Cherry Valley Rd.
Princeton, NJ 08540
(609)924-3131
Fax: (609)683-7524
E-mail: jaincorp@aol.com

Kemper Ventures
Princeton Forrestal Village
155 Village Blvd.
Princeton, NJ 08540

(609)936-3035
Fax: (609)936-3051

Penny Lane Parnters
One Palmer Sq., Ste. 309
Princeton, NJ 08542
(609)497-4646
Fax: (609)497-0611

Early Stage Enterprises L.P.
995 Route 518
Skillman, NJ 08558
(609)921-8896
Fax: (609)921-8703
Website: http://www.esevc.com

MBW Management Inc.
1 Springfield Ave.
Summit, NJ 07901
(908)273-4060
Fax: (908)273-4430

BCI Advisors, Inc.
Glenpointe Center W.
Teaneck, NJ 07666
(201)836-3900
Fax: (201)836-6368
E-mail: info@bciadvisors.com
Website: http://www.bcipartners.com

Demuth, Folger & Wetherill / DFW Capital Partners
Glenpointe Center E., 5th Fl.
300 Frank W. Burr Blvd.
Teaneck, NJ 07666
(201)836-2233
Fax: (201)836-5666
Website: http://www.dfwcapital.com

First Princeton Capital Corp.
189 Berdan Ave., No. 131
Wayne, NJ 07470-3233
(973)278-3233
Fax: (973)278-4290
Website: http://www.lytellcatt.net

Edelson Technology Partners
300 Tice Blvd.
Woodcliff Lake, NJ 07675
(201)930-9898
Fax: (201)930-8899
Website: http://www.edelsontech.com

New Mexico

Bruce F. Glaspell & Associates
10400 Academy Rd. NE, Ste. 313
Albuquerque, NM 87111
(505)292-4505
Fax: (505)292-4258

High Desert Ventures, Inc.
6101 Imparata St. NE, Ste. 1721

Albuquerque, NM 87111
(505)797-3330
Fax: (505)338-5147

New Business Capital Fund, Ltd.
5805 Torreon NE
Albuquerque, NM 87109
(505)822-8445

SBC Ventures
10400 Academy Rd. NE, Ste. 313
Albuquerque, NM 87111
(505)292-4505
Fax: (505)292-4528

Technology Ventures Corp.
1155 University Blvd. SE
Albuquerque, NM 87106
(505)246-2882
Fax: (505)246-2891

New York

Small Business Technology Investment Fund
99 Washington Ave., Ste. 1731
Albany, NY 12210
(518)473-9741
Fax: (518)473-6876

Rand Capital Corp.
2200 Rand Bldg.
Buffalo, NY 14203
(716)853-0802
Fax: (716)854-8480
Website: http://www.randcapital.com

Seed Capital Partners
620 Main St.
Buffalo, NY 14202
(716)845-7520
Fax: (716)845-7539
Website: http://www.seedcp.com

Coleman Venture Group
5909 Northern Blvd.
PO Box 224
East Norwich, NY 11732
(516)626-3642
Fax: (516)626-9722

Vega Capital Corp.
45 Knollwood Rd.
Elmsford, NY 10523
(914)345-9500
Fax: (914)345-9505

Herbert Young Securities, Inc.
98 Cuttermill Rd.
Great Neck, NY 11021
(516)487-8300
Fax: (516)487-8319

Sterling/Carl Marks Capital, Inc.
175 Great Neck Rd., Ste. 408
Great Neck, NY 11021
(516)482-7374
Fax: (516)487-0781
E-mail: stercrlmar@aol.com
Website: http://www.serlingcarlmarks
.com

Impex Venture Management Co.
PO Box 1570
Green Island, NY 12183
(518)271-8008
Fax: (518)271-9101

Corporate Venture Partners L.P.
200 Sunset Park
Ithaca, NY 14850
(607)257-6323
Fax: (607)257-6128

Arthur P. Gould & Co.
One Wilshire Dr.
Lake Success, NY 11020
(516)773-3000
Fax: (516)773-3289

Dauphin Capital Partners
108 Forest Ave.
Locust Valley, NY 11560
(516)759-3339
Fax: (516)759-3322
Website: http://www.dauphincapital.com

550 Digital Media Ventures
555 Madison Ave., 10th Fl.
New York, NY 10022
Website: http://www.550dmv.com

Aberlyn Capital Management Co., Inc.
500 Fifth Ave.
New York, NY 10110
(212)391-7750
Fax: (212)391-7762

Adler & Company
342 Madison Ave., Ste. 807
New York, NY 10173
(212)599-2535
Fax: (212)599-2526

Alimansky Capital Group, Inc.
605 Madison Ave., Ste. 300
New York, NY 10022-1901
(212)832-7300
Fax: (212)832-7338

Allegra Partners
515 Madison Ave., 29th Fl.
New York, NY 10022
(212)826-9080
Fax: (212)759-2561

The Argentum Group
The Chrysler Bldg.
405 Lexington Ave.
New York, NY 10174
(212)949-6262
Fax: (212)949-8294
Website: http://www.argentumgroup.com

Axavision Inc.
14 Wall St., 26th Fl.
New York, NY 10005
(212)619-4000
Fax: (212)619-7202

Bedford Capital Corp.
18 East 48th St., Ste. 1800
New York, NY 10017
(212)688-5700
Fax: (212)754-4699
E-mail: info@bedfordnyc.com
Website: http://www.bedfordnyc.com

Bloom & Co.
950 Third Ave.
New York, NY 10022
(212)838-1858
Fax: (212)838-1843

Bristol Capital Management
300 Park Ave., 17th Fl.
New York, NY 10022
(212)572-6306
Fax: (212)705-4292

**Citicorp Venture Capital Ltd.
(New York City)**
399 Park Ave., 14th Fl.
Zone 4
New York, NY 10043
(212)559-1127
Fax: (212)888-2940

CM Equity Partners
135 E 57th St.
New York, NY 10022
(212)909-8428
Fax: (212)980-2630

Cohen & Co., L.L.C.
800 Third Ave.
New York, NY 10022
(212)317-2250
Fax: (212)317-2255
E-mail: nlcohen@aol.com

Cornerstone Equity Investors, L.L.C.
717 5th Ave., Ste. 1100
New York, NY 10022
(212)753-0901
Fax: (212)826-6798
Website: http://www.cornerstone-equity
.com

CW Group, Inc.
1041 3rd Ave., 2nd fl.
New York, NY 10021
(212)308-5266
Fax: (212)644-0354
Website: http://www.cwventures.com

DH Blair Investment Banking Corp.
44 Wall St., 2nd Fl.
New York, NY 10005
(212)495-5000
Fax: (212)269-1438

Dresdner Kleinwort Capital
75 Wall St.
New York, NY 10005
(212)429-3131
Fax: (212)429-3139
Website: http://www.dresdnerkb.com

East River Ventures, L.P.
645 Madison Ave., 22nd Fl.
New York, NY 10022
(212)644-2322
Fax: (212)644-5498

Easton Hunt Capital Partners
641 Lexington Ave., 21st Fl.
New York, NY 10017
(212)702-0950
Fax: (212)702-0952
Website: http://www.eastoncapital.com

Elk Associates Funding Corp.
747 3rd Ave., Ste. 4C
New York, NY 10017
(212)355-2449
Fax: (212)759-3338

EOS Partners, L.P.
320 Park Ave., 22nd Fl.
New York, NY 10022
(212)832-5800
Fax: (212)832-5815
E-mail: mfirst@eospartners.com
Website: http://www.eospartners.com

Euclid Partners
45 Rockefeller Plaza, Ste. 3240
New York, NY 10111
(212)218-6880
Fax: (212)218-6877
E-mail: graham@euclidpartners.com
Website: http://www.euclidpartners.com

Evergreen Capital Partners, Inc.
150 East 58th St.
New York, NY 10155
(212)813-0758
Fax: (212)813-0754

Exeter Capital L.P.
10 E 53rd St.

New York, NY 10022
(212)872-1172
Fax: (212)872-1198
E-mail: exeter@usa.net

Financial Technology Research Corp.
518 Broadway
Penthouse
New York, NY 10012
(212)625-9100
Fax: (212)431-0300
E-mail: fintek@financier.com

4C Ventures
237 Park Ave., Ste. 801
New York, NY 10017
(212)692-3680
Fax: (212)692-3685
Website: http://www.4cventures.com

Fusient Ventures
99 Park Ave., 20th Fl.
New York, NY 10016
(212)972-8999
Fax: (212)972-9876
E-mail: info@fusient.com
Website: http://www.fusient.com

Generation Capital Partners
551 Fifth Ave., Ste. 3100
New York, NY 10176
(212)450-8507
Fax: (212)450-8550
Website: http://www.genpartners.com

Golub Associates, Inc.
555 Madison Ave.
New York, NY 10022
(212)750-6060
Fax: (212)750-5505

Hambro America Biosciences Inc.
650 Madison Ave., 21st Floor
New York, NY 10022
(212)223-7400
Fax: (212)223-0305

Hanover Capital Corp.
505 Park Ave., 15th Fl.
New York, NY 10022
(212)755-1222
Fax: (212)935-1787

Harvest Partners, Inc.
280 Park Ave, 33rd Fl.
New York, NY 10017
(212)559-6300
Fax: (212)812-0100
Website: http://www.harvpart.com

Holding Capital Group, Inc.
10 E 53rd St., 30th Fl.

New York, NY 10022
(212)486-6670
Fax: (212)486-0843

Hudson Venture Partners
660 Madison Ave., 14th Fl.
New York, NY 10021-8405
(212)644-9797
Fax: (212)644-7430
Website: http://www.hudsonptr.com

IBJS Capital Corp.
1 State St., 9th Fl.
New York, NY 10004
(212)858-2018
Fax: (212)858-2768

InterEquity Capital Partners, L.P.
220 5th Ave.
New York, NY 10001
(212)779-2022
Fax: (212)779-2103
Website: http://www.interequity-capital.
com

The Jordan Edmiston Group Inc.
150 East 52nd St., 18th Fl.
New York, NY 10022
(212)754-0710
Fax: (212)754-0337

Josephberg, Grosz and Co., Inc.
633 3rd Ave., 13th Fl.
New York, NY 10017
(212)974-9926
Fax: (212)397-5832

J.P. Morgan Capital Corp.
60 Wall St.
New York, NY 10260-0060
(212)648-9000
Fax: (212)648-5002
Website: http://www.jpmorgan.com

The Lambda Funds
380 Lexington Ave., 54th Fl.
New York, NY 10168
(212)682-3454
Fax: (212)682-9231

Lepercq Capital Management Inc.
1675 Broadway
New York, NY 10019
(212)698-0795
Fax: (212)262-0155

Loeb Partners Corp.
61 Broadway, Ste. 2400
New York, NY 10006
(212)483-7000
Fax: (212)574-2001

Madison Investment Partners
660 Madison Ave.
New York, NY 10021
(212)223-2600
Fax: (212)223-8208

MC Capital Inc.
520 Madison Ave., 16th Fl.
New York, NY 10022
(212)644-0841
Fax: (212)644-2926

McCown, De Leeuw and Co. (New York)
65 E 55th St., 36th Fl.
New York, NY 10022
(212)355-5500
Fax: (212)355-6283
Website: http://www.mdcpartners.com

Morgan Stanley Venture Partners
1221 Avenue of the Americas, 33rd Fl.
New York, NY 10020
(212)762-7900
Fax: (212)762-8424
E-mail: msventures@ms.com
Website: http://www.msvp.com

Nazem and Co.
645 Madison Ave., 12th Fl.
New York, NY 10022
(212)371-7900
Fax: (212)371-2150

Needham Capital Management, L.L.C.
445 Park Ave.
New York, NY 10022
(212)371-8300
Fax: (212)705-0299
Website: http://www.needhamco.com

Norwood Venture Corp.
1430 Broadway, Ste. 1607
New York, NY 10018
(212)869-5075
Fax: (212)869-5331
E-mail: nvc@mail.idt.net
Website: http://www.norven.com

Noveltek Venture Corp.
521 Fifth Ave., Ste. 1700
New York, NY 10175
(212)286-1963

Paribas Principal, Inc.
787 7th Ave.
New York, NY 10019
(212)841-2005
Fax: (212)841-3558

Patricof & Co. Ventures, Inc. (New York)
445 Park Ave.
New York, NY 10022

(212)753-6300
Fax: (212)319-6155
Website: http://www.patricof.com

The Platinum Group, Inc.
350 Fifth Ave, Ste. 7113
New York, NY 10118
(212)736-4300
Fax: (212)736-6086
Website: http://www.platinumgroup.com

Pomona Capital
780 Third Ave., 28th Fl.
New York, NY 10017
(212)593-3639
Fax: (212)593-3987
Website: http://www.pomonacapital.com

Prospect Street Ventures
10 East 40th St., 44th Fl.
New York, NY 10016
(212)448-0702
Fax: (212)448-9652
E-mail: wkohler@prospectstreet.com
Website: http://www.prospectstreet.com

Regent Capital Management
505 Park Ave., Ste. 1700
New York, NY 10022
(212)735-9900
Fax: (212)735-9908

Rothschild Ventures, Inc.
1251 Avenue of the Americas, 51st Fl.
New York, NY 10020
(212)403-3500
Fax: (212)403-3652
Website: http://www.nmrothschild.com

Sandler Capital Management
767 Fifth Ave., 45th Fl.
New York, NY 10153
(212)754-8100
Fax: (212)826-0280

Siguler Guff & Company
630 Fifth Ave., 16th Fl.
New York, NY 10111
(212)332-5100
Fax: (212)332-5120

Spencer Trask Ventures Inc.
535 Madison Ave.
New York, NY 10022
(212)355-5565
Fax: (212)751-3362
Website: http://www.spencertrask.com

Sprout Group (New York City)
277 Park Ave.
New York, NY 10172
(212)892-3600

Fax: (212)892-3444
E-mail: info@sproutgroup.com
Website: http://www.sproutgroup.com

US Trust Private Equity
114 W.47th St.
New York, NY 10036
(212)852-3949
Fax: (212)852-3759
Website: http://www.ustrust.com/
privateequity

Vencon Management Inc.
301 West 53rd St., Ste. 10F
New York, NY 10019
(212)581-8787
Fax: (212)397-4126
Website: http://www.venconinc.com

Venrock Associates
30 Rockefeller Plaza, Ste. 5508
New York, NY 10112
(212)649-5600
Fax: (212)649-5788
Website: http://www.venrock.com

Venture Capital Fund of America, Inc.
509 Madison Ave., Ste. 812
New York, NY 10022
(212)838-5577
Fax: (212)838-7614
E-mail: mail@vcfa.com
Website: http://www.vcfa.com

Venture Opportunities Corp.
150 E 58th St.
New York, NY 10155
(212)832-3737
Fax: (212)980-6603

Warburg Pincus Ventures, Inc.
466 Lexington Ave., 11th Fl.
New York, NY 10017
(212)878-9309
Fax: (212)878-9200
Website: http://www.warburgpincus.com

Wasserstein, Perella & Co. Inc.
31 W 52nd St., 27th Fl.
New York, NY 10019
(212)702-5691
Fax: (212)969-7879

Welsh, Carson, Anderson, & Stowe
320 Park Ave., Ste. 2500
New York, NY 10022-6815
(212)893-9500
Fax: (212)893-9575

Whitney and Co. (New York)
630 Fifth Ave. Ste. 3225
New York, NY 10111

(212)332-2400
Fax: (212)332-2422
Website: http://www.jhwitney.com

Winthrop Ventures
74 Trinity Place, Ste. 600
New York, NY 10006
(212)422-0100

The Pittsford Group
8 Lodge Pole Rd.
Pittsford, NY 14534
(716)223-3523

Genesee Funding
70 Linden Oaks, 3rd Fl.
Rochester, NY 14625
(716)383-5550
Fax: (716)383-5305

Gabelli Multimedia Partners
One Corporate Center
Rye, NY 10580
(914)921-5395
Fax: (914)921-5031

Stamford Financial
108 Main St.
Stamford, NY 12167
(607)652-3311
Fax: (607)652-6301
Website: http://www.stamfordfinancial
.com

Northwood Ventures LLC
485 Underhill Blvd., Ste. 205
Syosset, NY 11791
(516)364-5544
Fax: (516)364-0879
E-mail: northwood@northwood.com
Website: http://www.northwoodventures
.com

Exponential Business Development Co.
216 Walton St.
Syracuse, NY 13202-1227
(315)474-4500
Fax: (315)474-4682
E-mail: dirksonn@aol.com
Website: http://www.exponential-ny.com

Onondaga Venture Capital Fund Inc.
714 State Tower Bldg.
Syracuse, NY 13202
(315)478-0157
Fax: (315)478-0158

Bessemer Venture Partners (Westbury)
1400 Old Country Rd., Ste. 109
Westbury, NY 11590
(516)997-2300
Fax: (516)997-2371

E-mail: bob@bvpny.com
Website: http://www.bvp.com

Ovation Capital Partners
120 Bloomingdale Rd., 4th Fl.
White Plains, NY 10605
(914)258-0011
Fax: (914)684-0848
Website: http://www.ovationcapital.com

North Carolina

Carolinas Capital Investment Corp.
1408 Biltmore Dr.
Charlotte, NC 28207
(704)375-3888
Fax: (704)375-6226

First Union Capital Partners
1st Union Center, 12th Fl.
301 S College St.
Charlotte, NC 28288-0732
(704)383-0000
Fax: (704)374-6711
Website: http://www.fucp.com

Frontier Capital LLC
525 North Tryon St., Ste. 1700
Charlotte, NC 28202
(704)414-2880
Fax: (704)414-2881
Website: http://www.frontierfunds.com

Kitty Hawk Capital
2700 Coltsgate Rd., Ste. 202
Charlotte, NC 28211
(704)362-3909
Fax: (704)362-2774
Website: http://www.kittyhawkcapital
.com

Piedmont Venture Partners
One Morrocroft Centre
6805 Morisson Blvd., Ste. 380
Charlotte, NC 28211
(704)731-5200
Fax: (704)365-9733
Website: http://www.piedmontvp.com

Ruddick Investment Co.
1800 Two First Union Center
Charlotte, NC 28282
(704)372-5404
Fax: (704)372-6409

The Shelton Companies Inc.
3600 One First Union Center
301 S College St.
Charlotte, NC 28202
(704)348-2200
Fax: (704)348-2260

Wakefield Group
1110 E Morehead St.
PO Box 36329
Charlotte, NC 28236
(704)372-0355
Fax: (704)372-8216
Website: http://www.wakefieldgroup.com

Aurora Funds, Inc.
2525 Meridian Pkwy., Ste. 220
Durham, NC 27713
(919)484-0400
Fax: (919)484-0444
Website: http://www.aurorafunds.com

Intersouth Partners
3211 Shannon Rd., Ste. 610
Durham, NC 27707
(919)493-6640
Fax: (919)493-6649
E-mail: info@intersouth.com
Website: http://www.intersouth.com

Geneva Merchant Banking Partners
PO Box 21962
Greensboro, NC 27420
(336)275-7002
Fax: (336)275-9155
Website: http://www.genevamerchant
bank.com

The North Carolina Enterprise Fund, L.P.
3600 Glenwood Ave., Ste. 107
Raleigh, NC 27612
(919)781-2691
Fax: (919)783-9195
Website: http://www.ncef.com

Ohio

Senmend Medical Ventures
4445 Lake Forest Dr., Ste. 600
Cincinnati, OH 45242
(513)563-3264
Fax: (513)563-3261

The Walnut Group
312 Walnut St., Ste. 1151
Cincinnati, OH 45202
(513)651-3300
Fax: (513)929-4441
Website: http://www.thewalnutgroup.com

Brantley Venture Partners
20600 Chagrin Blvd., Ste. 1150
Cleveland, OH 44122
(216)283-4800
Fax: (216)283-5324

Clarion Capital Corp.
1801 E 9th St., Ste. 1120
Cleveland, OH 44114

(216)687-1096
Fax: (216)694-3545

Crystal Internet Venture Fund, L.P.
1120 Chester Ave., Ste. 418
Cleveland, OH 44114
(216)263-5515
Fax: (216)263-5518
E-mail: jf@crystalventure.com
Website: http://www.crystalventure.com

Key Equity Capital Corp.
127 Public Sq., 28th Fl.
Cleveland, OH 44114
(216)689-3000
Fax: (216)689-3204
Website: http://www.keybank.com

Morgenthaler Ventures
Terminal Tower
50 Public Square, Ste. 2700
Cleveland, OH 44113
(216)416-7500
Fax: (216)416-7501
Website: http://www.morgenthaler.com

National City Equity Partners Inc.
1965 E 6th St.
Cleveland, OH 44114
(216)575-2491
Fax: (216)575-9965
E-mail: nccap@aol.com
Website: http://www.nccapital.com

Primus Venture Partners, Inc.
5900 LanderBrook Dr., Ste. 2000
Cleveland, OH 44124-4020
(440)684-7300
Fax: (440)684-7342
E-mail: info@primusventure.com
Website: http://www.primusventure.com

Banc One Capital Partners (Columbus)
150 East Gay St., 24th Fl.
Columbus, OH 43215
(614)217-1100
Fax: (614)217-1217

Battelle Venture Partners
505 King Ave.
Columbus, OH 43201
(614)424-7005
Fax: (614)424-4874

Ohio Partners
62 E Board St., 3rd Fl.
Columbus, OH 43215
(614)621-1210
Fax: (614)621-1240

Capital Technology Group, L.L.C.
400 Metro Place North, Ste. 300

Dublin, OH 43017
(614)792-6066
Fax: (614)792-6036
E-mail: info@capitaltech.com
Website: http://www.capitaltech.com

Northwest Ohio Venture Fund
4159 Holland-Sylvania R., Ste. 202
Toledo, OH 43623
(419)824-8144
Fax: (419)882-2035
E-mail: bwalsh@novf.com

Oklahoma

Moore & Associates
1000 W Wilshire Blvd., Ste. 370
Oklahoma City, OK 73116
(405)842-3660
Fax: (405)842-3763

Chisholm Private Capital Partners
100 West 5th St., Ste. 805
Tulsa, OK 74103
(918)584-0440
Fax: (918)584-0441
Website: http://www.chisholmvc.com

Davis, Tuttle Venture Partners (Tulsa)
320 S Boston, Ste. 1000
Tulsa, OK 74103-3703
(918)584-7272
Fax: (918)582-3404
Website: http://www.davistuttle.com

RBC Ventures
2627 E 21st St.
Tulsa, OK 74114
(918)744-5607
Fax: (918)743-8630

Oregon

Utah Ventures II LP
10700 SW Beaverton-Hillsdale Hwy.,
Ste. 548
Beaverton, OR 97005
(503)574-4125
E-mail: adishlip@uven.com
Website: http://www.uven.com

Orien Ventures
14523 SW Westlake Dr.
Lake Oswego, OR 97035
(503)699-1680
Fax: (503)699-1681

OVP Venture Partners (Lake Oswego)
340 Oswego Pointe Dr., Ste. 200
Lake Oswego, OR 97034
(503)697-8766
Fax: (503)697-8863

E-mail: info@ovp.com
Website: http://www.ovp.com

Oregon Resource and Technology Development Fund
4370 NE Halsey St., Ste. 233
Portland, OR 97213-1566
(503)282-4462
Fax: (503)282-2976

Shaw Venture Partners
400 SW 6th Ave., Ste. 1100
Portland, OR 97204-1636
(503)228-4884
Fax: (503)227-2471
Website: http://www.shawventures.com

Pennsylvania

Mid-Atlantic Venture Funds
125 Goodman Dr.
Bethlehem, PA 18015
(610)865-6550
Fax: (610)865-6427
Website: http://www.mavf.com

Newspring Ventures
100 W Elm St., Ste. 101
Conshohocken, PA 19428
(610)567-2380
Fax: (610)567-2388
Website: http://www.newsprintventures
.com

Patricof & Co. Ventures, Inc.
455 S Gulph Rd., Ste. 410
King of Prussia, PA 19406
(610)265-0286
Fax: (610)265-4959
Website: http://www.patricof.com

Loyalhanna Venture Fund
527 Cedar Way, Ste. 104
Oakmont, PA 15139
(412)820-7035
Fax: (412)820-7036

Innovest Group Inc.
2000 Market St., Ste. 1400
Philadelphia, PA 19103
(215)564-3960
Fax: (215)569-3272

Keystone Venture Capital Management Co.
1601 Market St., Ste. 2500
Philadelphia, PA 19103
(215)241-1200
Fax: (215)241-1211
Website: http://www.keystonevc.com

Liberty Venture Partners
2005 Market St., Ste. 200

Philadelphia, PA 19103
(215)282-4484
Fax: (215)282-4485
E-mail: info@libertyvp.com
Website: http://www.libertyvp.com

Penn Janney Fund, Inc.
1801 Market St., 11th Fl.
Philadelphia, PA 19103
(215)665-4447
Fax: (215)557-0820

Philadelphia Ventures, Inc.
The Bellevue
200 S Broad St.
Philadelphia, PA 19102
(215)732-4445
Fax: (215)732-4644

Birchmere Ventures Inc.
2000 Technology Dr.
Pittsburgh, PA 15219-3109
(412)803-8000
Fax: (412)687-8139
Website: http://www.birchmerevc.com

CEO Venture Fund
2000 Technology Dr., Ste. 160
Pittsburgh, PA 15219-3109
(412)687-3451
Fax: (412)687-8139
E-mail: ceofund@aol.com
Website: http://www.ceoventurefund.com

Innovation Works Inc.
2000 Technology Dr., Ste. 250
Pittsburgh, PA 15219
(412)681-1520
Fax: (412)681-2625
Website: http://www.innovationworks.org

Keystone Minority Capital Fund L.P.
1801 Centre Ave., Ste. 201
Williams Sq.
Pittsburgh, PA 15219
(412)338-2230
Fax: (412)338-2224

Mellon Ventures, Inc.
One Mellon Bank Ctr., Rm. 3500
Pittsburgh, PA 15258
(412)236-3594
Fax: (412)236-3593
Website: http://www.mellonventures.com

Pennsylvania Growth Fund
5850 Ellsworth Ave., Ste. 303
Pittsburgh, PA 15232
(412)661-1000
Fax: (412)361-0676

Point Venture Partners
The Century Bldg.

130 Seventh St., 7th Fl.
Pittsburgh, PA 15222
(412)261-1966
Fax: (412)261-1718

Cross Atlantic Capital Partners
5 Radnor Corporate Center, Ste. 555
Radnor, PA 19087
(610)995-2650
Fax: (610)971-2062
Website: http://www.xacp.com

Meridian Venture Partners (Radnor)
The Radnor Court Bldg., Ste. 140
259 Radnor-Chester Rd.
Radnor, PA 19087
(610)254-2999
Fax: (610)254-2996
E-mail: mvpart@ix.netcom.com

TDH
919 Conestoga Rd., Bldg. 1, Ste. 301
Rosemont, PA 19010
(610)526-9970
Fax: (610)526-9971

Adams Capital Management
500 Blackburn Ave.
Sewickley, PA 15143
(412)749-9454
Fax: (412)749-9459
Website: http://www.acm.com

S.R. One, Ltd.
Four Tower Bridge
200 Barr Harbor Dr., Ste. 250
W Conshohocken, PA 19428
(610)567-1000
Fax: (610)567-1039

Greater Philadelphia Venture Capital Corp.
351 East Conestoga Rd.
Wayne, PA 19087
(610)688-6829
Fax: (610)254-8958

PA Early Stage
435 Devon Park Dr., Bldg. 500, Ste. 510
Wayne, PA 19087
(610)293-4075
Fax: (610)254-4240
Website: http://www.paearlystage.com

The Sandhurst Venture Fund, L.P.
351 E Constoga Rd.
Wayne, PA 19087
(610)254-8900
Fax: (610)254-8958

TL Ventures
700 Bldg.
435 Devon Park Dr.

Wayne, PA 19087-1990
(610)975-3765
Fax: (610)254-4210
Website: http://www.tlventures.com

Rockhill Ventures, Inc.
100 Front St., Ste. 1350
West Conshohocken, PA 19428
(610)940-0300
Fax: (610)940-0301

Puerto Rico

Advent-Morro Equity Partners
Banco Popular Bldg.
206 Tetuan St., Ste. 903
San Juan, PR 00902
(787)725-5285
Fax: (787)721-1735

North America Investment Corp.
Mercantil Plaza, Ste. 813
PO Box 191831
San Juan, PR 00919
(787)754-6178
Fax: (787)754-6181

Rhode Island

Manchester Humphreys, Inc.
40 Westminster St., Ste. 900
Providence, RI 02903
(401)454-0400
Fax: (401)454-0403

Navis Partners
50 Kennedy Plaza, 12th Fl.
Providence, RI 02903
(401)278-6770
Fax: (401)278-6387
Website: http://www.navispartners.com

South Carolina

Capital Insights, L.L.C.
PO Box 27162
Greenville, SC 29616-2162
(864)242-6832
Fax: (864)242-6755
E-mail: jwarner@capitalinsights.com
Website: http://www.capitalinsights.com

Transamerica Mezzanine Financing
7 N. Laurens St., Ste. 603
Greenville, SC 29601
(864)232-6198
Fax: (864)241-4444

Tennessee

Valley Capital Corp.
Krystal Bldg.

100 W Martin Luther King Blvd., Ste. 212
Chattanooga, TN 37402
(423)265-1557
Fax: (423)265-1588

Coleman Swenson Booth Inc.
237 2nd Ave. S
Franklin, TN 37064-2649
(615)791-9462
Fax: (615)791-9636
Website: http://www.colemanswenson
.com

Capital Services & Resources, Inc.
5159 Wheelis Dr., Ste. 106
Memphis, TN 38117
(901)761-2156
Fax: (907)767-0060

Paradigm Capital Partners LLC
6410 Poplar Ave., Ste. 395
Memphis, TN 38119
(901)682-6060
Fax: (901)328-3061

SSM Ventures
845 Crossover Ln., Ste. 140
Memphis, TN 38117
(901)767-1131
Fax: (901)767-1135
Website: http://www.ssmventures.com

Capital Across America L.P.
501 Union St., Ste. 201
Nashville, TN 37219
(615)254-1414
Fax: (615)254-1856
Website: http://www.capitalacross
america.com

Equitas L.P.
2000 Glen Echo Rd., Ste. 101
PO Box 158838
Nashville, TN 37215-8838
(615)383-8673
Fax: (615)383-8693

Massey Burch Capital Corp.
One Burton Hills Blvd., Ste. 350
Nashville, TN 37215
(615)665-3221
Fax: (615)665-3240
E-mail: tcalton@masseyburch.com
Website: http://www.masseyburch.com

Nelson Capital Corp.
3401 West End Ave., Ste. 300
Nashville, TN 37203
(615)292-8787
Fax: (615)385-3150

Texas

Phillips-Smith Specialty Retail Group
5080 Spectrum Dr., Ste. 805 W
Addison, TX 75001
(972)387-0725
Fax: (972)458-2560
E-mail: pssrg@aol.com
Website: http://www.phillips-smith.com

Austin Ventures, L.P.
701 Brazos St., Ste. 1400
Austin, TX 78701
(512)485-1900
Fax: (512)476-3952
E-mail: info@ausven.com
Website: http://www.austinventures
.com

The Capital Network
3925 West Braker Lane, Ste. 406
Austin, TX 78759-5321
(512)305-0826
Fax: (512)305-0836

Techxas Ventures LLC
5000 Plaza on the Lake
Austin, TX 78746
(512)343-0118
Fax: (512)343-1879
E-mail: bruce@techxas.com
Website: http://www.techxas.com

Alliance Financial of Houston
218 Heather Ln.
Conroe, TX 77385-9013
(936)447-3300
Fax: (936)447-4222

Amerimark Capital Corp.
1111 W Mockingbird, Ste. 1111
Dallas, TX 75247
(214)638-7878
Fax: (214)638-7612
E-mail: amerimark@amcapital.com
Website: http://www.amcapital.com

**AMT Venture Partners / AMT
Capital Ltd.**
5220 Spring Valley Rd., Ste. 600
Dallas, TX 75240
(214)905-9757
Fax: (214)905-9761
Website: http://www.amtcapital.com

Arkoma Venture Partners
5950 Berkshire Lane, Ste. 1400
Dallas, TX 75225
(214)739-3515
Fax: (214)739-3572
E-mail: joelf@arkomavp.com

Capital Southwest Corp.
12900 Preston Rd., Ste. 700
Dallas, TX 75230
(972)233-8242
Fax: (972)233-7362
Website: http://www.capitalsouthwest.com

Dali, Hook Partners
One Lincoln Center, Ste. 1550
5400 LBJ Freeway
Dallas, TX 75240
(972)991-5457
Fax: (972)991-5458
E-mail: dhook@hookpartners.com
Website: http://www.hookpartners.com

HO2 Partners
Two Galleria Tower
13455 Noel Rd., Ste. 1670
Dallas, TX 75240
(972)702-1144
Fax: (972)702-8234
Website: http://www.ho2.com

Interwest Partners (Dallas)
2 Galleria Tower
13455 Noel Rd., Ste. 1670
Dallas, TX 75240
(972)392-7279
Fax: (972)490-6348
Website: http://www.interwest.com

Kahala Investments, Inc.
8214 Westchester Dr., Ste. 715
Dallas, TX 75225
(214)987-0077
Fax: (214)987-2332

MESBIC Ventures Holding Co.
2435 North Central Expressway,
Ste. 200
Dallas, TX 75080
(972)991-1597
Fax: (972)991-4770
Website: http://www.mvhc.com

North Texas MESBIC, Inc.
9500 Forest Lane, Ste. 430
Dallas, TX 75243
(214)221-3565
Fax: (214)221-3566

Richard Jaffe & Company, Inc,
7318 Royal Cir.
Dallas, TX 75230
(214)265-9397
Fax: (214)739-1845

Sevin Rosen Management Co.
13455 Noel Rd., Ste. 1670
Dallas, TX 75240
(972)702-1100

Fax: (972)702-1103
E-mail: info@srfunds.com
Website: http://www.srfunds.com

Stratford Capital Partners, L.P.
300 Crescent Ct., Ste. 500
Dallas, TX 75201
(214)740-7377
Fax: (214)720-7393
E-mail: stratcap@hmtf.com

Sunwestern Investment Group
12221 Merit Dr., Ste. 935
Dallas, TX 75251
(972)239-5650
Fax: (972)701-0024

Wingate Partners
750 N St. Paul St., Ste. 1200
Dallas, TX 75201
(214)720-1313
Fax: (214)871-8799

Buena Venture Associates
201 Main St., 32nd Fl.
Fort Worth, TX 76102
(817)339-7400
Fax: (817)390-8408
Website: http://www.buenaventure.com

The Catalyst Group
3 Riverway, Ste. 770
Houston, TX 77056
(713)623-8133
Fax: (713)623-0473
E-mail: herman@thecatalystgroup.net
Website: http://www.thecatalyst
group.net

Cureton & Co., Inc.
1100 Louisiana, Ste. 3250
Houston, TX 77002
(713)658-9806
Fax: (713)658-0476

**Davis, Tuttle Venture Partners
(Dallas)**
8 Greenway Plaza, Ste. 1020
Houston, TX 77046
(713)993-0440
Fax: (713)621-2297
Website: http://www.davistuttle.com

Houston Partners
401 Louisiana, 8th Fl.
Houston, TX 77002
(713)222-8600
Fax: (713)222-8932

Southwest Venture Group
10878 Westheimer, Ste. 178
Houston, TX 77042

(713)827-8947
(713)461-1470

AM Fund
4600 Post Oak Place, Ste. 100
Houston, TX 77027
(713)627-9111
Fax: (713)627-9119

Ventex Management, Inc.
3417 Milam St.
Houston, TX 77002-9531
(713)659-7870
Fax: (713)659-7855

MBA Venture Group
1004 Olde Town Rd., Ste. 102
Irving, TX 75061
(972)986-6703

First Capital Group Management Co.
750 East Mulberry St., Ste. 305
PO Box 15616
San Antonio, TX 78212
(210)736-4233
Fax: (210)736-5449

The Southwest Venture Partnerships
16414 San Pedro, Ste. 345
San Antonio, TX 78232
(210)402-1200
Fax: (210)402-1221
E-mail: swvp@aol.com

Medtech International Inc.
1742 Carriageway
Sugarland, TX 77478
(713)980-8474
Fax: (713)980-6343

Utah

**First Security Business Investment
Corp.**
15 East 100 South, Ste. 100
Salt Lake City, UT 84111
(801)246-5737
Fax: (801)246-5740

Utah Ventures II, L.P.
423 Wakara Way, Ste. 206
Salt Lake City, UT 84108
(801)583-5922
Fax: (801)583-4105
Website: http://www.uven.com

Wasatch Venture Corp.
1 S Main St., Ste. 1400
Salt Lake City, UT 84133
(801)524-8939
Fax: (801)524-8941
E-mail: mail@wasatchvc.com

Vermont

North Atlantic Capital Corp.
76 Saint Paul St., Ste. 600
Burlington, VT 05401
(802)658-7820
Fax: (802)658-5757
Website: http://www.northatlanticcapital
.com

Green Mountain Advisors Inc.
PO Box 1230
Quechee, VT 05059
(802)296-7800
Fax: (802)296-6012
Website: http://www.gmtcap.com

Virginia

Oxford Financial Services Corp.
Alexandria, VA 22314
(703)519-4900
Fax: (703)519-4910
E-mail: oxford133@aol.com

Continental SBIC
4141 N. Henderson Rd.
Arlington, VA 22203
(703)527-5200
Fax: (703)527-3700

Novak Biddle Venture Partners
1750 Tysons Blvd., Ste. 1190
McLean, VA 22102
(703)847-3770
Fax: (703)847-3771
E-mail: roger@novakbiddle.com
Website: http://www.novakbiddle.com

Spacevest
11911 Freedom Dr., Ste. 500
Reston, VA 20190
(703)904-9800
Fax: (703)904-0571
E-mail: spacevest@spacevest.com
Website: http://www.spacevest.com

Virginia Capital
1801 Libbie Ave., Ste. 201
Richmond, VA 23226
(804)648-4802
Fax: (804)648-4809
E-mail: webmaster@vacapital.com
Website: http://www.vacapital.com

Calvert Social Venture Partners
402 Maple Ave. W
Vienna, VA 22180
(703)255-4930
Fax: (703)255-4931
E-mail: calven2000@aol.com

Fairfax Partners
8000 Towers Crescent Dr., Ste. 940
Vienna, VA 22182
(703)847-9486
Fax: (703)847-0911

Global Internet Ventures
8150 Leesburg Pike, Ste. 1210
Vienna, VA 22182
(703)442-3300
Fax: (703)442-3388
Website: http://www.givinc.com

Walnut Capital Corp. (Vienna)
8000 Towers Crescent Dr., Ste. 1070
Vienna, VA 22182
(703)448-3771
Fax: (703)448-7751

Washington

Encompass Ventures
777 108th Ave. NE, Ste. 2300
Bellevue, WA 98004
(425)486-3900
Fax: (425)486-3901
E-mail: info@evpartners.com
Website: http://www.encompassventures
.com

Fluke Venture Partners
11400 SE Sixth St., Ste. 230
Bellevue, WA 98004
(425)453-4590
Fax: (425)453-4675
E-mail: gabelein@flukeventures.com
Website: http://www.flukeventures.com

Pacific Northwest Partners SBIC, L.P.
15352 SE 53rd St.
Bellevue, WA 98006
(425)455-9967
Fax: (425)455-9404

Materia Venture Associates, L.P.
3435 Carillon Pointe
Kirkland, WA 98033-7354

(425)822-4100
Fax: (425)827-4086

OVP Venture Partners (Kirkland)
2420 Carillon Pt.
Kirkland, WA 98033
(425)889-9192
Fax: (425)889-0152
E-mail: info@ovp.com
Website: http://www.ovp.com

Digital Partners
999 3rd Ave., Ste. 1610
Seattle, WA 98104
(206)405-3607
Fax: (206)405-3617
Website: http://www.digitalpartners
.com

Frazier & Company
601 Union St., Ste. 3300
Seattle, WA 98101
(206)621-7200
Fax: (206)621-1848
E-mail: jon@frazierco.com

Kirlan Venture Capital, Inc.
221 First Ave. W, Ste. 108
Seattle, WA 98119-4223
(206)281-8610
Fax: (206)285-3451
Website: http://www.kirlanventure.com

Phoenix Partners
1000 2nd Ave., Ste. 3600
Seattle, WA 98104
(206)624-8968
Fax: (206)624-1907

Voyager Capital
800 5th St., Ste. 4100
Seattle, WA 98103
(206)470-1180
Fax: (206)470-1185
E-mail: info@voyagercap.com
Website: http://www.voyagercap.com

Northwest Venture Associates
221 N. Wall St., Ste. 628
Spokane, WA 99201
(509)747-0728
Fax: (509)747-0758
Website: http://www.nwva.com

Wisconsin

Venture Investors Management, L.L.C.
University Research Park
505 S Rosa Rd.
Madison, WI 53719
(608)441-2700
Fax: (608)441-2727
E-mail: roger@ventureinvestors.com
Website: http://www.ventureinvesters
.com

Capital Investments, Inc.
1009 West Glen Oaks Lane, Ste. 103
Mequon, WI 53092
(414)241-0303
Fax: (414)241-8451
Website: http://www.
capitalinvestmentsinc.com

Future Value Venture, Inc.
2745 N. Martin Luther King Dr., Ste. 204
Milwaukee, WI 53212-2300
(414)264-2252
Fax: (414)264-2253
E-mail: fvvventures@aol.com
William Beckett, President

Lubar and Co., Inc.
700 N. Water St., Ste. 1200
Milwaukee, WI 53202
(414)291-9000
Fax: (414)291-9061

GCI
20875 Crossroads Cir., Ste. 100
Waukesha, WI 53186
(262)798-5080
Fax: (262)798-5087

Organizations, Agencies, & Consultants

Glossary of Small Business Terms

Absolute liability

Liability that is incurred due to product defects or negligent actions. Manufacturers or retail establishments are held responsible, even though the defect or action may not have been intentional or negligent.

ACE

See Active Corps of Executives

Accident and health benefits

Benefits offered to employees and their families in order to offset the costs associated with accidental death, accidental injury, or sickness.

Account statement

A record of transactions, including payments, new debt, and deposits, incurred during a defined period of time.

Accounting system

System capturing the costs of all employees and/or machinery included in business expenses.

Accounts payable

See Trade credit

Accounts receivable

Unpaid accounts which arise from unsettled claims and transactions from the sale of a company's products or services to its customers.

Active Corps of Executives (ACE)

A group of volunteers for a management assistance program of the U.S. Small Business Administration; volunteers provide one-on-one counseling and teach workshops and seminars for small firms.

ADA

See Americans with Disabilities Act

Adaptation

The process whereby an invention is modified to meet the needs of users.

Adaptive engineering

The process whereby an invention is modified to meet the manufacturing and commercial requirements of a targeted market.

Adverse selection

The tendency for higher-risk individuals to purchase health care and more comprehensive plans, resulting in increased costs.

Advertising

A marketing tool used to capture public attention and influence purchasing decisions for a product or service. Utilizes various forms of media to generate consumer response, such as flyers, magazines, newspapers, radio, and television.

Age discrimination

The denial of the rights and privileges of employment based solely on the age of an individual.

Agency costs

Costs incurred to insure that the lender or investor maintains control over assets while allowing the borrower or entrepreneur to use them. Monitoring and information costs are the two major types of agency costs.

Agribusiness

The production and sale of commodities and products from the commercial farming industry.

Americans with Disabilities Act (ADA)

Law designed to ensure equal access and opportunity to handicapped persons.

Annual report

Yearly financial report prepared by a business that adheres to the requirements set forth by the Securities and Exchange Commission (SEC).

Antitrust immunity

Exemption from prosecution under antitrust laws. In the transportation industry, firms with antitrust immunity are permitted under certain conditions to set schedules and sometimes prices for the public benefit.

Applied research

Scientific study targeted for use in a product or process.

Assets

Anything of value owned by a company.

Audit

The verification of accounting records and business procedures conducted by an outside accounting service.

Average cost

Total production costs divided by the quantity produced.

Balance Sheet

A financial statement listing the total assets and liabilities of a company at a given time.

Bankruptcy

The condition in which a business cannot meet its debt obligations and petitions a federal district court either for reorganization of its debts (Chapter 11) or for liquidation of its assets (Chapter 7).

Basket clause

A provision specifying the amount of public pension funds that may be placed in investments not included on a state's legal list (see separate citation).

BDC

See Business development corporation

Benefit

Various services, such as health care, flextime, day care, insurance, and vacation, offered to employees as part of a hiring package. Typically subsidized in whole or in part by the business.

BIDCO

See Business and industrial development company

Billing cycle

A system designed to evenly distribute customer billing throughout the month, preventing clerical backlogs.

Blue chip security

A low-risk, low-yield security representing an interest in a very stable company.

Blue sky laws

A general term that denotes various states' laws regulating securities.

Bond

A written instrument executed by a bidder or contractor (the principal) and a second party (the surety or sureties) to assure fulfillment of the principal's obligations to a third party (the obligee or government) identified in the bond. If the principal's obligations are not met, the bond assures payment to the extent stipulated of any loss sustained by the obligee.

Bonding requirements

Terms contained in a bond (see separate citation).

Bonus

An amount of money paid to an employee as a reward for achieving certain business goals or objectives.

Brainstorming

A group session where employees contribute their ideas for solving a problem or meeting a company objective without fear of retribution or ridicule.

Brand name

The part of a brand, trademark, or service mark that can be spoken. It can be a word, letter, or group of words or letters.

Bridge financing

A short-term loan made in expectation of intermediateterm or long-term financing. Can be used when a company plans to go public in the near future.

Broker

One who matches resources available for innovation with those who need them.

Budget

An estimate of the spending necessary to complete a project or offer a service in comparison to cash-on-hand and expected earnings for the coming year, with an emphasis on cost control.

Business and industrial development company (BIDCO)

A private, for-profit financing corporation chartered by the state to provide both equity and long-term debt capital to small business owners (see separate citations for equity and debt capital).

Business birth

The formation of a new establishment or enterprise. The appearance of a new establishment or enterprise in the Small Business Data Base (see separate citation).

Business conditions

Outside factors that can affect the financial performance of a business.

Business contractions

The number of establishments that have decreased in employment during a specified time.

Business cycle

A period of economic recession and recovery. These cycles vary in duration.

Business death

The voluntary or involuntary closure of a firm or establishment. The disappearance of an establishment or enterprise from the Small Business Data Base (see separate citation).

Business development corporation (BDC)

A business financing agency, usually composed of the financial institutions in an area or state, organized to assist in financing businesses unable to obtain assistance through normal channels; the risk is spread among various members of the business development corporation, and interest rates may vary somewhat from those charged by member institutions. A venture capital firm in which shares of ownership are publicly held and to which the Investment Act of 1940 applies.

Business dissolution

For enumeration purposes, the absence of a business that was present in the prior time period from any current record.

Business entry

See Business birth

Business ethics

Moral values and principles espoused by members of the business community as a guide to fair and honest business practices.

Business exit

See Business death

Business expansions

The number of establishments that added employees during a specified time.

Business failure

Closure of a business causing a loss to at least one creditor.

Business format franchising

The purchase of the name, trademark, and an ongoing business plan of the parent corporation or franchisor by the franchisee.

Business license

A legal authorization issued by municipal and state governments and required for business operations.

Business name

Enterprises must register their business names with local governments usually on a "doing business as" (DBA) form. (This name is sometimes referred to as a "fictional name.") The procedure is part of the business licensing process and prevents any other business from using that same name for a similar business in the same locality.

Business norms

See Financial ratios

Business permit

See Business license

Business plan

A document that spells out a company's expected course of action for a specified period, usually including a detailed listing and analysis of risks and uncertainties. For the small business, it should examine the proposed products, the market, the industry, the management policies, the marketing policies, production needs, and financial needs. Frequently, it is used as a prospectus for potential investors and lenders.

Business proposal
See Business plan

Business service firm
An establishment primarily engaged in rendering services to other business organizations on a fee or contract basis.

Business start
For enumeration purposes, a business with a name or similar designation that did not exist in a prior time period.

Cafeteria plan
See Flexible benefit plan

Capacity
Level of a firm's, industry's, or nation's output corresponding to full practical utilization of available resources.

Capital
Assets less liabilities, representing the ownership interest in a business. A stock of accumulated goods, especially at a specified time and in contrast to income received during a specified time period. Accumulated goods devoted to production. Accumulated possessions calculated to bring income.

Capital expenditure
Expenses incurred by a business for improvements that will depreciate over time.

Capital gain
The monetary difference between the purchase price and the selling price of capital. Capital gains are taxed at a rate of 28% by the federal government.

Capital intensity
The relative importance of capital in the production process, usually expressed as the ratio of capital to labor but also sometimes as the ratio of capital to output.

Capital resource
The equipment, facilities and labor used to create products and services.

Catastrophic care
Medical and other services for acute and long-term illnesses that cost more than insurance coverage limits or that cost the amount most families may be expected to pay with their own resources.

CDC
See Certified development corporation

Certified development corporation (CDC)
A local area or statewide corporation or authority (for profit or nonprofit) that packages U.S. Small Business Administration (SBA), bank, state, and/or private money into financial assistance for existing business capital improvements. The SBA holds the second lien on its maximum share of 40 percent involvement. Each state has at least one certified development corporation. This program is called the SBA 504 Program.

Certified lenders
Banks that participate in the SBA guaranteed loan program (see separate citation). Such banks must have a good track record with the U.S. Small Business Administration (SBA) and must agree to certain conditions set forth by the agency. In return, the SBA agrees to process any guaranteed loan application within three business days.

Channel of distribution
The means used to transport merchandise from the manufacturer to the consumer.

Chapter 7 of the 1978 Bankruptcy Act
Provides for a court-appointed trustee who is responsible for liquidating a company's assets in order to settle outstanding debts.

Chapter 11 of the 1978 Bankruptcy Act
Allows the business owners to retain control of the company while working with their creditors to reorganize their finances and establish better business practices to prevent liquidation of assets.

Closely held corporation
A corporation in which the shares are held by a few persons, usually officers, employees, or others close to the management; these shares are rarely offered to the public.

Code of Federal Regulations
Codification of general and permanent rules of the federal government published in the Federal Register.

Code sharing

See Computer code sharing

Coinsurance

Upon meeting the deductible payment, health insurance participants may be required to make additional health care cost-sharing payments. Coinsurance is a payment of a fixed percentage of the cost of each service; copayment is usually a fixed amount to be paid with each service.

Collateral

Securities, evidence of deposit, or other property pledged by a borrower to secure repayment of a loan.

Collective ratemaking

The establishment of uniform charges for services by a group of businesses in the same industry.

Commercial insurance plan

See Underwriting

Commercial loans

Short-term renewable loans used to finance specific capital needs of a business.

Commercialization

The final stage of the innovation process, including production and distribution.

Common stock

The most frequently used instrument for purchasing ownership in private or public companies. Common stock generally carries the right to vote on certain corporate actions and may pay dividends, although it rarely does in venture investments. In liquidation, common stockholders are the last to share in the proceeds from the sale of a corporation's assets; bondholders and preferred shareholders have priority. Common stock is often used in firstround start-up financing.

Community development corporation

A corporation established to develop economic programs for a community and, in most cases, to provide financial support for such development.

Competitor

A business whose product or service is marketed for the same purpose/use and to the same consumer group as the product or service of another.

Consignment

A merchandising agreement, usually referring to secondhand shops, where the dealer pays the owner of an item a percentage of the profit when the item is sold.

Consortium

A coalition of organizations such as banks and corporations for ventures requiring large capital resources.

Consultant

An individual that is paid by a business to provide advice and expertise in a particular area.

Consumer price index

A measure of the fluctuation in prices between two points in time.

Consumer research

Research conducted by a business to obtain information about existing or potential consumer markets.

Continuation coverage

Health coverage offered for a specified period of time to employees who leave their jobs and to their widows, divorced spouses, or dependents.

Contractions

See Business contractions

Convertible preferred stock

A class of stock that pays a reasonable dividend and is convertible into common stock (see separate citation). Generally the convertible feature may only be exercised after being held for a stated period of time. This arrangement is usually considered second-round financing when a company needs equity to maintain its cash flow.

Convertible securities

A feature of certain bonds, debentures, or preferred stocks that allows them to be exchanged by the owner for another class of securities at a future date and in accordance with any other terms of the issue.

Copayment

See Coinsurance

Copyright

A legal form of protection available to creators and authors to safeguard their works from unlawful use or claim of ownership by others. Copyrights may be acquired for works of art, sculpture, music, and published or unpublished manuscripts. All copyrights should be registered at the Copyright Office of the Library of Congress.

Corporate financial ratios
The relationship between key figures found in a company's financial statement expressed as a numeric value. Used to evaluate risk and company performance. Also known as Financial averages, Operating ratios, and Business ratios.

Corporation
A legal entity, chartered by a state or the federal government, recognized as a separate entity having its own rights, privileges, and liabilities distinct from those of its members.

Cost containment
Actions taken by employers and insurers to curtail rising health care costs; for example, increasing employee cost sharing (see separate citation), requiring second opinions, or preadmission screening.

Cost sharing
The requirement that health care consumers contribute to their own medical care costs through deductibles and coinsurance (see separate citations). Cost sharing does not include the amounts paid in premiums. It is used to control utilization of services; for example, requiring a fixed amount to be paid with each health care service.

Cottage industry
Businesses based in the home in which the family members are the labor force and family-owned equipment is used to process the goods.

Credit Rating
A letter or number calculated by an organization (such as Dun & Bradstreet) to represent the ability and disposition of a business to meet its financial obligations.

Customer service
Various techniques used to ensure the satisfaction of a customer.

Cyclical peak
The upper turning point in a business cycle.

Cyclical trough
The lower turning point in a business cycle.

DBA (Doing business as)
See Business name

Death
See Business death

Debenture
A certificate given as acknowledgment of a debt (see separate citation) secured by the general credit of the issuing corporation. A bond, usually without security, issued by a corporation and sometimes convertible to common stock.

Debt
Something owed by one person to another. Financing in which a company receives capital that must be repaid; no ownership is transferred.

Debt capital
Business financing that normally requires periodic interest payments and repayment of the principal within a specified time.

Debt financing
See Debt capital

Debt securities
Loans such as bonds and notes that provide a specified rate of return for a specified period of time.

Deductible
A set amount that an individual must pay before any benefits are received.

Demand shock absorbers
A term used to describe the role that some small firms play by expanding their output levels to accommodate a transient surge in demand.

Demographics
Statistics on various markets, including age, income, and education, used to target specific products or services to appropriate consumer groups.

Demonstration
Showing that a product or process has been modified sufficiently to meet the needs of users.

Deregulation

The lifting of government restrictions; for example, the lifting of government restrictions on the entry of new businesses, the expansion of services, and the setting of prices in particular industries.

Disaster loans

Various types of physical and economic assistance available to individuals and businesses through the U.S. Small Business Administration (SBA). This is the only SBA loan program available for residential purposes.

Discrimination

The denial of the rights and privileges of employment based on factors such as age, race, religion, or gender.

Diseconomies of scale

The condition in which the costs of production increase faster than the volume of production.

Dissolution

See Business dissolution

Distribution

Delivering a product or process to the user.

Distributor

One who delivers merchandise to the user.

Diversified company

A company whose products and services are used by several different markets.

Doing business as (DBA)

See Business name

Dow Jones

An information services company that publishes the Wall Street Journal and other sources of financial information.

Dow Jones Industrial Average

An indicator of stock market performance.

Earned income

A tax term that refers to wages and salaries earned by the recipient, as opposed to monies earned through interest and dividends.

Economic efficiency

The use of productive resources to the fullest practical extent in the provision of the set of goods and services that is most preferred by purchasers in the economy.

Economic indicators

Statistics used to express the state of the economy. These include the length of the average work week, the rate of unemployment, and stock prices.

Economically disadvantaged

See Socially and economically disadvantaged

Economies of scale

See Scale economies

EEOC

See Equal Employment Opportunity Commission

8(a) Program

A program authorized by the Small Business Act that directs federal contracts to small businesses owned and operated by socially and economically disadvantaged individuals.

Electronic mail (e-mail)

The electronic transmission of mail via phone lines.

E-mail

See Electronic mail

Employee leasing

A contract by which employers arrange to have their workers hired by a leasing company and then leased back to them for a management fee. The leasing company typically assumes the administrative burden of payroll and provides a benefit package to the workers.

Employee tenure

The length of time an employee works for a particular employer.

Employer identification number

The business equivalent of a social security number. Assigned by the U.S. Internal Revenue Service.

Enterprise

An aggregation of all establishments owned by a parent company. An enterprise may consist of a single, independent establishment or include subsidiaries and other branches under the same ownership and control.

Enterprise zone
A designated area, usually found in inner cities and other areas with significant unemployment, where businesses receive tax credits and other incentives to entice them to establish operations there.

Entrepreneur
A person who takes the risk of organizing and operating a new business venture.

Entry
See Business entry

Equal Employment Opportunity Commission (EEOC)
A federal agency that ensures nondiscrimination in the hiring and firing practices of a business.

Equal opportunity employer
An employer who adheres to the standards set by the Equal Employment Opportunity Commission (see separate citation).

Equity
The ownership interest. Financing in which partial or total ownership of a company is surrendered in exchange for capital. An investor's financial return comes from dividend payments and from growth in the net worth of the business.

Equity capital
See Equity; Equity midrisk venture capital

Equity financing
See Equity; Equity midrisk venture capital

Equity midrisk venture capital
An unsecured investment in a company. Usually a purchase of ownership interest in a company that occurs in the later stages of a company's development.

Equity partnership
A limited partnership arrangement for providing start-up and seed capital to businesses.

Equity securities
See Equity

Equity-type
Debt financing subordinated to conventional debt.

Establishment
A single-location business unit that may be independent (a single-establishment enterprise) or owned by a parent enterprise.

Establishment and Enterprise Microdata File
See U.S. Establishment and Enterprise Microdata File

Establishment birth
See Business birth

Establishment Longitudinal Microdata File
See U.S. Establishment Longitudinal Microdata File

Ethics
See Business ethics

Evaluation
Determining the potential success of translating an invention into a product or process.

Exit
See Business exit

Experience rating
See Underwriting

Export
A product sold outside of the country.

Export license
A general or specific license granted by the U.S. Department of Commerce required of anyone wishing to export goods. Some restricted articles need approval from the U.S. Departments of State, Defense, or Energy.

Failure
See Business failure

Fair share agreement
An agreement reached between a franchisor and a minority business organization to extend business ownership to minorities by either reducing the amount of capital required or by setting aside certain marketing areas for minority business owners.

Feasibility study
A study to determine the likelihood that a proposed product or development will fulfill the objectives of a particular investor.

Federal Trade Commission (FTC)

Federal agency that promotes free enterprise and competition within the U.S.

Federal Trade Mark Act of 1946

See Lanham Act

Fictional name

See Business name

Fiduciary

An individual or group that hold assets in trust for a beneficiary.

Financial analysis

The techniques used to determine money needs in a business. Techniques include ratio analysis, calculation of return on investment, guides for measuring profitability, and break-even analysis to determine ultimate success.

Financial intermediary

A financial institution that acts as the intermediary between borrowers and lenders. Banks, savings and loan associations, finance companies, and venture capital companies are major financial intermediaries in the United States.

Financial ratios

See Corporate financial ratios; Industry financial ratios

Financial statement

A written record of business finances, including balance sheets and profit and loss statements.

Financing

See First-stage financing; Second-stage financing; Thirdstage financing

First-stage financing

Financing provided to companies that have expended their initial capital, and require funds to start full-scale manufacturing and sales. Also known as First-round financing.

Fiscal year

Any twelve-month period used by businesses for accounting purposes.

504 Program

See Certified development corporation

Flexible benefit plan

A plan that offers a choice among cash and/or qualified benefits such as group term life insurance, accident and health insurance, group legal services, dependent care assistance, and vacations.

FOB

See Free on board

Format franchising

See Business format franchising; Franchising

401(k) plan

A financial plan where employees contribute a percentage of their earnings to a fund that is invested in stocks, bonds, or money markets for the purpose of saving money for retirement.

Four Ps

Marketing terms referring to Product, Price, Place, and Promotion.

Franchising

A form of licensing by which the owner-the franchisor-distributes or markets a product, method, or service through affiliated dealers called franchisees. The product, method, or service being marketed is identified by a brand name, and the franchisor maintains control over the marketing methods employed. The franchisee is often given exclusive access to a defined geographic area.

Free on board (FOB)

A pricing term indicating that the quoted price includes the cost of loading goods into transport vessels at a specified place.

Frictional unemployment

See Unemployment

FTC

See Federal Trade Commission

Fulfillment

The systems necessary for accurate delivery of an ordered item, including subscriptions and direct marketing.

Full-time workers

Generally, those who work a regular schedule of more than 35 hours per week.

Garment registration number

A number that must appear on every garment sold in the U.S. to indicate the manufacturer of the garment, which may or may not be the same as the label under which the garment is sold. The U.S. Federal Trade Commission assigns and regulates garment registration numbers.

Gatekeeper

A key contact point for entry into a network.

GDP

See Gross domestic product

General obligation bond

A municipal bond secured by the taxing power of the municipality. The Tax Reform Act of 1986 limits the purposes for which such bonds may be issued and establishes volume limits on the extent of their issuance.

GNP

See Gross national product

Good Housekeeping Seal

Seal appearing on products that signifies the fulfillment of the standards set by the Good Housekeeping Institute to protect consumer interests.

Goods sector

All businesses producing tangible goods, including agriculture, mining, construction, and manufacturing businesses.

GPO

See Gross product originating

Gross domestic product (GDP)

The part of the nation's gross national product (see separate citation) generated by private business using resources from within the country.

Gross national product (GNP)

The most comprehensive single measure of aggregate economic output. Represents the market value of the total output of goods and services produced by a nation's economy.

Gross product originating (GPO)

A measure of business output estimated from the income or production side using employee

compensation, profit income, net interest, capital consumption, and indirect business taxes.

HAL

See Handicapped assistance loan program

Handicapped assistance loan program (HAL)

Low-interest direct loan program through the U.S. Small Business Administration (SBA) for handicapped persons. The SBA requires that these persons demonstrate that their disability is such that it is impossible for them to secure employment, thus making it necessary to go into their own business to make a living.

Health maintenance organization (HMO)

Organization of physicians and other health care professionals that provides health services to subscribers and their dependents on a prepaid basis.

Health provider

An individual or institution that gives medical care. Under Medicare, an institutional provider is a hospital, skilled nursing facility, home health agency, or provider of certain physical therapy services.

Hispanic

A person of Cuban, Mexican, Puerto Rican, Latin American (Central or South American), European Spanish, or other Spanish-speaking origin or ancestry.

HMO

See Health maintenance organization

Home-based business

A business with an operating address that is also a residential address (usually the residential address of the proprietor).

Hub-and-spoke system

A system in which flights of an airline from many different cities (the spokes) converge at a single airport (the hub). After allowing passengers sufficient time to make connections, planes then depart for different cities.

Human Resources Management

A business program designed to oversee recruiting, pay, benefits, and other issues related to the company's work force, including planning to determine the optimal use of labor to increase production, thereby increasing profit.

Idea

An original concept for a new product or process.

Import

Products produced outside the country in which they are consumed.

Income

Money or its equivalent, earned or accrued, resulting from the sale of goods and services.

Income statement

A financial statement that lists the profits and losses of a company at a given time.

Incorporation

The filing of a certificate of incorporation with a state's secretary of state, thereby limiting the business owner's liability.

Incubator

A facility designed to encourage entrepreneurship and minimize obstacles to new business formation and growth, particularly for high-technology firms, by housing a number of fledgling enterprises that share an array of services, such as meeting areas, secretarial services, accounting, research library, on-site financial and management counseling, and word processing facilities.

Independent contractor

An individual considered self-employed (see separate citation) and responsible for paying Social Security taxes and income taxes on earnings.

Indirect health coverage

Health insurance obtained through another individual's health care plan; for example, a spouse's employer-sponsored plan.

Industrial development authority

The financial arm of a state or other political subdivision established for the purpose of financing economic development in an area, usually through loans to non-profit organizations, which in turn provide facilities for manufacturing and other industrial operations.

Industry financial ratios

Corporate financial ratios averaged for a specified industry. These are used for comparison purposes and reveal industry trends and identify differences between the performance of a specific company and the performance of its industry. Also known as Industrial averages, Industry ratios, Financial averages, and Business or Industrial norms.

Inflation

Increases in volume of currency and credit, generally resulting in a sharp and continuing rise in price levels.

Informal capital

Financing from informal, unorganized sources; includes informal debt capital such as trade credit or loans from friends and relatives and equity capital from informal investors.

Initial public offering (IPO)

A corporation's first offering of stock to the public.

Innovation

The introduction of a new idea into the marketplace in the form of a new product or service or an improvement in organization or process.

Intellectual property

Any idea or work that can be considered proprietary in nature and is thus protected from infringement by others.

Internal capital

Debt or equity financing obtained from the owner or through retained business earnings.

Internet

A government-designed computer network that contains large amounts of information and is accessible through various vendors for a fee.

Intrapreneurship

The state of employing entrepreneurial principles to nonentrepreneurial situations.

Invention

The tangible form of a technological idea, which could include a laboratory prototype, drawings, formulas, etc.

IPO
See Initial public offering

Job description
The duties and responsibilities required in a particular position.

Job tenure
A period of time during which an individual is continuously employed in the same job.

Joint marketing agreements
Agreements between regional and major airlines, often involving the coordination of flight schedules, fares, and baggage transfer. These agreements help regional carriers operate at lower cost.

Joint venture
Venture in which two or more people combine efforts in a particular business enterprise, usually a single transaction or a limited activity, and agree to share the profits and losses jointly or in proportion to their contributions.

Keogh plan
Designed for self-employed persons and unincorporated businesses as a tax-deferred pension account.

Labor force
Civilians considered eligible for employment who are also willing and able to work.

Labor force participation rate
The civilian labor force as a percentage of the civilian population.

Labor intensity
The relative importance of labor in the production process, usually measured as the capital-labor ratio; i.e., the ratio of units of capital (typically, dollars of tangible assets) to the number of employees. The higher the capital-labor ratio exhibited by a firm or industry, the lower the capital intensity of that firm or industry is said to be.

Labor surplus area
An area in which there exists a high unemployment rate. In procurement (see separate citation), extra points are given to firms in counties that are designated a labor surplus area; this information is requested on procurement bid sheets.

Labor union
An organization of similarly-skilled workers who collectively bargain with management over the conditions of employment.

Laboratory prototype
See Prototype

LAN
See Local Area Network

Lanham Act
Refers to the Federal Trade Mark Act of 1946. Protects registered trademarks, trade names, and other service marks used in commerce.

Large business-dominated industry
Industry in which a minimum of 60 percent of employment or sales is in firms with more than 500 workers.

LBO
See Leveraged buy-out

Leader pricing
A reduction in the price of a good or service in order to generate more sales of that good or service.

Legal list
A list of securities selected by a state in which certain institutions and fiduciaries (such as pension funds, insurance companies, and banks) may invest. Securities not on the list are not eligible for investment. Legal lists typically restrict investments to high quality securities meeting certain specifications. Generally, investment is limited to U.S. securities and investment-grade blue chip securities (see separate citation).

Leveraged buy-out (LBO)
The purchase of a business or a division of a corporation through a highly leveraged financing package.

Liability
An obligation or duty to perform a service or an act. Also defined as money owed.

License
A legal agreement granting to another the right to use a technological innovation.

Limited Liability Company

A hybrid type of legal structure that provides the limited liability features of a corporation and the tax efficiencies and operational flexibility of a partnership. Depending on the state, the members can consist of a single individual (one owner), two or more individuals, corporations or other LLCs.

Limited liability partnerships

A business organization that allows limited partners to enjoy limited personal liability while general partners have unlimited personal liability

Liquidity

The ability to convert a security into cash promptly.

Loans

See Commercial loans; Disaster loans; SBA direct loans; SBA guaranteed loans; SBA special lending institution categories Local Area Network (LAN) Computer networks contained within a single building or small area; used to facilitate the sharing of information.

Local development corporation

An organization, usually made up of local citizens of a community, designed to improve the economy of the area by inducing business and industry to locate and expand there. A local development corporation establishes a capability to finance local growth.

Long-haul rates

Rates charged by a transporter in which the distance traveled is more than 800 miles.

Long-term debt

An obligation that matures in a period that exceeds five years.

Low-grade bond

A corporate bond that is rated below investment grade by the major rating agencies (Standard and Poor's, Moody's).

Macro-efficiency

Efficiency as it pertains to the operation of markets and market systems.

Managed care

A cost-effective health care program initiated by employers whereby low-cost health care is made available to the employees in return for exclusive patronage to program doctors.

Management Assistance Programs

See SBA Management Assistance Programs

Management and technical assistance

A term used by many programs to mean business (as opposed to technological) assistance.

Mandated benefits

Specific treatments, providers, or individuals required by law to be included in commercial health plans.

Market evaluation

The use of market information to determine the sales potential of a specific product or process.

Market failure

The situation in which the workings of a competitive market do not produce the best results from the point of view of the entire society.

Market information

Data of any type that can be used for market evaluation, which could include demographic data, technology forecasting, regulatory changes, etc.

Market research

A systematic collection, analysis, and reporting of data about the market and its preferences, opinions, trends, and plans; used for corporate decision-making.

Market share

In a particular market, the percentage of sales of a specific product.

Marketing

Promotion of goods or services through various media.

Master Establishment List (MEL)

A list of firms in the United States developed by the U.S. Small Business Administration; firms can be selected by industry, region, state, standard metropolitan statistical area (see separate citation), county, and zip code.

Maturity

The date upon which the principal or stated value of a bond or other indebtedness becomes due and payable.

Medicaid (Title XIX)

A federally aided, state-operated and administered program that provides medical benefits for certain low income persons in need of health and medical care who are eligible for one of the government's welfare cash payment programs, including the aged, the blind, the disabled, and members of families with dependent children where one parent is absent, incapacitated, or unemployed.

Medicare (Title XVIII)

A nationwide health insurance program for disabled and aged persons. Health insurance is available to insured persons without regard to income. Monies from payroll taxes cover hospital insurance and monies from general revenues and beneficiary premiums pay for supplementary medical insurance.

MEL

See Master Establishment List

Merchant Status

The relationship between a company and a bank or credit card company allowing the company to accept credit card payments

MESBIC

See Minority enterprise small business investment corporation

MET

See Multiple employer trust

Metropolitan statistical area (MSA)

A means used by the government to define large population centers that may transverse different governmental jurisdictions. For example, the Washington, D.C. MSA includes the District of Columbia and contiguous parts of Maryland and Virginia because all of these geopolitical areas comprise one population and economic operating unit.

Mezzanine financing

See Third-stage financing

Micro-efficiency

Efficiency as it pertains to the operation of individual firms.

Microdata

Information on the characteristics of an individual business firm.

Microloan

An SBA loan program that helps entrepreneurs obtain loans from less than $100 to $25,000.

Mid-term debt

An obligation that matures within one to five years.

Midrisk venture capital

See Equity midrisk venture capital

Minimum premium plan

A combination approach to funding an insurance plan aimed primarily at premium tax savings. The employer self-funds a fixed percentage of estimated monthly claims and the insurance company insures the excess.

Minimum wage

The lowest hourly wage allowed by the federal government.

Minority Business Development Agency

Contracts with private firms throughout the nation to sponsor Minority Business Development Centers which provide minority firms with advice and technical assistance on a fee basis.

Minority Enterprise Small Business Investment Corporation (MESBIC)

A federally funded private venture capital firm licensed by the U.S. Small Business Administration to provide capital to minority-owned businesses (see separate citation).

Minority-owned business

Businesses owned by those who are socially or economically disadvantaged (see separate citation).

Mission statement

A short statement describing a company's function, markets and competitive advantages.

Mom and Pop business

A small store or enterprise having limited capital, principally employing family members.

Multi-employer plan

A health plan to which more than one employer is required to contribute and that may be maintained through a collective bargaining agreement and required to meet standards prescribed by the U.S. Department of Labor.

Multi-level marketing

A system of selling in which you sign up other people to assist you and they, in turn, recruit others to help them. Some entrepreneurs have built successful companies on this concept because the main focus of their activities is their product and product sales.

Multiple employer trust (MET)

A self-funded benefit plan generally geared toward small employers sharing a common interest.

NASDAQ

See National Association of Securities Dealers Automated Quotations

National Association of Securities Dealers Automated Quotations

Provides price quotes on over-the-counter securities as well as securities listed on the New York Stock Exchange.

National income

Aggregate earnings of labor and property arising from the production of goods and services in a nation's economy.

Net assets

See Net worth

Net income

The amount remaining from earnings and profits after all expenses and costs have been met or deducted. Also known as Net earnings.

Net profit

Money earned after production and overhead expenses (see separate citations) have been deducted.

Net worth

The difference between a company's total assets and its total liabilities.

Network

A chain of interconnected individuals or organizations sharing information and/or services.

New York Stock Exchange (NYSE)

The oldest stock exchange in the U.S. Allows for trading in stocks, bonds, warrants, options, and rights that meet listing requirements.

Niche

A career or business for which a person is well-suited. Also, a product which fulfills one need of a particular market segment, often with little or no competition.

Nodes

One workstation in a network, either local area or wide area (see separate citations).

Nonbank bank

A bank that either accepts deposits or makes loans, but not both. Used to create many new branch banks.

Noncompetitive awards

A method of contracting whereby the federal government negotiates with only one contractor to supply a product or service.

Nonmember bank

A state-regulated bank that does not belong to the federal bank system.

Nonprofit

An organization that has no shareholders, does not distribute profits, and is without federal and state tax liabilities.

Norms

See Financial ratios

North American Free Trade Agreement (NAFTA)

Passed in 1993, NAFTA eliminates trade barriers among businesses in the U.S., Canada, and Mexico.

NYSE

See New York Stock Exchange

Occupational Safety & Health Administration (OSHA)

Federal agency that regulates health and safety standards within the workplace.

Operating Expenses

Business expenditures not directly associated with the production of goods or services.

Optimal firm size

The business size at which the production cost per unit of output (average cost) is, in the long run, at its minimum.

Organizational chart

A hierarchical chart tracking the chain of command within an organization.

OSHA

See Occupational Safety & Health Administration

Overhead

Expenses, such as employee benefits and building utilities, incurred by a business that are unrelated to the actual product or service sold.

Owner's capital

Debt or equity funds provided by the owner(s) of a business; sources of owner's capital are personal savings, sales of assets, or loans from financial institutions.

P & L

See Profit and loss statement

Part-time workers

Normally, those who work less than 35 hours per week. The Tax Reform Act indicated that part-time workers who work less than 17.5 hours per week may be excluded from health plans for purposes of complying with federal nondiscrimination rules.

Part-year workers

Those who work less than 50 weeks per year.

Partnership

Two or more parties who enter into a legal relationship to conduct business for profit. Defined by the U.S. Internal Revenue Code as joint ventures, syndicates, groups, pools, and other associations of two or more persons organized for profit that are not specifically classified in the IRS code as corporations or proprietorships.

Patent

A grant made by the government assuring an inventor the sole right to make, use, and sell an invention for a period of 17 years.

PC

See Professional corporation

Peak

See Cyclical peak

Pension

A series of payments made monthly, semiannually, annually, or at other specified intervals during the lifetime of the pensioner for distribution upon retirement. The term is sometimes used to denote the portion of the retirement allowance financed by the employer's contributions.

Pension fund

A fund established to provide for the payment of pension benefits; the collective contributions made by all of the parties to the pension plan.

Performance appraisal

An established set of objective criteria, based on job description and requirements, that is used to evaluate the performance of an employee in a specific job.

Permit

See Business license

Plan

See Business plan

Pooling

An arrangement for employers to achieve efficiencies and lower health costs by joining together to purchase group health insurance or self-insurance.

PPO

See Preferred provider organization

Preferred lenders program

See SBA special lending institution categories

Preferred provider organization (PPO)

A contractual arrangement with a health care services organization that agrees to discount its health care rates in return for faster payment and/or a patient base.

Premiums

The amount of money paid to an insurer for health insurance under a policy. The premium is generally paid periodically (e.g., monthly), and often is split between the employer and the employee. Unlike deductibles and coinsurance or copayments, premiums are paid for coverage whether or not benefits are actually used.

Prime-age workers

Employees 25 to 54 years of age.

Prime contract

A contract awarded directly by the U.S. Federal Government.

Private company

See Closely held corporation

Private placement

A method of raising capital by offering for sale an investment or business to a small group of investors (generally avoiding registration with the Securities and Exchange Commission or state securities registration agencies). Also known as Private financing or Private offering.

Pro forma

The use of hypothetical figures in financial statements to represent future expenditures, debts, and other potential financial expenses.

Proactive

Taking the initiative to solve problems and anticipate future events before they happen, instead of reacting to an already existing problem or waiting for a difficult situation to occur.

Procurement

A contract from an agency of the federal government for goods or services from a small business.

Product development

The stage of the innovation process where research is translated into a product or process through evaluation, adaptation, and demonstration.

Product franchising

An arrangement for a franchisee to use the name and to produce the product line of the franchisor or parent corporation.

Production

The manufacture of a product.

Production prototype

See Prototype

Productivity

A measurement of the number of goods produced during a specific amount of time.

Professional corporation (PC)

Organized by members of a profession such as medicine, dentistry, or law for the purpose of conducting their professional activities as a corporation. Liability of a member or shareholder is limited in the same manner as in a business corporation.

Profit and loss statement (P & L)

The summary of the incomes (total revenues) and costs of a company's operation during a specific period of time. Also known as Income and expense statement.

Proposal

See Business plan

Proprietorship

The most common legal form of business ownership; about 85 percent of all small businesses are proprietorships. The liability of the owner is unlimited in this form of ownership.

Prospective payment system

A cost-containment measure included in the Social Security Amendments of 1983 whereby Medicare payments to hospitals are based on established prices, rather than on cost reimbursement.

Prototype

A model that demonstrates the validity of the concept of an invention (laboratory prototype); a model that meets the needs of the manufacturing process and the user (production prototype).

Prudent investor rule or standard

A legal doctrine that requires fiduciaries to make investments using the prudence, diligence, and intelligence that would be used by a prudent person in making similar investments. Because fiduciaries make investments on behalf of third-party beneficiaries, the standard results in very conservative investments. Until recently, most state regulations required the fiduciary to apply this standard to each investment. Newer, more progressive regulations permit fiduciaries to apply this standard to the portfolio taken as a whole, thereby allowing a fiduciary to balance a portfolio with higher-yield, higher-risk investments. In states with more progressive regulations, practically every type of security is eligible for inclusion in the portfolio of investments made by a fiduciary, provided that the portfolio investments, in their totality, are those of a prudent person.

Public equity markets

Organized markets for trading in equity shares such as common stocks, preferred stocks, and warrants. Includes markets for both regularly traded and nonregularly traded securities.

Public offering

General solicitation for participation in an investment opportunity. Interstate public offerings are supervised by the U.S. Securities and Exchange Commission (see separate citation).

Quality control

The process by which a product is checked and tested to ensure consistent standards of high quality.

Rate of return

The yield obtained on a security or other investment based on its purchase price or its current market price. The total rate of return is current income plus or minus capital appreciation or depreciation.

Real property

Includes the land and all that is contained on it.

Realignment

See Resource realignment

Recession

Contraction of economic activity occurring between the peak and trough (see separate citations) of a business cycle.

Regulated market

A market in which the government controls the forces of supply and demand, such as who may enter and what price may be charged.

Regulation D

A vehicle by which small businesses make small offerings and private placements of securities with limited disclosure requirements. It was designed to ease the burdens imposed on small businesses utilizing this method of capital formation.

Regulatory Flexibility Act

An act requiring federal agencies to evaluate the impact of their regulations on small businesses before the regulations are issued and to consider less burdensome alternatives.

Research

The initial stage of the innovation process, which includes idea generation and invention.

Research and development financing

A tax-advantaged partnership set up to finance product development for start-ups as well as more mature companies.

Resource mobility

The ease with which labor and capital move from firm to firm or from industry to industry.

Resource realignment

The adjustment of productive resources to interindustry changes in demand.

Resources

The sources of support or help in the innovation process, including sources of financing, technical evaluation, market evaluation, management and business assistance, etc.

Retained business earnings

Business profits that are retained by the business rather than being distributed to the shareholders as dividends.

Return on investment

A profitability measure that evaluates the performance of a business by dividing net profit by net worth.

Revolving credit

An agreement with a lending institution for an amount of money, which cannot exceed a set maximum, over a specified period of time. Each time the borrower repays a portion of the loan, the amount of the repayment may be borrowed yet again.

Risk capital

See Venture capital

Risk management

The act of identifying potential sources of financial loss and taking action to minimize their negative impact.

Routing

The sequence of steps necessary to complete a product during production.

S corporations

See Sub chapter S corporations

SBA

See Small Business Administration

SBA direct loans

Loans made directly by the U.S. Small Business Administration (SBA); monies come from funds appropriated specifically for this purpose. In general, SBA direct loans carry interest rates slightly lower than those in the private financial markets and are available only to applicants unable to secure private financing or an SBA guaranteed loan.

SBA 504 Program

See Certified development corporation

SBA guaranteed loans

Loans made by lending institutions in which the U.S. Small Business Administration (SBA) will pay a prior agreed-upon percentage of the outstanding principal in the event the borrower of the loan defaults. The terms of the loan and the interest rate are negotiated between theborrower and the lending institution, within set parameters.

SBA loans

See Disaster loans; SBA direct loans; SBA guaranteed loans; SBA special lending institution categories

SBA Management Assistance Programs

Classes, workshops, counseling, and publications offered by the U.S. Small Business Administration.

SBA special lending institution categories

U.S. Small Business Administration (SBA) loan program in which the SBA promises certified banks a 72-hour turnaround period in giving its approval for a loan, and in which preferred lenders in a pilot program are allowed to write SBA loans without seeking prior SBA approval.

SBDB

See Small Business Data Base

SBDC

See Small business development centers

SBI

See Small business institutes program

SBIC

See Small business investment corporation

SBIR Program

See Small Business Innovation Development Act of 1982

Scale economies

The decline of the production cost per unit of output (average cost) as the volume of output increases.

Scale efficiency

The reduction in unit cost available to a firm when producing at a higher output volume.

SCORE

See Service Corps of Retired Executives

SEC

See Securities and Exchange Commission

SECA

See Self-Employment Contributions Act

Second-stage financing

Working capital for the initial expansion of a company that is producing, shipping, and has growing accounts receivable and inventories. Also known as Second-round financing.

Secondary market

A market established for the purchase and sale of outstanding securities following their initial distribution.

Secondary worker

Any worker in a family other than the person who is the primary source of income for the family.

Secondhand capital

Previously used and subsequently resold capital equipment (e.g., buildings and machinery).

Securities and Exchange Commission (SEC)

Federal agency charged with regulating the trade of securities to prevent unethical practices in the investor market.

Securitized debt
A marketing technique that converts long-term loans to marketable securities.

Seed capital
Venture financing provided in the early stages of the innovation process, usually during product development.

Self-employed person
One who works for a profit or fees in his or her own business, profession, or trade, or who operates a farm.

Self-Employment Contributions Act (SECA)
Federal law that governs the self-employment tax (see separate citation).

Self-employment income
Income covered by Social Security if a business earns a net income of at least $400.00 during the year. Taxes are paid on earnings that exceed $400.00.

Self-employment retirement plan
See Keogh plan

Self-employment tax
Required tax imposed on self-employed individuals for the provision of Social Security and Medicare. The tax must be paid quarterly with estimated income tax statements.

Self-funding
A health benefit plan in which a firm uses its own funds to pay claims, rather than transferring the financial risks of paying claims to an outside insurer in exchange for premium payments.

Service Corps of Retired Executives (SCORE)
Volunteers for the SBA Management Assistance Program who provide one-on-one counseling and teach workshops and seminars for small firms.

Service firm
See Business service firm

Service sector
Broadly defined, all U.S. industries that produce intangibles, including the five major industry divisions of transportation, communications, and utilities; wholesale trade; retail trade; finance, insurance, and real estate; and services.

Set asides
See Small business set asides

Short-haul service
A type of transportation service in which the transporter supplies service between cities where the maximum distance is no more than 200 miles.

Short-term debt
An obligation that matures in one year.

SIC codes
See Standard Industrial Classification codes

Single-establishment enterprise
See Establishment

Small business
An enterprise that is independently owned and operated, is not dominant in its field, and employs fewer than 500 people. For SBA purposes, the U.S. Small Business Administration (SBA) considers various other factors (such as gross annual sales) in determining size of a business.

Small Business Administration (SBA)
An independent federal agency that provides assistance with loans, management, and advocating interests before other federal agencies.

Small Business Data Base
A collection of microdata (see separate citation) files on individual firms developed and maintained by the U.S. Small Business Administration.

Small business development centers (SBDC)
Centers that provide support services to small businesses, such as individual counseling, SBA advice, seminars and conferences, and other learning center activities. Most services are free of charge, or available at minimal cost.

Small business development corporation
See Certified development corporation

Small business-dominated industry
Industry in which a minimum of 60 percent of employment or sales is in firms with fewer than 500 employees.

Small Business Innovation Development Act of 1982
Federal statute requiring federal agencies with large extramural research and development budgets to

allocate a certain percentage of these funds to small research and development firms. The program, called the Small Business Innovation Research (SBIR) Program, is designed to stimulate technological innovation and make greater use of small businesses in meeting national innovation needs.

Small business institutes (SBI) program

Cooperative arrangements made by U.S. Small Business Administration district offices and local colleges and universities to provide small business firms with graduate students to counsel them without charge.

Small business investment corporation (SBIC)

A privately owned company licensed and funded through the U.S. Small Business Administration and private sector sources to provide equity or debt capital to small businesses.

Small business set asides

Procurement (see separate citation) opportunities required by law to be on all contracts under $10,000 or a certain percentage of an agency's total procurement expenditure.

Smaller firms

For U.S. Department of Commerce purposes, those firms not included in the Fortune 1000.

SMSA

See Metropolitan statistical area

Socially and economically disadvantaged

Individuals who have been subjected to racial or ethnic prejudice or cultural bias without regard to their qualities as individuals, and whose abilities to compete are impaired because of diminished opportunities to obtain capital and credit.

Sole proprietorship

An unincorporated, one-owner business, farm, or professional practice.

Special lending institution categories

See SBA special lending institution categories

Standard Industrial Classification (SIC) codes

Four-digit codes established by the U.S. Federal Government to categorize businesses by type of economic activity; the first two digits correspond to major groups

such as construction and manufacturing, while the last two digits correspond to subgroups such as home construction or highway construction.

Start-up

A new business, at the earliest stages of development and financing.

Start-up costs

Costs incurred before a business can commence operations.

Start-up financing

Financing provided to companies that have either completed product development and initial marketing or have been in business for less than one year but have not yet sold their product commercially.

Stock

A certificate of equity ownership in a business.

Stop-loss coverage

Insurance for a self-insured plan that reimburses the company for any losses it might incur in its health claims beyond a specified amount.

Strategic planning

Projected growth and development of a business to establish a guiding direction for the future. Also used to determine which market segments to explore for optimal sales of products or services.

Structural unemployment

See Unemployment

Sub chapter S corporations

Corporations that are considered noncorporate for tax purposes but legally remain corporations.

Subcontract

A contract between a prime contractor and a subcontractor, or between subcontractors, to furnish supplies or services for performance of a prime contract (see separate citation) or a subcontract.

Surety bonds

Bonds providing reimbursement to an individual, company, or the government if a firm fails to complete a contract. The U.S. Small Business Administration guarantees surety bonds in a program much like the SBA guaranteed loan program (see separate citation).

Swing loan
See Bridge financing

Target market
The clients or customers sought for a business' product or service.

Targeted Jobs Tax Credit
Federal legislation enacted in 1978 that provides a tax credit to an employer who hires structurally unemployed individuals.

Tax number
A number assigned to a business by a state revenue department that enables the business to buy goods without paying sales tax.

Taxable bonds
An interest-bearing certificate of public or private indebtedness. Bonds are issued by public agencies to finance economic development.

Technical assistance
See Management and technical assistance

Technical evaluation
Assessment of technological feasibility.

Technology
The method in which a firm combines and utilizes labor and capital resources to produce goods or services; the application of science for commercial or industrial purposes.

Technology transfer
The movement of information about a technology or intellectual property from one party to another for use.

Tenure
See Employee tenure

Term
The length of time for which a loan is made.

Terms of a note
The conditions or limits of a note; includes the interest rate per annum, the due date, and transferability and convertibility features, if any.

Third-party administrator
An outside company responsible for handling claims and performing administrative tasks associated with health insurance plan maintenance.

Third-stage financing
Financing provided for the major expansion of a company whose sales volume is increasing and that is breaking even or profitable. These funds are used for further plant expansion, marketing, working capital, or development of an improved product. Also known as Third-round or Mezzanine financing.

Time management
Skills and scheduling techniques used to maximize productivity.

Trade credit
Credit extended by suppliers of raw materials or finished products. In an accounting statement, trade credit is referred to as "accounts payable."

Trade name
The name under which a company conducts business, or by which its business, goods, or services are identified. It may or may not be registered as a trademark.

Trade periodical
A publication with a specific focus on one or more aspects of business and industry.

Trade secret
Competitive advantage gained by a business through the use of a unique manufacturing process or formula.

Trade show
An exhibition of goods or services used in a particular industry. Typically held in exhibition centers where exhibitors rent space to display their merchandise.

Trademark
A graphic symbol, device, or slogan that identifies a business. A business has property rights to its trademark from the inception of its use, but it is still prudent to register all trademarks with the Trademark Office of the U.S. Department of Commerce.

Trend
A statistical measurement used to track changes that occur over time.

Trough

See Cyclical trough

UCC

See Uniform Commercial Code

UL

See Underwriters Laboratories

Underwriters Laboratories (UL)

One of several private firms that tests products and processes to determine their safety. Although various firms can provide this kind of testing service, many local and insurance codes specify UL certification.

Underwriting

A process by which an insurer determines whether or not and on what basis it will accept an application for insurance. In an experience-rated plan, premiums are based on a firm's or group's past claims; factors other than prior claims are used for community-rated or manually rated plans.

Unfair competition

Refers to business practices, usually unethical, such as using unlicensed products, pirating merchandise, or misleading the public through false advertising, which give the offending business an unequitable advantage over others.

Unfunded accrued liability

The excess of total liabilities, both present and prospective, over present and prospective assets.

Unemployment

The joblessness of individuals who are willing to work, who are legally and physically able to work, and who are seeking work. Unemployment may represent the temporary joblessness of a worker between jobs (frictional unemployment) or the joblessness of a worker whose skills are not suitable for jobs available in the labor market (structural unemployment).

Uniform Commercial Code (UCC)

A code of laws governing commercial transactions across the U.S., except Louisiana. Their purpose is to bring uniformity to financial transactions.

Uniform product code (UPC symbol)

A computer-readable label comprised of ten digits and stripes that encodes what a product is and how much it costs. The first five digits are assigned by the Uniform Product Code Council, and the last five digits by the individual manufacturer.

Unit cost

See Average cost

UPC symbol

See Uniform product code

U.S. Establishment and Enterprise Microdata (USEEM) File

A cross-sectional database containing information on employment, sales, and location for individual enterprises and establishments with employees that have a Dun & Bradstreet credit rating.

U.S. Establishment Longitudinal Microdata (USELM) File

A database containing longitudinally linked sample microdata on establishments drawn from the U.S. Establishment and Enterprise Microdata file (see separate citation).

U.S. Small Business Administration 504 Program

See Certified development corporation

USEEM

See U.S. Establishment and Enterprise Microdata File

USELM

See U.S. Establishment Longitudinal Microdata File

VCN

See Venture capital network

Venture capital

Money used to support new or unusual business ventures that exhibit above-average growth rates, significant potential for market expansion, and are in need of additional financing to sustain growth or further research and development; equity or equity-type financing traditionally provided at the commercialization stage, increasingly available prior to commercialization.

Venture capital company

A company organized to provide seed capital to a business in its formation stage, or in its first or second

Glossary of Small Business Terms

stage of expansion. Funding is obtained through public or private pension funds, commercial banks and bank holding companies, small business investment corporations licensed by the U.S. Small Business Administration, private venture capital firms, insurance companies, investment management companies, bank trust departments, industrial companies seeking to diversify their investment, and investment bankers acting as intermediaries for other investors or directly investing on their own behalf.

Venture capital limited partnerships

Designed for business development, these partnerships are an institutional mechanism for providing capital for young, technology-oriented businesses. The investors' money is pooled and invested in money market assets until venture investments have been selected. The general partners are experienced investment managers who select and invest the equity and debt securities of firms with high growth potential and the ability to go public in the near future.

Venture capital network (VCN)

A computer database that matches investors with entrepreneurs.

WAN

See Wide Area Network

Wide Area Network (WAN)

Computer networks linking systems throughout a state or around the world in order to facilitate the sharing of information.

Withholding

Federal, state, social security, and unemployment taxes withheld by the employer from employees' wages; employers are liable for these taxes and the corporate umbrella and bankruptcy will not exonerate an employer from paying back payroll withholding. Employers should escrow these funds in a separate account and disperse them quarterly to withholding authorities.

Workers' compensation

A state-mandated form of insurance covering workers injured in job-related accidents. In some states, the state is the insurer; in other states, insurance must be acquired from commercial insurance firms. Insurance rates are based on a number of factors, including salaries, firm history, and risk of occupation.

Working capital

Refers to a firm's short-term investment of current assets, including cash, short-term securities, accounts receivable, and inventories.

Yield

The rate of income returned on an investment, expressed as a percentage. Income yield is obtained by dividing the current dollar income by the current market price of the security. Net yield or yield to maturity is the current income yield minus any premium above par or plus any discount from par in purchase price, with the adjustment spread over the period from the date of purchase to the date of maturity.

Index

Listings in this index are arranged alphabetically by business plan type, then alphabetically by business plan name. Users are provided with the volume number in which the plan appears.

Index

Index

Index

Index